BIG ISLAND OF HAWAI'I

1st Edition

Where to Stay and Eat for All Budgets

Must-See Sights and Local Secrets

Ratings You Can Trust

Portions of this book appear in Fodor's Hawai'i

Fodor's Travel Publications New York, Toronto, London, Sydney, Auckland

www.fodors.com

FODOR'S BIG ISLAND OF HAWAI'I
Editors: Mary Beth Bohman, Amy B Wang, Joyce Eisenberg

Editorial Production: Evangelos Vasilakis
Editorial Contributors: Wanda Adams, Don Chapman, Jack Jeffrey, John Penisten, Cathy Sharpe, Cheryl Chee Tsutsumi, Amy Westervelt
Maps and Illustrations: Henry Columb and Monk Stroud, Moon Street Cartography; David Lindroth, Inc.; William Wu; Rebecca Baer and Bob Blake, *map editors*
Design: Fabrizio La Rocca, *creative director*; Guido Caroti, *art director*; Chie Ushio, *designer*; Moon Sun Kim, *cover designer*; Melanie Marin, *senior picture editor*
Production/Manufacturing: Colleen Ziemba
Cover Photo (Lava flowing from Kilauea volcano): G. Brad Lewis/age fotostock

First Edition

ISBN 978-1-4000-1778-2

ISSN 1934-5542

SPECIAL SALES
This book is available for special discounts for bulk purchases for sales promotions or premiums. Special editions, including personalized covers, excerpts of existing books, and corporate imprints, can be created in large quantities for special needs. For more information, write to Special Markets/Premium Sales, 1745 Broadway, MD 6-2, New York, New York 10019, or e-mail specialmarkets@randomhouse.com.

AN IMPORTANT TIP & AN INVITATION
Although all prices, opening times, and other details in this book are based on information supplied to us at press time, changes occur all the time in the travel world, and Fodor's cannot accept responsibility for facts that become outdated or for inadvertent errors or omissions. So **always confirm information when it matters,** especially if you're making a detour to visit a specific place. Your experiences—positive and negative—matter to us. If we have missed or misstated something, **please write to us.** We follow up on all suggestions. Contact the Hawai'i editors at editors@fodors.com or c/o Fodor's at 1745 Broadway, New York, NY 10019.

PRINTED IN THE UNITED STATES OF AMERICA

10 9 8 7 6 5 4 3 2

Be a Fodor's Correspondent

Your opinion matters. It matters to us. It matters to your fellow Fodor's travelers, too. And we'd like to hear it. In fact, we *need* to hear it.

When you share your experiences and opinions, you become an active member of the Fodor's community. That means we'll not only use your feedback to make our books better, but we'll publish your name and comments whenever possible. Throughout our guides, look for "Word of Mouth," excerpts of your unvarnished feedback.

Here's how you can help improve Fodor's for all of us.

Tell us when we're right. We rely on local writers to give you an insider's perspective. But our writers and staff editors—who are the best in the business—depend on you. Your positive feedback is a vote to renew our recommendations for the next edition.

Tell us when we're wrong. We're proud that we update most of our guides every year. But we're not perfect. Things change. Hotels cut services. Museums change hours. Charming cafés lose charm. If our writer didn't quite capture the essence of a place, tell us how you'd do it differently. If any of our descriptions are inaccurate or inadequate, we'll incorporate your changes in the next edition and will correct factual errors at fodors.com *immediately.*

Tell us what to include. You probably have had fantastic travel experiences that aren't yet in Fodor's. Why not share them with a community of like-minded travelers? Maybe you chanced upon a beach or bistro or B&B that you don't want to keep to yourself. Tell us why we should include it. And share your discoveries and experiences with everyone directly at fodors.com. Your input may lead us to add a new listing or highlight a place we cover with a "Highly Recommended" star or with our highest rating, "Fodor's Choice."

Give us your opinion instantly at our feedback center at 🌐 www.fodors.com/feedback. You may also e-mail editors@fodors.com with the subject line "Hawai'i Editor." Or send your nominations, comments, and complaints by mail to Hawai'i Editor, Fodor's, 1745 Broadway, New York, NY 10019.

You and travelers like you are the heart of the Fodor's community. Make our community richer by sharing your experiences. Be a Fodor's correspondent.

Aloha!

Tim Jarrell, Publisher

CONTENTS

MAPS & CHARTS

ABOUT THIS BOOK

Our Ratings

Sometimes you find terrific travel experiences and sometimes they just find you. But usually the burden is on you to select the right combination of experiences. That's where our ratings come in.

As travelers we've all discovered a place so wonderful that its worthiness is obvious. And sometimes that place is so experiential that superlatives don't do it justice: you just have to be there to know. These sights, properties, and experiences get our highest rating, **Fodor's Choice,** indicated by orange stars throughout this book.

Black stars highlight sights and properties we deem **Highly Recommended,** places that our writers, editors, and readers praise again and again for consistency and excellence.

By default, there's another category: any place we include in this book is by definition worth your time, unless we say otherwise. And we will.

Disagree with any of our choices? Care to nominate a place or suggest that we rate one more highly? Visit our feedback center at 🌐 www.fodors.com/feedback.

Budget Well

Hotel and restaurant price categories from ¢ to $$$$ are defined in the Where to Eat and Where to Stay chapters. Real prices are listed at the end of each restaurant and hotel review. For attractions, we always give standard adult admission fees; reductions are usually available for children, students, and senior citizens. Want to pay with plastic? **AE, D, DC, MC, V** following restaurant and hotel listings indicate if American Express, Discover, Diners Club, MasterCard, and Visa are accepted.

Restaurants

Unless we state otherwise, restaurants are open for lunch and dinner daily. We mention dress only when there's a specific requirement and reservations only when they're essential or not accepted—it's always best to book ahead.

Hotels

Hotels have private bath, phone, and TV, unless we state otherwise. We always list facilities but not whether you'll be charged an extra fee to use them, so when pricing accommodations, find out what's included.

Many Listings

- ★ Fodor's Choice
- ★ Highly recommended
- ✉ Physical address
- ✢ Directions
- 📫 Mailing address
- ☎ Telephone
- 📠 Fax
- 🌐 On the Web
- ✉ E-mail
- 🎟 Admission fee
- ⏲ Open/closed times
- 💳 Credit cards

Hotels & Restaurants

- 🏨 Hotel
- 🛏 Number of rooms
- 👍 Facilities
- 🍽 Meal plans
- ✕ Restaurant
- ✍ Reservations
- 👔 Dress code
- 🚬 Smoking
- 🍷 BYOB
- ✕🏨 Hotel with restaurant that warrants a visit

Outdoors

- ⛳ Golf
- ⛺ Camping

Other

- 👶 Family-friendly
- ℹ Contact information
- ⇨ See also
- ✉ Branch address
- ☞ Take note

Experience the Big Island

WORD OF MOUTH

"I love the vastness of the Big Island, the ever-changing landscape punctuated by hidden gems like black sand beaches, warm pools, and steam rooms. The Big Island had a peacefulness that I found was different [from other Hawaiian islands], deeper and more subtle, maybe more zen, as though the island is waiting to embrace you with a warm wind and whisper an ancient secret in your ear when you are ready to hear it."

—turn_it_on

www.fodors.com/forums

WELCOME TO THE BIG ISLAND

Getting Oriented

You could fit all of the other Hawaiian Islands onto the Big Island and still have a little room left over—hence the clever name. Locals refer to the island by side: Kona side to the west and Hilo side to the east. Most of the resorts, condos, and restaurants are crammed into 30 miles of the sunny Kona side, while the rainy, tropical Hilo side is much more local and residential.

Beautiful views make for pleasant drives, and the island's climate and vegetation change rapidly from one region to the next. Turn a corner from west to east on the north side of the island and you move quickly from hot, dry beaches to cool, lush valleys; the forty-mile drive to Waimea from Kailua-Kona affords awesome views of the coast below and the rolling pasture lands of the upcountry; and the drive east along the Hāmākua Coast from Waimea to Hilo (45 miles) is the stuff Hawaiian dreams are made of, with rainbows jumping over majestic cliffs and waterfalls, and green valleys hiding pristine swimming holes.

■ TIP→ **Directions on the island are often given as mauka (toward the mountains) and makai (toward the ocean).**

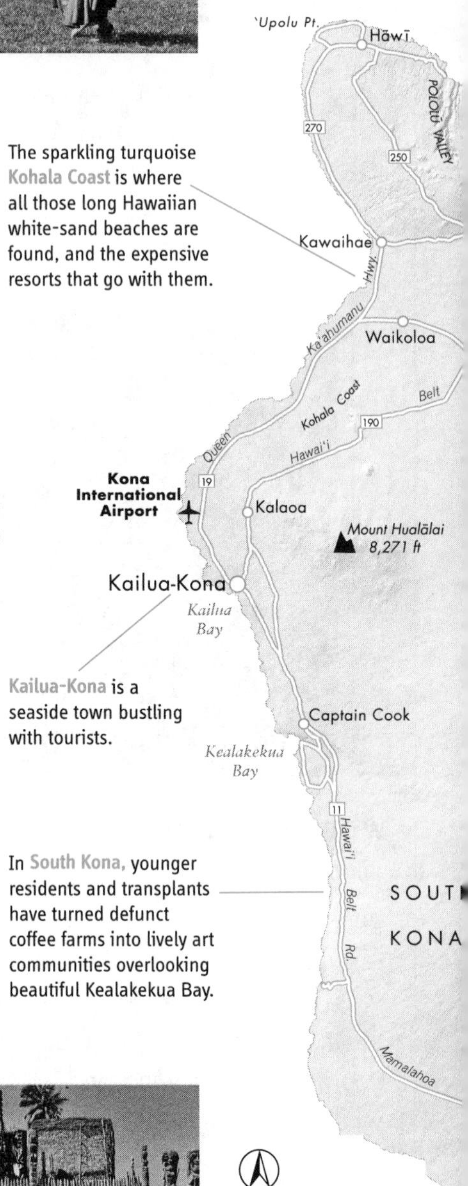

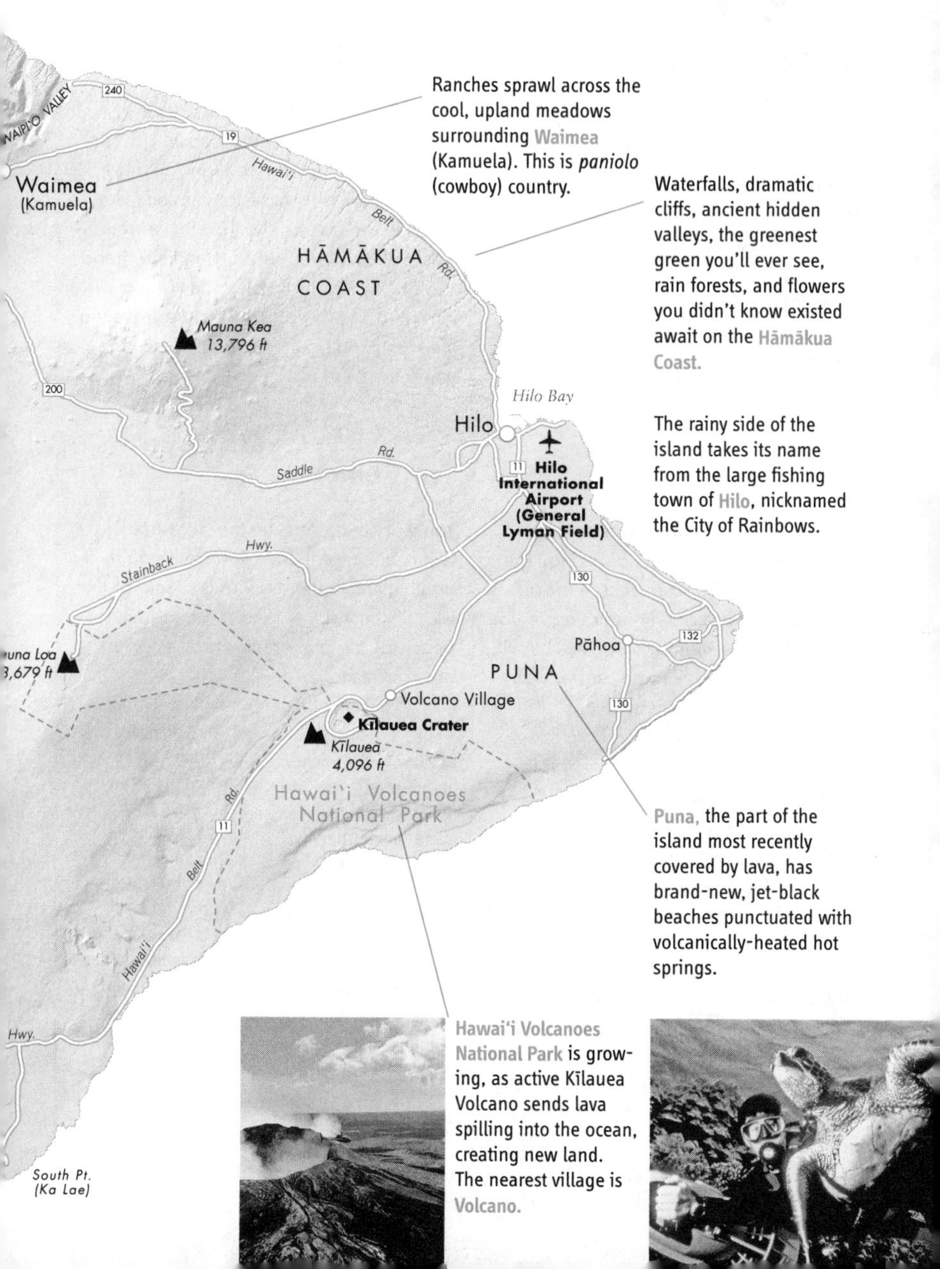

Ranches sprawl across the cool, upland meadows surrounding **Waimea** (Kamuela). This is *paniolo* (cowboy) country.

Waterfalls, dramatic cliffs, ancient hidden valleys, the greenest green you'll ever see, rain forests, and flowers you didn't know existed await on the **Hāmākua Coast.**

The rainy side of the island takes its name from the large fishing town of **Hilo**, nicknamed the City of Rainbows.

Puna, the part of the island most recently covered by lava, has brand-new, jet-black beaches punctuated with volcanically-heated hot springs.

Hawai'i Volcanoes National Park is growing, as active Kīlauea Volcano sends lava spilling into the ocean, creating new land. The nearest village is **Volcano.**

BIG ISLAND PLANNER

When You Arrive

The Big Island's two airports are directly across the island from each other. Kona International Airport on the west side is about a 10-minute drive from Kailua-Kona and 30 to 45 minutes from the Kohala Coast. On the east side, Hilo International Airport, 2 mi from downtown Hilo, is about 40 minutes from Volcanoes National Park. ■ TIP→ **The shortest, best route between Hilo and Kailua-Kona is the northern route, a 96-mi, 2½-hour drive. No time? Take a 20-minute flight on Island Air.**

Fitting It All In

Yes, it's big, and yes, there's a lot to see. If you're short on time, consider flying into one airport and out of the other. That will give you the opportunity to see both sides of the island without ever having to go backwards. Decide what sort of note you'd rather end on to determine your route—if you'd prefer to spend your last few days sleeping on the beach, go from east to west; if hiking through rain forests and showering in waterfalls sounds like a better way to end the trip, move from west to east. If you're short on time, head straight for Hawai'i Volcanoes National Park and briefly visit Hilo before traveling the Hāmākua Coast route and making your new base in Kailua-Kona.

Manta Rays

The Big Island is known for its scuba diving, and the visibility is amazing. The island's manta rays were scarce for a while, but they are slowly returning. If you book a nighttime manta-ray dive, you will probably actually see some, and it's an experience not to be missed.

Will I See Flowing Lava?

The best time to see lava is at night. However, you may or may not see flowing lava. Anyone who tries to tell you they can guarantee it or predict it is lying or trying to sell you something. Your best bet is to call the visitor center at the national park before you head out; even at that you could be pleasantly surprised or utterly disappointed. Keep in mind that the volcano is a pretty amazing sight even if it's not spewing fire.

Car Rentals

You will need a car on the Big Island. Get a four-wheel-drive vehicle if you're at all interested in exploring. Some of the island's best sights (and most beautiful beaches) are at the end of rough or unpaved roads.

TIPS→

- **Talk to the agency in advance if you want to pick up a car at one airport and drop it off at the other. Though they allow this, most charge an additional fee of up to $50. If you arrange it ahead of time, they can often be talked into waiving the fee.**
- **Most agencies make you sign an agreement that you won't drive on the Saddle Road, the path to Mauna Kea and its observatories. Though smoothly paved, the Saddle Road is remote, winding, unlighted, and bereft of gas stations. Harper's, a local rental company, is the sole exception.**

Timing Is Everything

You can see humpback whales clearly off the western coast of the island from about January until May. Technically, whale season is from November to May, but the migration doesn't really get going until January. The few scattered sightings in November and December are usually young males showing off. The Merrie Monarch Festival brings a full week of hula, both ancient and modern, to Hilo, beginning the week after Easter. Fish stories abound in Kailua-Kona every August during the week-long Hawaiian International Billfish Tournament. The Ironman Triathlon takes place every October in Kailua-Kona. Consider volunteering—you'll be inspired, and it's a great party.

Surfing

The Big Island is not known for its surf, but that doesn't mean that there isn't any, or that there aren't plenty of local surfers. Surf's up in winter, down in summer; the beautiful peaceful beach you went to last summer could be a rough and rowdy surfer beach in the winter.

Mix It Up

Consider spending part of your vacation at a resort and part of it at B&Bs. The big resorts sit squarely on some of the best beaches on the Island, and they have a lot to offer—spas, golf, and great restaurants for starters. The B&Bs, on the other hand, provide a more intimate experience in settings as diverse as an upcountry ranch, a jungle treehouse, and a Victorian mansion perched on sea cliffs. Several romantic B&Bs nestle in the rainforest surrounding Volcanoes National Park—very convenient after a nighttime lava hike.

Guided Activities

Factor activities into your budget and itinerary in advance. The Big Island is particularly well-known for deep-sea fishing (late summer to early fall is peak season), and it is also rapidly building a reputation as the golfer's island. Guided tours are handy for remote attractions like Mauna Kea stargazing and Waipi'o Valley.

ACTIVITY	COST
Deep-Sea Fishing (1/2 day)	$500-$600
Golf (Green Fee)	$15-$200
Horseback Riding (2 hr)	$85-$150
Kayak Tours (1/2 day)	$65-$160
Mauna Kea Astronomy Tour	$90-$185
Snorkel Cruise (1/2 day)	$90-$120
Surfing (2 hr group lesson)	$90-$120
Volcano Aerial Tour (2 hr)	$390
Whale-Watching	$70

Will It Rain?

The Kona side of the Big Island is arid and hot, with mile upon mile of black lava fields lining a shimmering coastline. The Hilo side, on the other hand, gets roughly 130 inches of rain a year, so the chances of getting rained on while driving along the Hāmākua Coast to Hilo are pretty high. That said, it tends to be sunny in the morning and early afternoon in Hilo, and clouds up for late afternoon showers that leave a handful of rainbows behind.

TOP BIG ISLAND EXPERIENCES

The Lava Show

(A) Watch as fiery red lava pours, steaming, into the ocean; stare in awe at nighttime lava fireworks; and hike across the floor of a crater at Volcanoes National Park. ⇨ *page 46*.

Green Sand Beach

(B) It's a hike, but this is the only place in the world to see green sand. And it happens to be surrounded by turquoise waters and dramatic cliffs. ⇨ *page 84*.

Exploring Waipi'o Valley

(C) Whichever way you choose to get there—on horseback, in a 4WD, or on foot—you'll discover that the "Valley of the Kings" is full of sky high waterfalls, lush green cliffs, and a mystical quality that can't quite be described or rivaled. ⇨ *page 63*.

A Window on the Universe

(D) Teams of astronomers from all over the world come to Mauna Kea for the clearest skies and best conditions anywhere. Head up the mountain in the late afternoon for the prettiest sunset on this island and the best stargazing on this planet. ⇨ *page 66*.

Play at a Perfect Beach

(E) Whether you follow the paved roads to Hāpuna, Kauna'oa (also known as Mauna Kea), or Kua Bay, or brave the rocky routes to Makalawena, you'll find that the Big Island is full of postcard-perfect beaches. ⇨ *page 75*.

A Swim Through Coral Gardens

(F) Diving or snorkeling in the crystal clear, warm waters off the coast is like being let loose in your very own ocean-sized aquarium. Bright yellow, purple, and rose-

colored coral creates surreal kingdoms ruled by octopi, turtles, rays, dolphins, and fish in every color of the rainbow. ⇨ *page 106.*

Stunning Waterfalls

(G) Watch rainbows forming in the mist then take a refreshing dip in the cold, deep pools fed by the powerful waterfalls spilling over the dramatic cliffs of the Hāmākua Coast. ⇨ *page 61.*

Snooze with a Sea Turtle

(H) Hang out at Punalu'u Beach, where sea turtles surf the waves and nap on the black sands. ⇨ *page 85.*

A Healing Lomi Lomi Massage

(I) Beginning with a chant, the lomi lomi technique uses a combination of arms, elbows, hands, and breath to impart the overall sense of well-being associated with this ancient healing tradition. ⇨ *page 141.*

A Kona Coffee Farm Tour

Spend an hour discovering why it is that Kona coffee commands those high prices. Watch as "cherries" become beans, enjoy the smoky coffee smell of the roasting process, then indulge in the freshest cup of coffee you'll ever have. Did we mention that it's all free? ⇨ *page 42.*

Whale the Day Away

(J) From December to May, you can sit on any beach on the west side of the island and watch the humpback whale migration. The sight of their backs, glistening as they move through the water, or the occasional perfect fluke cutting through the surface, is a matchless experience. ⇨ *page 108.*

GREAT 1-DAY ITINERARIES

Sun & Stars

Spend the day lounging on a Kohala Coast beach (Hāpuna, Kauna'oa—also known as Mauna Kea—or Kua Bay), but throw jackets and boots in the car because you'll be catching the sunset from Mauna Kea's summit. Bundle up and stick around after darkness falls for some of the world's best stargazing. Book a tour or head straight for the visitor center, join their free tour of the summit at sunset, and return to the center to use their telescopes.

Hike Volcanoes

Devote a full day (at least) to Volcanoes National Park. Head out on the Kīlauea Iki trail—a 4-mi loop at the summit—by late morning. Grab a sandwich at the Volcano House when you've finished and take in their fantastic views of the craters. After lunch, head down Chain of Craters Road to the coast and the active lava flows. Bring water, snacks, and a flashlight if you intend to hike out to the end of the road where the lava flows into the ocean. Start your hike during the day (by 4 PM or earlier) to ensure that you're as close as you can safely be when night falls and to prepare yourself for a spectacular nighttime lava show.

Majestic Waterfalls & Kings' Valleys

Take a day to enjoy the splendors of the Hāmākua Coast—any gorge you see on the road is an indication of a waterfall waiting to be explored. For a sure bet, head to beautiful Waipi'o Valley. Book a horseback, hiking, or 4WD tour or walk on in yourself (just keep in mind that it's an arduous hike back up—25% grade for a little over a mile). Once in the valley, take your first right to get to the black sand beach. Take a moment to sit here—the ancient Hawaiians believed this was where souls crossed over to the afterlife. Whether you believe it or not, there's something unmistakably special about this place. Waterfalls abound in the valley, depending on the amount of recent rainfall. Your best bet is to follow the river from the beach to the back of the valley, where a waterfall and its lovely pool await.

Underwater Day

Explore the colorful reefs populated with tropical fish off the Big Island's coast for one day, and we defy you to stop thinking about the world beneath the waves when you're back on land. Our favorite spots include Two Step (near the Place of Refuge), Kealakekua Bay, and the Kapoho Tide Pools. Early morning is the best time to see the Hawaiian spinner dolphins that frolic off this coast, but you're likely to see turtles any time of day, along with yellow and white angel fish, spotted Moray eels, trumpet fish, and a myriad of other brightly colored varieties.

Volcano Hotsprings & Boiling Pots

Most tourists skip Puna. Venture into this remote area for a morning, and you'll be rewarded with lava tube hikes (Kīlauea Caverns of Fire), volcanically heated pools (Ahalanui Beach Park), and tide pools brimming with colorful coral, fish, and the occasional turtle (Kapoho). Head to Hilo in the afternoon to catch a glimpse of the Boiling Pots waterfalls, Banyan Drive, and Queen Lili'uokalani Gardens, before dining at one of Hilo's great restaurants.

Pololū & Paniolo Country

North Kohala is a world away from the resorts of the coast. Visit the quaint artists' community of Hāwī, then head to Pololū Valley for amazing views. A steep-ish ½-mi hike leads to a fantastic black sand beach surrounded by beautiful sheer green cliffs. Back on the road, head up Highway 250 to Waimea and the pastures of paniolo country. Indulge in a memorable meal at one of the fantastic restaurants (we recommend Merriman's, Daniel Thiebaut, or Edelweiss).

Go Off-Road

Book an ATV tour or take your 4WD for a spin to check out some of the Big Island's isolated beaches. There are green beaches (in addition to "the" Green Sand Beach) waiting in the Ka'u region and ruggedly beautiful white beaches with perfect turquoise water along the Kohala Coast; deal with the tough, 4WD-only roads into these beaches and you're likely to be rewarded with a pristine tropical beach all to yourself.

THE QUICKEST WAY . . .

From Kailua-Kona to Volcano: Take the southern route, following Highway 11 through South Kona and Ka'u around South Point to Volcano (125 mi, just under three hours).

Between Kailua-Kona and Hilo: Starting in Kailua-Kona, take Highway 190 east to Highway 19. Follow 19 through Waimea to Hilo (96 mi, two hours or less).

From Kohala to Waimea: Take Highway 11 to Waikoloa Road (9 mi south of Hāpuna Beach) and follow it 10 mi to Highway 190. Turn left on 190 and follow it another 11 mi to Waimea (30 mi, 40 minutes).

WEDDINGS & HONEYMOONS

There's no question that Hawai'i is one of the country's foremost honeymoon destinations. Romance is in the air here, and the white, sandy beaches and turquoise water and swaying palm trees and balmy tropical breezes and perpetual summer sunshine put people in the mood for love. It's easy to understand why Hawai'i is fast becoming a popular wedding destination as well, especially as the cost of airfare has gone down, and new resorts and hotels entice visitors. A destination wedding is no longer exclusive to celebrities and the super rich. You can plan a traditional ceremony in a place of worship followed by a reception at an elegant resort, or you can go barefoot on the beach and celebrate at a lū'au. There are almost as many wedding planners in the islands as real estate agents, which makes it oh-so-easy to wed in paradise, and then, once the knot is tied, stay and honeymoon as well.

The Big Day

Choosing the Perfect Place. When choosing a location, remember that you really have two choices to make: the ceremony location and where to have the reception, if you're having one. For the former, there are beaches, bluffs overlooking beaches, gardens, private residences, resort lawns, and, of course, places of worship. It really depends on you. As for the reception, there are these same choices, as well as restaurants and even lū'au. If you decide to go outdoors, remember the seasons—yes, Hawai'i has seasons. If you're planning a winter wedding outdoors, be sure you have a backup plan (such as a tent), in case it rains. Also, if you're planning an outdoor wedding at sunset—which is very popular—be sure you match the time of your ceremony to the time the sun sets at that time of year. If you choose indoors, be sure to ask for pictures of the environs when you're planning. You don't want to plan a pink wedding, say, and wind up in a room that's predominantly red. Or maybe you do. The point is, it should be your choice.

Finding a Wedding Planner. If you're planning to invite more than a minister and your loved one to your wedding ceremony, seriously consider an on-island wedding planner who can help select a location, help design the floral scheme and recommend a florist as well as a photographer, help plan the menu and choose a restaurant, caterer, or resort, and suggest any special Hawaiian traditions to incorporate into your ceremony. And more: Will you need tents? Of course, a cake. Music. Maybe transportation. Lodging. Many planners have relationships with vendors, providing packages—which mean savings.

If you're planning a resort wedding, most have on-site wedding coordinators; however, there are many independents around the island and even those who specialize in certain types of ceremonies—by locale, size, religious affiliation, and so on. A simple "Big Island weddings" Google search will reveal dozens. What's important is that you feel comfortable with your coordinator. Ask for references—and call them. Share your budget. Get a proposal—in writing. Ask how long they've been in business, how they charge, how often you'll meet with them, and how they select vendors. Request a detailed list of the exact services they'll provide. If your idea of your wedding doesn't match their services, try someone else. If you can afford it, you might want to consider meeting the planner in person.

Getting Your License. The good news about marrying in Hawai'i is that no waiting period, no residency or citizenship requirements, and no blood tests or shots are required. However, both the bride and groom must appear together in person before a marriage license agent to apply for a marriage license. You'll need proof of age—the legal age to marry is 18. Upon approval, a marriage license is immediately issued and costs $60, cash only. After the ceremony, your officiant will mail the marriage license to the state. Approximately 120 days later, you will receive a copy in the mail. (For $10 extra, you can expedite this process. Ask your marriage license agent when you apply for your license.) For more detailed information, visit www.hawaii.gov or call 808/241–3498.

Also—this is important—the person performing your wedding must be licensed by the Hawai'i Department of Health, even if he or she is a licensed minister. Be sure to ask.

Wedding Attire. In Hawai'i, basically anything goes, from long, formal dresses with trains to white bikinis. Floral sundresses are fine, too. For the men, tuxedos are not the norm; a pair of solid-colored slacks with a nice aloha shirt is. In fact, tradition in Hawai'i for the groom is a plain white aloha shirt (they do exist) with slacks or long shorts and a colored sash around the waist. If you're planning a wedding on the beach, barefoot is the way to go.

If you decide to marry in a formal dress and tuxedo, don't expect to find such on the Big Island. It's possible but not easy. Instead, make your selections on the mainland and hand-carry them aboard the plane. Yes, it can be a pain, but ask your wedding gown retailer to provide a special carrying bag. After all, you don't want to chance losing your wedding dress in a wayward piece of luggage. And when it comes to fittings, again, that's something you'll want to take care of before you arrive on the Big Island.

Local customs. When it comes to traditional Hawaiian wedding customs, the most obvious is the lei exchange in which the bride and groom take turns placing a lei around the neck of the other—with a kiss. Bridal lei are usually floral, whereas the groom's is typically made of maile, a green leafy garland that drapes around the neck and is open at the ends. Brides often also wear a haku lei—a circular floral headpiece. Other Hawaiian customs include the blowing of the conch shell, hula, chanting, and Hawaiian music.

The Honeymoon

Do you want champagne and strawberries delivered to your room each morning? A maze of a swimming pool in which to float? A five-star restaurant in which to dine? Then a resort is the way to go. If, however, you prefer the comforts of a home, try a bed-and-breakfast. A B&B is also good if you're on a tight budget or don't plan to spend much time in your room. On the other hand, maybe you want your own private home in which to romp naked—or just laze around recovering from the wedding planning. Maybe you want your own kitchen in which to whip up a gourmet meal for your loved one. In that case, a private vacational rental home is the answer. Or maybe a condominium resort. That's another beautiful thing about Hawai'i: the lodging accommodations are almost as plentiful as the beaches, and there's one to match your tastes and your budget.

KIDS & FAMILIES

With dozens of adventures, discoveries, and fun-filled beach days, Hawai'i is a blast with *keiki* (kids). The entire family (parents included) will enjoy surf lessons, discovering a waterfall in the rain forest, and snorkeling with sea turtles. And there are plenty of organized activities for kids that will free parents' time for a few romantic beach strolls.

Choosing a Place to Stay

Resorts: All of the big resorts make kids' programs a priority, and it shows. A handful go above and beyond kid friendly, with exotic animals, monorails, and the sort of pool slides that make kids squeal with delight. When you are booking your room, ask about "kids eat free" deals and the number of kids' pools. Also, check out the size of the groups in the children's programs and find out whether the cost of the programs includes lunch, equipment, or other activities.

The Hilton Waikoloa is every kid's fantasy vacation come true, with dozens of pool slides, one lagoon for snorkeling and one filled with dolphins, and even a choice between riding a monorail or taking a boat to your room. Not to be outdone, the Four Seasons Hualālai Resort has a fantastic program that will keep your little ones happy and occupied all day, as does the Kona Village Resort, which also offers a kids' dinner and a teens' dinner seating to give parents the option of a solo date night.

Condos: Condos and vacation rentals are a fantastic value for families. You can cook your own food, which is cheaper than eating out and sometimes easier (especially if you have a finicky eater in your group), and you'll get twice the space of a hotel room for about a quarter of the price. If you decide to go the condo route, be sure to ask about the size of the complex's pool (some try to pawn a tiny soaking tub off as a pool) and whether barbecues are available.

Condos in Kailua-Kona (on or near Ali'i Drive) are the best value on the Big Island. We like Kona Pacific for its pool, barbecues, size of the units, and proximity to town; Casa de Emdeko for its ocean-front pool and on-site convenience store; and Hale Puhako for its tiny private beach. Affordable food is available at restaurants in Kona, if you are looking for a family night out or, even better, for date night.

Ocean Activities

On the Beach: Most people like being in the water, but toddlers and school-age kids tend to be especially enamored of it. The swimming pool at your condo or hotel is always an option, but don't be afraid to hit the beach with a little one in tow. There are several beaches that are nearly as safe as a pool—completely protected bays with pleasant white sand beaches. As always, use your good judgment and heed all posted signs and lifeguard warnings.

Calm beaches to try include Kamakahonu Beach and Kahalu'u in Kailua-Kona; Spencer Beach Park, Kauna'oa (aka Mauna Kea Beach), and Hāpuna Beach in Kohala; and Onekahakaha Beach Park in Hilo.

On the Waves: Surf lessons are a great idea for the older kids. Beginner lessons are always on safe and easy waves and tend to last anywhere from two to four hours.

For school-age and older kids, book a four-hour surfing lesson with Ocean Eco Tours and either join them out on the break or say aloha to a little parents-only time.

The Underwater World: If your kids are ready to try snorkeling, Hawai'i is a great place to introduce them to the underwa-

ter world. Even without the mask and snorkel, they'll be able to see colorful fish darting this way and that, and they may also spot turtles and dolphins at many of the island beaches.

Kahaluʻu Beach in Kailua-Kona is a great introductory snorkel spot. You can see fish darting just below the surface even before you get into the water, and Hawaiian sea turtles often waddle up on to the rocks or swim around close to the shore.

On the southern tip of the island, Punaluʻu provides opportunities to see the sea turtles up close—though the water can be rough, the sea turtles nest here and there are nearly always one or two napping on the black sand beach. At nighttime, head to the Mauna Kea Beach Resort, the Sheraton Keauhou, or Huggo's on the Rocks in Kailua-Kona to view manta rays; each spot shines a bright spotlight on the water to attract the rays. Anyone, but especially kids, could sit and watch them fly through the ocean in graceful circles for hours. No snorkel required!

Another great option is to book a snorkel cruise or opt to stay dry inside the Atlantis Submarine. Kids love crawling down into a real-life submarine and viewing the ocean world through its little portholes.

Land Activities

In addition to beach experiences, Hawaiʻi has rain forests, botanical gardens, and even petting zoos and hands-on kids' museums that will keep your kids entertained and out of the sun for a day.

On the Big Island, Volcanoes National Park is a must on a family vacation. Even grumpy teenagers will acknowledge the coolness of lava tubes, steaming earth, and a fiery nighttime lava show.

On the Hilo side, the Panaʻewa Rainforest Zoo is small, but free, and lots of fun for the little ones, with a small petting zoo. Just a few miles north, on the Hāmākua Coast, the Hawaiʻi Tropical Botanical Garden is beautiful and fun to meander through, checking out huge lily pads and the noisy local frogs.

School-age and older kids will get a kick out of the ATV tours at Kahua Ranch or the Parker Ranch in Waimea, and horseback rides through Waipiʻo Valley with Naʻalapa Stables.

After Dark

At nighttime, younger kids get a kick out of lūʻaus, and many of the shows incorporate young audience members, adding to the fun. The older kids might find it all a bit lame, but there are a handful of new shows in the islands that are more modern, incorporating acrobatics, lively music, and fire dancers. On the Big Island, teens and adults alike are sure to enjoy the music, lighting, acrobatics, fire eating, and overall theatrical quality of "Kamahaʻo–The Wondrous Myths of Hawaiʻi" at the Sheraton Keauhou.

Stargazing from Mauna Kea is another treat. The visitor center has telescopes set up for all visitors to use. If you'd rather leave the planning to someone else, book a tour with Hawaiʻi Forest and Trail. Their guides are also unbelievably knowledgeable and great at sharing that knowledge in a narrative form that kids—and adults for that matter—enjoy.

CRUISING THE HAWAIIAN ISLANDS

Cruising has become extremely popular in Hawai'i. For first-time visitors, it's an excellent way to get a taste of all the islands; and if you fall in love with one or even two, you know how to plan your next trip. It's also a comparatively inexpensive way to see Hawai'i. The limited amount of time in each port can be an argument against cruising—there's enough to do on any island to keep you busy for a week, so some folks feel shortchanged by cruise itineraries.

Cruising to Hawai'i

Until 2001 it was illegal for any cruise ships to stop in Hawai'i unless they originated from a foreign port, or were including a foreign port in their itinerary. The law has changed, but most cruises still include a stop in the Fanning Islands, Ensenada, or Vancouver. Gambling is legal on the open seas, and your winnings are tax-free; most cruise ships offer designated smoking areas and now enforce the U.S. legal drinking age (21) on Hawai'i itineraries.

Carnival Cruises. They call them "fun ships" for a reason—Carnival is all about keeping you busy and showing you a good time, both on board and on shore. Great for families, Carnival always plans plenty of kid-friendly activities, and their children's program rates high with the little critics. Carnival offers itineraries starting in Ensenada, Vancouver, and Honolulu. Their ships stop on Maui (Kahului and Lahaina), the Big Island (Kailua-Kona and Hilo), O'ahu, and Kaua'i. ☎ *888/227–6482* 🌐 *www.carnival.com.*

Celebrity Cruises. Celebrity's focus is on service, and it shows. From their waitstaff to their activity directors to their fantastic Hawaiian cultural experts, every aspect of your trip has been well thought out. They cater more to adults than children, so this may not be the best line for families. Celebrity's Hawai'i cruises depart from Los Angeles and stop in Maui (Lahaina), O'ahu, the Big Island (Hilo and Kailua-Kona), and Kaua'i. ☎ *800/647–2251* 🌐 *www.celebrity.com.*

Holland America. The grande dame of cruise lines, Holland America has a reputation for service and elegance. Holland America's Hawai'i cruises leave and return to San Diego, CA, and stop on Maui (Lahaina), the Big Island (Kailua-Kona and Hilo), O'ahu, and for half a day on Kaua'i. ☎ *877/724–5425* 🌐 *www.hollandamerica.com.*

Norwegian Cruise Lines. Norwegian has traditionally been one of the more casual cruise lines and offers a variety of service, activity, and excursion options. The latest addition to their fleet, *Pride of Hawai'i,* has expensive suites; but all the boats maintain a family-friendly focus. The only line with ships not required to stop in foreign ports, NCL itineraries originate either in Vancouver or Honolulu and include stops on Maui (Kahului and Lahaina), O'ahu, the Big Island (Hilo and Kona), and Kaua'i (Nawiliwili). ☎ *800/327–7030* 🌐 *www.ncl.com.*

Princess Cruises. Princess strives to offer affordable luxury. Their prices start out a little higher, but you get more bells and whistles (more affordable balcony rooms, nice decor, more restaurants to choose from, personalized service). They're not fantastic for kids, but they do a great job of keeping teenagers occupied. Princess's Hawaiian cruise is 15 days, round-trip from Los Angeles, with a service call in Ensenada. The *Island Princess* stops in Maui (Lahaina), the Big Island (Hilo and Kailua-Kona), O'ahu, and Kaua'i. ☎ *800/774–6237* 🌐 *www.princess.com.*

Royal Caribbean. Royal Caribbean's cruises originate in Los Angeles only, and stop in Maui (Lahaina), Kaua'i, O'ahu and the Big Island (both Hilo and Kailua-Kona). In keeping with its reputation for being all things to all people, Royal Caribbean offers a huge variety of activities and services on board and more excursions on land than any other cruise line. ☎ *800/521–8611* 🌐 *www.royalcaribbean.com.*

Cruising within Hawai'i

If you'd like to cruise from island to island, Norwegian is the only major cruise line option. For a different experience, Hawai'i Nautical offers cruises on smaller boats.

Norwegian Cruise Lines. Norwegian is the only major operator to offer interisland cruises in Hawai'i. Several of their ships cruise the islands—the main ones are *Pride of Aloha* (older, Hawaiian-themed, priced lowest), *Pride of Hawai'i* (newest, suites available, Hawaiian themed, slightly pricier), and *Pride of America* (Vintage Americana theme, very new, big family focus with lots of connecting staterooms and suites). All offer 7-day or longer itineraries within the islands, stopping on Maui, O'ahu, the Big Island, and overnighting in Kaua'i. ☎ *800/327–7030* 🌐 *www.ncl.com.*

Hawai'i Nautical. Offering a completely different sort of experience, Hawai'i Nautical provides private multiple-day interisland cruises on their catamarans, yachts, and sailboats. Prices are higher, but service is completely personal, right down to the itinerary. ☎ *808/234–7245* 🌐 *www.hawaiinautical.com.*

TIPS

1. On all but the *Pride of America*, *Pride of Hawai'i*, and *Pride of Aloha* cruises (operated by Norwegian Cruise Lines), you must bring a passport, as you will be entering foreign ports of call.
2. Think about booking your own excursions directly (except on Maui). You'll often pay less for greater value. For example, if you want to take a surfing lesson on O'ahu, visit one of the beachside shacks to find excellent instructors who offer better deals to individuals than they do to the cruise lines.
3. Tendering in Maui can be a tedious process—if you want to avoid a little bit of the headache (and hours waiting in the sun), be sure to book an excursion there through the ship and you'll have smooth sailing.
4. Most mainland cell phones will work without a hitch on board between the islands and at all Hawaiian ports of call.

Exploring the Big Island

WORD OF MOUTH

"The Big Island is my favorite. It's host to the most active volcano–an incredible sight to see! The mountains (Mauna Kea and Mauna Loa) are often snowcapped in the winter months. There's so much to see and do without the huge commercialization that has happened on O'ahu and Maui."

–CityOfRefuge

By Amy Westervelt

NICKNAMED "THE BIG ISLAND," Hawai'i the island is a microcosm of Hawai'i, the state. From long white-sand beaches and crystal clear bays to rain forests, waterfalls, lū'aus, exotic flowers, and birds, all things quintessentially Hawaiian are well represented here. But an assortment of happy surprises also distinguish the Big Island from the rest of Hawai'i—an active volcano (Kīlauea) oozing red lava and creating new earth every day, the clearest place in the world to view stars in the night sky (Mauna Kea), and some seriously good coffee (Kona, of course).

Sometimes referred to as an "adventurer's island," the Big Island can be daunting for first-time visitors because it is, in fact, big, and it can seem wild and unruly. But if all you want is a mai tai and a beach, the Big Island has got you covered. If you like to hike but don't consider yourself an adventurer, nature walks and pleasant strolls to match your ability and interest abound. Golfers have long flocked to the Big Island for their pick of a dozen or so award-winning golf courses. Don't worry if you're a non-golfer being dragged along on a golf day—the courses tend to be within spitting distance of a beach, a pool, a spa, or all three. A foodie in your group? The Big Island has enough award-winning chefs and locally sourced ingredients to please even the most discerning palate.

If you have sought out the Big Island for that adventurous reputation, prepare to have your expectations met and exceeded. From scuba diving to surfing, from kayaking to kiteboarding, the waters surrounding the Big Island will not disappoint. The gorges and valleys of the Hāmākua Coast offer dozens of hikes, ranging from moderate to extreme and typically including a dip in a waterfall-fed pool. And, because even a beach day can be an adventure, some of the island's most beautiful beaches lie at the end of a hike over fields of black lava.

Whether your goal is relaxation, adventure, or a bit of both, the first secret to enjoying the Big Island is to rent a car, ideally one with four-wheel drive. The second: stay more than three days, or return again and again to really explore this fascinating place. With 266 mi of coastline made up of white coral, black lava, and a dusting of green-olivine beaches, interspersed with lava cliffs, emerald gorges, and splashing waterfalls, the Big Island can be overwhelming. Depending on the number of days you have available, it would be best to divide your time between the Hilo and Kona sides of the island in order to take in the attractions of each.

The Big Island is also the youngest and (no surprises here) the largest of the Hawaiian Islands (still growing, thanks to Kīlauea). It is the birthplace of King Kamehameha, the leader credited with uniting the separate island kingdoms into one Hawai'i. And it is the place where the ancient Hawaiians first interacted with western explorers.

It is easy to forget that you are in America when you visit the Big Island. Though the island is young compared to the rest of the Islands, it is nonetheless thousands of years old, and the culture and traditions of its people date back to long before Columbus sailed the ocean blue. The ancient Hawaiians are descended from a mix of Tahitian, Marquesan, and Polynesian explorers who landed in Hawai'i between AD 500 and 700, bringing with them livestock (pigs and chickens), plants and seedlings (they introduced coconut and taro to the Islands, along with several other species), stowaway insects and rats, a vibrant culture, and a tribal hierarchy system. The history of the Big Island's early people is evident in the ancient *heiau* (temples) and monuments that dot its coast, the rituals still practiced by its people, and the welcoming spirit of aloha. It is still considered *kapu* (forbidden, according to an ancient Hawaiian social code) to take lava rock from Kīlauea or to pick a Lehua flower from an Ohi'a tree, and locals still leave offerings of gin and flowers around the Kīlauea crater to Pele, the Volcano Goddess. Each May, Hilo fills to capacity with dancers and admirers in town for the Merrie Monarch Festival, the largest hula festival in the world. The festival's name honors King Kalakaua (he ruled from 1874 to 1891), who was responsible for reinstating many ancient Hawaiian cultural traditions in the Islands during the late 1800s, including the hula. The Big Island is also home to the ancient Place of Refuge, where kapu breakers sought refuge when exiled from the rest of the Islands for social indiscretions.

THE KOHALA DISTRICT

If you had only a weekend to spend on the Big Island, this is where you'd want to go. Kohala is a mix of the island's best beaches and swankiest hotels just minutes from ancient valleys and temples, waterfalls, and funky artist enclaves.

North of Kona International Airport, along Highway 19, brightly colored bougainvillea stand out in relief against miles of black lava fields stretching from the mountain to the sea. Most of the lava flows are from the last eruptions of Mt. Hualālai, in 1800 and 1801. Technically Mt. Hualālai is not dormant just yet. If it sticks to the schedule it has been on for the last few thousand years, it may be due to blow again soon. For now, however, the area around the long silent crater makes for some surprisingly beautiful hiking.

Back down at the coast, the black lava fields created by those 1800 flows are interrupted only by green oases of irrigated golf courses surrounding the glamorous luxury resorts of the Kona-Kohala Coast. The resorts lay claim to some of the island's finest restaurants and its only destination spas. But the real attractions here are the island's best beaches. On a clear day you can see Maui from the Kohala Coast, and during the winter months, glistening humpback whales cleave the waters just offshore.

The arid coast suddenly gives way to the lush green valley of Pololū in North Kohala, and hot sunny days at the beach become cool misty evenings in the Kohala mountains. In the sugar-plantations-turned-artsy enclaves of Hāwī and Kapa'au, new galleries are interspersed with charming reminders of old Hawai'i—wooden boardwalks, quaint local stores, delicious neighborhood restaurants, friendly locals, and a delightfully slow pace. With beaches, waterfalls, resorts, and villages within a

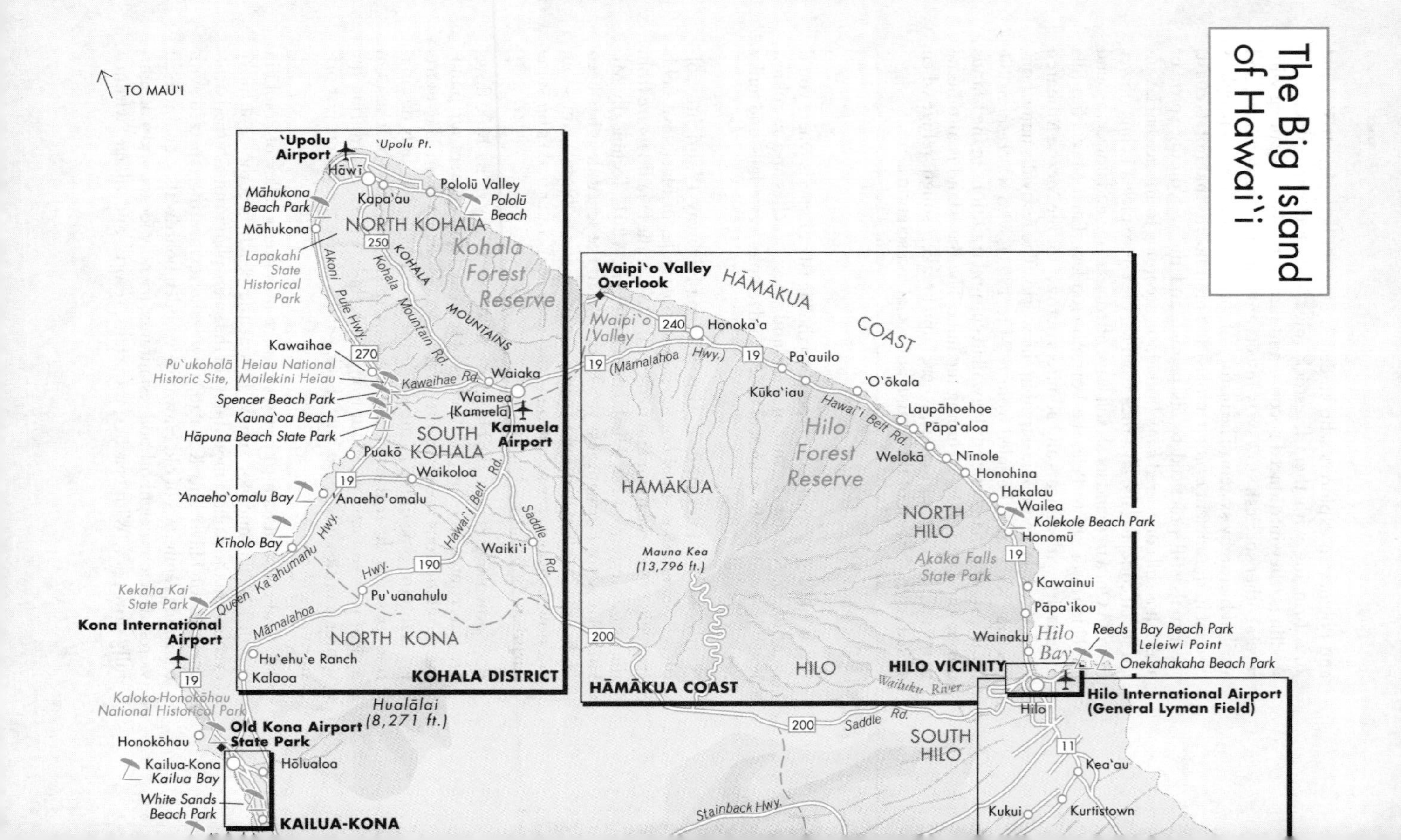

The Big Island of Hawai`i
TO MAU'I
`Upolu Airport
`Upolu Pt.
Hāwī
Kapa`au
Pololū Valley
Pololū Beach
Māhukona Beach Park
Māhukona
NORTH KOHALA
250
Kohala Forest Reserve
KOHALA MOUNTAINS
Kohala Mountain Rd.
Akoni Pule Hwy.
Lapakahi State Historical Park
Kawaihae
270
Pu`ukoholā Heiau National Historic Site, Mailekini Heiau
Spencer Beach Park
Kauna`oa Beach
Hāpuna Beach State Park
Kawaihae Rd.
Waiaka
Waimea (Kamuela)
Kamuela Airport
SOUTH KOHALA
Puakō
Waikoloa
19
`Anaeho`omalu Bay
'Anaeho'omalu
Kīholo Bay
Queen Ka`ahumanu Hwy.
Hawai`i Belt Rd.
Saddle Rd.
Waiki`i
Hwy.
190
Pu`uanahulu
Māmalahoa
Kekaha Kai State Park
Kona International Airport
NORTH KONA
Hu`ehu`e Ranch
Kalaoa
KOHALA DISTRICT
Kaloko-Honokōhau National Historical Park
Hualālai (8,271 ft.)
Old Kona Airport State Park
Honokōhau
Kailua-Kona
Kailua Bay
Hōlualoa
White Sands Beach Park
KAILUA-KONA
Waipi`o Valley Overlook
Waipi`o Valley
HĀMĀKUA COAST
240
Honoka`a
19 (Māmalahoa Hwy.)
Pa`auilo
Kūka`iau
`O`ōkala
Hawai`i Belt Rd.
Laupāhoehoe
Pāpa`aloa
Hilo Forest Reserve
Welokā
Nīnole
Honohina
HĀMĀKUA
Hakalau
Wailea
NORTH HILO
Kolekole Beach Park
Honomū
Mauna Kea (13,796 ft.)
Akaka Falls State Park
Kawainui
Pāpa`ikou
200
Wainaku
Hilo Bay
Reeds Bay Beach Park
Leleiwi Point
Onekahakaha Beach Park
HILO
HILO VICINITY
HĀMĀKUA COAST
Wailuku River
Hilo
Hilo International Airport (General Lyman Field)
Saddle Rd.
SOUTH HILO
11
Kea`au
Kukui
Kurtistown
Stainback Hwy.

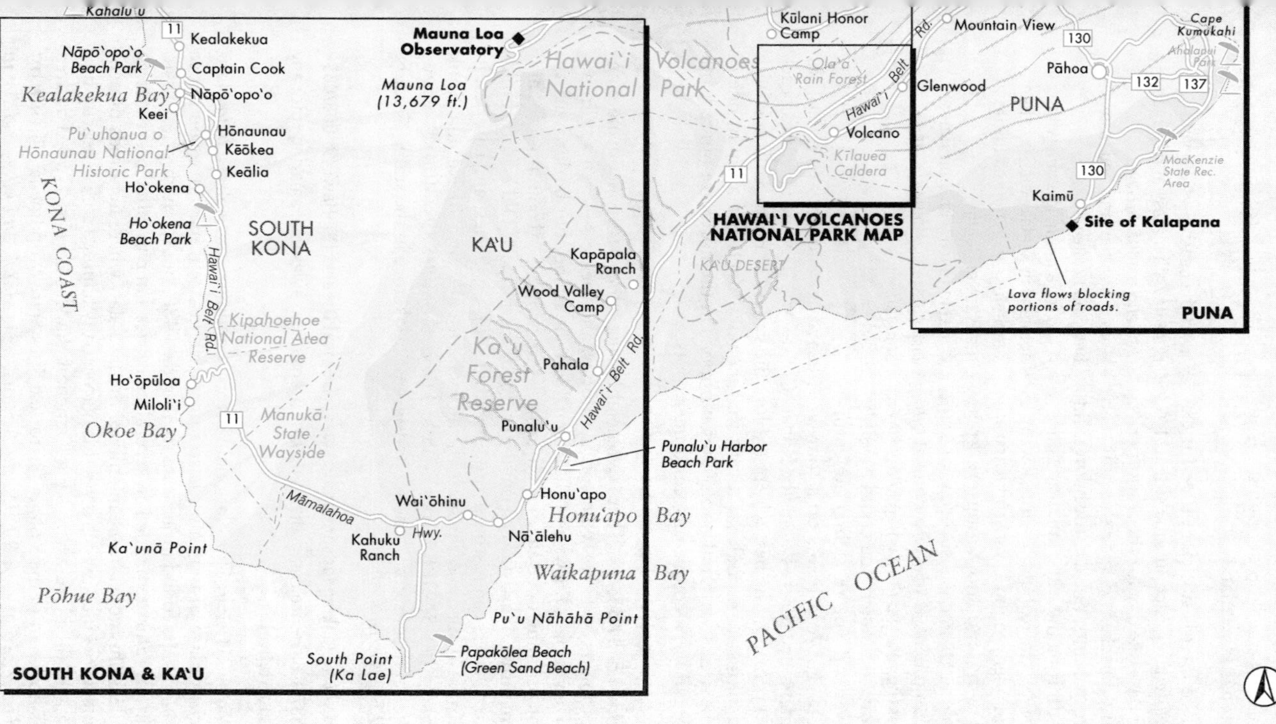

SOUTH KONA & KA'U
Kahalu'u
11
Kealakekua
Nāpō'opo'o Beach Park
Captain Cook
Kealakekua Bay
Nāpō'opo'o
Keei
Pu'uhonua o Hōnaunau National Historic Park
Hōnaunau
Kēōkea
Keālia
Ho'okena
Ho'okena Beach Park
KONA COAST
SOUTH KONA
Hawai'i Belt Rd.
Kipahoehoe National Area Reserve
Ho'ōpūloa
Miloli'i
Okoe Bay
Manukā State Wayside
Māmalahoa Hwy.
Ka'unā Point
Pōhue Bay
Kahuku Ranch
Wai'ōhinu
Nā'ālehu
South Point (Ka Lae)
Papakōlea Beach (Green Sand Beach)
Pu'u Nāhāhā Point
Waikapuna Bay
Honu'apo Bay
Honu'apo
Punalu'u
Punalu'u Harbor Beach Park
Ka'u Forest Reserve
Pahala
Wood Valley Camp
Kapāpala Ranch
KA'U
Mauna Loa Observatory
Mauna Loa (13,679 ft.)
Hawai'i Volcanoes National Park
Kūlani Honor Camp
Ola'a Rain Forest
Volcano
Kīlauea Caldera
Hawai'i Belt Rd.
HAWAI'I VOLCANOES NATIONAL PARK MAP
KA'U DESERT
Glenwood
Mountain View
130
Pāhoa
132
137
Cape Kumukahi
PUNA
MacKenzie State Rec. Area
Kaimū
Site of Kalapana
Lava flows blocking portions of roads.
PUNA
PACIFIC OCEAN

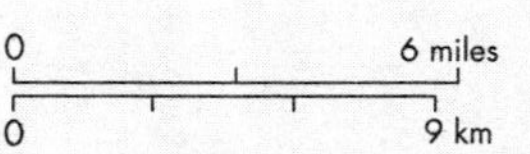

0
6 miles
0
9 km

few short miles of each other, Kohala is one-stop shopping for all things Hawaiian.

LOGISTICS Two days is sufficient time for experiencing each unique side of Kohala—one day for the resort perks: the beach, the spa, the golf, the restaurants; one day for hiking and admiring the waterfalls and valleys of North Kohala, coupled with a wander around Hāwī and Kapa'au. Diving and snorkeling are great along this coast, so bring or rent equipment. If you're staying at one of the resorts, they will usually have any equipment you could possibly want. If you're feeling adventurous, get your hands on a four-wheel-drive car and head to one of the unmarked beaches along the Kohala Coast—you may end up with a beach to yourself. The best way to explore the valleys of north Kohala is with a hiking tour. Look for a tour that includes lunch and a dip in one of the area's waterfall pools. Lunch options in the north are limited, but Hāwī has a couple of great dinner spots.

FUN THINGS TO DO: KONA SIDE

- Hit the beach. Live out your Blue Hawai'i fantasy at Hāpuna or 'Anaeho'omalu (A-Bay).
- Tour a coffee farm and taste the best Kona coffee.
- Go for a morning swim with dolphins in Kealakekua Bay, then seek refuge with the sea turtles at the Place of Refuge.
- Get in touch with your inner artist in Hāwī, Hōlualoa, or Kainaliu.

Main Attractions

❺ **Hāwī and Kapa'au.** These two neighboring villages thrived during plantation days. There were hotels, saloons, and theaters—even a railroad. They took a hit when "Big Sugar" left the island, but both towns are blossoming once again today, thanks to strong local communities and an influx of artists keen on honoring the towns' past. Old historic buildings have been restored and now hold shops, galleries, and eateries. In Kapa'au, browse through the Hawaiian collection of **Kohala Book Shop** (✉ 54-3885 Akoni Pule Hwy. ☎ 808/889–6400 🌐 www.kohalabooks.com), the second-largest bookstore in the state. ✉ *Hwy. 270, North Kohala.*

NEED A BREAK? **If you're looking for something sweet, Tropical Dreams (✉ Hāwī ☎ 808/889–5577) makes ice cream that is *da kine* (translation: awesome, amazing—pick any superlative).**

★ ❹ **Mo'okini Heiau.** This National Historic Landmark, an isolated *heiau* (ancient place of worship), is so impressive in size it may give you goose bumps. Its foundations date to about AD 480, but the high priest Pa'ao from Tahiti expanded it several centuries later to offer sacrifices to please his gods. You can still see the lava slab where hundreds of people were killed, which gives this place a truly haunted feel. A nearby sign marks the place where King Kamehameha was born in 1758. The area is now part of the Kohala Historical Sites State Monument. ✉ *Turn off Hwy. 270 at sign for 'Upolu Airport, near Hāwī, and hike or drive in a four-wheel-drive vehicle 1½ mi southwest* ☎ *808/974–6200.*

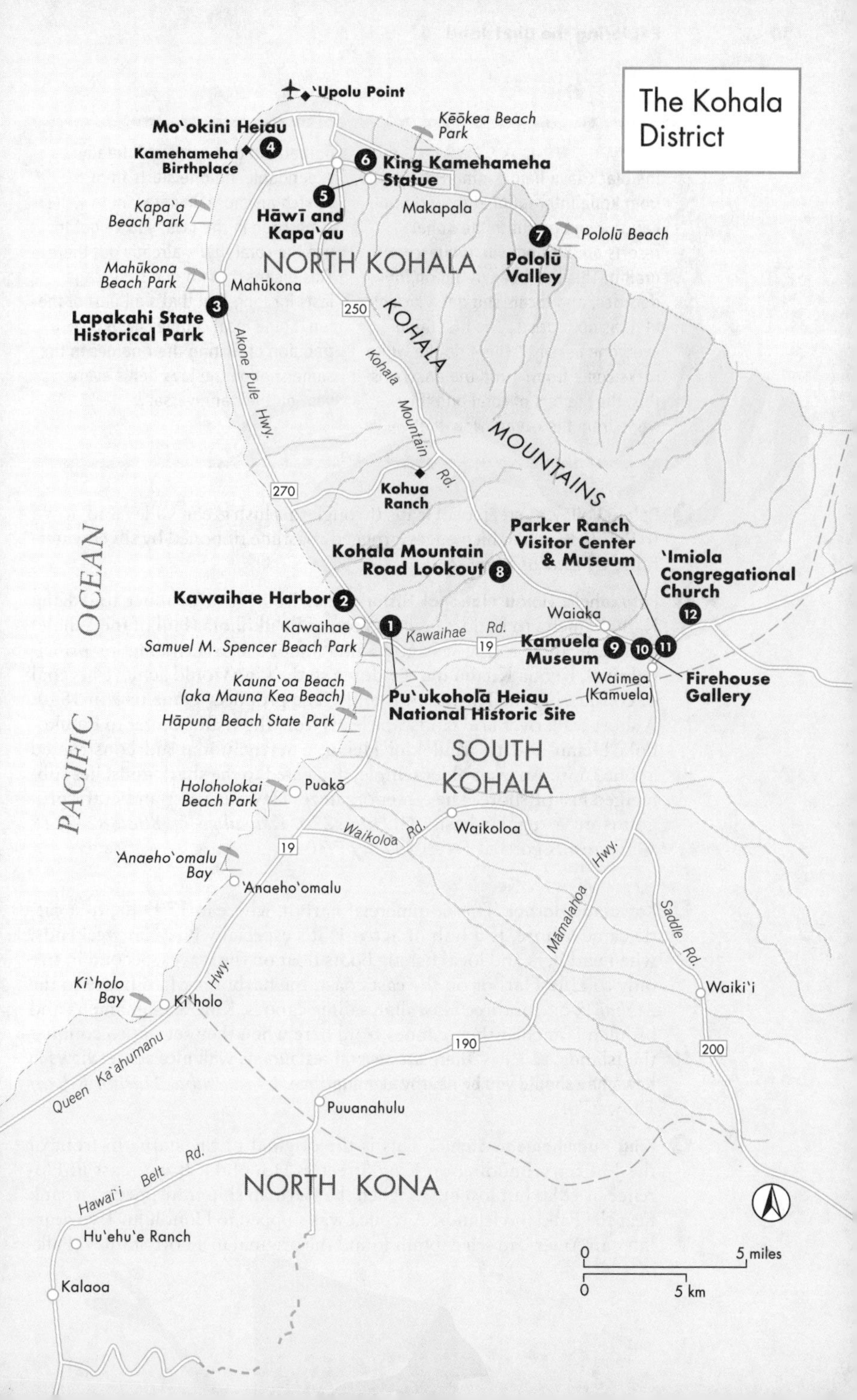

The Kohala District
'Upolu Point
Mo'okini Heiau
Kamehameha Birthplace
Kēōkea Beach Park
King Kamehameha Statue
Hāwī and Kapa'au
Makapala
Kapa'a Beach Park
Pololū Beach
Pololū Valley
NORTH KOHALA
Mahūkona Beach Park
Mahūkona
Lapakahi State Historical Park
250
KOHALA
Kohala Mountain Rd.
Akone Pule Hwy.
MOUNTAINS
270
Kohua Ranch
Parker Ranch Visitor Center & Museum
Kohala Mountain Road Lookout
'Imiola Congregational Church
Kawaihae Harbor
Kawaihae
Kawaihae Rd.
Waiaka
Samuel M. Spencer Beach Park
19
Kamuela Museum
Waimea (Kamuela)
Firehouse Gallery
Kauna'oa Beach (aka Mauna Kea Beach)
Pu'ukoholā Heiau National Historic Site
Hāpuna Beach State Park
PACIFIC OCEAN
SOUTH KOHALA
Holoholokai Beach Park
Puakō
Waikoloa Rd.
Waikoloa
'Anaeho'omalu Bay
'Anaeho'omalu
Māmalahoa Hwy.
Saddle Rd.
Ki'holo Bay
Ki'holo
Waiki'i
Queen Ka'ahumanu Hwy.
190
200
Puuanahulu
NORTH KONA
Hawai'i Belt Rd.
Hu'ehu'e Ranch
Kalaoa
0
5 miles
0
5 km

CLOSE UP

Graffiti

YOU WILL NO DOUBT NOTICE that the black-lava fields lining Highway 19 from Kona International Airport into Kailua-Kona or out to the Kohala resorts are littered with white-coral graffiti. This has been going on for decades, and locals still get a kick out of it, as do tourists. The first thing everyone asks is "where do the white rocks come from?" and the answer is this: they're bits of coral and they come from the ocean. Now that we've figured out that coral isn't totally expendable, no one starts from scratch anymore. If you want to write a message in the lava, you've got to use the coral that's already out there. This means that no one's message lasts for long, but that's all part of the fun. Some local couples even have a tradition of writing their names in the same spot on the lava fields every year on their anniversary.

7 **Pololū Valley.** A steep trail leads through this lush green valley and down to Pololū Beach, which edges a rugged coastline ribboned by silver waterfalls. ✉ *End of Hwy. 270.*

★ 1 **Pu'ukoholā Heiau National Historic Site.** In 1790 a prophet told King Kamehameha to build a *heiau* on top of Pu'ukoholā (Hill of the Whale) and dedicate it to the war god Kūkā'ilimoku by sacrificing his principal rival, Keōua Kūahu'ula. By doing so the king would achieve his goal of conquering the Hawaiian Islands. The prophecy came true in 1810. A short walk over arid landscape leads from the visitor center to **Pu'ukoholā Heiau** and to **Mailekini Heiau,** a navigational aid constructed about 1550. An even older temple, dedicated to the shark gods, lies submerged just offshore. The center organizes Hawaiian arts-and-crafts programs on a regular basis. ✉ *Hwy. 270, Kawaihae* ☎ *808/882–7218* 🌐 *www.nps.gov* 🎫 *Free* ⏲ *Daily 7:30–4.*

Also Worth Seeing

2 **Kawaihae Harbor.** This commercial harbor, where in 1793 the first cattle came ashore, is a hub of activity. It's especially busy on weekends, when paddlers and local fishing boats float on the waves. Second in size only to Hilo Harbor on the east coast, the harbor is often home to the *Makali'i,* one of three Hawaiian sailing canoes. King Kamehameha and his men launched their canoes from here when they set out to conquer the Islands. ■ TIP→ **There are several restaurants with nice sunset views in Kawaihae should you be nearby at dinnertime.** ✉ *Kawaihae Harbor Rd. off Hwy. 270.*

6 **King Kamehameha Statue.** This is the original of the statue in front of the Judiciary Building on King Street in Honolulu. It was cast in Florence in 1880 but lost at sea when the German ship transporting it sank near the Falkland Islands. A replica was shipped to Honolulu. Two years later an American sea captain found the original in a Port Stanley (Falk-

land Islands) junkyard and brought it to the Big Island. The legislature voted to erect it near Kamehameha's birthplace. Every year, on King Kamehameha Day (June 11), a magnificent abundance of floral lei adorns the image of Hawai'i's great king. It's in front of the old Kohala Courthouse next to the highway. ✉ *Hwy. 270, Kapa'au.*

NEED A BREAK?

Kohala Rainbow Cafe (☎ 808/889-0099), across from the King Kamehameha statue in Kapa'au, serves wraps, salads, smoothies, and sandwiches all day long. Try the Kamehameha wrap–filled with Hawaiian-style kālua pork, organic greens, tomatoes, onions, cheeses, and Maui onion dressing. Open Monday and Wednesday to Friday 10–6, weekends 11–5.

★ ❸ **Lapakahi State Historical Park.** A self-guided, 1-mi walking tour leads through the ruins of the once-prosperous fishing village Koai'e, which dates as far back as the 15th century. Displays illustrate early Hawaiian fishing and farming techniques, salt gathering, games, and legends. A park guide is often on-site to answer questions. Since the shoreline near the state park is an officially designated Marine Life Conservation District, and part of the site itself is considered sacred, swimming is discouraged. For some reason a distinction is made between swimming and snorkeling; the latter is allowed and superb. ✉ *Hwy. 270, between Kawaihae and Māhukona, North Kohala* ☎ *808/974–6200 or 808/882–6207* 🎫 *Free* ⏲ *Daily 8–4.*

WAIMEA

Just up the hill from Kohala, past Saddle Road (the route to Mauna Kea), Waimea offers a completely different experience from the rest of the island. Rolling green hills, large open pastures, cool evening breezes and morning mists, cattle everywhere, and regular rodeos are just a few of the surprises you'll stumble upon here in *paniolo* (Hawaiian for "cowboy") country. In addition to the horses and cattle, this is also where some of the island's top resort chefs are sent out to pasture, which makes Waimea an ideal place to find yourself stranded at dinnertime. In keeping with the recent Big Island restaurant trend toward locally farmed ingredients, a handful of Waimea farms and ranches supply most of the restaurants on the island, and many sell to the public as well. With its galleries, restaurants, and museum, as well as the Parker Ranch, Waimea is well worth a stop if you're heading to Hilo or Mauna Kea. And the short highway that connects Waimea to North Kohala (Hwy. 170) affords some of our favorite Big Island views.

LOGISTICS You can see most of what Waimea has to offer in one day, but if you're heading up to Mauna Kea for stargazing (which you should), it could easily be stretched to two. If you stay in Waimea overnight (there are a few B&B options), or just got up really early, you could go for a morning horseback ride around the Parker Ranch, spend the afternoon browsing through town or touring some of the area's fantastic farms and ranches, then indulge in a gourmet dinner—all before heading up Saddle Road for world-renowned stargazing atop Mauna Kea. One word to the wise—there are no services or gas stations on Saddle Road, the only way to reach Mauna Kea. Fill up on gas and bring water and/or snacks with you (there are plenty of gas stations, cafés, and shops in Waimea).

WAIMEA OR KAMUELA?

Both, actually. The name of the Waimea post office is Kamuela, while the name of the town itself is Waimea. Some say the post office is named for the son of the founder of Parker Ranch.

Main Attractions

8 **Kohala Mountain Road Lookout.** The lookout here provides a splendid view of the Kohala Coast and Kawaihae Harbor far below. On clear days, you can see well beyond the resorts. It's one of the most scenic spots on the island and great for a picnic. Often, thick mists drift in, casting an eerie feeling. ✉ *Kohala Mountain Rd., Hwy. 250.*

Merriman's Farm Visits and Dinner. Hawai'i Forest & Trail operates this half-day tour, which is one of the best ways to delve into the Big Island's burgeoning food scene. Chef Peter Merriman, the godfather of Hawai'i regional cuisine, put together the itinerary. It includes visits to Kahua Ranch where all of the top chefs buy their pork and beef and to Honopua Farms, a top organic produce farm. Honopua Farms is also home to lei maker and native Hawaiian Marie McDonald, who was named a "living treasure" by the Smithsonian Institution. After touring the farms, the group returns to Merriman's Restaurant in Waimea for a gourmet four-course meal comprised of various farm-fresh items. ☎ *800/464–1993* 🌐 *www.hawaii-forest.com* 🎫 *$155, including dinner* ⏲ *Mon.–Thurs., from 2:30–7:30.*

11 **Parker Ranch Visitor Center & Museum.** The center chronicles the life of John Palmer Parker (and his descendants), who founded Parker Ranch in 1847. Parker married the granddaughter of King Kamehameha and bought two acres of land from the king for the sum of $10. Purchase your tickets here for the **Parker Ranch Historic Homes,** a couple of miles south of town. The original family residence, Mānā, is built entirely from native woods such as koa. Pu'ōpelu, added to the estate in 1879, was the residence of Richard Smart, a sixth-generation Parker who expanded the house to make room for his European art collection. On Friday, Hawaiian crafts demonstrations take place at the homes. A wagon ride allows you a comfortable, albeit old-fashioned, visit to the pastures. Also available are horseback rides, ATV rides, and guided hunting or walking tours (⇨ Cowboys of Hawai'i ATV Rides *in* Chapter 5, Golf, Hiking & Outdoor Activities). ✉ *Parker Ranch Shopping Center, 67-1185 Māmalahoa Hwy., Waimea* ☎ *808/885–7655 or 808/885–5433, 800/262–7290 toll-free* 🌐 *www.parkerranch.com* 🎫 *Museum $7, homes $8.50, both $14* ⏲ *Museum Mon.–Sat. 9–5, homes daily 10–5.*

Also Worth Seeing

10 **Firehouse Gallery.** Walk across the Parker Ranch Shopping Center parking lot to a historic 77-year-old fire station, now a gallery, to glimpse what the artists in Hāmākua and Kohala are up to. The Waimea Arts

‘Akaka Falls, ‘Akaka Falls State Park, Hāmākua Coast.

(top left) Kona coffee beans. (top right) The "Lobster Claw" *Heliconia* plant.
(bottom) The Gemini and Canada-France-Hawaii telescopes at the summit of Mauna Kea.

(top) Lava flows at Hawai'i Volcanoes National Park. (bottom) A pristine beach at Kua Bay.

(top) What's better than a hot stone massage? A hot stone massage on the beach. (bottom) A diver observes as a green sea turtle is cleaned by yellow tang and lined bristletooth fish.

Horseback riding in Waipi‘o Valley.

(top) Hula dancers perform in a traditional lū'au. (bottom) Humpback whales can be spotted from early December through April.

(top) Driving through Waimea, with snowcapped Mauna Kea in the background. (bottom) Rowing at sunrise, Kailua Bay.

Lava rocks in the Waipi'o Valley, Hāmākua Coast.

Council sponsors free *kaha ki'is* (one-person shows). ✉ *Near main stoplight in Waimea, toward Kailua-Kona on Hwy. 190, Waimea* ☎ *808/887–1052.*

⓬ **'Imiola Congregational Church.** Stop here to admire the dark koa interior and the unusual wooden calabashes hanging from the ceiling. Be careful not to walk in while a service is in progress, as the front entry of this church, which was established in 1832 and rebuilt in 1857, is behind the pulpit. ✉ *65-1084 Mamalahoa Hwy., on "Church Row", Waimea* ☎ *808/885–4987.*

❾ **Kamuela Museum.** This small private museum has a fascinating collection of artifacts from Hawai'i and around the world. The eclectic collection includes Hawaiian weapons and a satiny-smooth koa table that once graced 'Iolani Palace in Honolulu. There are also period furniture pieces, artwork, and military and war memorabilia. ✉ *Hwys. 19 and 250, Waimea* ☎ *808/885–4724* *$5* ⏲ *Daily 8–5.*

NEED A BREAK?

At Aioli's (✉ 'Opelo Plaza, Hwy. 19 and 'Opelo Rd., Waimea ☎ 808/885–6325) you can pick up ready-to-go box lunches or opt for a custom-made sandwich. They also offer a delicious bistro menu that changes often to make use of local produce and fresh fish. Stop by Waimea Coffee & Company (✉ Parker Sq., 65-1279 Kawaihae Rd., Waimea ☎ 808/885–4472) for a steaming latté and a warm pastry. Sit out on their veranda, and try to believe you're in Hawai'i.

KAILUA-KONA

A fun and funky seaside village, Kailua-Kona has the souvenir shops and open-air restaurants you'd expect in a major tourist hub, but with the added bonus of a surprising number of historic sites. Except for the rare deluge, the sun shines year-round. Mornings offer cooler weather, smaller crowds, and more birds singing in the banyan trees; you'll see dozens of tourists and locals out running on Ali'i Drive, the town's main drag, by about 5 AM every morning. Afternoon and evenings are great for cool drinks, brilliant sunsets, and lazy hours spent gazing out over the ocean. Though there are better beaches north of the town on the Kohala Coast, Kailua-Kona is nonetheless home to a few gems, including a fantastic snorkeling beach (Kahalu'u) and a tranquil bay perfect for kids (Kamakahonu Beach, in front of the King Kamehameha Hotel).

Scattered amongst the shops, restaurants, and condo complexes of Ali'i Drive are King Kamehameha I's resting place (he died here in 1819), the last royal palace in the U.S., and a battle ground dotted with the graves of ancient Hawaiians who fought for their land and lost. It was also here in Kailua-Kona that Kamehameha's successor, King Liholiho, broke and officially abolished the ancient *kapu* (roughly translating as "forbidden," it was the name for the strict code of conduct islanders were compelled to follow) system by publicly sitting and eating with women. The following year, on April 4, 1820, the first Christian missionaries came ashore here, changing the islands forever. If you want to know more about the village's fascinating past, arrange for a 75-minute guided walking tour with the **Kona Historical Society** (✉ 81-6551 Māmalahoa Hwy. ☎ 808/323–3222 🌐 www.konahistorical.org).

LOGISTICS Half a day is plenty of time to explore Kailua-Kona; most of the town's sights are located in or near the downtown area. Still, if you add in a beach trip (Kahalu'u Beach has some of the best and easiest snorkeling on the island), it's easy to while away the bulk of a day. Another option for making a day of it is to tack on a short trip to the charming artists' village of Hōlualoa or to the coffee farms in the mountains just above the village. There are a few great restaurants here that are far more affordable than those on the Kohala Coast and in Waimea. The town closest to the Kona International Airport (it's about 7 mi away), Kailua-Kona is a convenient home-base from which to explore the island.

WHERE DO I PARK?

The easiest place to park your car is at King Kamehameha's Kona Beach Hotel ($3). Some free parking is also available: when you enter Kailua via Palani Road (Hwy. 190), turn left onto Kuakini Highway; drive for a half block, and turn right into the small marked parking lot. Walk *makai* (toward the ocean) on Likana Lane a half block to Ali'i Drive and you'll be in the heart of Kailua-Kona.

Main Attractions

Hōlualoa. Hugging the hillside above Kealakekua Bay, the tiny village of Hōlualoa is just up winding Hualālai Road from Kailua-Kona. A charming surprise, it's the kind of place where locals sit on their porches or in front of the stores and "talk story" (Hawaiian for shoot the breeze) all day long. It's comprised almost entirely of galleries in which all types of artists, from woodworkers to jewelry-makers and more traditional painters, work in their studios in back and sell the finished product up front. Formerly the exclusive domain of coffee plantations, there are still quite a few coffee farms offering free tours and cups of joe. Duck into the only café in town, the cleverly named **Hōluakoa Cafe** (✉ 76-5900 Mamalahoa Hwy. ☎ 808/322–2233), and grab a cup to sip while you stroll through town.

18 **Kona Inn Shopping Village.** Originally a hotel, the Kona Inn was built in 1928 to woo a new wave of wealthy travelers. As newer condos and resorts opened along the Kona and Kohala coasts, it lost much of its appeal, and was eventually transformed into a low-rise mall with dozens of clothing boutiques, art galleries, gift shops, and island-style eateries. Broad lawns with coconut trees on the ocean side are lovely for afternoon picnics and the open-air Kona Inn restaurant is a local favorite for evening mai tais. Prior to the construction of the inn, the personal *heiau* of King Liholiho stood on this shore. ✉ *75-5744 Ali'i Dr.*

NEED A BREAK?

Grab a tasty croissant sandwich and knock back some of Kona's best coffee at Hula Bean (✉ 75-5719 Ali'i Dr. ☎ 808/329–6152), directly across from the Kona Village Shopping Center. If it's late afternoon, it's time to unwind with one of those umbrella drinks. For cocktails head to the Kona Inn Restaurant (✉ 75-5744 Ali'i Dr. ☎ 808/329–4455), a local favorite.

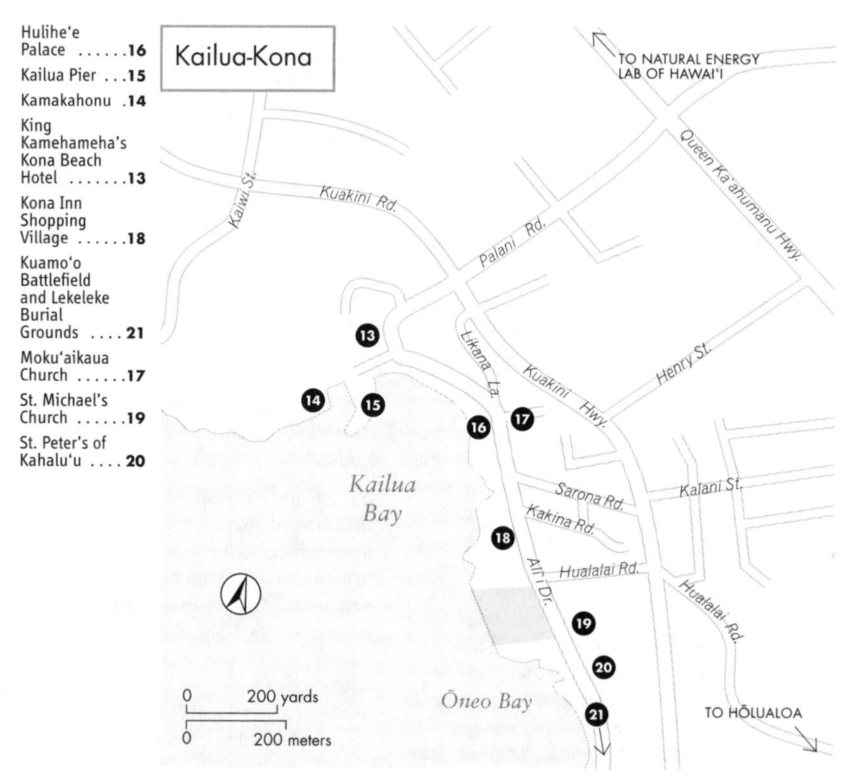

2

Natural Energy Lab of Hawai'i. Driving south from the Kona International Airport towards Kailua-Kona you'll spot a large mysterious group of buildings with an equally large and mysterious photovoltaic (solar) panel installation just inside its gate. Although it looks like some sort of top-secret military station, this is the site of the Natural Energy Lab of Hawaii, NELHA for short, where scientists, researchers, and entrepreneurs are developing and marketing everything from new uses for solar power to energy-efficient air-conditioning systems and environmentally friendly aqua-culture techniques. Visitors are welcome at the lab, and there are 1½-hr tours for those interested in learning more about the experiments being conducted. ✉ *73-4460 Queen Ka'ahumanu Hwy., #101* ☎ *808/329–7341* 🌐 *www.nelha.org* 🎫 *Free, $8 tour* ⏲ *Weekdays 8–4; Tours Tues., Wed., Thurs. at 10.*

Also Worth Seeing

16 **Hulihe'e Palace.** A lovely rambling old stone home surrounded by jewel-green grass and sweeping ocean views and fronted by an elaborate wrought-iron gate, Hulihe'e Palace is one of only three royal palaces in America. The two-story residence was built by Governor John Adams Kuakini in 1838, a year after he completed Moku'aikaua Church. Dur-

CLOSE UP

Green Hawai'i

WITH ITS ISOLATED LOCATION, MULTIPLE CLIMATE ZONES, agriculture, and unique cultural and natural resources, the Big Island has long been considered a "living classroom" by geologists, biologists, anthropologists, and environmental scientists. In recent years, rapid development has also made the island a study in conservation—what works, what doesn't, and what can be reversed. The scarcity of natural resources is more striking on an island than in most other places, and in the Big Island this holds especially true. The last two decades of rapid growth have the island and its infrastructure bursting at the seams. Small island roads that have never known traffic are piled up bumper to bumper during rush hour, a concept that was foreign to this island until recently. Locals, priced out of the expensive new housing market, have been pushed farther and farther away from their jobs, creating longer commutes and more traffic. Even fresh water is at a premium.

Local residents, scientists, and the government have teamed together in the last several years to push for sustainable development on the Big Island and in Hawai'i in general. Affordable housing developments for locals are in the works; resorts and new developments must retain at least one staff member who is well-versed in Hawaiian history and culture to protect the island's traditions; and the Kohala Coast resorts have instituted organic landscaping techniques and marine protection programs to mitigate their environmental impact.

Scientists are also devising ways to maximize the island's resources. Researchers at the Natural Energy Lab of Hawai'i are particularly concerned with alternative energy sources, as the island has no natural sources of fossil fuels. In addition to solar power, lab scientists have pioneered uses for deep sea water. The super cold water pumped from the depths of the ocean keeps virtually energy-free air-conditioning units running at the labs and surrounding offices, a practice that will soon be adopted by the hotels and shops of downtown Honolulu.

But the green side of the Big Island is not solely of interest to scientists. Many visitors to the island are curious to learn about its natural resources and protection of them. Of particular interest are the **Natural Energy Lab of Hawai'i** (⇨ Kailua-Kona); the **'Imiloa Astronomy Center** (⇨ Hilo) which informs visitors about Mauna Kea conservation efforts, the mountain's spiritual significance in Hawaiian tradition, and the impact that research there has on both the scientific community and the world at large; and several **Botanical Gardens** throughout the island. You might also try a nature hike with **Hawai'i Forest and Trail** (☎ 800/464-1993 🌐 www.hawaii-forest.com), whose guides are full of information about endangered native plants and birds, as well as about protection efforts.

For more information on the island's ongoing conservation movement, pick up a copy of **Environment Hawai'i** (🌐 www.environment-hawaii.org) magazine, or visit their Web site.

ing the 1880s it served as King David Kalākaua's summer palace. It's constructed of local materials, including lava, coral, koa wood, and *'ōhi'a* timber. The oversize doors and furniture bear witness to the size of some of the Hawaiian people. On weekday afternoons hula schools rehearse on the grounds. Hulihe'e Palace is operated by the Daughters of Hawai'i, a nonprofit focused on maintaining the heritage of the Islands. ✉ *75-5718 Ali'i Dr.* ☎ *808/329–1877* 🌐 *www.huliheepalace.org* 🎟 *$4.*

⓯ **Kailua Pier.** Though most fishing boats use Honokōhau Harbor, this pier dating from 1918 is still a hub of ocean activity. Outrigger canoe teams practice, and tour boats depart from these docks most days. Along the seawall children and old-timers cast their lines daily, careful not to hook the pair of sea turtles nesting nearby. For youngsters, a bamboo pole and hook are easy to come by, and plenty of locals are willing to give pointers. Each October close to 1,500 international athletes swim 2.4 mi from the pier to begin the grueling Ironman Triathlon competition. ✉ *Next to King Kamehameha's Kona Beach Hotel; seawall is between Kailua Pier and Hulihe'e Palace on Ali'i Dr.*

★ ⓮ **Kamakahonu.** King Kamehameha spent his last years, from 1812 to 1819, near what is now King Kamehameha's Kona Beach Hotel. Part of what was once a 4-acre homestead complete with several houses and religious sites has been swallowed by Kailua Pier, but a replica of the temple, **Ahu'ena Heiau,** keeps history alive. Free tours start from King Kamehameha's Kona Beach Hotel. Small but pleasant King Kamehameha Beach is a great place to lie in the sun and take an easy swim after the tour. ✉ *75-5660 Palani Rd.* ☎ *808/329–2911* 🎟 *Free* ⏲ *Tours weekdays at 1:30.*

⓭ **King Kamehameha's Kona Beach Hotel.** Stroll through the high-ceiling lobby of this Kailua-Kona fixture to view displays of Hawaiian artifacts and mounted marlin from Hawaiian International Billfish tournaments (from when Kailua Pier was still the weigh-in point). These "granders," marlin weighing 1,000 pounds or more, are the big attraction here. Classes in Hawaiian arts and crafts are given regularly. ✉ *75-5660 Palani Rd.* ☎ *808/923–4511 or 800/367–6060* 🌐 *www.konabeachhotel.com.*

㉑ **Kuamo'o Battlefield and Lekeleke Burial Grounds.** In 1819 an estimated 300 Hawaiians were killed on this vast, black-lava field, and you can still see their burial mounds there today. After the death of his father, King Kamehameha, Liholiho was crowned king; shortly thereafter he ate at the table of women, thereby breaking the ancient *kapu* (taboo) system. Chief Kekuaokalani, who held radically different views about religious traditions, unsuccessfully challenged King Liholiho in battle here. ✉ *South end of Ali'i Dr.*

★ ⓱ **Moku'aikaua Church.** A thatch hut, erected on this site by missionaries in 1820, served as the first Christian church on the Islands. A more permanent structure was built in 1836 with black stone from an abandoned *heiau.* The stone was mortared with white coral and topped by an impressive steeple. Inside, behind a panel of gleaming koa wood, is a model of the brig *Thaddeus.* ✉ *75-5713 Ali'i Dr.* ☎ *808/329–0655.*

19 **St. Michael's Church.** The site of Kona's first Catholic church, built in 1840, is marked by a small thatch structure to the left of the present church, which dates from 1850. In front of the church a coral grotto shrine holds 2,500 coral heads, harvested in 1940, when preservation was not yet an issue. ✉ *75-5769 Ali'i Dr.* ☎ *808/326–7771.*

NEED A BREAK?

The laid-back Island Lava Java (✉ 75-5799 Ali'i Dr. ☎ 808/327-2161), in the Ali'i Sunset Plaza, has great coffee and the best and biggest cinnamon rolls on the island. In the afternoon stop by for fresh fish or *kālua* pig tacos, sandwiches, fruit smoothies, and ice cream. The large outdoor seating area has a bird's-eye view of the ocean. Locals hang out here to read the paper, play board games, or just watch the surf.

20 **St. Peter's of Kahalu'u.** The definition of "quaint" with its crisp white and blue trim, this tiny old-fashioned steeple church sits on the rocks overlooking the ocean near Kahalu'u Beach. It has appeared on many a Kailua-Kona postcard, and its charm and views bring hundreds of visitors every year. ✉ *Ali'i Dr., north of mile marker 5.*

SOUTH KONA & KEALAKEKUA BAY

South of Kailua-Kona, Highway 11 hugs splendid coastlines, leaving busy streets behind. A detour along the winding narrow roads in the mountains above takes you straight to the heart of coffee country where lush plantations and jaw-dropping views offer a taste of what Hawai'i was like before the resorts took over. Tour one of the coffee farms to find out what the big deal is about Kona coffee, and snag a free sample while you're at it. A half-hour back on the highway will lead you to magical Kealakekua Bay, where Captain James Cook arrived in 1778, changing the Islands forever. Hawaiian spinner dolphins frolic in the bay, now a marine preserve nestled alongside impossibly high green cliffs more reminiscent of Ireland than posters of Hawai'i. Snorkeling is superb here, as it is a protected marine reserve, so you may want to bring your gear and spend an hour or so exploring the coral reefs. This is also a nice kayaking spot; the bay is extremely calm. One of our favorite ways to spend a morning is to throw some snorkel gear in a kayak, paddle across the bay, go for a swim and a snorkel, and paddle back, dodging dolphins along the way (⇨ Chapter 4, Water Activities & Tours).

The winding road above Kealakekua Bay is home to a quaint little painted church, as well as several reasonably priced B&Bs with great views. The communities surrounding the bay (Kainaliu and Captain Cook) are brimming with local and transplanted artists, making them great places to stop for a meal, some unique gifts, or an afternoon stroll.

LOGISTICS Between the coffee plantations, artsy towns, and Kealakekua Bay, South Kona has plenty of activities to keep you occupied for a day. Bring a swimsuit and snorkel gear, and hit Kealakekua Bay first thing in the morning. You'll have a better chance of a dolphin sighting, and you'll beat the large snorkel cruise groups. Follow the signs off Highway 11 to the

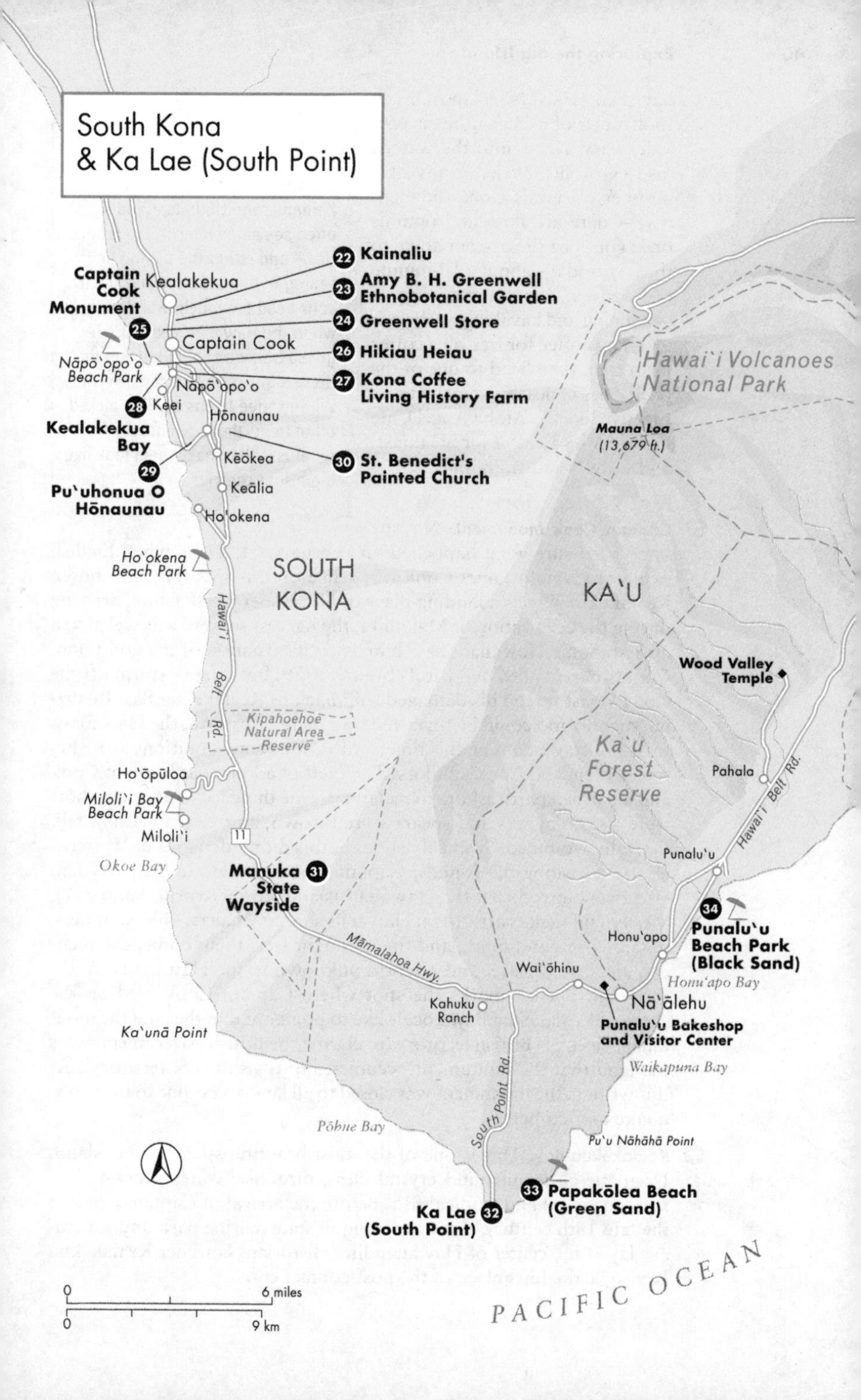

South Kona
& Ka Lae (South Point)
Kealakekua
Captain Cook Monument
25
Captain Cook
Nāpō`opo`o Beach Park
Nāpō`opo`o
28 Keei
Kealakekua Bay
Hōnaunau
29
Pu`uhonua O Hōnaunau
Kēōkea
Keālia
Ho`okena
Ho`okena Beach Park
22 Kainaliu
23 Amy B. H. Greenwell Ethnobotanical Garden
24 Greenwell Store
26 Hikiau Heiau
27 Kona Coffee Living History Farm
30 St. Benedict's Painted Church
SOUTH KONA
Hawai`i Belt Rd.
Kipahoehoe Natural Area Reserve
Ho`ōpūloa
Miloli`i Bay Beach Park
Miloli`i
11
Okoe Bay
Manuka State Wayside 31
Māmalahoa Hwy.
Ka`unā Point
Kahuku Ranch
Wai`ōhinu
Nā`ālehu
Punalu`u Bakeshop and Visitor Center
Hawai`i Volcanoes National Park
Mauna Loa (13,679 ft.)
KA`U
Ka`u Forest Reserve
Wood Valley Temple
Pahala
Hawai`i Belt Rd.
Punalu`u
34 Punalu`u Beach Park (Black Sand)
Honu`apo
Honu`apo Bay
Waikapuna Bay
South Point Rd.
Pōhue Bay
Pu`u Nāhāhā Point
33 Papakōlea Beach (Green Sand)
Ka Lae (South Point) 32
PACIFIC OCEAN
0 6 miles
0 9 km

bay, then park at Nāpō'opo'o Beach (not much of a beach, but it provides easy access into the water). You can rent kayaks at any of a number of stands along the highway—there are no rental options once you start the descent down to the bay, and it's about a 10-minute trek down. After a morning of swimming and kayaking, grab your morning coffee for free on a coffee farm tour, then head to one of the great cafés in nearby Kainaliu to refuel (we like the Aloha Angel Cafe in the Aloha Theater for breakfast, and Cafe Nasturtium for lunch).

HAWAIIAN CHERRIES

Driving around the towns of South Kona–Hōnaunau, Captain Cook, Kainaliu, and Hōlualoa–you'll often see signs referring to "cherries," and either the buying or selling of them. Before you scratch your head too much, wondering when the Hawaiian cherry trade got so hot, we should tell you that these signs refer to coffee cherries. When coffee beans are first picked off of trees, they are encased in red husks that make them look like big bright cherries.

Main Attractions

25 **Captain Cook Monument.** No one knows for sure what happened on February 14, 1779, when English explorer Captain James Cook was killed on this spot. He had chosen Kealakekua Bay as a landing place in November 1778. Cook, arriving during the celebration of Makahiki, the harvest season, was welcomed at first. Some Hawaiians saw him as an incarnation of the god Lono. Cook's party sailed away in February 1779, but a freak storm off the Kona Coast forced his damaged ship back to Kealakekua Bay. Realizing that no god could be thwarted by a mere rainstorm, the Hawaiians were not so welcoming this time, and various confrontations arose between them and Cook's sailors. The theft of a longboat brought Cook and an armed party ashore to reclaim it. One thing led to another: shots were fired, daggers and spears were thrown, and Captain Cook fell, mortally wounded. Strangely enough, this didn't deter other Westerners from visiting the Islands; Captain James Cook and his party had effectively introduced the Hawaiian Islands to the world. Soon after, Western influences arrived on Hawai'i's shores: whalers, sailors, traders, missionaries, and more, and they brought with them crime, debauchery, alcohol, disease, and a world unknown to the Hawaiians. A 27-foot-high obelisk marks the spot where Captain Cook died on the shore of Kealakekua Bay. Locals like to point out that the land the monument sits on is British territory (to clarify: the British government owns the land that the monument occupies, but it's still U.S. territory). At this writing, the monument was closed to all land access due to the earthquake of October 2006.

28 **Kealakekua Bay.** This is one of the most beautiful spots on the island. Dramatic cliffs surround crystal clear, turquoise water chock-full of stunning coral and tropical fish. Before the arrival of Captain Cook in the late 18th century, this now tranquil state marine park and sanctuary lay at the center of Hawaiian life. Historians consider Kealakekua Bay to be the birthplace of the post-contact era.

Fodor'sChoice ★

The term "beach" is used a bit liberally for **Nāpō'opo'o Beach,** on the south side of the bay. There's no real beach to speak of, but there are easy ways to enter the water. To the left of the parking lot is an old cement pier that serves as a great ladder for swimmers going into or coming out of the bay. This is a nice place to swim as it's well protected from weather or currents, so the water is almost always calm and clear. ■ TIP→ **At this writing, a portion of the bay remained closed to water activities and hiking, a safety zone established after the 2006 earthquake.** Excellent snorkel cruises can still be booked through Fair Wind Cruises (⇨ Chapter 4, Water Activities & Tours), the only company allowed to dock in Kealakekua. ✉ *Bottom of Nāpō'opo'o Rd.*

NEED A BREAK?

Before or after winding down Nāpō'opo'o Road, treat yourself to awesome views of Kealakekua Bay at the Coffee Shack (✉ 83-5799 Māmalahoa Hwy. ☎ 808/328-9555 🌐 www.coffeeshack.com), a deli and pizza place with just nine tables on an open, breezy lānai. The bread is home-baked, the eggs Benedict is a local breakfast favorite, the sandwiches are generous, and the staff is friendly.

★ 29 **Pu'uhonua O Hōnaunau** (Place of Refuge). This 180-acre National Historic Park was once considered a place of refuge. It was a safe haven for women in times of war as well as for *kapu* breakers, criminals, and prisoners of war—anyone who could get inside the 1,000-foot-long wall, which was 10 feet high and 17 feet thick, could avoid punishment. **Hale-o-Keawe Heiau,** built in 1650 as the burial place of King Kamehameha's ancestor Keawe, has been restored. South of the park, tide pools offer another delight—most notably the crowd of sea turtles feeding there regularly. Demonstrations of poi pounding, canoe making, and local games are occasionally scheduled. ✉ *Rte. 160, about 20 mi south of Kailua-Kona* ☎ *808/328–2288* 🌐 *www.nps.gov/puho* 🎫 *$3–$5* 🕑 *Park Mon.–Thurs. 6 AM–8 PM, Fri.–Sun. 6 AM–11 PM; visitor center daily 8 AM–4:30 PM.*

Also Worth Seeing

23 **Amy B. H. Greenwell Ethnobotanical Garden.** Often overlooked, this garden fosters a wealth of Hawaiian cultural traditions. On 12 acres grow 250 types of plants that were typical in an early Hawaiian *ahupua'a,* pie-shape land divisions that ran from the mountains to the sea. Call to find out about guided tours or drop in between 8:30 AM and 5 PM. ✉ *82-6188 Māalahoa Hwy., Captain Cook* ☎ *808/323–3318* 🌐 *www.bishopmuseum.org/greenwell.*

24 **Greenwell Store.** Established in 1850, the homestead of Henry N. Greenwell served as cattle ranch, sheep station, store, post office, and family home all in one. Now, all that remains is the 1875 stone structure, which is listed on the National Register of Historic Places. It houses a fascinating museum that has exhibits on ranching and coffee farming. It's also headquarters for the **Kona Historical Society,** which organizes walking tours of Kailua-Kona. ✉ *81-6551 Māmalahoa Hwy.* ☎ *808/323–3222* 🌐 *www.konahistorical.org* 🎫 *Donations accepted* 🕑 *Weekdays 9–3.*

CLOSE UP

Kona Coffee

EVEN IF YOU'RE NOT a java fiend, it's easy to get into the history and culture surrounding Kona coffee. From the hundreds of cafés, stores, and restaurants selling Kona coffee to the farm tours to the annual Gevalia Kona Coffee Cupping Competition, coffee is a major part of life on the Big Island and represents one of only a few non-tourism-related industries in Hawai'i. Hawai'i is the only U.S. producer of commercially grown coffee, and, though it may seem like the Kona coffee craze is a relatively recent thing, coffee has been growing here since 1828, when Reverend Samuel Ruggles, an American missionary, brought a cutting over from the O'ahu farm of Chief Boki, O'ahu's governor. That initial coffee plant was a strain of Ethiopian coffee called Coffee Arabica, and it is the same coffee being produced on the Big Island today, although a Guatemalan strain of Arabica introduced in the late 1800s is produced in far higher quantities.

In the latter half of the 1800s, many coffee plantations closed to make room for more lucrative sugar plantations, and by the early 1900s, the era of the large Hawaiian coffee plantation had ended. Plantation owners subdivided their lots and began leasing smaller parcels to local tenant farmers, a practice that continues today. The majority of the tenant farmers were Japanese families who managed their farms as family businesses with no outside labor. At one point in the 1930s, local schools switched summer vacation to "coffee vacation" from August to November so that the kids could help with the coffee harvest, a practice that held until 1969.

Coffee is harvested as "cherries"—the beans are encased in a hard red shell. The cherries are shelled, and the green beans (more gray in color than green) inside are roasted to produce the dark brown beans seen in coffee shops all over the world. Despite family control of the harvest, the coffee production process was controlled by just two firms up until the late 1950s when farmers and farmer cooperatives began to buy and operate their own mills. Today, most farms—owned and operated by a variety of Japanese-American families, west coast Mainland transplants, native Hawaiians, and descendents of Portuguese and Chinese immigrants—take control of the entire coffee chain from harvest to cup.

COFFEE-FARM TOURS

Several coffee farms around the South Kona and Upcountry Kona coffee-belt area welcome visitors with tours that let you in on the whole coffee process, from harvesting green beans to packaging. Some tours are self-guided, and most are free, with the exception of the Kona Coffee Living History Farm. The brew, of course, is always ready.

Greenwell Farms. ✉ *81-6581 Māmalahoa Hwy., Kealakekua* ☎ *808/323-2862.*

Hōlualoa-Kona Coffee Company. ✉ *77-6261 Old Māmalahoa Hwy., Hwy. 180, Hōlualoa* ☎ *808/322-9937 or 800/334-0348.*

Kona Coffee Living History Farm (D. Uchida Farm). ⇨ Exploring South Kona & Kealakekua Bay

Royal Kona Coffee Museum & Coffee Mill. ✉ *83-5427 Māmalahoa Hwy., next to tree house in Hōnaunau* ☎ *808/328-2511.*

26 **Hikiau Heiau.** This stone platform was once an impressive temple dedicated to the god Lono. When Captain Cook arrived in 1778, ceremonies in his honor were held here. ✉ *Bottom of Nāpō'opo'o Rd.*

22 **Kainaliu.** Like many of the Big Island's old plantation towns, Kainaliu is experiencing a bit of a renaissance. In addition to a ribbon of funky old stores, many of them traditional Japanese family-operated shops, a handful of new galleries and shops have sprung up in the last few years. Browse around Oshima's, established in 1926, and Kimura's, established in 1927, to find authentic Japanese goods beyond tourist trinkets, then pop into Cafe Nasturtium for a tasty vegetarian snack. Cross the street to peek into the 1932 Aloha Theatre, where community-theater actors might be practicing a Broadway revue. ✉ *Hwy. 11, mile markers 112–114.*

27 **Kona Coffee Living History Farm.** Known as the D. Uchida Farm, this site is on the National Register of Historic Places. Completely restored by the Kona Historical Society, it includes a 1913 farmhouse surrounded by coffee trees, a Japanese bathhouse, *kuriba* (coffee-processing mill), and *hoshidana* (traditional drying platform). Tours of the farm are available by reservation only and cost $20. ✉ *81-6551 Māmalahoa Hwy., Kealakekua* ☎ *808/323–3222* 🌐 *www.konahistorical.org.*

30 **St. Benedict's Painted Church.** The walls, columns, and ceiling of this Roman Catholic church depict colorful biblical scenes through the paintbrush of Belgian-born priest Father Velghe. Mass is still held every weekend. ■ TIP→ **The view of Kealakekua Bay from the entrance is amazing.** ✉ *Painted Church Rd. off Hwy. 160, Hōnaunau* ☎ *808/328–2227.*

KA'U & KA LAE (SOUTH POINT)

The most desolate region of the island, Ka'u is nonetheless home to some spectacular sights. Mark Twain wrote some of his finest prose here, where macadamia-nut farms, green-sand beaches, and tiny villages offer largely undiscovered beauty. The 50-mi drive from Kailua-Kona to windswept South Point, where the first Polynesians came ashore as early as AD 750, winds away from the ocean through a surreal moonscape of lava-covered forests. Past South Point, glimpses of the ocean return and hidden Green Sand Beach tempts hikers to stop awhile before the highway narrows and returns to the coast, passing verdant cattle pastures and sheer cliffs on the way to the black-sand beach of Punalu'u, the nesting place of the Hawaiian sea turtle.

LOGISTICS Ka'u and Ka Lae are destinations usually combined with a quick trip to the volcano from Kona. This is probably cramming too much into one day, however. The volcano fills up a day and then some, and the sights of this region are worth more than a cursory glance. Our recommendation? Make Green Sand Beach or Punalu'u your destination for a beach day at some point during your stay, and stop to see some of the other sights on the way there or back. Bring sturdy shoes if Green Sand Beach is your choice (reaching the beach requires a steep hike) and snorkeling gear if you're heading to Punalu'u. The drive from Kailua-Kona to Ka Lae is a long one (roughly 2½ hours). It's a good idea to fill up on gasoline and pack a lunch before you leave, as there are few amenities along the way. There are a few places to eat if you forget or can't be bothered, but what's better than a beach picnic? As with the rest of the island, a 4-wheel-drive vehicle will make it much easier to explore this area. Weather tends to be warm, dry, and windy.

Main Attractions

★ 32 **Ka Lae (South Point).** Windswept Ka Lae is the southernmost point of land in the United States. It's thought that the first Polynesians came ashore here. Check out the old canoe-mooring holes that are carved through the rocks, possibly by settlers from Tahiti as early as AD 750. Some artifacts, thought to have been left by early voyagers who never settled here, date to AD 300. Driving down to the point, you pass Kama'oa Wind Farm; although the rows of windmill turbines are still fueled by the nearly constant winds sweeping across this coastal plain, the equipment and facilities are falling into disrepair due to neglect. Indeed, some of the windmills no longer turn at all. Continue down the road (parts at the end are unpaved, but driveable), bear left when the road forks and park in the lot at the end; walk past the boat hoists toward the little lighthouse. South Point is just past the lighthouse at the southernmost cliff. ■ TIP→ **Don't leave anything of value in your car, and you don't have to pay for parking. It's a free, public park, so anyone trying to charge you is likely running some sort of scam.** ✉ *Turn right past mile marker 70 on Māmalahoa Hwy., then drive 12 mi down South Point Rd.*

> **GREEN SAND?**
>
> Formed by the lava flows of Mauna Loa, Papakōlea (Green Sand Beach) gets its color from eroded olivine crystals. Wind and heavy surf have intensified the beach's color by stripping away lighter grains of sand (made from volcanic ash), leaving the denser olivine crystals behind. Though this is commonly thought to be the only green sand beach on the Big Island, there are actually two others nearby, formed by the same lava flow.

33 **Papakōlea Beach (Green Sand Beach).** It takes awhile to get down and even longer to get back, but where else are you going to see a green sand beach? Add to that the fact that the rock formations surrounding the beach are surreally beautiful, and this is a detour worth taking (⇨ Chapter 3, Beaches). ✉ *2½ mi northeast of South Point.*

34 **Punalu'u Beach Park (Black Sand Beach).** This easily accessed beach is well worth at least a short stop for two reasons: it's a beautiful black-sand beach, and it's where the Hawaiian sea turtles like to nest so the water's swarming with them. The turtles are used to people by now, and have no problem swimming right alongside you (⇨ Chapter 3, Beaches). ✉ *Turn right down driveway into beach off Hwy. 11 south. Beach is well marked off hwy.*

NEED A BREAK?

Punalu'u Bakeshop & Visitor Center (✉ Hwy. 11, Na'alehu ☎ 808/366-3501 ⏲ Daily 9–5) is a bit of a tourist trap, but it's also a good spot to grab a snack before heading back out on the road. Try some Portuguese sweet bread or a

homemade ice-cream sandwich paired with some local Ka'u coffee (that's right, not Kona, but equally tasty). If you're in the mood for a healthier treat, head up the road a bit to the Na'alehu Fruit Stand (✉ Main St., Hwy. 11, Na'alehu ☎ 808/929-9009 ⏲ Mon.-Thurs. 9-6, Fri.-Sat. 9-7, Sun. 9-5) for a great salad, fish sandwich, or fresh fruit. Fear not, indulgences abound here as well—their baked goods are locally renowned.

Also Worth Seeing

(31) **Manuka State Wayside.** This dry, upland forest spreads across several lava flows. A rugged trail follows a 2-mi loop past a pit crater and winds around ancient trees such as *hau* and *kukui*. It's an okay spot to get out of the car and stretch your legs—you can wander through the well-maintained arboretum, snap a few photos of the eerie forest, and let the kids scramble around trees so large they can't get their arms around them. However, we don't recommend spending too much time here, especially if you're planning on driving all the way down to South Point. The pathways are not well maintained, but restrooms, picnic areas, and telephones are available. ✉ *Hwy. 11, north of mile marker 81* ☎ *808/974–6200* 🎟 *Free* ⏲ *Daily 7–7.*

OFF THE BEATEN PATH

PAHALA – About 16 mi east of Na'lehu, beyond Punalu'u Beach Park, Highway 11 flashes past this little town. You'll miss it if you blink. Pahala is a perfect example of a sugar-plantation town. Behind it, along a wide cane road, you enter Wood Valley, once a prosperous community, now just a road heavily scented by eucalyptus trees, coffee blossoms, and night-blooming jasmine. Here you'll find **Wood Valley Temple** (☎ 808/928–8539 🌐 www.nechung.org), a serene and beautiful Tibetan Buddhist temple dedicated by the Dalai Lama during his 1980 visit. Today, you can explore the gardens and the temple, attend a service, or book lodging in the Temple's guest house for a complete Buddhist retreat.

THE VOLCANO

Few visitors realize that in addition to "the Volcano" there's also Volcano, the town. Conveniently located next to—you guessed it—Hawai'i Volcanoes National Park, Volcano (also known as Volcano Village) is a charming little hamlet in the woods that offers a dozen or so inns and B&Bs, a decent Thai restaurant, some killer (although strangely expensive) pizza, and a handful of things to see and do that don't include the village's namesake. For years, writers, artists, and meditative types have been coming to the Volcano to seek inspiration, and many of them have settled in and around Volcano Village. Artist studios (open to the public by appointment) are scattered throughout the hills, and writers' retreats are hidden in the tranquil rainforests surrounding the area. If you plan to explore the Volcano, spending a night or two in Volcano Village is the ideal way to go about it. Spend the day hiking over lava, then spend the evening lounging around on your cushy bed in front of the fireplace, indulging in gourmet pizza and waxing poetic.

Continued on page 52

HAWAI'I VOLCANOES NATIONAL PARK

Exploring the surface of the world's most active volcano—from the moonscape craters at the summit to the red-hot lava flows on the coast to the kīpuka, pockets of vegetation miraculously left untouched—is the ultimate ecotour and one of Hawai'i's must-dos.

The park sprawls over 520 square miles and encompasses Kīlauea and Mauna Loa, two of the five volcanoes that formed the Big Island nearly half a million years ago. Kīlauea, youngest and most rambunctious of the Hawaiian volcanoes, erupted at its summit from the 19th century through the 1950s. Since then, the top of the volcano has been more or less quiet, frequently shrouded in mists.

The real action, however, began on January 3, 1983, when Kīlauea's eastern side sprang to life, shooting molten lava four stories high. The eruption has been ongoing, and lava flows are generally steady and slow, appearing and disappearing from view. Over 500 acres have been added to Hawai'i's eastern coast since the activity began, and scientists say this eruptive phase is not likely to end anytime soon.

If you're lucky, you'll be able to catch creation at its most elemental—when molten lava meets the ocean, cools, and solidifies into brand-new stretches of coastline. Even if lava-viewing conditions aren't ideal, you can hike 150 miles of trails; camp amid wide expanses of *'a'ā* (rough) and *pahoehoe* (smooth) lava; or sip cocktails at Volcano House, a hotel perched on the rim of Kīlauea Caldera. There's nothing quite like it.

P.O. Box 52, Hawai'i Volcanoes National Park, HI 96718

808/985-6000

www.nps.gov/havo

$10 per vehicle; $5 for pedestrians and bicyclists. Ask about passes. Admission is good for seven consecutive days.

The park is open daily, 24 hours. Kīlauea Visitor Center: 7:45 am–5 pm. Thomas A. Jaggar Museum: 8:30–5. Volcano Art Center Gallery: 9–5.

(top) Kīlauea Iki Trail
(left) Fuming rim of Pu'u' Ō'ō, source of the current eruption

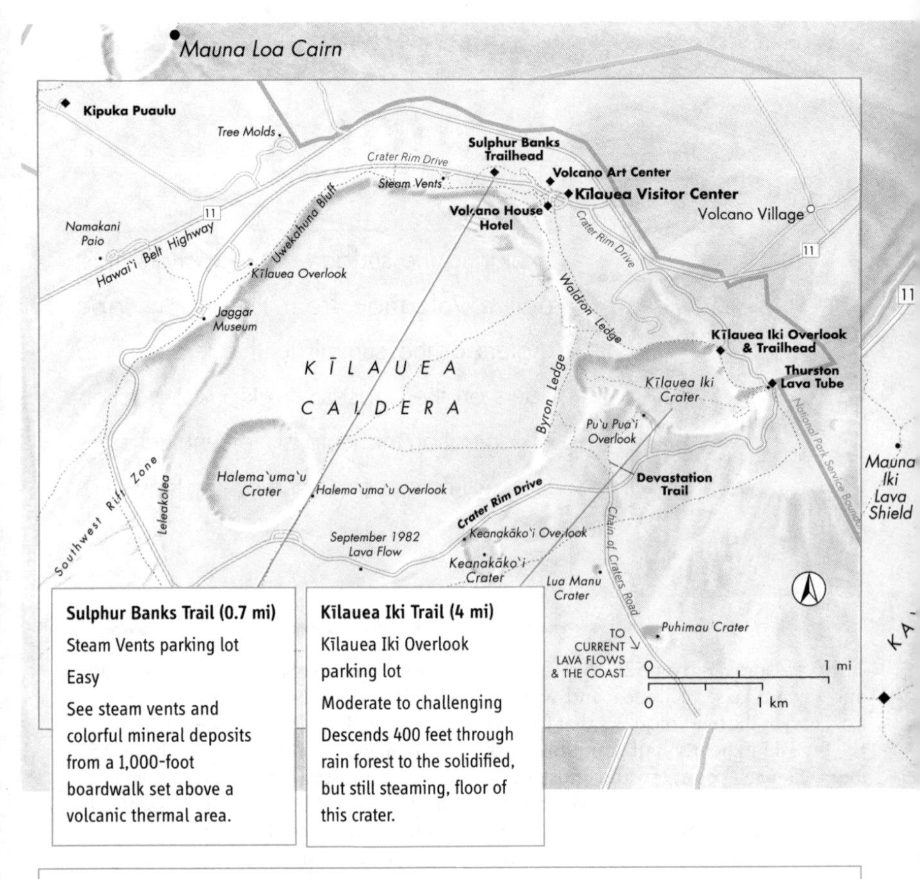

SEEING THE SUMMIT

The best way to explore the summit of Kīlauea is to cruise 11-mile Crater Rim Drive, which encircles the volcano's massive caldera. Volcano House's dining room offers front-row views of this eerie, awe-inspiring spot, which bears an uncanny resemblance to those old Apollo moon photos.

Depending on the number of stops you make, it'll take one to three hours to complete the circuit. Highlights include sulfur and steam vents, a walk-through lava tube, and the southwest rift zone—deep fissures, fractures, and gullies along Kīlauea's flanks.

There's also Halema'uma'u Crater, an awesome depression in Kīlauea Caldera measuring 3,000 feet across and nearly 300 feet deep. When skies are clear, this is a good place to see Mauna Loa and Mauna Kea.

The Thomas A. Jaggar Museum offers breathtaking looks at Halema'uma'u and Kīlauea Caldera, geologic displays, video presentations of volcanic eruptions, and exhibits of seismographs once used by volcanologists at the adjacent Hawaiian Volcano Observatory (not open to the public).

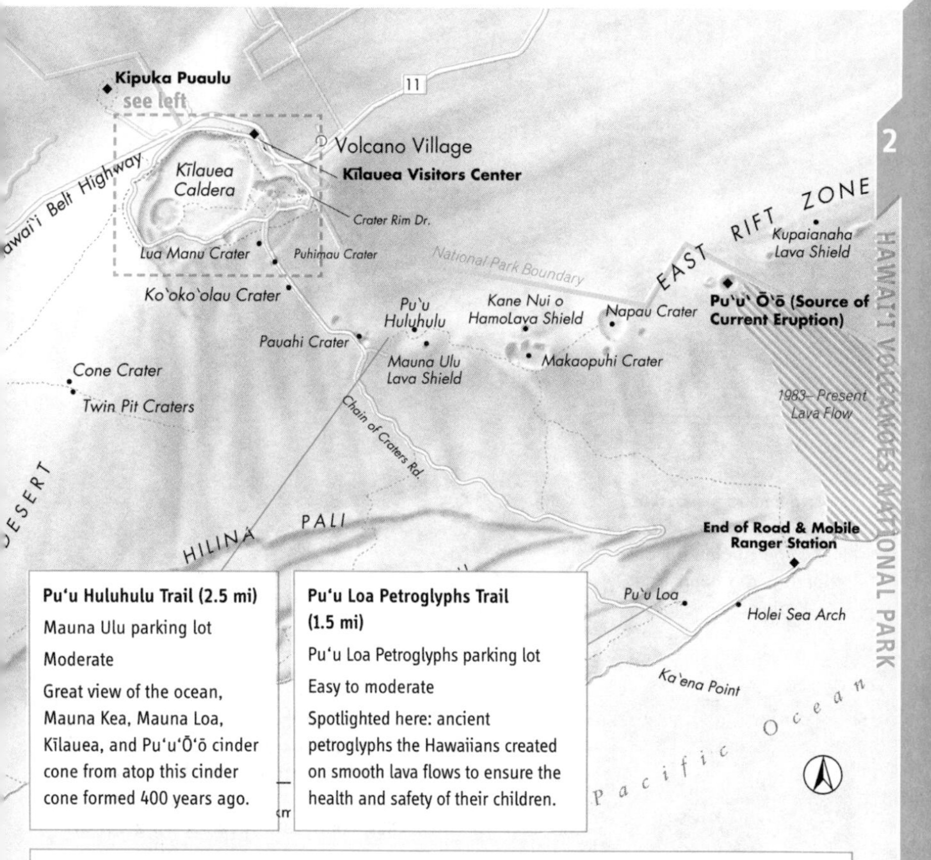

Pu'u Huluhulu Trail (2.5 mi)

Mauna Ulu parking lot

Moderate

Great view of the ocean, Mauna Kea, Mauna Loa, Kīlauea, and Pu'u'Ō'ō cinder cone from atop this cinder cone formed 400 years ago.

Pu'u Loa Petroglyphs Trail (1.5 mi)

Pu'u Loa Petroglyphs parking lot

Easy to moderate

Spotlighted here: ancient petroglyphs the Hawaiians created on smooth lava flows to ensure the health and safety of their children.

SEEING LAVA

Before you head out to find flowing lava, pinpoint the safe viewing spots at the Visitor Center. One of the best places usually is at the end of 19-mile Chain of Craters Road. Magnificent plumes of steam rise where the rivers of liquid fire meet the sea.

There are three guarantees about lava flows in HVNP. First: They constantly change. Second: Because of that, you can't predict when and where you'll be able to see them. Third: New land formed when lava meets the sea is highly unstable and can collapse at any time. Never go into areas that have been closed.

■ TIP→→ **The view of brilliant red-orange lava flowing from Kīlauea's east rift zone is most dramatic at night.**

People watching lava flow at HVNP

PLANNING YOUR TRIP TO HVNP

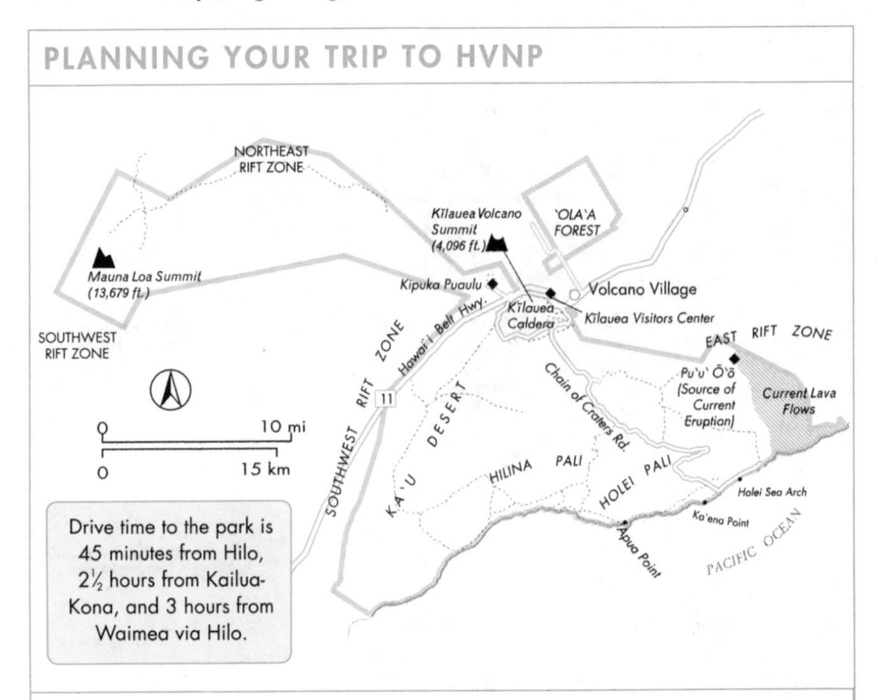

Lava entering the ocean

WHERE TO START

Begin your visit at the Visitor Center, where you'll find maps, books, and DVDs; information on trails, ranger-led walks, and special events; and current weather, road, and lava-viewing conditions. Free volcano-related film showings, lectures, and other presentations are regularly scheduled.

WEATHER

Weather conditions fluctuate daily, sometimes hourly. It can be rainy and chilly even during the summer; the temperature usually is 14° cooler at the 4,000-foot-high summit of Kīlauea than at sea level.

Expect hot, dry, and windy coastal conditions at the end of Chain of Craters Road. Bring rain gear, and wear layered clothing, sturdy shoes, sunglasses, a hat, and sunscreen.

Hardened lava across Kalapana

FOOD

Volcano House has the only food concessions at HVNP; it's a good idea to bring your own favorite snacks and beverages. Stock up on provisions in Volcano Village, 1½ miles away.

PARK PROGRAMS

Rangers lead daily walks into different areas; check with the Visitor Center for details as times and destinations depend on weather conditions.

Over 60 companies hold permits to lead hikes at HVNP. Good choices are Hawai'i Forest & Trail (www.hawaii-forest.com), Hawaiian Walkways (www.hawaiianwalkways.com), and Native Guide Hawai'i (www.nativeguidehawaii.com).

CAUTION

"Vog" (volcanic smog) can cause headaches; breathing difficulties; lethargy; irritations of the skin, eyes, nose, and throat; and other health problems. Pregnant women, young children, and people with asthma and heart conditions are most susceptible, and should avoid areas such as Halema'uma'u Crater where fumes are thick.

Wear long pants and boots or closed-toe shoes with good tread for hikes on lava. Stay on marked trails and step carefully. Lava is composed of 50% silica (glass) and can cause serious injury if you fall.

Carry at least 2 quarts of water on hikes. Temperatures near lava flows can rise above 100°F, and dehydration, heat exhaustion, and sunstroke are common consequences of extended exposure to intense sunlight and high temperatures.

Help protect the endangered *nēnē* (Hawaiian goose), Hawai'i's state bird. Watch out for them when driving and don't feed them; *nēnē* seeking handouts often are hit by moving vehicles.

Volcanologists inspecting a vent in the East Rift Zone

LOGISTICS There are a handful of dining options, a couple of stores, and a gas station available in Volcano, so most of your needs should be covered. If you can't find what you're looking for, Hilo is only about a 30-minute drive away. Bring a fleece or a sweater if you plan to stay the night; temperatures drop at night and mornings are cool and misty. One of the main reasons people choose to stay the night in Volcano is to do the night hike to the lava flow in the park. If you're planning on making the trek, bring hiking shoes, a flashlight (check the batteries), and water. Also make sure you have enough gas to get down to the flow and back up. The entrance to Volcanoes National Park is about one minute from Volcano Village, but the drive down is nearly 30 minutes. Remember that you'll be coming back from the hike at around midnight, long after the rangers have gone home.

Extra-Volcanic Activity

Kīlauea Caverns of Fire. Strap on a miners hat and gloves and get ready to explore the underbelly of the world's largest active volcano. Tours through these fascinating caves and lava tubes underneath the volcano must be arranged in advance, but are well worth a little extra planning. Located off Highway 11 between Hilo and Volcanoes National Park, the Caverns are comprised of four main tubes, each 500–700 years old and full of stalactites, stalagmites, and a variety of different colored flowstone. The largest lava tube in the world is here—40 mi long, it has 80-foot ceilings and is 80 feet wide. Tours can range from safe and easy (safe enough for children five years old and up) to long and adventurous. For those not so sure about "spelunking," an easy walking tour through the lava tube can also be arranged. ✉ *Off Hwy. 11, between Kurtistown and Mountain View* ☎ *808/217–2363* 🌐 *www.kilaueacavernsoffire.com* 🎫 *$29 for walking tour* ⏲ *By appointment only.*

Volcano Farmers Market. Local produce, flowers, and food products are on offer every Sunday morning at one of the better farmers' markets on the island. It's not swarmed with people the way the Hilo market can be, but it's best to get there early as vendors tend to sell out. The revolving schedule of additional events includes "meet public officials day" (2nd Sunday of the month) and "arts and crafts day" (4th Sunday). There are also more prepared-food vendors at the Volcano market than Hilo, with such temptations as a gourmet picnic lunch, fresh-baked croissants and pastries, or homemade Thai food. ✉ *Cooper Center, Wright Rd.* ☎ *808/967–7800* 🌐 *www.volcanogallery.com/volcano_farmers.htm* ⏲ *Sun. 8–10 AM.*

NEED A BREAK?

Lava Rock Cafe (✉ Old Volcano Hwy., Volcano ☎ 808/967–8526) is not great for a sit-down meal (slow service), but their to-go "seismic sandwiches" are perfect to bring along for a day of hiking around the park or exploring the rest of the area.

Volcano Garden Arts. Located on the former Hopper Estate, the Volcano Garden Arts complex includes a gallery, several acres of landscaped sculpture gardens, and dozens of art studios all housed in redwood buildings built in 1908. The grounds are immaculately maintained, and there are several trails leading up to and through the surrounding rain forest. A recently renovated one-bedroom "artist's cottage" is available for rent on the estate grounds as well. ✉ *19-3438 Old Volcano Rd.* ☎ *808/985-8979* 🌐 *www.volcanogardenarts.com* 💳 *Free* ⏲ *Tues.–Sat. 10–4.*

Volcano Golf Course and Country Club. Don't let the "country club" bit fool you, this is nothing like the snooty courses on the Kohala coast. First off, the green fees are way lower; second, the course is well maintained but not overly manicured; and third, there are rarely crowds so play is continuous and moves quickly. The course itself is reasonably challenging—an 18-hole, par 72 course—but the real draws are the views and the location. It might be the only course in the world built on an active volcano (Kīlauea), with views of Mauna Kea and Mauna Loa, as well as frequent hawk, wild turkey, and nēnē sightings. The small golf course restaurant also serves a great (and cheap) breakfast or lunch. ✉ *Pi'i Mauna Dr., across from the entrance to Volcanoes National Park* ☎ *808/967-7331* 🌐 *www.volcanogolfshop.com* 💳 *$63* ⏲ *Daily 7–5.*

Volcano Winery. Lava rock may not seem like ideal soil for the cultivation of grapes, but that hasn't stopped the Volcano Winery from producing award-winning wines combining their Volcano-grown grapes with various island ingredients. Their Macadamia Nut Honey Wine works well as an after-dinner drink, although it may be a touch too sweet for some. Their white Symphony wines have garnered the most praise from critics and visitors to the winery. The wines here are good, but not amazing. The primary reason to visit is the novelty of the winery itself—wine produced from an active volcano is undeniably interesting and appealing. And it makes for a great, unique (and fairly reasonable) gift to bring home. The winery is in a pleasant setting, looking out over the vineyard and nearby golf course; staff are friendly and helpful; and their gift store has a well-chosen selection of local crafts and goods. ✉ *35 Pi'i Mauna Dr.* ☎ *808/967-7772* 🌐 *www.volcanowinery.com* 💳 *Free tasting* ⏲ *Daily 10–5:30.*

HILO

When compared to Kailua-Kona, Hilo is often described as "the real Hawai'i." With fewer tourists than residents, more historic buildings, and more Hawaiian cultural events, life does seem more Hawaiian on this side of the island. This quaint, traditional fishing village stretches from the banks of the Wailuku River to Hilo Bay, where a few hotels line stately Banyan Drive. The wonderful old buildings that make up Hilo's downtown have recently been spruced up as part of a revitalization effort. Nearby, the 30-acre Lili'uokalani Gardens, a formal Japanese garden with arched bridges and waterways, was created in the early 1900s to honor the area's Japanese sugar-plantation laborers. It also became a safety zone after a devastating tidal wave swept away businesses and homes on May 22, 1960, killing 60 people.

With a population of almost 50,000 in the entire district, Hilo is the fourth-largest city in the state and home to the University of Hawai'i at Hilo. Although it is the center of government and commerce for the is-

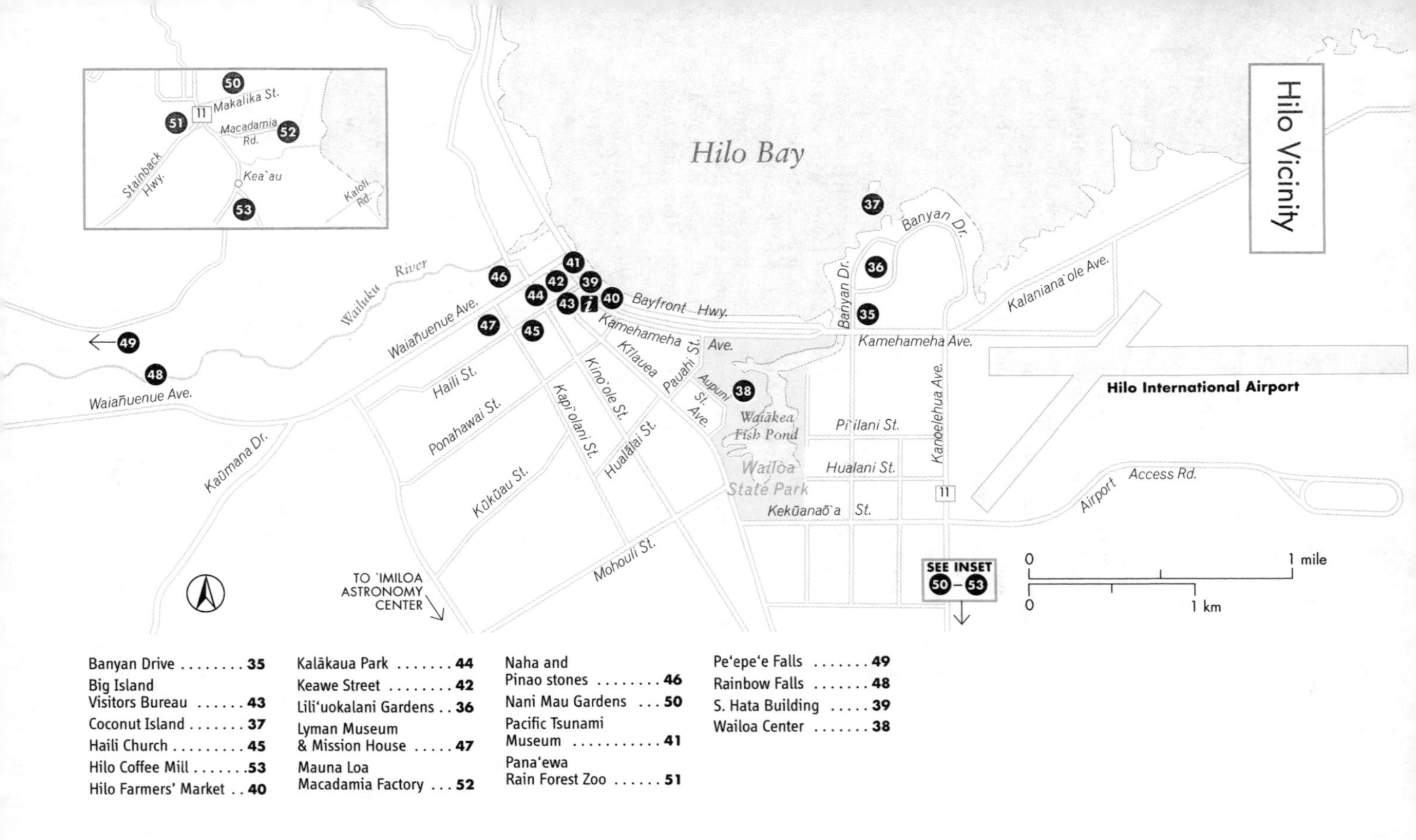
Hilo Vicinity
Hilo Bay
Hilo International Airport
Makalika St.
Macadamia Rd.
Stainback Hwy.
Kea`au
Kaloli Rd.
Wailuku River
Waiānuenue Ave.
Bayfront Hwy.
Kamehameha Ave.
Kīlauea Ave.
Pauahi St.
Aupuni St.
Haili St.
Ponahawai St.
Kapi`olani St.
Kino`ole St.
Hualālai St.
Kūkūau St.
Kaūmana Dr.
Mohouli St.
Banyan Dr.
Kalaniana`ole Ave.
Kanoelehua Ave.
Pi`ilani St.
Hualani St.
Kekūanaō`a St.
Waiākea Fish Pond
Wailoa State Park
Airport Access Rd.
TO `IMILOA ASTRONOMY CENTER
SEE INSET 50–53
0 1 mile
0 1 km
Banyan Drive 35
Big Island Visitors Bureau 43
Coconut Island 37
Haili Church 45
Hilo Coffee Mill 53
Hilo Farmers' Market . . 40
Kalākaua Park 44
Keawe Street 42
Lili'uokalani Gardens . . 36
Lyman Museum & Mission House 47
Mauna Loa Macadamia Factory . . . 52
Naha and Pinao stones 46
Nani Mau Gardens . . . 50
Pacific Tsunami Museum 41
Pana'ewa Rain Forest Zoo 51
Pe'epe'e Falls 49
Rainbow Falls 48
S. Hata Building 39
Wailoa Center 38

land, Hilo is primarily a residential town. Mansions with yards of lush tropical foliage surround older wooden houses with rusty corrugated roofs. It's a friendly community, populated primarily by descendants of the contract laborers—Japanese, Chinese, Filipino, Puerto Rican, and Portuguese—brought in to work the sugarcane fields during the 1800s.

One of the main reasons visitors have tended to steer clear of the east side of the island is its weather. With an average rainfall of 130 inches per year, it's easy to see why Hilo's yards are so green, its buildings so weather-worn. Hilo is rain forests and waterfalls, very unlike the hot and dry white-sand beaches of the Kohala Coast. But when the sun does shine, the snow glistens on Mauna Kea, 25 mi in the distance, and the town sparkles. Most days the rain blows away by noon, leaving behind the colorful arches that earn Hilo its nickname: the City of Rainbows.

LOGISTICS Hilo is a great base for exploring the eastern and southern parts of the island, just be sure to bring an umbrella for the afternoon showers. If you're just passing through town or making a day trip, make the first right turn into the town off Highway 19 (it comes up fast) and grab a parking spot in the lot on your left or on any of the surrounding streets. Downtown Hilo is best experienced on foot. The **Downtown Hilo Improvement Association** (✉ 329 Kamehameha Ave. ☎ 808/935–8850 ⊕ www.downtownhilo.com ⏲ Mon.–Fri. 8:30–4:30) provides an excellent and free self-guided walking tour to downtown Hilo. The tour includes historical information, a map, and directions to 18 historic sites. You can download it from their Web site or pick it up in person at their downtown Hilo office.

There are plenty of gas stations and restaurants in the area. Hilo is a good spot to load up on food and supplies—just south of downtown there are several large budget chains. The Merrie Monarch Hula Festival takes place in Hilo every year during the second week of April, and dancers and admirers flock to the city from all over the world. If you're planning a stay in Hilo during this time, be sure to book your room well in advance.

Main Attractions

★ 40 **Hilo Farmers' Market.** An abundant and colorful market draws farmers and shoppers from all over the island. Bright orchids, anthuriums, and birds-of-paradise create a feast for the eyes, while exotic vegetables, tropical fruits, and baked goods satisfy the stomach. Craft and jewelry makers and clothing vendors round out the market. Don't dawdle, as it closes in the early afternoon. ✉ *Mamo and Kamehameha Sts.* ⏲ *Wed. and Sat. 6:30 AM–2:30 PM.*

'Imiloa Astronomy Center. Part Hawaiian cultural center, part astronomy museum, the 'Imiloa Astronomy Center provides an educational and cultural complement to the research being conducted atop Mauna Kea. Although visitors are welcome at Mauna Kea, its primary function is research center—not observatory, museum, or education center. Those roles have been taken on by 'Imiloa in a big way. With its exhibits, full-dome planetarium shows, and regularly scheduled talks and events, the

BIRTH OF THE ISLANDS

How did the volcanoes of the Hawaiian Islands evolve here, in the middle of the Pacific Ocean? The ancient Hawaiians believed that the volcano goddess Pele's hot temper was the key to the mystery; modern scientists contend that it's all about plate tectonics and one very hot spot.

Plate Tectonics & the Hawaiian Question: The theory of plate tectonics says that the Earth's surface is comprised of plates that float around slowly over the planet's molten interior. The vast majority of earthquakes and volcanic eruptions occur near plate boundaries—the San Francisco earthquakes in 1906 and 1989, for example, were the result of activity along the nearby San Andreas Fault, where the Pacific and North American plates meet. Hawai'i, more than 1,988 miles from the nearest plate boundary, is a giant exception. For years scientists struggled to explain the island chain's existence—if not a fault line, what caused the earthquakes and volcanic eruptions that formed these islands?

What's a hotspot? In 1963, J. Tuzo Wilson, a Canadian geophysicist, argued that the Hawaiian volcanoes must have been created by small concentrated areas of extreme heat beneath the plates. Wilson hypothesized that there is a hotspot beneath the present-day position of the Big Island. Its heat produced a persistent source of magma by partly melting the Pacific Plate above it. The magma, lighter than the surrounding solid rock, rose through the mantle and crust to erupt onto the sea floor, forming an active seamount. Each flow caused the seamount to grow until it finally emerged above sea level as an island volcano. Plausible so far, but why then, is there not one giant Hawaiian island?

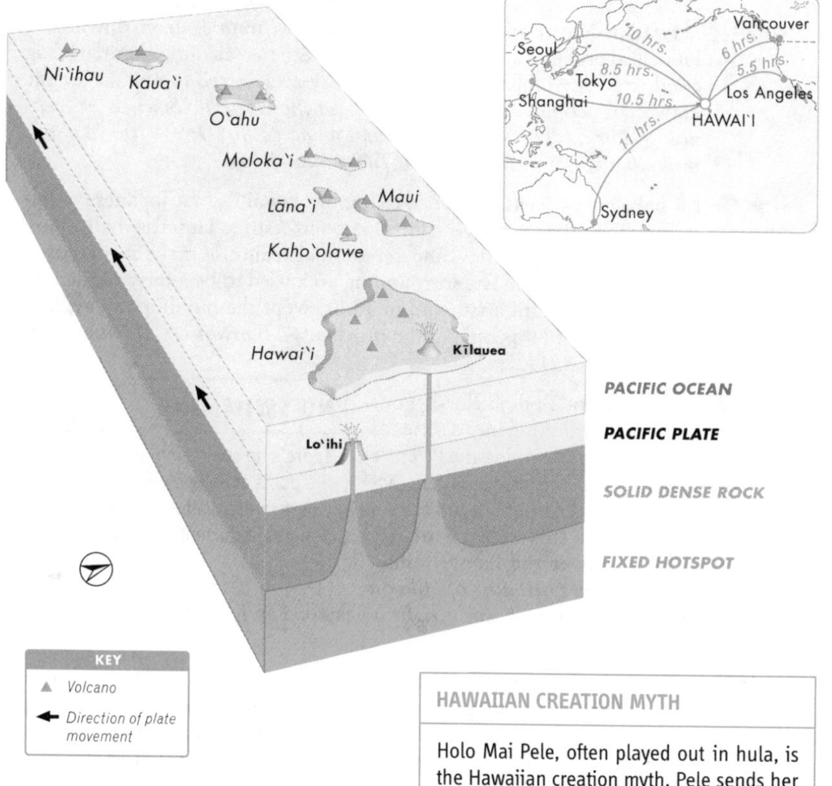

Volcanoes on the Move: Wilson further suggested that the movement of the Pacific Plate itself eventually carries the island volcano beyond the hotspot. Cut off from its magma source, the island volcano becomes dormant. As the plate slowly moved, one island volcano would become extinct just as another would develop over the hotspot. After several million years, there is a long volcanic trail of islands and seamounts across the ocean floor. The oldest islands are those farthest from the hotspot. The exposed rocks of Kaua'i, for example, are about 5.5 million years old, but those on the Big Island are less than .7 million years old, with new volcanic rock still being formed.

HAWAIIAN CREATION MYTH

Holo Mai Pele, often played out in hula, is the Hawaiian creation myth. Pele sends her sister Hi'iaka on an epic quest to fetch her lover Lohi'au. Overcoming many obstacles, Hi'iaka reaches full goddess status and falls in love with Lohi'au herself. When Pele finds out, she destroys everything dear to her sister, killing Lohi'au and burning Hi'iaka's 'ohi'a groves. Each time lava flows from a volcano, 'ohi'a trees sprout shortly after, in a constant cycle of destruction and renewal.

An Island on the Way: Off the coast of the Big Island, the volcano known as Lo'ihi is still submerged but erupting. Scientists long believed it to be a retired seamount volcano, but in the 1970s they discovered both old and new lava on its flanks, and in 1996 it erupted with a vengeance. It is believed that several thousand years from now, Lo'ihi will be the newest addition to the Hawaiian Islands.

center is a must-see for anyone interested in the stars, the planets, or Hawaiian culture and history. The center, five minutes from downtown Hilo, also provides an important link between the scientific research being conducted at Mauna Kea and its history as a sacred mountain for the Hawaiian people. ✉ *600 'Imiloa Pl., at the UH Hilo Science & Technology Park, off of Nowelo and Komohana* ☎ *808/969–9700* 🌐 *www.imiloahawaii.org* 🎫 *$14.50* ⏲ *Tues.–Sun., 9–4.*

★ 36 **Lili'uokalani Gardens.** Designed to honor Hawai'i's first Japanese immigrants, the 30-acre park's fish-filled ponds, stone lanterns, half-moon bridges, elegant pagodas, and ceremonial teahouse make it a favorite Sunday destination. The surrounding area used to be a busy residential neighborhood until a tsunami in 1960 swept the buildings away, taking the lives of 60 people in the process. ✉ *Banyan Dr. at Lihiwai St.* ☎ *808/961–8311.*

49 **Pe'epe'e Falls** (Boiling Pots). Four separate streams fall into a series of circular pools, forming the Pe'epe'e Falls. The resulting turbulent action—best seen after a good rain—has earned this stretch of the Wailuku River the name Boiling Pots. ✉ *3 mi northwest of Hilo on Waiānuenue Ave.; keep to right when road splits and look for a green sign for Boiling Pots.*

NO SWIMMING

There's no swimming allowed in the pools at Pe'epe'e Falls, or anywhere in the Wailuku River, due to dangerous currents and undertows.

★ 48 **Rainbow Falls.** After a hard rain, these falls thunder into the Wailuku River gorge. If the sun peeks out in the morning hours, rainbows form above the mist. ✉ *Take Waiānuenue Ave. west of town 1 mi; when road forks, stay on right of Waiānuenue Ave.; look for Hawaiian warrior sign.*

Also Worth Seeing

★ 35 **Banyan Drive.** The more than 50 leafy banyan trees with aerial roots dangling from their limbs were planted some 60 to 70 years ago by visiting celebrities. You'll find such names as Amelia Earhart and Franklin Delano Roosevelt on plaques affixed to the trees. ✉ *Begin at Hawai'i Naniloa Resort, 93 Banyan Dr.*

43 **Big Island Visitors Bureau.** Marked by a red-and-white Hawaiian warrior sign, the bureau is worth a visit for brochures, maps, and up-to-date, friendly insider advice. ✉ *250 Keawe St., at Haili St.* ☎ *808/961–5797* 🌐 *www.bigisland.org* ⏲ *Weekdays 8–4:30.*

★ 37 **Coconut Island.** This small island, just offshore from Lili'uokalani Gardens, is accessible via a footbridge. It was considered a place of healing in ancient times. Today children play in the tide pools while fisherfolk try their luck. ✉ *Lili'uokalani Gardens, Banyan Dr.*

45 **Haili Church.** This church was originally constructed in 1859 by New England missionaries, but the church steeple was rebuilt in 1979 following a fire. ■ TIP→ **Haili Church is known for its choir, which sings hymns in Hawaiian during services.** ✉ *211 Haili St.* ☎ *808/935–4847.*

CLOSE UP

If Trees Could Talk

THE HISTORY OF THE TREES lining Hilo's Banyan Drive is one of the Big Island's most interesting and least-known stories. Banyan Drive was named for these trees, which were planted by VIP visitors to Hilo. Altogether, some 50 or so banyans were planted between 1933 and 1972.

The majority are Chinese banyans, and each one is marked with a sign naming the VIP who planted it and the date on which it was planted. The first trees were planted on October 20, 1933, by a Hollywood group led by director Cecil B. DeMille, who was in Hilo making the film *Four Frightened People*. Soon after, on October 29, 1933, another banyan was planted by the one and only George Herman "Babe" Ruth, who was in town playing exhibition games. President Franklin D. Roosevelt planted a tree on his visit to Hilo on July 25, 1934. And in 1935, famed aviatrix Amelia Earhart put a banyan in the ground just days before she became the first person to fly solo across the Pacific Ocean.

Trees continued to be planted along Banyan Drive until World War II. The tradition was then revived in 1952 when a young and aspiring U.S. senator, Richard Nixon of California, planted a banyan tree. Nixon's tree was later toppled by a storm and was replanted by his wife, Pat, during a Hilo visit in 1972. On a bright, sunny day, strolling down Banyan Drive is like going through a green, shady tunnel. The banyans form a regal protective canopy over Hilo's own "Walk of Fame."

53 **Hilo Coffee Mill.** With all the buzz about Kona coffee, it's easy to forget that coffee is produced throughout the rest of the island as well. The Hilo Coffee Mill is a pleasant reminder of that fact. In addition to farming their own coffee on-site, the Mill has partnered with several local small coffee farmers in East Hawai'i in an effort to put the region on the world's coffee map. You can sample the efforts of all of the farmers, as well as touring the Mill and watching the roasters in action. The shop sells coffee and other locally produced goods. Even if you don't have time for the tour or shopping, the Mill's café is a great pit stop on the way to Volcanoes National Park from Hilo. ✉ *17-995 Volcano Rd., between mile markers 12 and 13, Mountain View* ☎ *808/968–1333* 🌐 *www.hilocoffeemill.com* 🎫 *Free* ⏲ *Mon.–Fri. 8–4.*

44 **Kalākaua Park.** King Kalākaua, who revived the hula, was the inspiration for Hilo's Merrie Monarch Festival. A bronze statue, erected in 1988, depicts the king with a taro leaf in his left hand to signify the Hawaiian peoples' bond with the land. The park also has a huge spreading banyan tree and small fishponds, but no picnic or recreation facilities. In a local tradition, families that have had recent funerals often leave leftover floral displays and funeral wreaths along the fishpond walkway as a way of honoring and celebrating their loved ones. It makes for a unique and colorful display. ✉ *Kalākaua and Kino'ole Sts.*

NEED A BREAK?

For breads and sandwiches, soups, mouthwatering apple pies, croissants, and biscotti, O'Keefe & Sons Bread Bakers (✉ 374 Kino'ole St. ☎ 808/934-9334) is the place to go. The tiny retail shop is filled with specialties such as five-grain sourdough, banana bread, and cinnamon toast.

42 **Keawe Street.** Buildings here have been restored to their original 1920s and '30s plantation styles. Although most shopping is along Kamehameha Avenue, the ambience on Keawe Street offers a nostalgic sampling of Hilo as it might have been 80 years ago.

47 **Lyman Museum & Mission House.** Built in 1839 for David and Sarah Lyman, Congregationalist missionaries, the Lyman House is the oldest frame building on the island. In the adjacent museum, dedicated in 1973, there's a realistic magma chamber and exhibits on the islands' formation. There's also an interesting section on Hawaiian flora and fauna. The gift shop sells Hawaiian books, cards, gifts, and music. ✉ *276 Haili St.* ☎ *808/935–5021* 🌐 *www.lymanmuseum.org* *$10* *Mon.–Sat. 9:30–4:30.*

52 **Mauna Loa Macadamia Factory.** Acres of macadamia trees lead to a processing plant with viewing windows. A videotape depicts the harvesting and preparation of the nuts, and there are free samples in the visitor center. Children can run off their energy on the nature trail. ✉ *Macadamia Rd. off Hwy. 11, 5 mi south of Hilo* ☎ *808/966–8618* 🌐 *www.maunaloa.com* *Daily 8:30–5:30.*

46 **Naha and Pinao stones.** These two huge, oblong stones are legendary. The Pinao stone is purportedly an entrance pillar of an ancient temple built near the Wailuku River. King Kamehameha is said to have moved the 5,000-pound Naha stone when he was still in his teens. Legend decreed that he who did so would become king of all the islands. They're in front of the Hilo Public Library. ✉ *300 Waiānuenue Ave.*

★ 50 **Nani Mau Gardens.** The name means "forever beautiful" in Hawaiian, and that's a good description of this 20-acre botanical garden filled with several varieties of fruit trees and hundreds of varieties of ginger, orchids, anthuriums, and other exotic plants. A botanical museum details the history of Hawaiian flora, and guided tours by tram are available. There's also a café with a lunch buffet. ✉ *421 Makalika St., off Hwy. 11* ☎ *808/959–3500* 🌐 *www.nanimau.com* *$10, tram tour $15* *Daily 8–5.*

41 **Pacific Tsunami Museum.** A memorial to all those who lost their lives in the tragedies that have struck this side of the island, this small museum offers a poignant history of tsunamis. In a 1931 C. W. Dickey–designed building—the former home of the First Hawaiian Bank—you'll find an interactive computer center, a science room, a theater, a replica of Old Hilo Town, a *keiki* (children's) corner, and a knowledgeable, friendly staff. In the background, a striking quilt tells a silent story. ✉ *130 Kamehameha Ave.* ☎ *808/935–0926* 🌐 *www.tsunami.org* *$7* *Mon.–Sat. 9–4.*

51 **Pana'ewa Rain Forest Zoo.** Children enjoy the spider monkeys, the pygmy hippopotamus, and the white tiger (feedings are every day at 3:30) in

this quiet zoo, the only rain-forest zoo in the United States. There are a variety of native Hawaiian species, such as the state bird, the nēnē (Hawaiian goose), as well as a small petting zoo every Saturday 1:30–2:30. ✉ *Left on Mamaki off Hwy. 11, just past the "Kulani 19, Stainback Hwy" sign* ☎ *808/959–7224* 🌐 *www.hilozoo.com* 🎫 *Free* ⏲ *Daily 9–4.*

39 **S. Hata Building.** Erected as a general store in 1912 by Sadanosuke Hata and his family, this historic structure now houses shops, restaurants, offices, and a museum called Mokupapapa: Discovery Center for Hawaii's Remote Coral Reefs. During World War II the Hatas were interned and the building confiscated by the U.S. government. When the war was over, a daughter repurchased it for $100,000. A beautiful example of Renaissance-revival architecture, it won an award from the state for the authenticity of its restoration. ✉ *308 Kamehameha Ave., at Mamo St.*

FUN THINGS TO DO, HILO SIDE

- Enjoy the best shower you've ever had beneath an ancient waterfall.
- Watch the world's largest active volcano make the earth beneath your feet.
- Take in a starry night on the tallest mountain in the world, Mauna Kea.
- Swim with sea turtles at Punalu'u Black Sand Beach, then hike into Green (yes, green) Sand Beach.
- Relax in nature's hot tub—the volcanically heated springs of Puna.

Wailoa Center. This circular exhibition center, adjacent to Wailoa State Park, has shows by local artists that change monthly. There's also a photographic exhibit of the 1946 and 1960 tsunamis. Just in front of the center is a 12-foot-high bronze statue of King Kamehameha I, made in Italy in the late 1980s. Check out his gold Roman sandals. ✉ *Pi'opi'o St. off Kamehameha Ave.* ☎ *808/933–0416* ⏲ *Mon., Tues., Thurs., and Fri. 8:30–4:30, Wed. noon–4:30, Sat. 9:30–3.*

HĀMĀKUA COAST

The spectacular waterfalls, mysterious jungles, emerald fields, and stunning ocean vistas along Highway 19 northwest of Hilo are collectively referred to as the Hilo–Hāmākua Heritage Coast. Brown signs featuring a sugarcane tassel reflect the area's history: thousands of acres of sugarcane are now idle, with no industry to support since "King Sugar" left the island in the early 1990s. The 45-mi drive winds through little plantation towns, Pāpa'ikou, Laupāhoehoe, and Pa'auilo among them. It's a great place to wander off the main road and see "real" Hawai'i—untouched valleys, overgrown banyan trees, tiny coastal villages. In particular, the "Heritage Drive," a 4-mi loop just off the main highway, is well worth the detour. Once back on Highway 19, you'll pass the road to Honoka'a, which leads to the end of the road bordering Waipi'o Val-

ley, ancient home to Hawaiian royalty. The isolated valley floor has maintained the ways of old Hawai'i, with taro patches, wild horses, and a handful of houses.

LOGISTICS Any turn off along this coast could lead to an incredible view, so take your time and go exploring. Where there's a gorge there's usually a waterfall, and many of them fall into lovely swimming holes, so you might want to bring both hiking shoes and a swimsuit. Gas stations, stores, and restaurants are hard to come by on the coast, so it's a good idea to fuel up your car and your tummy before hitting the road. If you're driving from Kailua-Kona, rather than driving around the northern tip of the island, cut across on the Mamalahoa Highway (190) to Waimea and then catch the 19 to the coast.

If you've stopped to explore the quiet little villages with wooden boardwalks and dogs dozing in backyards, or if you've spent several hours in Waipi'o Valley, night will undoubtedly be falling by the time you've had your fill of the Hāmākua Coast. Don't worry: the return to Hilo via Highway 19 only takes about an hour, or you can continue on the same road to stop for dinner in Waimea (30 minutes) before heading back to the Kohala Coast resorts (another 25 to 45 minutes). Although you shouldn't have any trouble exploring the Hāmākua coast in a day, a handful

WAIPI'O VALLEY TOURS

If the steep climb out of Waipi'o Valley is not an appealing prospect, or if your time is limited, consider taking a guided tour. Costs range from about $40 to $145, depending on the company and the transport mode.

- **Na'alapa Stables** (☎ 808/775-0419 🌐 www.naalapastables.com) Horseback riding trips.
- **Waipi'o Ridge Stables and Waipi'o Rim Backroad Adventures** (☎ 808/775-7291 for stables, 808/775-1122 for backroad adventures 🌐 www.waipioridgestables.com, www.topofwaipio.com) Horseback riding trips, 4x4 or ATV trips.
- **Waipi'o Valley Shuttle** (☎ 808/775-7121 🌐 www.waipiovalleytour.com) Four-wheel-drive tours.
- **Waipi'o Valley Wagon Tours** (☎ 808/775-9518 🌐 www.waipiovalleywagontours.com) Mule-drawn wagon tours.

of romantic B&Bs are available along the coast if you want to spend more time.

Main Attractions

★ 55 **'Akaka Falls State Park.** A meandering 10-minute loop trail takes you to the best spots to see the two cascades, **'Akaka** and **Kahuna.** The 400-foot Kahuna Falls is on the lower end of the trail. The majestic upper 'Akaka Falls drops more than 442 feet, tumbling far below into a pool drained by Kolekole Stream amid a profusion of fragrant white, yellow, and red torch ginger. ✉ *4 mi inland off Hwy. 19, near Honomū* ☎ *808/974-6200* 💵 *Free* ⏲ *Daily 7–7.*

63 Fodor's Choice ★ **Waipi'o Valley.** Bounded by 2,000-foot cliffs, the Valley of the Kings was once a favorite retreat of Hawaiian royalty. Waterfalls drop 1,200 feet from the Kohala Mountains to the valley floor, and the sheer cliff faces make access difficult. Though completely off the grid today, Waipi'o was once the center of Hawaiian life; somewhere between 4,000 and 20,000 people made it their home between the 13th and 17th centuries. In 1780 Kamehameha I was singled out here as a future ruler by reigning chiefs. In 1791 he fought Kahekili in his first naval battle at the mouth of the valley. In 1823 the first white visitors found 1,500 people living in this Eden-like environment amid fruit trees, banana groves, taro fields, and fishponds. The 1946 tidal wave drove most residents to higher ground.

Now, as then, waterfalls frame the landscape, but the valley has become one of the most isolated places in the state. To preserve this pristine part of the island, commercial transportation permits are limited—only four outfits offer organized valley trips—and Sunday the valley rests. A four-wheel-drive road leads down from the **Waipi'o Valley Overlook** (✣ Follow Hwy. 240 8 mi northwest of Honoka'a), but only four-wheel-drive vehicles should attempt the steep road. The walk down into the valley is less than a mile from here—but keep in mind, the climb back up is strenuous in the hot sun. A crescent of black sand makes it a popular spot for surfers. ■ TIP→ **Continued overuse of the beach area and lack of** sanitary facilities have caused serious unhealthy conditions to persist since 2003. Until it's cleaned up we don't recommend getting into the water.

SEE THE SIGN

In addition to looking cool and hearkening back to the days when sugar was king, the brown and white Hilo-Hāmākua Heritage Coast signs mark various sites of historical interest, as well as scenic views along the 40-mi stretch of coastline. Keep an eye out for these signs and try to stop at the sights mentioned—you won't be disappointed.

Also Worth Seeing

★ 54 **Hawai'i Tropical Botanical Garden.** Eight miles north of Hilo, stunning coastline views appear around each curve of the 4-mi scenic jungle drive that accesses the privately owned nature preserve beside Onomea Bay. Paved pathways in the 17-acre botanical garden lead past ponds, waterfalls, and more than 2,000 species of plants and flowers, including palms, bromeliads, ginger, heleconia, orchids, and ornamentals. *27-717 Old Māmalahoa Hwy., Pāpa'ikou 808/964–5233 www.hawaiigarden.com $15 Daily 9–4.*

62 **Honoka'a.** In 1881 Australian William Purvis planted the first macadamia-nut trees in Hawai'i near what is now this funky little town. But Honoka'a's true heyday came when sugar was king in the early part of the 20th century. During World War II, this was the place for soldiers stationed around Waimea to cut loose. Today, little eateries and stores crammed with knickknacks, secondhand goods, and antiques occupy its historic buildings. *Mamane St., Hwy. 240.*

NEED A BREAK?

A quick stop at Tex Drive-In (45-690 Pakalana St. and Hwy. 19 808/775–0598) will give you a chance to taste the snack that made it famous: *malassada*, a puffy, doughy Portuguese doughnut without a hole. These deep-fried beauties are best eaten hot. They also come in cream-filled versions, including vanilla, chocolate, and coconut.

56 **Honomū.** A plantation past is reflected in the wooden boardwalks and tin-roof buildings of this small, struggling town. It's fun to poke through old dusty shops such as Glass from the Past, where you'll find an assortment of old bottles. The Woodshop Gallery/Café showcases local artists. *2 mi inland from Hwy. 19 en route to 'Akaka Falls State Park.*

★ 61 **Kalōpā State Park.** Past the old plantation town of Pa'auilo, at a cool elevation of 2,000 feet, lies this 100-acre state park. There's a lush forested area with picnic tables and restrooms, and an easy ¾-mi loop trail with additional paths in the adjacent forest reserve. Small signs identify some of the plants. *12 mi north of Laupāhoehoe and 3 mi inland off Hwy. 19 808/775–8852 Free Daily 7–7 or by permit.*

57 **Kolekole Beach Park.** This rocky beach on the Kolekole River offers an idyllic setting for a barbecue or picnic. A large banyan tree leans over the river, and its rope swing is a hit with local kids during lazy summer days. An old train bridge crosses the river where it empties into the ocean. The surf can be rough, so only experienced swimmers should venture

CLOSE UP

Pele & the Night Marchers

THE BEST-KNOWN DEITY in Hawaiian lore is Pele, the beautiful volcano goddess. Although visitors are warned not to remove lava rocks from Pele's domain without her permission, some do and find themselves dogged by bad luck until they return the stolen items. The Hawai'i Volcanoes National Park Service often receives packages containing chunks of lava along with letters describing years of misfortune. Tales of Pele's fiery temper are legendary. She battled Poli'ahu, ruler of snowcapped Mauna Kea on the Big Island, in a fit of jealousy over the snow goddess's extraordinary beauty. She picked fights with her peace-loving sister, Hi'iaka, turning the younger goddess's friends into pillars of stone. And her recurring lava-flinging spats with suitor Kamapua'a, a demigod who could change his appearance at will, finally drove him into the sea, where he turned into a fish to escape her wrath. In addition to battling the elements and each other, gods were thought to have intervened in the daily lives of early Hawaiians. Storms that destroyed homes and crops, a fisherman's poor catch, or a loss in battle were blamed on the wrath of angry gods.

According to legend, an industrious race of diminutive people called *menehune* built aqueducts, fishponds, and other constructs requiring advanced engineering knowledge unavailable to early Hawaiians. Living in remote hills and valleys, these secretive workers toiled only in darkness and completed complex projects in a single night. Their handiwork can still be seen on all the Islands.

Also at night, during certain lunar periods, a traveler might inadvertently come across the Night Marchers—armies of dead warriors, chiefs, and ancestral spirits whose feet never touch the ground. They float along the ancient highways, chanting and beating their drums, pausing only to claim the spirits of their brethren who died that night. It was believed that such an encounter would bring certain death unless a relative among the marchers pleaded for the victim's life.

past the river's mouth. Back on the road, a scenic drive takes you from the top of the park through the old town of Wailea back to Highway 19. ✉ *Off Hwy. 19* ☎ *808/961–8311* 🎫 *Free* ⏲ *Daily 7 AM–sunset.*

59 **Laupāhoehoe Point Park.** Come here to watch the surf pound the jagged black rocks at the base of the stunning point. This is not a safe place for swimming, however. Still vivid in the minds of longtime area residents is the 1946 tragedy in which 21 schoolchildren and three teachers were swept to sea by a tidal wave. ✉ *On northeast coastline, Hwy. 19, makai side, north of Laupāhoehoe* ☎ *808/961–8311* 🎫 *Free* ⏲ *Daily 7 AM–sunset.*

60 **Laupāhoehoe Train Museum.** Behind the stone-loading platform of the once-famous Hilo Railroad, constructed around the turn of the 20th century, the former manager's house is a poignant reminder of the era when sugar was the local cash crop. The railroad, used to transport sugar from

the plantations to the port, was one of the most expensive built in its time. It was washed away by the 1946 tsunami. Today one of the old engines is running again on a short Y-track at the museum. ✉ *Hwy. 19, Laupāhoe-hoe* ☎ *808/962–6300* 🎫 *$3* ⏲ *Weekdays 9–4:30, weekends 10–2.*

58 **World Botanical Gardens.** About 300 acres of former sugarcane land are slowly giving way to a botanical center, which includes native Hawaiian plants such as orchids, palms, gingers, hibiscus, and heliconias. In the 10-acre arboretum children love to wind their way through a maze made of shrubs. From within the gardens you have access to splendid views of one of the prettiest waterfalls on the isle, triple-tiered **Umauma Falls.** You may feel a little bit cheated, since it's $8 per person to essentially drive in, park, get out, and view the falls from a distance, but unfortunately this is the only place to see Umauma without some pretty rigorous hiking and scrambling. ✉ *Hwy. 19, from Hilo just past mile marker 16* ☎ *808/963–5427* 🌐 *www.wbgi.com* 🎫 *$8* ⏲ *Mon.–Sat. 9–5:30.*

MAUNA KEA

You can go snowboarding in Hawai'i. Seriously. You do have to be in pretty good shape and a close-to-expert boarder to get up the mountain and down again with no lifts, but lack of snow is definitely not a problem. Mauna Kea is the antithesis of the typical island experience. Freezing temperatures and arctic conditions are common at the summit, and snowstorms can occur year-round. From its base below the ocean's surface to its summit, Mauna Kea is the tallest island mountain on the planet. It's also home to Lake Waiau, one of the highest lakes in the world.

In addition to being a unique spot in all the ways mentioned above, Mauna Kea's summit—at 13,796 feet—is reputedly the clearest place in the world for viewing the night sky. For this reason, the summit is home to the world's largest astronomical observatory. Research teams from eleven different countries operate 13 telescopes on Mauna Kea, several of which are record-holders: the world's largest optical/infrared telescopes (the Keck telescopes), the world's largest dedicated infrared telescope (UKIRT), and the largest submillimeter telescope (the JCMT).

Mauna Kea is tall, but there are taller mountains in the world, so what makes this spot so great for astronomy? It has more to do with atmosphere than with height. A tropical inversion cloud layer below the summit keeps moisture from the ocean and other atmospheric pollutants down at lower elevations. As a result, the air around the Mauna Kea summit is extremely dry, which helps in the measurement of infrared and submillimeter radiation from stars, planets, and the like. There are also no clouds; the annual number of clear nights here blows every other place out of the water. And, because the mountain is far away from any interfering lights (not a total coincidence—in addition to the fact that the nearest town is nearly 30 mi away, there is an official ordinance limiting light on the island) skies are dark for the astronomers' research. To quote the staff at the observatory, astronomers here are able to "observe the faintest galaxies that lie at the very edge of the observable Universe."

CLOSE UP

2

Team Mauna Kea

THERE'S A MEETING OF THE MINDS on the mountaintop, with 13 telescopes operated by astronomers from around the world. A roll call:

UH 0.6-m telescope University of Hawai'i

UH 2.2-m telescope University of Hawai'i

IRTF (NASA Infrared Telescope Facility) NASA

CFHT (Canada-France-Hawai'i Telescope) Canada/France/University of Hawai'i

UKIRT (United Kingdom Infrared Telescope) United Kingdom

Keck I (W. M. Keck Observatory) Caltech/University of California

Keck II (W. M. Keck Observatory) Caltech/University of California

Subaru (Subaru Telescope) Japan

Gemini (Gemini Northern Telescope) USA/UK/Canada/Argentina/Australia/Brazil/Chile

CSO (Caltech Submillimeter Observatory) Caltech/National Science Foundation (NSF)

JCMT (James Clerk Maxwell Telescope) UK/Canada/Netherlands

SMA (Submillimeter Array) Smithsonian Astrophysical Observatory/Taiwan

VLBA (Very Long Baseline Array) National Radio Astronomers Observatory (NRAO)/Associated Universities, Inc. (AUI)/NSF

Although the telescopes are owned and operated by various countries and organizations, any research teams can book time on the equipment. A U.S.-Japan team comprising astronomers from the University of Hawai'i, University of Tokyo, Tohoku University, and Japan's Institute of Space and Astronautical Science made an important discovery of distant galaxies obscured by cosmic dust, using the JCMT telescope, which is jointly owned and operated by the United Kingdom, Canada, and the Netherlands. Similarly, a team of astronomers from the University of Hawai'i recently used the Keck telescopes (owned/operated by Caltech and the University of California) to discover a distant galaxy that gives astronomers a glimpse of the Dark Ages, when galaxies and stars were first forming in the universe.

Teams from various universities have used the telescopes on Mauna Kea to make major astronomical discoveries, including new satellites around Jupiter and Saturn, new "Trojans" (asteroids that orbit, similar to moons) around Neptune, new moons and rings around Uranus, and new moons around Pluto. Their studies of galaxies are changing the way scientists think about time and evolution.

What does all this mean for you? In addition to the best sunrises and sunsets—we're gonna go ahead and say it—in the world, a visit to Mauna Kea is a chance to see more stars than you've likely ever seen before and an opportunity to learn more about mind-boggling scientific discoveries in the very spot where these discoveries are being made. A trip to Mauna Kea may just be the highlight of your trip.

If you have a budding interest in astronomy, be sure to visit the 'Imiola Astronomy Center in Hilo (⇨ Hilo, *above*).The Center has presentations and planetarium films about the mountain and the science being conducted there.

LOGISTICS Mauna Kea is only 34 miles from Hilo and 18 from Waimea, but the drive takes an hour to an hour and a half from Hilo and half an hour to an hour from Waimea thanks to some rough driving. Between the ride there, sunset on the summit, and stargazing, we recommend allotting about four hours for your Mauna Kea visit.

There are a few potential obstacles to enjoying Mauna Kea, but nothing you can't avoid with a little planning. The first hurdle is getting there. To reach the summit, you must drive on Saddle Road. Saddle Road, which is a shortcut across the island, is a steep and winding road with no services, and parts of it are unpaved and rough. The road to the Visitor Center at Mauna Kea is fine, but the road from there to the summit is a bit more precarious, unpaved, and very steep. Most car rental companies make you sign a statement that you won't drive on Saddle Road, even if you rent a four-wheel-drive vehicle. Harper's, an independent company that rents cars, trucks, and motor homes in Hilo and Kailua-Kona is the sole exception. If you haven't rented a car that can make the drive, you can still head for the summit with one of a handful of tour operators who will take care of everything. If you plan to drive yourself, fill up on gas and bring water and snacks with you, as there is nowhere along the way to stock up.

The second thing, which is extremely important to remember, is the altitude. Whether you're hiking or driving to the summit, take the change in altitude seriously—stop at the visitor center for at least half an hour, and don't overexert yourself, especially at the top. Scuba divers must wait at least 24 hours before attempting a trip to the summit to avoid getting the bends. The observatory recommends that children under 16, pregnant women, and those with heart, respiratory, or weight problems not go higher than the Visitor Center.

The last potential obstacle: it's cold. The military personnel stationed in Hawai'i do their cold-weather training atop Mauna Kea. It is cold, and the snow never completely melts. It's difficult to find cold weather clothing in Hawai'i, so, if you plan to visit Mauna Kea, pack your favorite warm things from home.

Onizuka Visitor Center

64 **Onizuka Center for International Astronomy Visitor Information Station.** At a 9,300-foot elevation, this is the best amateur observation site on the planet, with three telescopes and a knowledgeable staff. It hosts nightly stargazing sessions from 6 to 10. This is also where you should stop to acclimate to the altitude if you're heading for the summit. On weekends the Onizuka Center offers escorted summit tours, heading up the mountain in a caravan. Reservations are not required for the free tours, which depart at 1 PM. To get here from Hilo, which is about 34 mi away, take

Highway 200 (Saddle Rd.), and turn right at mile marker 28 onto the John A. Burns Way, which is the access road to the summit. ☎ *808/961–2180* 🌐 *www.ifa.hawaii.edu/info/vis* ⏲ *Daily 9 AM–10 PM.*

The Summit

65 The summit is your destination just before sunset. Check out the telescopes (only the astronomers are allowed to use the equipment) and the scenery, then watch the sun sink into the horizon. When darkness falls, you really must descend to the Visitor Center for stargazing.

If you haven't rented a four-wheel-drive vehicle, don't want to deal with driving to the summit, or don't want to fight over the handful of telescopes at the visitor's center, consider booking a tour. Operators provide transportation to and from the summit and expert guides; some also provide parkas, gloves, telescopes, dinner, hot beverages, and snacks. Excursion fees range from $90 to $185.

Arnott's Lodge & Hiking Adventures. A bit cheaper than the others at $90 per person, Arnott's tours leave from Hilo; their tour does not include dinner, and they do not bring warm clothing for guests or their own telescope. Focusing more on the experience of the mountain than astronomy, Arnott's brings binoculars for each guest and provides an informative lesson on major celestial objects and Polynesian navigational stars. ☎ *808/969–7097* 🌐 *www.arnottslodge.com.*

Hawai'i Forest & Trail. This outfitter stops for dinner along the way at a historic ranch, and brings parkas, gloves, and their own telescope along. Cookies and hot chocolate make cold stargazing more pleasant. The price is $165 per person. ☎ *808/331–8505 or 800/464–1993* 🌐 *www.hawaii-forest.com.*

Jack's Tours. Jack's follows the same itinerary as the other tours—sunset on the summit, followed by stargazing from the visitor center. They take larger groups than the other outfitters, and their guides speak English and Japanese. Boxed dinner, hot tea, bottled water, light snack, telescopes, and use of jackets and gloves are included. The price is $165 per person. ☎ *800/442–5557* 🌐 *www.jackstours.com.*

Mauna Kea Summit Adventures. As the first company to specialize in tours to the mountain and the only company to offer only Mauna Kea tours, Mauna Kea Summit Adventures has a bit more cred than the rest of the pack. They use cushy new van coaches for their tours, bring along parkas and gloves, and serve dinner at the visitor center before heading up to sunset on the summit. They also bring along their own powerful telescope. The price is $185 per person. ☎ *808/322–2366* 🌐 *www.maunakea.com.*

Onizuka Visitor Center Tours. If you want to charge the summit with a group but don't fancy paying for one of the tours above, consider joining one of the Visitor Center's free summit tours, which depart from 1 PM to 5 PM every Saturday and Sunday. Reservations are not required, but a 4-wheel-drive vehicle is—The staff leads visitors up the summit in a caravan of their own cars. ☎ *808/961–2180* 🌐 *www.ifa.hawaii.edu/info/vis.*

PUNA

The Puna District is a wild place in every sense of the word. The jagged black coastline is changing all the time; the trees are growing out of control, forming canopies over the few paved roads; the land is dirt-cheap and there are no building codes; and the people, well, there's something about living in an area that could be destroyed by lava at any moment (as Kalapana was in 1990) that makes the laws of modern society seem silly. So it is that Puna has its well-deserved reputation as the "outlaw" region of the Big Island. That said, it's a unique place that's well worth a detour, especially if you're in this part of the island anyway. There are volcanically heated springs, tide pools bursting with interesting sea life, and some mighty fine people-watching opportunities in Pāhoa, a funky little town that the outlaws call home. This is also farm country (yes, that kind of farm, but also the legal sort). Local farmers grow everything from orchids and anthuriums to papayas, bananas, and macadamia nuts. Several of the island's larger, rural residential subdivisions are between Kea'au and Pāhoa, including Hawaiian Paradise Park, Orchidland Estates, Hawaiian Acres, Hawaiian Beaches, and others. When night falls the air fills with the high-pitched symphony of hundreds of coqui frogs. Though they look cute on the signs and sound harmless, the coqui frogs are a pest both to local crops and to locals, tired of their loud, shrill all-night song.

SLOW DOWN, BRA

Speed limits in this area are low for a reason. Paved roads can become unpaved within a few feet; heed the speed limits so that you don't go flying onto a bumpy dirt road at 70 mph. There are also tons of kids riding around on ATVs (and some of them might be going way faster than you're allowed to). It's best to be able to dodge them without landing in a palm tree.

LOGISTICS Puna is close to both Hilo and Volcano, and, if you're staying in either place for the night, driving around Puna is a great way to spend a morning. The roads connecting Pāhoa to Kapoho and the Kalapana coast form a loop that's about 25 mi long; driving times are from two to three hours, depending on the number of stops you make and the length of time at each stop. There are restaurants, stores, and gas stations in Pāhoa, but services elsewhere in the region are spotty. There are long stretches of the road that may be completely isolated at any given point; this can be a little scary at night but beautiful and tranquil during the day. Compared to big city living, it's pretty tame, but there is a bit of a "locals only" vibe in parts of Puna, and a growing drug problem in Pāhoa, so don't go wandering around at night.

Main Attractions

(68) **Cape Kumukahi Lighthouse.** The lighthouse, 1½ mi east of the intersection of highways 132 and 137, was miraculously unharmed during the 1960 volcano eruption here that destroyed the town of Kapoho. The lava flowed directly up to the lighthouse's base but instead of pushing it over, actually flowed around it. According to Hawaiian legend, Pele,

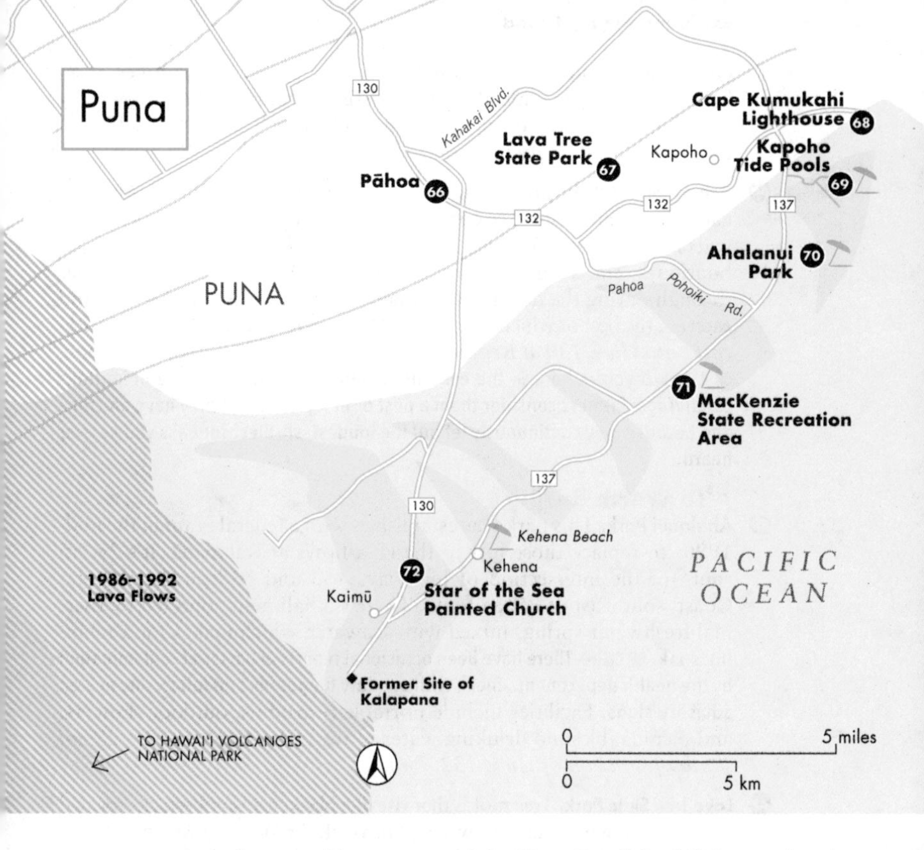

the volcano goddess, protected the Hawaiian fisherfolk by sparing the lighthouse. The lighthouse itself is a simple metal-frame structure with a light on top, similar to a tall electric-line transmission tower. Seeing the hardened lava flows skirting directly around the lighthouse is worth the visit. ⊠ *Past intersection of Hwys. 132 and 137, Kapoho.*

69 **Kapoho Tide Pools.** This network of tide pools at the end of Kapoho-Kai Road is great for a swim or a snorkel, or even just a beautiful view of new coastline. Some of the pools are volcanically heated, so if your back's a little sore from exploring the island, stop for a 10-minute soak and you'll feel better immediately. Take the road to the end, turn left, and park. Some of the pools are on private property, but those closest to the ocean, Wai'ōpae (ponds), are open to all. ⊠ *End of Kapoho-Kai Rd., off Hwy. 137.*

71 **MacKenzie State Recreation Area.** This is a coastal park located on rocky shoreline cliffs in a breezy, cool ironwood grove. There are picnic tables, restrooms, and a tent-camping area; bring your own drinking water. The park is significant for the restored section of the old "King's Highway" trail system, which circled the coast in the era before Hawai'i was discovered by the Western world. In those days, tribal kings and chiefs used these trails to connect the coastal villages, allowing them to

collect taxes and maintain control over the people. Short hikes of an hour or less are possible along the existing sections of the rough rocky trail. There are views of rugged coast, rocky beach, and coastal dry forest. ✉ *Hwy. 137, Puna District.*

66 **Pāhoa.** Sort of like an outlaw town from the Wild West, but with renegade Hawaiians instead of cowboys, this little town is all wooden boardwalks and rickety buildings. The secondhand stores, tie-dye clothing boutiques, and art galleries in quaint old buildings are fun to wander through during the day. Pāhoa's main street boasts a handful of island eateries, the best of which is **Luquin's Mexican Restaurant.** ✉ *Turn southeast onto Hwy. 130 at Kea'au, drive 11 mi to right turn marked Pāhoa.* ■ TIP→ **If you're here in the evening, listen for the sound of the ubiquitous coqui frogs; farmers consider them a pest both for the effect they have on crops and because they continuously let out the loudest, shrillest squeaks you've ever heard.**

Also Worth Seeing

70 **Ahalanui Park.** This park was established with a federal grant in the mid-1990s to replace those lost to the lava flows at Kalapana. It's 2½ mi south of the intersection of highways 132 and 137 on the Kapoho Coast, southeast of Pāhoa town. There's a half-acre pond fed by thermal freshwater springs mixed with seawater, which makes for a relaxing soak. ■ TIP→ **There have been occasional reports of bacterial contamination by the health department. Check with on-duty lifeguards and follow any posted advisory signs.** Facilities include portable restrooms, outdoor showers, and picnic tables; no drinking water is available. ✉ *Hwy. 137, 2½ mi south of junction of Hwy. 132, Puna.*

67 **Lava Tree State Park.** Tree molds that rise like blackened smokestacks formed here in 1790 when a lava flow swept through the *'ōhi'a* forest. Some reach as high as 12 feet. The meandering trail provides close-up looks at some of Hawai'i's tropical plants and trees. There are restrooms and a couple of picnic pavilions and tables. ■ TIP→ **Mosquitoes live here in abundance, so be sure to bring repellent.** ✉ *Hwy. 132, Puna District* ☎ *808/974–6200* *Free* ⏲ *Daily 30 min before sunrise–30 min after sunset.*

72 **Star of the Sea Painted Church.** This historic church, now a community center, was moved to its present location in 1990 just ahead of the advancing lava flow that destroyed the Kalapana area. The church, which dates from the 1930s, was built by a Belgian Catholic missionary priest, Father Evarest Gielen, who also did the detailed paintings on the church's interior. Though similar in style, the Star of the Sea and St. Benedict's were actually painted by two different Belgian Catholic missionary priests. Star of the Sea also has several lovely stained-glass windows. ✉ *Hwy. 130, 1 mi north of Kalapana.*

A CIRCLE ISLAND TOUR

Given the large amount of territory to cover, we recommend that those interested in circling the Big Island stay at different spots throughout. This also allows you to break up your time between hotels, vacation rentals, and B&Bs, which keeps things interesting and usually drives your lodging costs down (a real bonus considering the cost of gas). Following are routes around the island originating in either Hilo or Kona. These are seven-day itineraries, but they can easily be shortened by leaving out stops and increasing the amount of driving per day.

Starting in Hilo

Book a night at a B&B in **Hilo** and get up early to explore the town. By late morning, head to **Volcano.** It's less than an hour away (just over 28 slow-driving miles, about 40 minutes), but we recommend staying the night so that you can take the nighttime lava walk and spend quality time in Volcanoes National Park. In the morning, head south on Highway 11 to Ka Lae (South Point), stopping on the way at Punaluʻu Beach (30 mi/35 minutes from Volcano) for a quick swim with the sea turtles. Once at South Point (15 mi/20 minutes from Punaluʻu), park and hike down to Papakōlea Beach (Green Sand Beach). Back on the road, drive north 45 mi/one hour on Highway 11 to **Kealakekua Bay.** Stay the night, and get up early to spend the morning kayaking and snorkeling in Kealakekua Bay and exploring the ancient Place of Refuge. Drive back up the hill from these sites to spend some time in Kainaliu or take a coffee farm tour. A 10- to 15-minute drive north will get you to Kailua-Kona. Get out to wander around, then make a beeline to Huggo's on the Rocks or the Kona Inn for a sunset mai tai and pūpū. Stay either in **Kailua-Kona** or on the **Kohala Coast** (30 mi north of Kailua-Kona). Spend the next day at local favorite Hāpuna Beach. In the morning of the following day, set out north on Highway 11 and veer left to continue north on Highway 270 deeper into the North Kohala region. You'll pass through the charming village of Kapaʻau and dead-end at the Pololū Valley lookout. Head back through Kapaʻau and turn onto Highway 250 to Hāwī. Next it's up the hill to Waimea. This road offers our favorite views on the island—it's only about 20 mi, but it will likely take you an hour, between the slow curves and the photo ops. Check into a B&B and spend the rest of the day exploring **Waimea,** dining at one of the town's terrific restaurants. In the morning, drive south on Highway 19 to the Hāmākua Coast; follow the brown and white Heritage Coast signs to points of interest along the way, then turn off at Honokaʻa to check out Waipiʻo Valley. The drive from Waimea to Honokaʻa is under 15 mi and should take you 20 minutes or less. Spend the rest of the day exploring the coastline and stay the night on the **Hāmākua Coast.** It's just over 40 mi to the Hilo airport, a trip that should take you 50 minutes to an hour.

Starting in Kona

We recommend overnighting in the same towns if you start in Kailua-Kona, and just reversing the order. If you fly into Kona, stay your first and second nights in either Kailua-Kona or Kohala (Kailua-Kona is 7 mi southeast of the airport; the nearest Kohala resort is 7 mi north, the farthest 27 mi) then head north around the island to North Kohala, then Waimea, then the Hāmākua Coast, followed by Hilo, the Volcano, Punaluʻu, South Point, and Green Sand Beach, finishing up in Kealakekua Bay and South Kona. If you choose to stay near Kealakekua Bay on your last night, the trip to the airport is 20 mi.

BIG ISLAND SIGHTSEEING TOURS

GUIDED TOURS on the island are great for specific things: seeing Mauna Kea, exploring Waipi'o Valley, maybe even touring Volcanoes National Park (especially if your time is short). Sticking to a guided tour the whole time, though, would not be a great idea. Half the fun of the island is in exploring it on your own. Plus, if you stick to a guided tour, you'll only see the major tourist attractions, none of the Big Island's many hidden treasures.

Local tour-bus operators conduct volcano tours and circle-island tours, with pickup at the major resorts. Costs range from $38 to $160, depending on pickup location and length of tour. The circle-island tour is a full 12-hour day, but Jack's and Polynesian Adventure Tours also offer half-day tours to the volcano, Mauna Kea observatory, and around Kailua-Kona. Hawai'i Forest & Trail offers a volcano tour, Mauna Kea tour, several other specific sights tours, and the option of customizing a private tour.

Jack's Tours. ☎ *808/329-2555 in Kona, 808/961-6666 in Hilo, 800/442-5557* 🌐 *www.jackstours.com.*

Polynesian Adventure Tours. ☎ *808/329-8008 in Kona, 800/622-3011* 🌐 *www.polyad.com.*

Roberts Hawai'i. ☎ *808/329-1688 in Kona, 808/966-5483 in Hilo, 800/831-5541* 🌐 *www.robertshawaii.com.*

Hawai'i Forest & Trail. ☎ *808/464-1993* 🌐 *www.hawaii-forest.com.*

The Quickest Way . . .

From Kailua-Kona to Volcano: Take the southern route, following Highway 11 through South Kona and Ka'u around South Point to Volcano (125 mi, just under three hours).

Between Kailua-Kona and Hilo: Starting in Kailua-Kona, take Highway 190 east to Highway 19. Follow 19 through Waimea to Hilo (96 mi, two hours or less).

From Kohala to Waimea: Take Highway 11 to Waikoloa Road (9 mi south of Hāpuna Beach) and follow it 10 mi to Highway 190. Turn left on 190 and follow it another 11 mi to Waimea (30 mi, 40 minutes).

Beaches

WORD OF MOUTH

"The Punalu'u Black Sand Beach on the Big Island is very nice. When we were there, there were several turtles riding the surf. The beach is very wide and there are lots of picnic tables and palm trees."
–ChristieP

"If you want to experience sandy beaches and safer waters for the kids to swim in, then the Kona area is a good choice. We rented a small house on Ali'i Drive just south of Kona proper, and it was very convenient."
–bon100

www.fodors.com/forums

By John Penisten

DON'T BELIEVE ANYONE who tells you that the Big Island lacks beaches. It's just one of the myths about Hawai'i's largest island that has no basis in fact.

It's not so much that the Big Island has fewer than the other islands, just that there's more island, so getting to the beaches can be slightly less convenient. That said, there are plenty of those perfect white beaches you think of when you hear "Hawai'i," and the added bonus of black- and green-sand beaches, thanks to the age of the island and its active volcanoes. New beaches appear—and disappear—regularly, created and destroyed by volcanic activity. In 1989 a black-sand beach, Kamoamoa, formed when molten lava shattered as it hit cold ocean waters; it was closed by new lava flows in 1992. It's part of the ongoing process of the volcano's creation and change dynamic.

The bulk of the island's beaches are on the northwest part of the island, along the Kohala Coast. Black-sand beaches and green-sand beaches are in the southern region, along the coast nearest the volcano. On the eastern side of the island, beaches tend to be of the rocky-coast–surging-surf variety, but there are still a few worth visiting, and this is where the Hawaiian shoreline is at its most picturesque.

KOHALA COAST

Most of the white sandy beaches are found on the Kohala Coast, which is, understandably, home to the majority of the island's first-class resorts. Hawai'i's beaches are public property. The resorts are required to provide public access to the beach, so don't be frightened off by a guard shack and a fancy sign. There is some limited public parking as well. The resort beaches aside, there are some real hidden gems on the Kohala Coast accessible only by boat, four-wheel drive, or a 15- to 20-minute hike. It's well worth the effort to get to at least one of these. ■ TIP→ **The west side of the island tends to be calmer, but still the surf gets rough in winter.** The beaches here are listed in order from north (farthest from Kona) to south.

Pololū Valley Beach. On the North Kohala peninsula is one of the Big Island's most scenic black sand beaches. About 8 mi past Hāwī town, Highway 270 terminates at the overlook of remote Pololū Valley. Beach access is gained by a 20-minute hike down (twice as long back up) a generally steep and difficult trail that can be muddy and slippery. Caution is advised. The beach itself is a nice wide expanse of fine black sand backed by high dunes with some rocky outcroppings. ■ TIP→ **This is not a safe swimming beach even though locals do swim, bodyboard, and surf here. Dangerous rip currents and usually rough surf pose a real hazard.** And because this is a remote, isolated area far from emergency help, extreme caution is advised. The valley leading back from the beach was once farmed with taro patches but is no longer being used. There is very limited parking at the turnaround and along the roadside here. ✉ *End of Hwy. 270* ☞ *No facilities.*

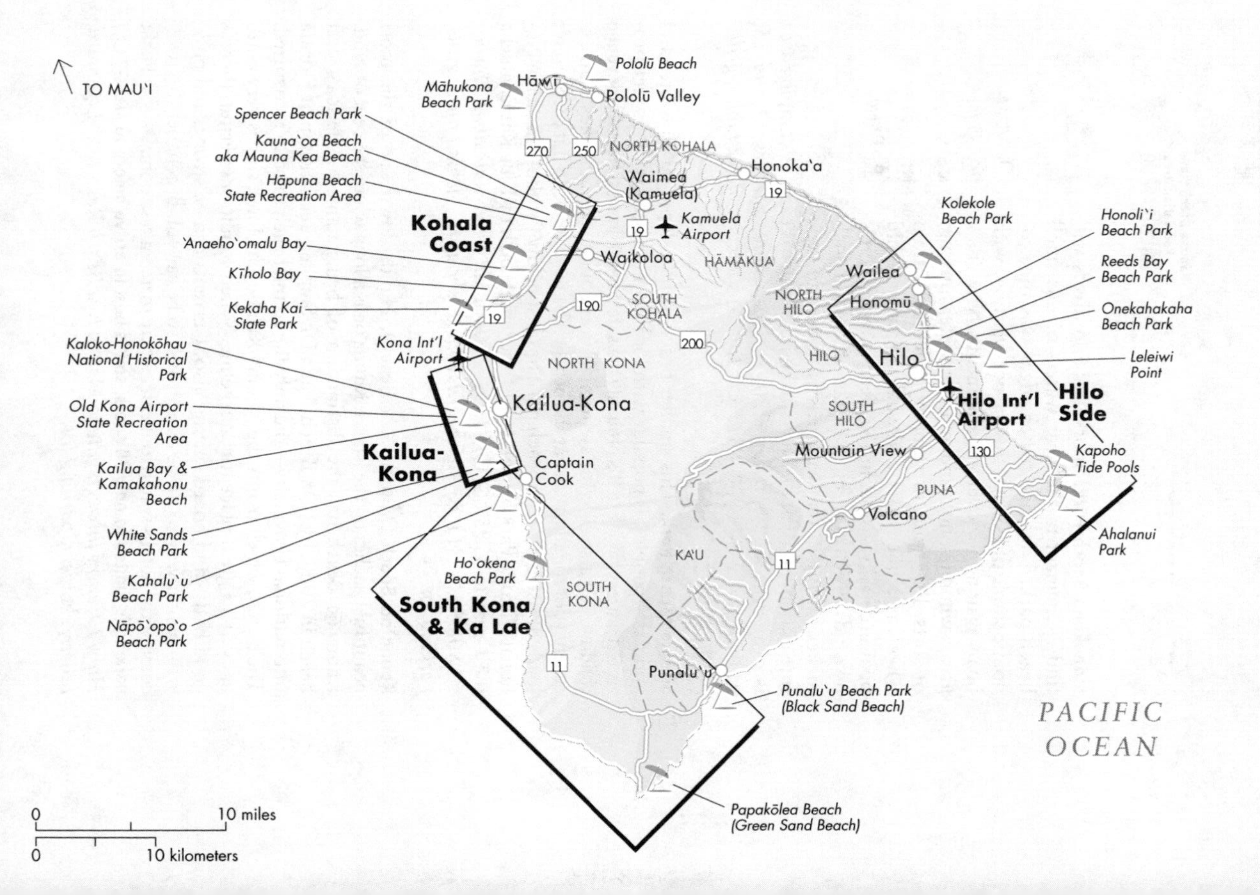
Big Island Beaches
TO MAU`I
Pololū Beach
Pololū Valley
Hāwī
Māhukona Beach Park
Spencer Beach Park
Kauna`oa Beach aka Mauna Kea Beach
Hāpuna Beach State Recreation Area
Kohala Coast
`Anaeho`omalu Bay
Kīholo Bay
Kekaha Kai State Park
Kona Int'l Airport
Kaloko-Honokōhau National Historical Park
Old Kona Airport State Recreation Area
Kailua Bay & Kamakahonu Beach
Kailua-Kona
White Sands Beach Park
Kahalu`u Beach Park
Nāpō`opo`o Beach Park
Captain Cook
Ho`okena Beach Park
South Kona & Ka Lae
NORTH KOHALA
Honoka`a
Waimea (Kamuela)
Kamuela Airport
Waikoloa
HĀMĀKUA
SOUTH KOHALA
NORTH KONA
SOUTH KONA
KA'U
Punalu`u
Punalu`u Beach Park (Black Sand Beach)
Papakōlea Beach (Green Sand Beach)
Kolekole Beach Park
Wailea
Honomū
NORTH HILO
HILO
Hilo
Honoli`i Beach Park
Reeds Bay Beach Park
Onekahakaha Beach Park
Leleiwi Point
Hilo Int'l Airport
Hilo Side
SOUTH HILO
Mountain View
PUNA
Volcano
Kapoho Tide Pools
Ahalanui Park
PACIFIC OCEAN
270
250
19
190
200
130
11
0
10 miles
10 kilometers

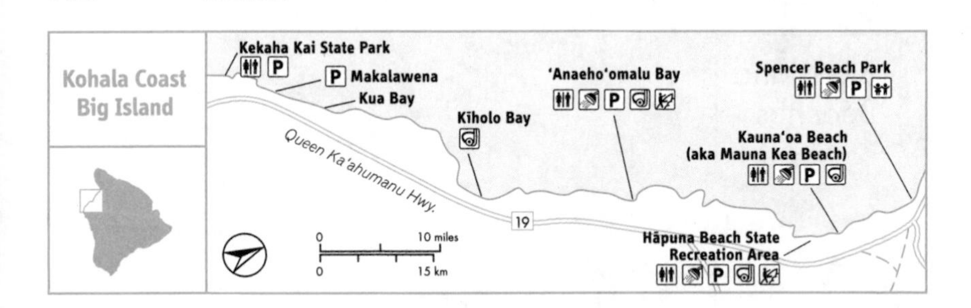

Māhukona Beach Park. Snorkelers and divers will find excitement in the clear waters of this small beach park. Long ago, when sugar was the economic staple of Kohala, this harbor was busy with boats waiting for overseas shipments. Now it's a great swimming hole and an underwater museum of sorts. Remnants of shipping machinery, train wheels and other parts, and what looks like an old boat are easily visible in the clear water. There's no sandy beach here, but a ladder off the old dock makes getting in the water easy. It's best to venture out only on tranquil days, when the water is calm. A camping area is available. ✉ *Off Hwy. 270, between mile markers 14 and 15, Māhukona* ☎ *808/961–8311* ☞ *Toilets, showers, picnic tables, grills, parking lot.*

Spencer Beach Park. This smaller beach, gently sloping with white sand and a few pebbles, is popular with local families because of its reef-protected waters. ■ TIP→ **It's probably the safest beach in west Hawai'i for young children.** It's also safe for swimming year-round, which makes it an excellent spot for a lazy day at the beach. The water is clear, but there aren't loads of fish here. The beach park lies just below Pu'ukoholā Heiau National Historic Park, site of the historic temple built by King Kamehameha the Great in 1795. ✉ *Off Hwy. 270, uphill from Kawaihae Harbor* ☎ *808/961–8311* ☞ *Lifeguard, toilets, showers, picnic tables, grills, parking lot.*

Fodor's Choice ★ **Kauna'oa Beach** (Mauna Kea Beach). Hands-down one of the most beautiful beaches on the island, Kauna'oa is a long white crescent of sand. Kauna'oa Beach has the distinction of being named America's best beach in 2000, by "Dr. Beach," aka Dr. Stephen Leatherman of Florida International University—the only Big Island beach to be so recognized. The beach, which fronts the Mauna Kea Beach Hotel, slopes very gradually. It's a great place for snorkeling. When conditions permit, there is good body- and board surfing also. Currents can be strong, and powerful winter waves can be dangerous, so be careful. Beachgoers are welcome at the hotel's waterfront café, where there's a restroom. ■ TIP→ **Public parking is limited to only 30 spots, so it's best to arrive before 10 AM.** ✉ *Off Hwy. 19; entry through gate to Mauna Kea Beach Resort* ☞ *Lifeguard, toilets, showers, parking lot.*

BEACH SAFETY

The Big Island's beaches, protected coves and bays, and beach parks are popular attractions. And because many of them are not easily accessible, those that are get heavy use on a regular basis. However, on any given day you may find that you are the only person on a long stretch of golden sand or in a secluded beach cove.

The old Hawaiians had a firm respect for the ocean. A rule they followed is still apt today: "Never turn your back to the sea." The reason is that many people have drowned because they were knocked over by unexpected large waves. They were caught off guard in the sand at the water's edge, on rocks along the shoreline, or even on high sea cliffs where they felt safe.

Keeping Safe in the Water

- Remember the rule of safe swimming anywhere: Use the buddy system and never swim or snorkel alone.
- Few public beaches have lifeguards. To be safe, try to stick to those that do.
- Get into the water only when you see other swimmers.
- Before you enter the water, ask lifeguards or local folks about the surf, rip currents, and any special hazards. Read and heed any warning signs of heavy surf, slippery rocks, jellyfish, or other unsafe conditions.
- Try to duck or dive beneath breaking waves before they reach you to avoid being knocked over and tumbled about.
- If you get caught in a rip current carrying you away from the shore, don't swim against it; you will tire rapidly. Instead, try to swim sideways across the current to get back to shore.
- Know this: alcohol and swimming don't mix.
- If you have any reason to doubt your ability to swim in the ocean, wear an inflatable flotation device such as a life vest. Don't use an air mattress or other device from which you can become separated.
- Closely supervise young children. Make them wear a flotation device and watch them constantly. Don't let them wander into rough water or near the breaking surf line. Even a small wave can knock them over, easily rendering them helpless in the water.
- Don't dive into unfamiliar places. Jump feet first to protect your head, neck, and spine.
- Being in the water is tiring, so know your limits. Avoid fatigue and get out when you are tired.
- Don't take glass containers to the beach, as broken glass is a hazard to bare feet; make fires only where allowed in designated areas in barbecue grills or fireplaces.
- Don't put yourself and loved ones at risk by getting close to the water's edge on slippery rocks or a high sea cliff or posing for a photo near big surf breaking in the background.

Fodor's Choice ★ **Hāpuna Beach State Recreation Area.** By any measurement, this is one fine beach. Guidebooks usually say it's a toss-up between Hāpuna and Kauna'oa for "best beach" on the island, but most locals give the prize to Hāpuna. There is ample parking so you don't have to get here at dawn, although it can fill up by midday. And while the north end of the beach fronts the Hāpuna Beach Prince Hotel, it's still a public beach and not just for hotel guests. The beach itself is a long (½-mi), white, perfect crescent, one of the Big Island's largest. The turquoise water is very calm in summer, with just enough rolling waves to make bodysurfing or boogie boarding fun. There's some excellent snorkeling around the jagged rocks that border the beach on either side, but a strong current means it's only for experienced swimmers. In winter, surf can be very rough. Hāpuna tends to get a little windy in the late afternoon; even that can have a benefit, as everyone else leaves just in time to give you a private, perfect sunset. ■ TIP→ **There are a couple of small protected coves at the north end of the beach with shallow, sandy-bottomed pools ideal for youngsters.** ✉ *Hwy. 19, near mile marker 69, at Hāpuna Beach Prince Hotel* ☎ *808/974–6200* ☞ *Lifeguard, toilets, showers, food concession, picnic tables, grills/firepits, parking lot.*

TOP BEACHES

- Kauna'oa Beach (also known as Mauna Kea Beach) is a beautiful palm-lined golden crescent.
- Hāpuna Beach is a wide expanse of fine sandy playground and aquamarine water.
- 'Anaeho'omalu Beach's lovely curving crescent provides lots of water sports options.
- Makalawena has fine sand, turquoise water, and is generally uncrowded.
- Honokōhau Beach is a find in a historic location.

★ **'Anaeho'omalu Beach (A-Bay).** This expansive beach of golden sand mixed with black lava grains fronts the Waikoloa Beach Marriott and is perfect for swimming, windsurfing, snorkeling, and diving. It's a well-protected bay, so even when surf is rough on the rest of the island, it's fairly calm here. Snorkel gear, kayaks, and boogie boards are available for rent at the north end. Graceful coconut palms line the beach and behind it are two old Hawaiian fishponds, Ku'uali'i and Kahapapa, that served the Hawaiian royalty in the old days. A walking trail follows the coastline to the Hilton Waikoloa Village next door, passing by tide pools and ponds. Footwear is recommended for the trail. ✉ *Follow Waikoloa Beach Dr. to Kings' Shops, then turn left; parking lot and beach right-of-way south of Waikoloa Beach Marriott* ☞ *Toilets, showers, food concession, picnic tables, parking lot.*

Kīholo Bay. The brilliant turquoise waters of this bay are a cooling invitation on a warm Kohala day, and happily a new gravel road to the shoreline makes it an absolute must-see (previously you'd have to hike over lava for 20 minutes). Thanks to Mauna Loa, what was once the site of King Kamehameha's gigantic fishpond is now several freshwater ponds encircling a beautiful little bay. The water's a bit cold and hazy because of the mix of fresh and salty water, but there are tons of green sea turtles in residence year-round here, and the snorkeling is great. If you follow the shoreline southwest toward Kona, just past the big yellow house is another public beach where you'll find some naturally occurring freshwater pools inside a lava tube. This area, called Queen's Bath, is as cool as it sounds. ✉ *Hwy. 19, gravel road between mile markers 82 and 83* ☞ *No facilities.*

Kua Bay. Remoteness does have its merits at this lovely beach, the northernmost beach in the stretch of coast that comprises Kekaha Kai State Park. At one time you had to hike over a few miles of unmarked, rocky trail to get here, which kept many people out. Now, a newly paved road leads to Kua Bay, and while locals are pretty unhappy about it, this beach is still uncrowded compared to others. It's easy to understand why area residents would be so protective. This is one of the most beautiful bays you will ever see—the water is crystal clear, deep aquamarine, and peaceful in summer. Rocky shores on either side keep the beach from getting too windy in the afternoon. The surf here can get very rough in winter. ✉ *Hwy. 19, north of mile marker 88* ☞ *No facilities.*

Makalawena. Makalawena is a long white crescent, dotted with little coves and surrounded by dunes and trees. The sand is powdery fine, the water is perfect, and the place is deserted. If it weren't so hard to get to, this would be the unanimous choice for best beach on the island. Like Kua Bay, Mahai'ula and Ka'elehuluhulu, it is within Kekaha Kai State Park, but it is the most remote. You either have to rent a boat and anchor there, walk 20 minutes over a rough coastal trail over lava rock terrain, or take a brutal four-wheel-drive jaunt over the lava. (You still have to walk the last 5 to 10 minutes.) But it's worth it. Makalawena is more than just a great beach—it's a truly magical place. An afternoon here is a recipe for delirious happiness. Sometimes people are so happy they just want to frolic around naked (forgetting that nude sunbathing/swimming is against the law here). Did we mention that there are wild goats hanging around? There's a freshwater pond that beats hosing off at one of those water-spigot showers at the marked public beaches. ✉ *Hwy. 19, between mile markers 88 and 89; if you're walking, park in lot at Kekaha Kai State Park and follow footpath along the shore* ☞ *No facilities.*

Kekaha Kai State Park. A 1.5-mi narrow, bumpy gravel road leads off Highway 19 to this recently developed beach park. Mahai'ula is to the south while Ka'elehuluhulu is to the north. The wide expanse of good sandy beach provides a lot of space here, so it doesn't feel crowded. There are high sand dunes and tidal pools for snorkeling and swimming. The sand is a salt and pepper mix of golden and black lava grains and pebbles. Caution is advised for rough surf and strong currents. You can hike along a historic 4½-mi trail from one to the other, but be prepared for the heat and bring lots of drinking water. ✉ *Hwy. 19, sign about 2 mi north of Keāhole–Kona International Airport marks rough Rd.* ☎ *808/327–4958 or 808/974–6200* ☞ *Parking lot at entrance, Mahai'ula: Toilets, picnic area; Ka'elehuluhulu: No facilities.*

KAILUA-KONA

There are a few good sandy beaches in the area near Kailua-Kona town. However, the coastline is generally rugged black lava rock, so don't expect long stretches of wide golden sand. The beaches near Kailua-Kona get lots of use by local residents but visitors will find them attractive as well. There are excellent snorkeling and scuba diving, good swimming, kayaking, and other water sports activities to enjoy.

Kaloko–Honokōhau National Historical Park. There are few beaches with as many old Hawaiian archaeological ruins as these three, sheltered in a 1,160-acre park near Honokōhau Harbor, just north of Kailua-Kona town. All are good for swimming. **'Ai'opio** (☞ Toilets), a few yards north of the harbor, is a small beach with calm, protected swimming areas (good for kids) and great snorkeling in the water near the archaeological site of Hale o Mono. **Honokōhau Beach** (☞ No facilities) a ¾-mi stretch with ruins of ancient fishponds, is also north of the harbor. At the north end of the beach, a historic trail leads *mauka* (toward the mountain) across the lava to a pleasant freshwater pool called Queen's Bath. A Hawaiian settlement until the 19th century, the area is being developed as a cultural and historical site. **'Alula** (☞ No facilities) is a slip of white sand at the south end of the harbor, a short walk over lava to the left of the harbor entrance. The park, which is still undergoing development, seeks to preserve early Hawaiian archaeological resources including *heiau* (an ancient Hawaiian place of worship), house platforms, fishponds, petroglyph rock etchings, and more. The park's wetlands provide refuge to a number of waterbirds, including the endemic Hawaiian stilt and coot. For information about the park, visit its headquarters, a 5- to 10-minute drive away. ✉ *74-425 Kealakehe Pkwy. off Hwy. 19* ☎ *808/329–6881* 🌐 *www.nps.gov* 🕒 *Park road gate 8 AM–3:30 PM* ☞ *Toilets, food concession, parking lot.*

Old Kona Airport State Recreation Area. The unused runway—great for jogging—is still visible above this palm-tree-lined beach at Kailua Park, a popular place to picnic, beachcomb, sunbathe, and more. It's especially busy on weekends. The generally rocky beachline has a few small pocket coves of white sand with safe entry to the water and tide pools for children, but for adults it's better for snorkeling than swimming. Conditions are best here on calmer days. An offshore surfing break known as Old Airport is popular with local surfers. ✉ *North end of Kuakini Hwy., Kailua-Kona* ☎ *808/327–4958 or 808/974–6200* ☞ *Toilets, showers, picnic tables, parking lot.*

ADMIRING THE MARINE LIFE

Big Island beach tidal pools and shallow reef areas are exciting places to explore and discover unique marine life. To be safe: Wear protective gloves and proper footwear. Watch for any high surf activity. Avoid sharp rocks and coral heads, as cuts can be painful and get infected. Many marine creatures have natural defenses like sharp teeth, spines, stingers, and even venom. So don't pick up unknown creatures or don't stick fingers into crevices in rocks or reefs where creatures may lurk.

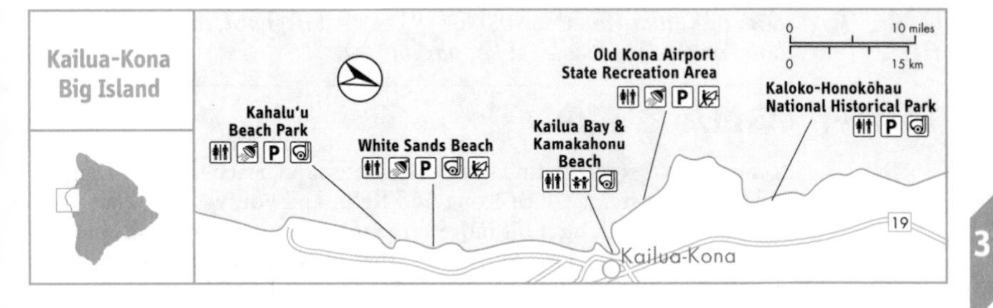

Kailua Bay & Kamakahonu Beach. Kids will especially enjoy this small pocket beach where they can play in the sand, ride waterbikes, paddle kayaks, and splash in the calm water. Fronting the King Kamehameha's Kona Beach Hotel and next to Kailua Pier, this little crescent of white sand is the only beach in downtown Kailua-Kona. Protected by the harbor, the calm water makes this a perfect spot for kids; for adults it's a great place for a swim and a lazy beach day. The water is surprisingly clear for being surrounded by an active pier. Snorkeling can be good, especially if you move south from the beach. There's a kiosk with snorkeling and kayaking equipment rentals. ■ TIP→ **A little family of sea turtles likes to hang out next to the seawall, so keep an eye out.** On a small peninsula protecting the beach is the reconstructed Ahu'ena Heiau, the recognized temple of King Kamehameha the Great, who spent the last years of his life here at Kamakahonu. ✉ *Ali'i Dr.* ☞ *Toilets available on the adjacent boat pier.*

White Sands, Magic Sands, or Disappearing Sands Beach. Towering coconut trees provide some shade and lend a touch of tropical beauty to this pretty little beach park, which may well be the Big Island's most intriguing beach. A migratory beach of sorts, it goes away in winter and returns in summer: Winter waves wash away the small white-sand parcel. In summer it re-forms; you'll know you've found it when you see the body- and board surfers. Though not really a great beach, this is a really popular summer hangout for young locals. ✉ *Ali'i Dr., 4½ mi south of Kailua-Kona* ☎ *808/961–8311* ☞ *Lifeguard, toilets, showers, food concession, parking lot.*

Kahalu'u Beach Park. Snorkelers can actually hand feed the unusually tame reef fish at this spot, which was a favorite of King Kalākaua, whose summer cottage is on the grounds of the neighboring Outrigger Keauhou Beach Resort. The salt and pepper beach is a combination of white and black sand mixed with lava and coral pebbles. This is one of the Big Island's most popular swimming and snorkeling sites, thanks to the fringing reef that helps keep the waters calm. But outside the reef there are very strong rip currents, so caution is advised. Experienced surfers find good waves to ride beyond the reef, and scuba divers like the shore dives—shallow ones inside the breakwater, deeper ones outside. A narrow path leads directly to the hotel's Kalanikai Bar & Grill (open daily 11 AM–4 PM), which serves beverages, sandwiches, and plate lunches. ✉ *Ali'i Dr., 5½ mi* *south of Kailua-Kona ☎ 808/961–8311 ☞ Lifeguard, toilets, showers, food concession, picnic tables, parking lot.*

SOUTH KONA & KA'Ū

You wouldn't expect to find sparkling white-sand beaches on the rugged and rocky coasts of South Kona and Ka'ū, and you won't. What you will find is something a bit more rare and well worth the visit: black- and green-sand beaches. And there's the chance to see the endangered Hawaiian green sea turtles close up. Beaches are listed here from north to south.

Nāpō'opo'o Beach Park. There's no real beach here, but don't let that deter you—this is a great spot and a historically significant one. It's where Captain James Cook landed in late 1778 to refurbish his ships; when he returned in 1779 he was killed in a skirmish with Hawaiians. A monument marks the spot on the north end of the bay. Kealakekua Bay is surrounded by high green cliffs, so the water's usually fairly calm and clear, making it ideal for swimming. Bring a mask along, as the snorkeling in the Kealakekua Bay Underwater Marine Reserve is superb. It's a great place to spot varied marine life, schools of colorful reef fish, corals, and more. This is also a great kayaking spot, and there are several shops in the villages of Honalo, Kainaliu, Kealakekua, and Captain Cook along Highway 11 that rent kayaks, in addition to snorkel gear. You can also take a snorkel, scuba, or glass-bottom boat tour from Keauhou Bay. ✉ *End of Nāpō'opo'o Rd., off Hwy. 11, Kealakekua Bay* ☎ *808/961–8311* ☞ *Parking lot.*

Ho'okena Beach Park. Driving south on Highway 11 from Kealakekua Bay, you'll see the sign for Ho'okena Beach Park. The road down to the quiet, out-of-the-way beach is narrow and steep, but the views are great. Plus you'll feel like you're venturing off the beaten path. By Hawaiian standards, this is an average beach (the water's nice for swimming, and there's a bit of snorkeling but nothing amazing), but that still makes it great for the rest of us. It's frequented mostly by the people from the nearby village; it's rarely crowded, except on weekends. The smallish beach, blessed with a few shade trees, is composed of black and white sand mixed with lava debris, which gives the sand an overall gray color. The bay is usually calm for swimming, snorkeling, and diving but caution is advised during high surf periods. ✉ *2-mi drive down road bordered by ruins of stone wall off Hwy. 11, 23 mi south of Kailua-Kona* ☎ *808/961–8311* ☞ *Toilets, showers, picnic tables, parking lot.*

★ **Papakōlea Beach (Green Sand Beach).** Tired of the same old gold, white, or black sand beach? Then how about a green sand beach? You'll need good hiking shoes to get to this greenish black crescent, one of the most unusual beaches on the island. It lies at the base of Pu'u o Mahana, at Mahana Bay, where a cinder cone formed during an early eruption of Mauna Loa. The greenish tint is caused by an accumulation of olivine crystals that form in volcanic eruptions. The dry barren landscape is totally surreal. The surf is often rough and swimming is hazardous due

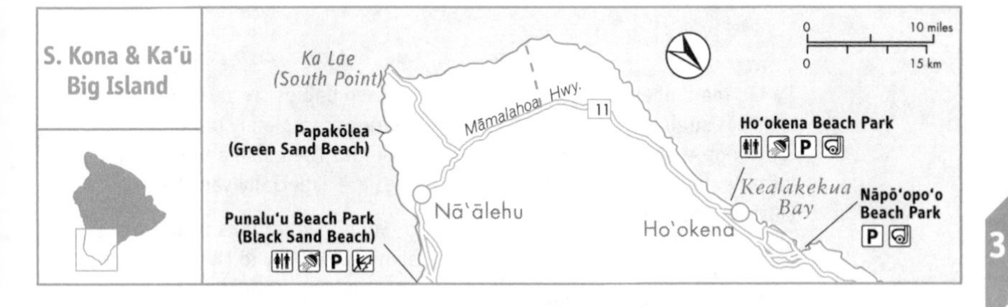

to strong currents, so caution is advised. Take the road toward the left at the end of the paved road to Ka Lae (South Point) about 12 mi off Highway 11. Park at the end of the road. (Anyone trying to charge you for parking is running a scam.) Hikers can follow the 2-mi coastal trail, which will end in a steep and dangerous descent down the cliff side on an unimproved trail. Note: While hikers can cross the private Hawaiian Home Lands without a permit to get to the beach, those wanting to take a 4WD vehicle along the rugged coast trail must first contact the Department of Hawaiian Home Lands in Hilo (☎ 808/974–4250). ■ TIP➔ **There is no guarantee of open access to 4WD vehicles, and sometimes the trail is completely closed to all vehicle and foot traffic. So check first.** ✉ *2½ mi northeast of South Point, off Hwy. 11* ☞ *No facilities.*

★ **Punalu'u Beach Park (Black Sand Beach).** Want to get up close and personal with a green sea turtle? ■ TIP➔ **The endangered Hawaiian green sea turtle nests in the black sand of this beautiful and easily accessible beach.** You can see them feeding on the seaweed along the surfbreak. You can even swim with the turtles; they're used to people and will swim along right next to you. (Resist the urge to touch them, though.) Strong shoreward currents make being in the water here a hazard. Don't venture far out, and avoid going out past the boat ramp as very strong rip currents are active. The beach is a long black sand crescent backed by low dunes with some rocky outcroppings at the shoreline. At its northern end, near the boat ramp, lie the ruins of Kane'ele'ele Heiau, an old Hawaiian temple. This area used to be a sugar port until the tidal wave of 1946 destroyed the buildings. Inland is a memorial to Henry 'Ōpūkaha'ia. In 1809, when he was 17, 'Ōpūkaha'ia swam out to a fur-trading ship in the harbor and asked to sign up as a cabin boy. When he reached New England, he entered the Foreign Mission School in Connecticut, but he died of typhoid fever in 1818. His dream of bringing Christianity to the Islands inspired the American Board of Missionaries to send the first Protestant missionaries to Hawai'i in 1820. ✉ *Hwy. 11, 27 mi south of Hawai'i Volcanoes National Park* ☎ *808/961–8311* ☞ *Toilets, showers, food concession, grills/firepits, parking lot.*

HILO

Hilo isn't exactly known for its beautiful white beaches, but there are a few in the Hilo and east Hawai'i area that provide good swimming and snorkeling opportunities. Beaches are listed from north to south.

SUN SAFETY

By far, the biggest danger on the island is sunburn. The tropical sun is strong: At about 20 degrees latitude, the Big Island is much closer to the equator than any other area of the United States. It's the tradewinds that fool you. It feels cool and refreshing on the beach, but you'll quickly get burnt to a crisp. Even on cloudy days, UV rays can penetrate and reflect off sand, water, and concrete. Follow these steps to keep safe in the sun.

- Even at 9 AM, sunscreen with 30 SPF or higher is a must. Apply sunscreen about 30 minutes before you go outside.
- Reapply sunscreen every two to three hours and after sweating or swimming.
- Limit your time in the sun between 10 AM and 4 PM when the rays are the strongest.
- During peak sunshine hours, cover up with tightly woven, loose-fitting clothing or a rash guard—those clingy-looking lycra swim shirts.
- Wear a hat and sunglasses. Make sure the sunglasses label ensures 100% UV protection.
- Keep babies six months and younger completely out of direct sunlight. Their skin and developing eyes are especially sensitive.
- Some medications increase the skin's sensitivity to UV rays, so check with your doctor or pharmacist to see if this applies to you. If so, take extra care to be sun safe.

Treating a Sunburn

To relieve pain and discomfort:

- Take a cool—not cold—bath, or gently apply cool wet compresses to the skin.
- Apply pure aloe vera gel to any sunburned areas. It's available at most pharmacies.
- Oral pain relievers like acetaminophen or ibuprofen, or "after sun" sprays and lotions can also help.
- Moisturizing creams help rehydrate the skin; for bad sunburns use 1% hydrocortisone cream.
- If the sunburn is severe and blistering develops, contact your physician.

Reeds Bay Beach Park. No, there really isn't ice in the swimming hole; it just feels that way on a hot sultry day. Safe swimming, proximity to downtown Hilo, and a freshwater-fed swimming hole called "the Ice Pond" that flows into the backwaters of Hilo Bay are the enticements of this cove. The large pond, between Hilo Seaside Hotel and Harrington's Restaurant, is a favorite of local kids who enjoy jumping into and frolicking in the chilly fresh and salt water mix. There is no real beach here, however. ✉ *Banyan Dr. and Kalaniana'ole Ave., Hilo* ☎ *808/961–8311* ☞ *No facilities.*

Onekahakaha Beach Park. A white-sand beach with a shallow, enclosed tide pool makes this a favorite for Hilo families with small children. The

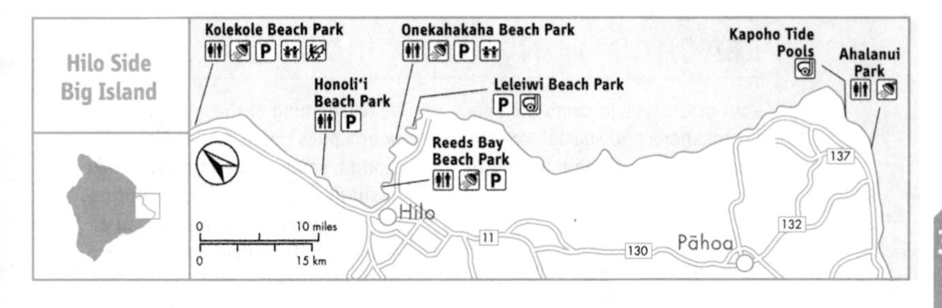

protected tidal pools are great places to look for Hawaiian marinelife such as small fish, brittle stars, sea cucumbers, seashells, sea urchins, and more. The water is usually rough beyond the line of large boulders protecting the inner tide pools. Caution is advised in times of heavy surf. ✉ *Kalaniana'ole Ave., 3 mi east of Hilo* ☎ *808/961–8311* ☞ *Lifeguard, toilets, showers, picnic tables, parking lot.*

Leleiwi Beach Park and Richardson Ocean Park. There's hardly any sand here near road's end in Keaukaha, east of Hilo, but these two beaches make up one beautiful spot—laced with bays, inlets, lagoons, and pretty parks. It's a peaceful setting for a lazy day at the beach; the grassy area is ideal for picnics. Rocky outcrops provide shelter for schools of reef fish, and snorkeling can be great, as turtles and dolphins frequent this area. Local kids use the small black sand pocket beach for body boarding. ✉ *2349 Kalaniana'ole Ave., 4 mi east of Hilo* ☎ *808/961–8311* ☞ *Lifeguard (on weekends), picnic tables, parking lot.*

HĀMĀKUA COAST

Honoli'i Beach Park. There aren't many places along the east Hawai'i coastline to catch the waves when the surf's up, but this is one of the best. It's popular among the local surf crowd, and it's fun to watch the surfers paddle out to catch the waves when the surf's up and running. ■ TIP→ **The presence of surfers is not an indication that an area is safe for swimmers.** The sandy beach is minimal here, a mix of sand and coral rubble debris along the mostly rocky coast. There's limited parking beside the narrow roadside. ✉ *1.5 mi north of Hilo on Hwy. 19* ☎ *808/961–8311* ☞ *Toilets.*

Kolekole Beach Park. This small beach park is a picture postcard of tropical Hawai'i. The Kolekole Stream meets the ocean here between 'Akaka and Umauma Falls, just below a high bridge that crosses the gulch along Highway 19. The beach is composed of large, smooth, waterworn lava rocks. Although the shoreline is rocky, the stream is calm and great for swimming. There's even a rope swing tied to a banyan tree on the opposite side. The stream flows from the lovely tropical 'Akaka Falls Park located about 4 mi upstream. Even though the park is only fair for beach activities, it's surrounded by lush vegetation and is ideal for a picnic amid Hawai'i's tropical environment. Local surfers like this spot

BEACHCOMBING WITH KIDS

Youngsters love to comb the beach for seashells and special treasures. The following will help maximize the results.

- Find a tide chart in the local newspaper, on TV, or online to check the times of high and low tides.
- Check out the beach with a walk at low tide. Note the high tide lines by observing the location of the debris piles.
- Return at high tide or just after the next morning. Begin your beachcombing at those high tide debris piles noted earlier. Bring along a small garden trowel or rake to sift through the sand. Also bring a nylon mesh bag–a plastic bag or a small container will also work–to collect seashells.
- Back at the hotel, repeatedly rinse your seashells in fresh water. Buff and polish the best ones for your collection.
- Back home, check online arts and crafts sites for seashell projects children can do.

in the winter. Where the stream meets the ocean, the surf is rough and the currents strong. Only very experienced swimmers should venture here. ✉ *Off Hwy. 19* ☎ *808/961–8311* *Free* ⏲ *Daily 7 AM–sunset* ☞ *Toilets, showers, picnic tables, grills, parking lot.*

PUNA

As the region closest to Kīlauea, Puna's few beaches have some unique attributes—swaths of black sand, volcano-heated springs, and a coastline that is beyond dramatic (sheer walls of lava rock dropping into the bluest ocean you've ever seen). Beaches here are listed in order from north to south along Highway 137, the Kehena-Pohoiki scenic coastal drive.

Kapoho Tide Pools. Snorkelers will find tons of coral and the fish who feed off it in this network of tide pools at the end of Kapoho-Kai Road. This is a great place for getting close-up looks at Hawai'i's interesting marinelife and reef fish. Some of the pools have been turned into private swimming pools; those closest to the ocean are open to all. The pools are usually very calm, and some are volcanically heated. It's best to come during the week, as the pools can get crowded on the weekend. Note: There is no real sandy beach here. Take the road to the end, then turn left and park. ✉ *End of Kapoho-Kai Road, off Hwy. 13, about 9 mi southeast of Pāhoa town* ☞ *No facilities.*

Ahalanui Park. This 3-acre beach park, surrounded by a coconut palm grove, has a ½-acre pond—fresh spring water mixed with sea water—heated by volcanic steam. There's nothing like swimming in this geothermal pool, but the nearby ocean is rough. ■ TIP→ **The pool has had ongoing bacterial contamination problems that are typical of some ocean tidal**

pools in Hawai'i. Those with skin lesion problems, or chronic conditions like psoriasis, etc., may want to avoid the water here. Others should have no problem. However, check with the lifeguard on duty and heed all posted signs. The park was established with federal funds to replace the famous black sand beaches of Kalapana, which were covered by lava flows in the 1990s. ✉ *Hwy. 137, 2½ mi south of junction of Hwy. 132* ☎ *808/961–8311* ☞ *Lifeguard, toilets, showers, picnic tables, grills.*

RESPECT MOTHER NATURE

Mother Nature is still creating the Big Island's beaches, thanks to its flowing lava. While it's tempting to take a souvenir container of black, green, or golden sand, you can assist in protecting and preserving the Big Island's beaches by not removing sand. As the old slogan goes, "Take nothing but pictures, and leave nothing but footprints."

Water Activities & Tours

WORD OF MOUTH

"From late December to mid- to late April the whales come to Hawai'i, especially the Big Island and Maui. It is one of my favorite times to be there." —Lauricelli

"The Kapoho tidepools were amazing. I saw at least 10 sea turtles." —merridith165

"Don't miss kayaking and snorkeling in Kealakekua Bay (Captain Cook Monument)." —sceneisle

www.fodors.com/forums

By John Penisten

THE ANCIENT HAWAIIANS, who took much of their daily sustenance from the ocean, also enjoyed playing in the water. In fact, surfing was the sport of kings. Though it's easy to be lulled into whiling away the day baking in the sun on a white, golden, black, or green sand beach—surrounded by sheer cliffs that plunge to the sea—getting into and onto the water will be a highlight of your trip to the Big Island.

All of the Hawaiian Islands are surrounded by the Pacific Ocean, making them some of the world's greatest natural playgrounds. But certain experiences are even better on the Big Island: Nighttime scuba diving trips to see manta rays; deep sea fishing in Kona's fabled waters, where dozens of Pacific blue marlin of 1,000 pounds or more have been caught; kayaking among the dolphins in Kealakekua Bay; and sighting humpback whales on a whale-watching cruise. With underwater coral reefs and marine preserves harboring endemic and endangered species, such as the Hawaiian green sea turtle and the Hawaiian monk seal, plus tropical fish in a rainbow of colors, snorkelers are in paradise.

From any point on the Big Island, the ocean is never far away. With the variety of water sports that can be enjoyed—from boogie boarding and snorkeling to jet skiing and surfing—there is something for everyone. For most activities, you can rent gear and go it alone or sign up for a group excursion with an experienced guide, who can offer security as well as special insights about Hawaiian marine life and culture. Want to try surfing? You can take lessons as well.

The Kona and Kohala Coasts of west Hawai'i boast the largest number of ocean sports outfitters and tour operators. They operate from the small boat harbors and piers in Kailua-Kona, Keauhou, and at the Kohala Coast resorts. There are also several outfitters in the east Hawai'i and Hilo areas.

As a general rule, the waves are gentler here than on other Islands, but there are a few things to be aware of before heading to the shore. First, don't turn your back on the ocean. It's unlikely, but if conditions are right a wave could come along and push you face first into the sand or drag you out to sea. Conditions can change quickly, so keep your eyes open. Second, realize that ultimately you must keep yourself safe. We strongly encourage you to obey lifeguards and park rangers stationed on the beaches of the Big Island, and to heed the advice of outfitters from whom you rent equipment. It could save your trip, or even your life.

BOOGIE BOARDING & BODYSURFING

According to the movies, in the Old West there was always friction between cattle ranchers and sheep ranchers. Some will say the same situation exists between surfers and boogie boarders. Sure, there's some good-natured trash-talking between the groups, but nothing more. The truth is, boogie boarding is a blast. The only surfers who don't do it are hardcore surfing purists, and almost none of that type live on this island.

Novice boogie boarders should use smooth-bottom boards, wear protective clothing (or at least T-shirts), and catch shore waves only. You'll need a pair of short fins to get out to the bigger waves offshore (not rec-

BOAT TOURS & CHARTERS

OUTFITTER	Tour(s) Available	Food Included?	Price
Sailing Charters			
Honu Sail Charters	Half-day and full-day charters	Sandwiches, snacks, cold drinks	$96 half-day, $144 full-day
Maile Charters	Half-day and full-day charters	No	$148 half-day, $248 full day
Scuba Diving			
Aloha Dive Company	2-tank boat dive	Snacks, cold drinks	$95–$105
Dive Makai	2-tank boat dive	Snacks, cold drinks	$125
Jack's Diving Locker	2-tank boat dive	Snacks, cold drinks	$125
Kona Coast Divers	2-tank boat dive	Snacks, cold drinks	$125
Ocean Eco Tours	2-tank boat dive	Snacks, cold drinks	$95
Aloha Dive Company	1-tank manta-ray night dive	Snacks, cold drinks	$75
Jack's Diving Locker	2-tank manta-ray night dive	Snacks, cold drinks	$145
Kona Coast Divers	2-tank manta-ray night dive	Snacks, cold drinks	$145
Ocean Eco Tours	2-tank manta-ray night dive	Snacks, cold drinks	$145
Sightseeing Tours			
Aloha Kayak Co.	Half-day snorkel/sea cave tour	Lunch	$65
Kona Boys	Half-day Kealakekua Bay tour	Lunch	$159
Ocean Safari's Kayak Adventures	Half-day sea cave tour	Snacks, cold drinks	$64
Ocean Safari's Kayak Adventures	2-hour early morning tour	No	$35
Snorkel Cruises			
Captain Zodiac Raft Cruises	Half-day cruise	Snacks, cold drinks	$93
Fair Wind Snorkel Cruises	Half-day cruise	Lunch (morning only)	$105 morning, $69 afternoon
Kamanu Catamaran Snorkel Sails	Half-day cruise	Lunch	
Whale-Watch Cruises			
Captain Dan McSweeney's	3-hour cruise	Snacks, cold drinks	$70
Living Ocean Adventures	4-hour cruise	Snacks, cold drinks	$67

ommended for newbies). As for bodysurfing, just catch a wave and make like Superman going faster than a speeding bullet.

Best Spots

When conditions are right, **Hāpuna Beach State Recreation Area** (✉ Hwy. 19, near mile marker 69) is fabulous. The water is very calm in summer, with just enough rolling waves for bodysurfing or boogie boarding. But this beach north of Kailua-Kona isn't known as the "broken-neck capital" for nothing. Ask the lifeguards about conditions before heading into the water. ■ TIP→ **Remember that if almost no one is in the water, there's a good reason for it.**

Much of the sand at **White Sands, Magic Sands, or Disappearing Sands Beach Park** (✉ Ali'i Dr., 4½ mi south of Kailua-Kona) washes out to sea and forms a sandbar just offshore. This causes the waves to break in a way that's great for intermediate or advanced boogie boarding. No wonder the Magic Sands Bodysurfing Contest, which brings out hardcore bodysurfers each winter, is held here. This small beach can get pretty crowded. There can be nasty rip currents at high tide. ■ TIP→ **If you're not using fins, wear reef shoes because of the rocks.**

North of Hilo, **Honoli'i Cove** (✉ Access road off Hwy. 19, just past mile marker 4) is the best boogie boarding–surfing spot on the east side of the island. Keep in mind that it is also one of the few good boarding spots in east Hawai'i, so boogie boarders and surfers need to share the space.

Equipment Rentals

Equipment rental shacks are located at many beaches and boat harbors, along the highway, and at most resorts. Boogie board rental rates are $10 to $12 per day and $50 to $60 per week. Ask the vendor if he'll throw in a pair of fins—some will for no extra charge.

Honolua Surf Company ✉ *75-5744 Ali'i Dr., Kona Shopping Village, Kailua-Kona* ☎ *808/329–1001.*

Orchid Land Surf Shop ✉ *262 Kamehameha Ave., Hilo* ☎ *808/935–1533* 🌐 *www.orchidlandsurf.com.*

Pacific Vibrations ✉ *75-5702 Likana La., at Ali'i Dr., Kailua-Kona* ☎ *808/329–4140.*

DEEP-SEA FISHING

Along the Kona Coast you can find some of the world's most exciting "blue-water" fishing. Although July, August, and September are peak months, with the best fishing and a number of tournaments, charter fishing goes on year-round. You don't have to compete to experience the thrill of landing a Pacific blue marlin or other big-game fish. More than 60 charter boats, averaging 26 to 58 feet, are available for hire, most of them out of **Honokōhau Harbor,** north of Kailua-Kona.

For an exclusive charter, prices generally range from $300 to $600 for a half-day trip (about four hours) and $500 to $900 for a full day at sea (about eight hours). For share charters, rates range from $80 to $140 per person for a half-day and $190 for a full day. If fuel prices continue increasing, expect charter costs to rise. Most boats are licensed to take up to six passengers, in addition to the crew. Tackle, bait, and ice are furnished, but you'll usually have to bring your own lunch. You won't be able to keep your catch, although if you ask, many captains will send you home with a few fillets.

Big fish are weighed in daily at **Honokōhau Harbor's Fuel Dock.** Show up at 11 AM to watch the weigh-in of the day's catch from the morning charters, or 3:30 PM for the afternoon charters. If you're lucky, you'll get to see a "grander" weighing in at 1,000-plus pounds. A surprising num-

CLOSE UP

Kona's Grander Alley

KONA HAS THE REPUTATION of producing large marlin, mostly the Pacific blue variety. According to records, 63 marlin weighing 1,000 pounds or more have been caught off the Kona Coast, which has come to be known as "Grander Alley," a reference to the number of big fish that inhabit its waters. The largest "grander" ever, caught in 1984, weighed in at 1,649 pounds.

These prize big game fish have been sought after by deep sea fishermen from all over the world who come to dip a line in Kona's fabled waters, most notably during the Hawaiian International Billfish Tournament www.hibtfishing.com. Held each August since 1959, this granddaddy of big game fishing tourneys has attracted teams from around the globe. The HIBT hosts various community events during its annual run including a parade, daily weigh-ins, and more.

Tournament records note that the largest marlin caught during the tourney was an 1,166-pound Pacific blue marlin taken on 50-pound test line in 1993. That's an awful lot of sashimi!

4

ber of these are caught just outside Kona Harbor. TIP→ **On Kona's Waterfront Row look for the "Grander's Wall" of anglers with their prizes.**

Booking Agencies

Before you sign up with anyone, think about the kind of trip you want. Looking for a romantic cruise? A rockin' good time with your buddies? Serious fishing in one of the "secret spots"? A family-friendly excursion? Be sure to describe your expectations so your booking agent can match you with a captain and a boat that suits your style.

Charter Locker. This company can provide information on various charter boat fishing trips and make all the arrangements—they can even book you on the luxurious *Blue Hawai'i,* which has air-conditioned staterooms for overnight trips. *74-425 Kealakehe Pkwy., Honokōhau Harbor, Kailua-Kona 808/326–2553 www.charterlocker.com.*

Charter Services Hawai'i. This booking service represents several Kona fishing boats and can assist with all the details in arranging a charter. *Box 5234, Kailua-Kona 96745 808/334–1881 or 800/567–2650 www.konazone.com.*

Honokōhau Harbor Charter Desk. With 50 boats on the books, this place can take care of almost anyone. You can make arrangements through your hotel activity desk, but we suggest you go down to the desk at the harbor and look things over for yourself. *74-381 Kealakehe Pkwy., Kailua-Kona 808/329–5735 or 888/566–2487 www.charterdesk.com.*

Kona Charter Skippers Association. In business since 1956, this company can help arrange half-day and full-day exclusive or share charters on several boats. The *Pamela* (⇨ Boats & Charters) is their featured boat. ✉ *Box 806, 74-857 Iwalani Pl., Kailua-Kona* ☎ *808/329–3600 or 800/762–7546* 🌐 *www.konabiggamefishing.com.*

Boats & Charters

Humdinger Sportfishing. This game fisher guide has over three decades of fishing experience in Kona waters. The experienced crew are marlin specialists. The 37-foot *Humdinger* has the latest in electronics and top line rods and reels. Half-day exclusive charters begin at $550, full-day exclusives at $850. ☎ *808/936–3034 or 800/926–2374* 🌐 *www.humdinger-online.com.*

Illusions Sportfishing. Captain Tim Hicks is one of Kona's top fishing tourney producers with several years' experience. The 39-foot *Illusions* is fully equipped with galley, restrooms, an air-conditioned cabin for guest comfort, plus the latest in fishing equipment. Half-day exclusive charters begin at $500, full-day exclusives at $750. ☎ *808/883–0180, 808/960–7371 (cell), or 800/482–3474* 🌐 *www.illusionssportfishing.com.*

Pamela Big Game Fishing. This family-operated company has been in the business since 1967. The 38-foot *Pamela* is captained by either Peter Hoogs or his son. They've also got an informative Web site with information on sportfishing. Half-day exclusive charters begin at $600, full-day exclusives at $900. ☎ *808/329–3600 or 800/762–7546* 🌐 *www.konabiggamefishing.com.*

BIG ISLAND, BIG FISH

Along the Kona Coast, deep sea fishermen pursue several species of game fish. The most sought after is, of course, the Pacific blue marlin, averaging 300 to 400 pounds, though "granders" of 1,000 pounds and up are not unusual. Mid-size catches include the striped marlin (averaging 150 pounds), the black marlin (around 200 pounds), and the broadbill swordfish (up to 250 pounds). The much sought after *ahi* (yellowfin tuna) can range up to 300 pounds. The smaller guys, weighing in from about 20 to 50 pounds, include spearfish, sailfish, *aku* (skipjack tuna), *ono* (wahoo), and the prized *mahi mahi* (dolphin fish).

DOLPHIN ENCOUNTERS

Few other marine creatures gravitate to humans quite like the curious dolphin, which swims, jumps, and spins around boats and swimmers. While the large humpback whales are only seen seasonally (December to April), Hawai'i has a year-round resident population of spinner, spotted, and bottlenose dolphins. You can see pods of them—plus pilot, sperm, false killer, and other whales—on cruise and snorkel excursions on the Kona Coast. For a more interactive adventure, sign up for the educational and hands-on Dolphin Quest program at the Hilton Waikoloa Village resort on the Kohala Coast.

Blue Sea Cruises Inc. The *Makai,* a 46-foot double deck catamaran, cruises along the Kona Coast twice a day on two-hour tours. The boat has all the comforts, including snack bar and his/hers restrooms. The narrated tour covers Hawai'i's marine wildlife and the history and culture of the Islands. Sightings include spinner, spotted, and bottlenose dolphins, resident pilot whales, and seasonal humpbacks. Tours depart from Kailua Pier at 8:30 AM and include snacks and cold beverages. The 11 AM tour includes a light lunch. Rates start at $49 per person. ✉ *Box 2429, Kailua-Kona* ☎ *808/331–8875* 🌐 *www.blueseacruisesinc.com.*

★ **Captain Dan McSweeney's Whale Watch.** This longtime Kona tour operator, who made his name in whale-watching, also offers year-round excursions to spot Hawai'i's resident spinner, spotted, and bottlenose dolphins. The *Lady Ann* is a comfortable double-deck cruise boat with partial shade, cushioned seats, and restrooms. Captain Dan offers guaranteed sightings or an invitation to come again. The 3½-hour tours depart daily at 7:15 AM and 11:15 AM. Per person rates of $70 include snacks and cold juices. ✉ *Honokōhau Harbor, Kailua-Kona* ☎ *808/322–0028 or 888/942–5376* 🌐 *www.ilovewhales.com.*

Dolphin Discoveries. The captains, certified marine mammal specialists, lead educational dolphin and whale-watching cruises on the Kona Coast in rigid-hull inflatable crafts. They sight Hawaiian spinner, spotted, and bottlenose dolphins (passengers can participate in their photo-ID research program), plus pilot whales, humpbacks, and more on daily year-round cruises. Cruises, which include fresh tropical fruits, snacks, and cold drinks, depart from Keauhou Bay. Four-hour morning cruises are $94 per person and three-hour afternoon cruises are $69 per person. ✉ *77-116 Queen Kalama Ave., Kailua-Kona* ☎ *808/322–8000 or 808/324–0433* 🌐 *www.dolphindiscoveries.com.*

Dolphin Quest. Under the guidance of professional animal experts, participants interact with dolphins in the protected lagoons of the Hilton Waikoloa Village resort. This was the first location of the Dolphin Quest program, which works to foster public education and conservation efforts of marine wildlife. Various encounters, geared toward different age groups, range in length from 10 to 90 minutes and in price from $150 to $330 per person. Participants learn to give commands to the dolphins to perform maneuvers, dives, jumps, etc. They also feed the dolphins and have personal contact in the water. All ages, from 5 and up, are welcome. Book well in advance; the encounters almost always sell out. ✉ *425 Waikoloa Beach Dr., Waikoloa* ☎ *808/886–1234* 🌐 *www.dolphinquest.org.*

JET SKIING

Kailua Bay in Kona has generally calm waters that are perfect for jet skiing.

Aloha Jet Ski Rentals. The only outfitter on the island charges $95 an hour or $60 for 30 minutes for a Jet Ski that can accommodate up to three passengers. Extra riders are $15. Drivers must be at least 16 and must stay in a designated area south of the pier. Ask about an early-bird discount. ✉ *Kailua Pier, across from King Kamehameha's Kona Beach Hotel, Palani Road at Ali'i Dr., Kailua-Kona* ☎ *808/329–2754* 🌐 *www.mauiwatersports.com.*

JET SKIING SAFETY

- Don't do it unless you're a good swimmer.
- Wear a life vest or jacket.
- Be familiar with local laws governing the use of Jet Skis.
- Follow the traffic pattern of the waterway, and obey speed or no-wake zones.
- Keep on alert for swimmers and surfers; go slow until clear of the shore, dock, and swimming areas.
- Don't pass close to other craft to jump their wakes.
- Go out with a buddy.
- Don't drink and drive.

KAYAKING

The leeward west coast areas of the Big Island are protected for the most part from the Northeast Trade Winds, making for ideal near-shore kayaking conditions. There are literally miles and miles of uncrowded Kona and Kohaha coastline to explore, presenting closeup views of stark raw lava rock shores and cliffs, lava tube sea caves, pristine secluded coves, and deserted beaches.

Ocean kayakers can get in close to shore—where the commercial snorkel and dive cruise boats can't reach. This opens up all sorts of possibilities for adventure, such as near-shore snorkeling among the expansive coral reefs and lava rock formations that teem with colorful tropical fish, Hawaiian green sea turtles, and more. You can pull ashore at a quiet cove for a picnic and a plunge into a deep turquoise pool. With a good coastal map and some advice from the kayak vendor, you can explore inland, where you might find ancient battle grounds, burial sites, bathing ponds for Hawaiian royalty, or old villages.

Kayaking experiences can be enjoyed via a guided tour or on a self-guided paddling excursion. Either way, the kayak outfitter can brief you on recommended routes, manageable currents, and how you can help preserve and protect Hawai'i's ocean resources and coral reef system.

Best Spots

The likelihood of seeing dolphins makes **Kealakekua Bay** (✉ Bottom of Nāpō'opo'o Rd., south of Kailua-Kona) one of the most popular kayak spots on the Big Island. The bay is usually calm, and the kayaking is not difficult—except during high surf. If you're there in the morning, you're likely to see spinner dolphins. Depending on your strength and enthusiasm, you'll cross the bay in 30–60 minutes and put in at the ancient canoe landing about 50 yards to the left of the **Captain Cook Monument.** The monument marks the landfall of Captain James Cook in 1778, the first European to visit Hawai'i. The coral around the monument itself is too fragile to land a kayak, but it makes for fabulous snorkeling.

There are several rental outfitters on Highway 11 between mile markers 110 and 113. There's also one unofficial stand at the shore, at the house on the corner just across from the parking lot. After you've loaded your kayak onto the roof of your car, follow the 2-mi road down the rather steep hill to the parking lot below. ■ TIP→ **There are usually local guys who will set up your kayak and get you into (and out of) the water; tips of between $5 and $10 are encouraged, expected, and appreciated.**

DOLPHINS AT REST

Kealakekua Bay is a designated marine refuge where the dolphins return to rest after feeding. Kayakers occasionally pursue the dolphins in an aggressive way. Because of the actions of a few, some environmental activists are working to close the bay to all kayakers. Those who charge after dolphins may be videotaped and have complaints filed against them (as well as suffer the ephemeral but very real consequences of behaving without the aloha spirit). If you behave in a calm, nonthreatening manner, the dolphins are very likely to come to you.

Ōneo Bay (✉ Ali'i Dr., south of Kailua-Kona) is usually quite a placid place to kayak. It's easy to get to and great for all skill levels. If you can't find a parking spot along Ali'i Drive, there's a parking lot across the street near the farmers' market.

Hilo Bay (✉ 2349 Kalaniana'ole Ave., about 4 mi east of Hilo) is a favorite kayak spot. The best place to put in is at **Richardson's Ocean Beach Park.** Most afternoons you can share the bay with local paddling clubs. Stay inside the breakwater unless the ocean is calm (or you're feeling unusually adventurous). Conditions range from extremely calm to quite choppy.

Equipment Rentals & Tours

Aloha Kayak Co. This Honalo outfitter offers guided Wet-N-Wild Kayak Snorkel/Cave Tours—a four-hour morning tour ($65 per person) and a 2½-hour afternoon version ($50 per person). Morning tour includes sandwich lunch, snacks, and cold drinks; afternoon tour includes snacks and drinks. Tours depart from Keauhou Bay. Daily kayak rental rates: single $25, double $40. ■ TIP→ **Ask about renting one of their glass kayaks, for a clear and close-up view of the marinelife below you.** ✉ *79-7428 Mamalahoa Hwy., Honalo* ☎ *808/322–2868 or 877/322–1444* 🌐 *www.alohakayak.com.*

Kona Boys. On the highway above Kealakekua Bay, this full-service outfitter handles kayaks, boogie boards, and related equipment. Single-seat kayaks are $47 daily, doubles $67, weekly single $200, double $275. Dive kayaks with a well for an air tank are also available. The Boys also lead a guided trip to Kealakekua that includes kayaking, snorkeling, and hiking around a lava rock point (½-day starting at $159 per person, includes lunch, snacks, and drinks), a Sunset Kayak & Snorkel Tour for $125 per person, as well as customized overnight camping–kayaking trips to Miloli'i, Pololū, or our favorite, Waipi'o Valley. ✉ *79-7539 Mamalahoa Hwy., Kealakekua* ☎ *808/328–1234* 🌐 *www.konaboys.com.*

Ocean Safari's Kayak Adventures. On the guided 3½-hour morning Sea Cave Tour that begins in Keauhou Bay, you can visit lava tube sea caves along the coast, then swim ashore for a snack. The kayaks are on the

KAYAK SAFETY

- Whether a beginner or experienced kayaker, choose appropriate water and weather conditions for your kayak excursion.
- Ask the outfitter about local conditions and hazards, such as tides and currents.
- Beginners, especially, should practice getting into and out of the kayak and capsizing in shallow water.
- Before departing, secure the kayak's hatches, etc., to prevent water intake.
- Use a line to attach the paddle to the kayak to avoid losing it.
- Always use a life vest or jacket.
- Wear a helmet if kayaking in and around rough water and rocks.
- Carry appropriate amounts of water and food.
- Don't kayak alone. Create a float plan; tell someone where you're going and when you will return.

beach, so you don't have to hassle with transporting them. The cost is $64 per person. A two-hour Early Riser Dolphin Quest Tour leaves at 7 AM on Tuesdays. It's $35 per person. Kayak daily rental rates are single $25, double $40. ✉ *End of Kamehameha III Rd., Kailua-Kona* ☎ *808/326–4699* 🌐 *www.oceansafariskayaks.com.*

PARASAILING

Parasailing, gliding on the winds with a parachute while being pulled behind a power boat, is a relaxing and thrilling experience. If you can handle heights, you'll revel in the experience of being suspended in air while soaring above Kailua Bay. The water is so clear you can almost see the ocean floor. And no swimming is required; takeoffs and landings are from the back of the boat.

UFO Parasail. This is the sole parasailing outfitter in Kona. The parasailing adventures run across Kailua Bay and along the Kona Coast in rides up to 800 feet high for bird's-eye views and real thrills (an optional "freefall" that stops short of the water recreates the rush of a parachute descent). A power boat and winch provide dry takeoffs and landings; parasailors can "fly" alone or in tandem. Though the flight is short, the boat ride takes about one hour. Rates: standard 400 feet, 7 minutes, $60; deluxe 800 feet, 10 minutes, $70; non-flyers boat ride only, $30. ✉ *55-5669 Ali'i Dr., Kailua-Kona* ☎ *888/359–4UFO or 808/325–5836* 🌐 *www.ufoparasailing.com.*

SAILING

For old salts and novice sailors alike, there's nothing like a cruise on the Kona or Kohala coasts of the Big Island. Calm waters, serene shores, and the superb scenery of Mauna Kea, Mauna Loa, and Hualālai, the Big Island's primary volcanic peaks, make for a great sailing adventure. You can drop a line over the side and try your luck at catching dinner, or grab some snorkel gear and explore when the boat drops anchor in one of the quiet coves and bays. A cruise may well be the most relaxing and adventurous part of a Big Island visit.

Honu Sail Charters. The fully equipped 32-foot cutter-rigged sloop *Honu* (Hawaiian for sea turtle) carries six passengers on full-day, half-day, and sunset sailing excursions along the scenic Kona Coast, which include time to snorkel in clear waters over coral reefs. This friendly outfitter allows passengers to get some hands-on sailing experience or just to kick back and relax. Rates run from $72 per person for the two-hour Sunset Sail to $144 per person for the full-day sail. Prices include food, snorkel equipment, towels, etc. ✉ *Honokōhau Harbor, Kailua-Kona* ☎ *808/896–4668* 🌐 *www.sailkona.com.*

Maile Charters. Ralph Blancato and Kalia Potter offer unique around-the-Islands sailing adventures that range from half-day excursions to five-day journeys to Maui, Moloka'i, or Lāna'i. Private cabins and hot showers keep you comfortable, and island-style meals keep you satisfied. Fees start at $590 for six passengers for a half-day charter to $5,000 for five days with a maximum of four adult passengers. The price includes food and use of water sports equipment. ✉ *Kawaihae Harbor, Kawaihae* ☎ *808/326–5174 or 800/726–7245* 🌐 *www.adventuresailing.com.*

SCUBA DIVING

The Big Island's underwater world is the setting for a dramatic diving experience. With generally calm waters, vibrant coral reefs and rock formations, and plunging underwater dropoffs, the Kona and Kohala coasts provide some great scuba diving. There are also some good dive locations in east Hawai'i, not far from the Hilo area. Divers will find much to occupy their time, including marine reserves teeming with unique Hawaiian reef fish, Hawaiian green sea turtles, an occasional and rare Hawaiian monk seal, and even some feisty Hawaiian spinner dolphins. On special night dives to see manta ray, divers descend with bright underwater lights that attract plankton, which in turn attracts these otherworldly creatures. The best spots to dive are listed in order from north to south; all are on the west coast.

Best Spots

Hāpuna Beach State Recreation Area (✉ Hwy. 19, near mile marker 69) in Kohala can be a good shore dive. Just south of the state park is **Puako** (✉ Puako Rd., off Hwy. 19). Public access to the beach from Puako Road provides easy entry to some fine reef diving. Deep chasms, sea caves, rock arches, and more abound with varied marinelife.

The water is usually very clear at **Pawai Bay Marine Reserve** (✉ Just north of Old Kona Airport Beach Park, at the beginning of Kuakini Hwy.). This bay near Kailua-Kona has numerous underwater sea caves, arches, and rock formations, plus lots of marinelife. It can be busy with snorkel boats but is an easy dive spot. **Plane Wreck Point,** off Keāhole Point, is for expert divers only. Damselfish, fantail, and filefish hover around in the shadows.

One of Kona's best night dive spots is **Manta Village** (✉ off the Sheraton Keauhou Bay Resort at Keauhou). A booking with a scuba/snorkel night dive operator is required for the short boat ride to the area. If you're a diving or snorkeling fanatic, it's well worth it for the experience of seeing the manta rays.

Dive boats come to **Pu'uhonua O Hōnaunau** (Place of Refuge) (✉ Rte. 160, about 20 mi south of Kailua-Kona 🌐 www.nps.gov/puho) for the steep drop-offs and dramatic views. You can also get in the water from the shore on the north end.

Equipment Rentals & Dive Tours

There are quite a few good dive shops on the Kona Coast. Most are happy to take on all customers, but a few focus on specific types of trips. Trip prices vary, depending on whether you're already certified and whether you're diving from a boat or from shore. Instruction with PADI, SDI, or TDI certification in three to five days costs $400–$650. Most instructors rent out dive equipment and snorkel gear, and many rent underwater cameras. A few organize otherworldly manta-ray dives at night or whale-watching cruises in season.

★ **Aloha Dive Company.** Native-born Hawaiian and PADI master dive instructor Mike Nakachi, together with wife Buffy (a registered nurse and PADI dive instructor), and Earl Kam (a videographer and PADI dive master) have been instructing since 1990. Although they'll take anybody, they're biased in favor of experienced divers who want unique locations and know how to take care of themselves in deep water. Their boat is fast enough to take you places other companies can't reach. They're fun people with great attitudes and operate the only true *kamā'aina* (Hawai'i born-and-raised) outfitter around. Rates begin at $75 for a manta ray night dive and go up to $200 for a three-tank remote dive. ☎ *808/325–5560 or 800/708–5662* 🌐 *www.alohadive.com.*

★ **Body Glove Cruises.** This company offers primarily snorkel cruises but can also accommodate several divers. It's a good choice for families where at least one member is a certified diver and the rest want to snorkel. The 51-foot catamaran sets off from the Kailua Pier daily for a 4½-hour dive and snorkel cruise, which includes breakfast and a buffet lunch; the three-hour afternoon cruise includes snacks and drinks. Snorkelers pay $66–$105 per adult and $44–$65 per child. Scuba divers pay the snorkel rate plus $57–$67 per person with or without gear. ✉ *Kailua Pier, Kailua-Kona* ☎ *808/329–4807 or 800/551–8911* 🌐 *www.bodyglovehawaii.com.*

★ **Jack's Diving Locker.** The best place for novice and intermediate divers (certified to 60 feet), Jack's Diving Locker has trained and certified tens of thousands of divers since opening in 1981. The company has two boats

FUN FACTS ABOUT HAWAI'I'S MANTA RAYS

Manta rays, one of Hawai'i's most fascinating marinelife species, can be seen on some nighttime diving excursions along the Kona and Kohala Coasts. They are generally harmless to divers and don't normally attack people. If you don't want to get wet, head to the beach fronting the Mauna Kea Beach Hotel on the Kohala Coast, where each evening, visitors gather under the lights to watch manta rays feed in the shallows.

- The manta ray (*manta birostris*), called the devil fish by some, is known as *hahalua* by Hawaiians.
- Its wing-like fins, reaching up to 20 feet wide, allow the ray to glide through the water like a bird gliding through air.
- The manta ray uses the two large flap-like lobes extending from its eyes to funnel food to its mouth. It eats microscopic plankton, small fish, and tiny crustaceans.
- The manta ray, closely related to the shark, can weight more than 3,000 pounds.
- Its skeleton is made of cartilage, not bone.
- A female ray gives birth to one or two young at a time; pups can be 45 inches long and weigh 20 pounds at birth.

that can each take 12 divers. It does a good job looking out for customers and protecting the coral reef. Before each charter the dive master briefs divers on various options and then everyone votes on where to go. Jack's also runs the biggest dive shop on the island and has classrooms and a dive pool for beginning instruction. ■ TIP→ **Kona's best dive bargain for newbies is the introductory shore dive from Kailua Pier for $55.** ✉ *75-5813 Ali'i Dr., Kailua-Kona* ☎ *800/345–4807 or 808/329–7585* 🌐 *www.jacksdivinglocker.com.*

★ **Ocean Eco Tours.** Ecofriendly and full-service, this outfit is eager to share a wealth of knowledge. It's close to a number of good reefs and other prime locations. They offer various dives from an intro dive ($125) to shore dives ($85) and multi-day boat dive packages (three two-tank dives for $255). The PADI open-water certification classes can be completed in three to four days. ✉ *Honokōhau Harbor, 74-425 Kealakehe Pkwy., Kailua-Kona* ☎ *808/324–7873* 🌐 *www.oceanecotours.com.*

SNORKELING

A favorite pastime on the Big Island, snorkeling is perhaps one of the easiest and most enjoyable water activities for visitors. By ducking underwater, you'll see lava rock formations, sea arches, sea caves, and coral reefs teeming with colorful tropical fish. While the Kona and Kohala coasts have more beaches, bays, and quiet coves to snorkel, the east side around Hilo and at Kapoho are also great places to get in the water.

If you don't bring your own equipment, you can easily rent all the gear needed from a beach activities vendor, who will happily provide directions to the best sites for snorkeling in the area. For access to deeper water and assistance from an experienced crew, you can opt for a snorkel cruise. Excursions generally range from two to five hours; be sure you know what equipment and food is included.

Best Spots

★ **Kealakekua Bay** (✉ Bottom of Nāpō'opo'o Rd., south of Kailua-Kona) is, hands down, the best snorkel spot on the island, with fabulous coral reefs around the Captain Cook monument and generally calm waters. Besides, you'll probably get to swim with dolphins. Overland access is difficult, so you can opt for one of several guided snorkel cruises or kayak across the bay to get to the monument. ■ TIP→ **Be on the lookout for kayakers who might not notice you swimming beneath them.**

The snorkeling just north of the boat launch at **Pu'uhonua O Hōnaunau** (Place of Refuge) (✉ Rte. 160, about 20 mi south of Kailua-Kona 🌐 www.nps.gov/puho) is almost as good as Kealakekua Bay, and it's much easier to reach. It's also a popular scuba diving spot.

White Sands, Magic Sands, or Disappearing Sands Beach Park (✉ Ali'i Dr., 4½ mi south of Kailua-Kona) is a great place for beginning and intermediate snorkelers. In winter it's also a good place to see whales.

Since ancient times, the waters around **Kahalu'u Beach Park** (✉ Ali'i Dr., 5½ mi south of Kailua-Kona) have been a traditional net fishing area. The swimming is good, and the snorkeling is even better. You'll see angelfish, parrotfish, needlefish, pufferfish, and a lot more. ■ TIP→ **Stay inside the breakwater and don't stray too far, as dangerous and unpredictable currents swirl outside the bay.**

Kapoho Tide Pools (✉ End of Kapoho-Kai Rd., off Hwy. 137) has the best snorkeling on the Hilo side. Fingers of lava from the 1960 flow (that destroyed the town of Kapoho) jut into the sea to form a network of tide pools. Conditions near the shore are excellent for beginners, and challenging enough farther out for experienced snorkelers.

Cruises & Equipment Rentals

Captain Zodiac Raft Expedition. The exciting four-hour trip on an inflatable raft takes you along the Kona Coast to explore gaping lava-tube caves, search for dolphins and turtles, and snorkel around Kealakekua Bay. The captain often throws in Hawaiian folklore and Kona history; the company started up in 1974. The morning trip departs at 8:15 AM, the afternoon at 1 PM. Adults pay $93 and kids $77. A seasonal (Dec.–Apr.) three-hour whale watch cruise is adults $70, kids $60. ✉ *Honokōhau Harbor, Kailua-Kona* ☎ *808/329–3199* 🌐 *www.captainzodiac.com.*

★ **Fair Wind Cruises.** This outfit offers both a 4½-hour morning and 3½-hour afternoon snorkeling excursions to Kealakekua Bay, and a luxury cruise that sails into three different secret snorkeling spots a day. Snorkel gear is included (ask about prescription masks), but bring your own towel. On morning cruises you'll get a Continental breakfast and a barbecue lunch. These trips are great for families with small kids (lots of pint-size flotation equipment), and they provide underwater viewing devices for those who don't want to use a mask–snorkel setup. Morning cruises cost $105 for adults and $65 for kids; afternoon cruises are cheaper, but you're less likely to see dolphins in the bay. The spring–summer afternoon deluxe cruise includes a late barbecue lunch and snorkel time; adults $99, kids $59. ✉ *78-7130 Kaleiopapa St., Keauhou Bay, Kailua-Kona* ☎ *808/322–2788 or 800/677–9461* 🌐 *www.fair-wind.com.*

Snorkel Bob's. You're likely to see his wacky ads in your airline inflight magazine. The company actually delivers what it promises, and you can make reservations online before beginning your trip. Basic gear package of mask, fins, and snorkel rents for $9–$22 per week; children's equipment and prescription masks are available. ✉ *75-5831 Kahakai St., Kailua-Kona* ☎ *808/329–0770 or 800/262–7725* 🌐 *www.snorkelbob.com.*

4

SNUBA

Snuba—a cross between scuba and snorkeling—is a great choice for nonscuba divers who want to go a step beyond snorkeling. You and an instructor dive off a raft attached to a 25-foot hose and regulator; you can dive as deep as 20 feet or so. This is a good way to explore reefs a bit deeper than you can get to by snorkeling. If you get frightened or need a rest, the raft is right there, ready to support you.

Snuba Big Island. Rendezvous with your instructor across from King Kamehameha's Kona Beach Hotel in Kailua-Kona for 30 minutes of instruction and a one-hour dive in Kailua Bay ($79 per person). Boat dives lasting three hours leave from Honakahou Harbor ($125 per person). You can also dive in Kealakekua Bay. The minimum age for snuba is 8, but kids 4–7 can come along on the Snuba Doo program, which keeps them snorkeling safely on the surface. ☎ *808/326–7446* 🌐 *www.snubabigisland.com.*

SUBMARINE TOURS

Fodor's Choice ★

***Atlantis VII* Submarine.** Want to stay dry while exploring the undersea world? Climb aboard the 48-foot *Atlantis VII* submarine anchored off Kailua Pier, across from King Kamehameha's Kona Beach Hotel in Kailua-Kona. A large glass dome in the bow and 13 viewing ports on the sides allow clear views of the aquatic world more than 100 feet down. This is a great trip for kids and nonswimmers. Each one-hour voyage costs $90 for adults and $45 for children under 12. The company also operates on O'ahu and Maui. ☎ *808/329–6626 or 800/548–6262* 🌐 *www.atlantisadventures.com.*

SURFING

The Big Island does not have the variety of great surfing spots found on O'ahu or Maui, but it does have decent waves and a thriving surf culture. Local kids and avid surfers frequent a number of places up and

Continued on page 108

SNORKELING IN HAWAI'I

The waters surrounding the Hawaiian Islands are filled with life—from giant manta rays cruising off the Big Island's Kona Coast to humpback whales giving birth in Maui's Mā'alaea Bay. Dip your head beneath the surface to experience a spectacularly colorful world: pairs of milletseed butterfly fish dart back and forth, red-lipped parrot fish snack on coral algae, and spotted eagle rays flap past like silent spaceships. Sea turtles bask at the surface while tiny wrasses give them the equivalent of a shave and a haircut. The water quality is typically outstanding; many sites afford 30 foot-plus visibility. On snorkel cruises, you can often stare from the boat rail right down to the bottom.

Certainly few destinations are as accommodating to every level of snorkeler as Hawai'i. Beginners can tromp in from sandy beaches while more advanced divers descend to shipwrecks, reefs, craters, and sea arches just offshore. Because of Hawai'i's extreme isolation, the island chain has fewer fish species than Fiji or the Caribbean—but many of the fish that are here exist nowhere else. The Hawaiian waters are home to the highest percentage of endemic fish in the world.

The key to enjoying the underwater world is slowing down. Look carefully. Listen. You might hear the strange crackling sound of shrimp tunneling through coral, or you may hear whales singing to one another during winter. A shy octopus may drift along the ocean's floor beneath you. If you're hooked, pick up a waterproof fishkey from Long's Drugs. You can brag later that you've looked the Hawaiian turkeyfish in the eye.

Picasso Triggerfish	Milletseed Butterfly Fish*	Yellow Tang
Moorish Idol	Hawaiian Whitespotted Toby*	Saddleback Wrasse*
Red-lipped Parrot Fish	Hawaiian Turkeyfish*	Zebra Moray Eel
Stocky Hawkfish	Green Sea Turtle	Spotted Eagle Ray

*endemic to Hawai'i

POLYNESIA'S FIRST CELESTIAL NAVIGATORS: HONU

Honu **is the Hawaiian name for two native sea turtles, the hawksbill and the green sea turtle. Little is known about these dinosaur-age marine reptiles, though snorkelers regularly see them foraging for *limu* (seaweed) and the occasional jellyfish in Hawaiian waters. Most female honu nest in the uninhabited Northwestern Hawaiian Islands, but a few sociable ladies nest on Maui beaches. Scientists suspect that they navigate the seas via magnetism—sensing the earth's poles. Amazingly, they will journey up to 800 miles to nest—it's believed that they return to their own birth sites. After about 60 days of incubation, nestlings emerge from the sand at night and find their way back to the sea by the light of the stars.**

down the Kona and Kohala Coasts of west Hawai'i. Expect high surf in winter and much calmer activity during summer. The surf scene is much more active on the Kona side.

Among the best places to catch the waves are **Pine Trees** (✉ Off Hwy. 11 and south of the Kona Airport and the Natural Energy Lab of Hawai'i on an unimproved beach road) and **Kahalu'u Beach Park** (✉ Ali'i Dr., 5½ mi south of Kailua-Kona next to Outrigger Keauhou Beach Hotel). **Banyans** (✉ Ali'I Dr. near the Kona Bali Kai condos) is popular with local surfers. **Old Kona Airport State Recreation Area** (✉ Kuakini Rd. at the old Kona Airport) is also a good place for catching wave action. On the east side near Hilo, try **Honoli'i Cove** (✉ Access road off Hwy. 19, just past mile marker 4).

Surf Shops & Schools

Hawai'i Lifeguard Surf Instructors. This certified school with experienced instructors helps novice surfers become wave riders; their surf tours take more experienced riders to Kona's top surfing spots. Though they offer a one-hour introductory lesson ($72 for a small group, $98 for private instruction), they recommend the two-hour lesson to get you ready to surf. You can try a two-hour tandem lesson on a board for two. ✉ *75-159 Lunapule Rd., Kailua-Kona* ☎ *808/936–SURF or 808/324–0442* 🌐 *www.surflessonshawaii.com.*

Ocean Eco Tours Surf School. This surf school emphasizes the basics of safe surfing and specializes in beginners. All lessons are taught by certified CPR-trained lifeguard instructors, and they guarantee that you will surf! If you're hooked, you can sign up for a three-lesson package for $270. ✉ *74-425 Kealakehe Pkwy., Kailua-Kona* ☎ *808/324–7873* 🌐 *www.oceanecotours.com.*

Orchid Land Surf Shop. The shop has a wide variety of water sports and surf equipment for sale or rent. They stock professional custom surfboards, bodyboards, and surf apparel and do repairs. ✉ *262 Kamehameha Ave., Hilo* ☎ *808/935–1533* 🌐 *www.orchidlandsurf.com.*

Pacific Vibrations. This surf shop carries a full line of surfboards, body boards, and related gear. They also rent a variety of water sports equipment. ✉ *75-5702 Likana La., at Ali'i Dr. a block south of Kailua Pier, Kailua-Kona* ☎ *808/329–4140.*

WHALE-WATCHING

Each winter, some two-thirds of the North Pacific humpback whale population (about 4,000–5,000 animals) migrate over 3,500 mi from the icy Alaska waters to the warm Hawaiian ocean to give birth to and nurse their calves. Recent reports indicate that the whale population is on the upswing—a few years ago one even ventured into the mouth of Hilo Harbor, which marine biologists say is quite rare. Humpbacks are spotted here from early December through the end of April, but other species, like sperm, pilot, and beaked whales, can be seen year-round. Most ocean tour companies offer whale outings during the season, but two owner–operators do it full time. They are much more familiar with

CLOSE UP

Protecting the Humpback Whale

THE WATERS AROUND THE HAWAIIAN Islands are one of the North Pacific humpback whales' most significant habitats: the only place in the United States coastal waters where humpbacks are known to reproduce and give birth to their young.

The Hawaiian Islands Humpback Whale National Marine Sanctuary 🌐 www.hawaiihumpbackwhale.noaa.gov was established in 1997 to protect humpback whales and their habitat and to educate the public about whales and the Hawai'i marine environment. The 1,400-square-mi sanctuary includes five protected areas around the main Hawaiian Islands.

Did you know?

- Humpback whales are the fifth largest of the world's great whales; a mature whale can be up to 45 feet long and weigh about 42–45 tons.
- Their top jaw has fleshy knobs called tubercles. Each tubercle has a strand of hair and many nerve endings believed to serve some sensory function.
- Their throats have expandable pleats, allowing the animal to ingest over 500 gallons of prey and water in a single gulp. They primarily eat zooplankton and small fish.
- Their tongues can weigh up to one ton.
- The calves have a 10- to 12-month gestation period. On average, newborns weigh 1.5 tons and are 10–16 feet long.
- Calves nurse on the mother's rich milk for six to eight months and grow fast, nearly doubling their length by the end of the first year.
- Humpback whales live about 40 to 60 years.

whale behavior and you're more likely to have a quality whale-watching experience. ■ TIP→ **If you take the morning cruise, you're likely to see dolphins as well.**

★ **Captain Dan McSweeney's Year-Round Whale Watching Adventures.** This is probably the most experienced small operation on the island. Captain Dan McSweeney offers three-hour trips on his 40-foot boat. In addition to humpbacks in the winter, he'll show you some of the six other whale species that live off the Kona Coast year-round. Three-hour tours cost $70 per adult and $60 for kids under 12 (snacks and juices included). McSweeney guarantees you'll see a whale or he'll take you out again free. ✉ *Honokōhau Harbor, Kailua-Kona* ☎ *808/322–0028 or 888/942–5376* 🌐 *www.ilovewhales.com.*

Living Ocean Adventures. Captain Tom Bottrell leads whale-watching excursions (combined with deep-sea fishing, if desired) for up to six people on the *Spinner,* his 31-foot fishing boat. If you book the whole boat, his four-hour rate is $400 for six people; it goes up to $575 for a six-hour outing. Bottled water is included, but you have to bring your own snacks. ✉ *Honokōhau Harbor, Kailua-Kona* ☎ *808/325–5556* 🌐 *www.livingoceanadventures.com.*

WINDSURFING

Windsurfers will find good waters and winds in the coves and bays along the Kohala Coast. The surf is usually choppy when the wind comes up but not so much that windsurfers can't get out. Unlike surfing, windsurfing requires no paddling. Instead, you have to hang on to a sail flapping in the wind and pick up speed. Coordination and balance are crucial.

One of the best windsurfing locations on the Big Island is at **'Anaeho'omalu Beach** (✉ Follow Waikoloa Beach Dr. to Kings' Shops, then turn left) in North Kohala. The beach fronts the Waikoloa Beach Marriott.

Equipment Rentals & Lessons

Ocean Sports & Activities. This beach concession shack fronting the Waikoloa Beach Marriott has a full line of water sports and beach equipment rentals and can arrange various tours and excursions. They offer windsurfing lessons at $60 per person and claim you'll learn how to sail in just one lesson. ✉ *69-275 Waikoloa Beach Dr., Waikoloa* ☎ *808/886–6666 or 888/724–5234* 🌐 *www.hawaiioceansports.com.*

Golf, Hiking & Outdoor Activities

5

WORD OF MOUTH

"Going to Hawai'i Volcanoes National Park and hiking over lava at the end of the Chain of Craters road is amazing. We also took a helicopter tour of the Big Island and it was incredible!"

–DebitNM

"[The Ironman] is like a big party at the finish line and so much fun and inspiring! If you are nearby, it's a must-see. Yes, roads are closed, but you can get around, park, and walk around and cheer on these athletes."

–beachkomer

www.fodors.com/forums

By John Penisten & Don Chapman

WITH THE BIG ISLAND'S PREDICTABLY MILD year-round climate, it's no wonder the lifestyle emphasis is on outdoor activities. After all, this is the home of the annual Ironman Triathlon World Championship. Whether you are an avid hiker or a beginning bicyclist, a casual golfer or a tennis buff, there are plenty of land-based activities to lure you away from the sun and surf.

You can explore by ATV, bike, helicopter, or horse, or you can put on your hiking boots and use your own horsepower. No matter how you get around, you'll be treated to breathtaking backdrops along and beyond the Big Island's 266-mile coastline. Aerial tours take in the latest eruption activity and lava flows, as well as the island's gorgeous tropical valleys, gulches, and coastal areas. Trips into the backcountry wilderness explore the rain forest, private ranch lands, coffee farms, and sugar plantation villages that give a glimpse of Hawai'i's earlier days.

Golfers will find acclaimed, championship-caliber golf courses at Mauna Kea Resort, Mauna Lani Resort, Waikoloa Resort, and Four Seasons at Hualalai, among others. And during the winter, if snow conditions allow, you can go skiing on top of Mauna Kea (elevation: 13,796 ft). It's a skiing experience unlike any other.

AERIAL TOURS

There's nothing quite like the aerial view of a waterfall that drops a couple of thousand feet into multiple pools, or seeing lava flow to the ocean, where clouds of steam billow into the air. You can get this bird's-eye view from a helicopter or a small fixed-wing aircraft. Although there have been a few cases of pilots violating flight paths and altitudes over resident communities in recent years, most operators are reputable and fly with strict adherence to FAA safety rules. How to get the best experience for your money? ■ TIP→ **Before you hire a company, be a savvy traveler and ask the right questions. What kind of aircraft do they fly? Do they have two-way headsets so you can talk with the pilot? What is their safety record?**

For more on Hawai'i Volcanoes National Park, see page 46.

Island Hoppers. Despite the name, this isn't a helicopter line. They fly fixed-wing three- to six-passenger Cessna aircraft from both the Hilo and Kona airports. Every seat is a window seat with panoramic views. There are three air tours, from a 50-minute Volcano Waterfall tour at $64 per person to a two-hour Full Circle Island Tour for $287. ☎ *808/329–0018 or 800/538–7590* 🌐 *www.hawaiiislandhoppers.com.*

Mokulele Airlines. In addition to regular inter-island scheduled flights, this commuter line offers a 1½-hour Circle Island Tour in a nine-passenger twin-engine aircraft. The air tour departs Kona Airport and goes over Hawai'i Volcanoes National Park, the Hilo-Hāmākua Coast, and the Kohala Coast. Rates are $299 per person; ask about senior discounts. ☎ *808/326–7070 or 866/260–7070* 🌐 *www.mokulele.com.*

Paradise Helicopters. Paradise flies six-passenger Bell 470 and four-passenger MD-500 helicopters. Everyone has a window seat in these highly maneuverable helicopters. The friendly and knowledgeable pilots communicate with passengers over two-way headsets. Paradise operates from Kona and Hilo, which is better for volcano-viewing. The 50-minute Volcano & Waterfall Adventure (from Hilo) is $185 per person; the top-of-the-line tour is a three-hour Volcanoes & Valley Adventure (from Kona) for $530 per person, including lunch. For an additional thrill and an even better view, you can choose a Doors-Off Experience from Hilo; you can literally feel the heat radiating from the lava. ✉ *Hilo Airport, Kona Airport* ☎ *808/356–1800, 808/329–6601 or 888/349–7888* 🌐 *www.paradisecopters.com.*

Sunshine Helicopters. Ride the "Black Beauties" or the luxurious WhisperSTAR EC-130 helicopters on these exciting air tours that take in the ocean cliffs and valleys of the Kohala-Hāmākua Coast, or, from Hilo, the formations of the Kīlauea Volcano. Narrated tours range from 45 minutes ($185) to two hours ($390); the longer tour covers both regions. Afterwards, you can buy a DVD of your flight experience. ✉ *Helipad at Hāpuna Beach Prince Hotel and Hilo Airport* ☎ *Hāpuna Beach Prince Hotel: 808/882–1223; Hilo: 808/969–7501 or 800/469–3000* 🌐 *www.sunshinehelicopters.com.*

5

ATV TOURS

A different way to experience the Big Island's rugged coastline and wild ranch lands is through an off-road adventure—a real backcountry experience. At higher elevations, weather can be nippy and rainy, but views can be awesome. Protective gear is provided. Generally, you have to be 16 or older to ride your own ATV, though some outfitters allow children 7 and older to be a passenger.

ATV Outfitters Hawai'i. These trips take in the scenic beauty of the rugged North Kohala Coast, traveling along coastal cliffs and into the forest in search of waterfalls. The ATV outfitter's three adventures are priced from $109 per person for the 1½-hour Ocean Cliff Adventure to $249 per person for the 22-mi three-hour Deluxe Rainforest & Waterfall Adventure. ✉ *Old Sakamoto Store, Hwy. 270, Kapa'au* ☎ *808/889–6000 or 888/288–7288* 🌐 *www.outfittershawaii.com.*

ATV Ranch Ride. This 2½-hour ATV adventure on a working ranch takes in the Hāmākua Coast and the Waipi'o Valley: dramatic ocean cliffs, quiet forests, and remnants of Hawai'i's once-thriving sugar cane industry. Prices begin at $100 per person. ✉ *Honoka'a* ☎ *808/775–7291 or 877/775–7291* 🌐 *www.waipioonhorseback.com.*

Cowboys of Hawai'i ATV Rides. Riders cruise Parker Ranch to Holoholo Hill for an incomparable panorama of the ranch's 175,000 acres and thousands of cattle or follow the Mana Road, in the shadow of towering Mauna Kea. Rates for the two-hour ride begin at $95 per person. ✉ *Parker Ranch Center, 67-1435 Mamalahoa Hwy., Waimea* ☎ *808/885–5006* 🌐 *www.cowboysofhawaii.com.*

Kahuā Ranch ATV Rides. On this working ranch, you can ride the range, from upslope rain forest to midlevel mountain desert. Dramatic cinder cones and backcountry pastures offer scenic views. ■ TIP→ **Ride later in**

the day, and stay for a ranch barbecue with the family; afterwards, you can stargaze through their powerful telescope and learn how to rope. Rates for the two-hour ride begin at $95 per person (not including dinner). ✉ *Hwy. 250, 10 mi north of Waimea* ☎ *808/882–7954 or 808/882–4646* 🌐 *www.kahuaranch.com.*

Kukui ATV & Adventures. On this Waipi'o Valley ride, you'll see expansive black sand beaches, 1,200-foot Hi'ilawe Falls, and the lush rain forest surrounding the top edge of the valley. Rates for the three-hour rim tour begin at $135 per person. ✉ *Waipi'o Valley Artworks Bldg., 48-5416 Kukuihaele Rd., Kukuihaele* ☎ *808/775–1701 or 877/757–1414* 🌐 *www.topofwaipio.com.*

BIKING

The Big Island's biking trails range from easy to moderate coastal rides to rugged backcountry wilderness treks that will challenge the most serious bikers. En route, bikers can soak up some of the island's storied scenic vistas and varied geography—from tropical rain forest to rolling ranch country, from high country mountain meadows to dry lava deserts. It's dry, windy, and hot on leeward coastal trails and cool, wet, and muddy in upcountry windward areas. There are long distances between towns and few services available in the Ka'u, Puna, South Kona, and Kohala Coast areas, so bikers need to plan accordingly for weather, water, food, and lodging before setting out.

The nonprofit **Big Island Mountain Bike Association** (📫 Box 6819, Hilo 96720-8934 🌐 www.interpac.net/~mtbike) has tons of information on biking the Big Island. It provides maps and detailed descriptions of rides for all ability levels. ■ TIP→ **For other suggested rides, see the Web site run by Alternative Hawai'i (🌐 www.alternative-hawaii.com/activity/biecotrb.htm).**

Best Routes

Fodor'sChoice ★ *Mountain Bike* magazine voted **Kulani Trails,** south of Hilo, the best ride in the state. To reach the trailhead from the intersection of Highways 11 and 19, take Highway 19 south about 4 mi, then turn right onto Stainback Highway and continue on 2½ mi, then turn right at the Waiakea Arboretum. Park near the gate. This technically demanding ride, which passes majestic eucalyptus trees, is for advanced cyclists.

The **Old Puna Trail** (✉ Trailhead: From Hwy. 130, about 3 mi south of Kea'au town, take Kaloli Rd. to Beach Rd.) is a 10½-mi ride through the subtropical jungle in Puna, one of the island's most isolated areas. You'll start out on a cinder road, which becomes a four-wheel-drive trail. If it's rained recently, you'll have to deal with some puddles—the first few of which you'll gingerly avoid until you give in and go barreling through the rest of them for the sheer fun of it. This is a great ride for all abilities that takes about 90 minutes.

Guided Rides

Orchid Isle Bicycling. This is the only Big Island outfitter currently offering daily bicycle tours. Geared to cyclists of varying abilities, options range from challenging 3,500-foot climbs up Kohala Mountain to

CLOSE UP

Ironman & Friends

Run annually since 1978, the **Ironman Triathlon World Championship** (☎ 808/329-0063 🌐 www.ironmanlive.com) is the granddaddy of them all. For about a week prior to Race Day (the 3rd Saturday of October), Kailua-Kona takes on the air of an Olympic Village as top athletes from across the globe arrive to compete for glory and $580,000 in prize money at the world's premiere swim/bike/run endurance event. To watch these 1,700 competitors push themselves to the ultimate in this grueling event is an inspiring testament to the human spirit. The competition starts at Kailua Pier with a 2.4-mi open-water swim, immediately followed by a 112-mi bicycle ride, then a 26.2-mi marathon. The Ironman wouldn't happen without the 7,000 volunteers who donate their time and services. To volunteer, register online at the Ironman Web site.

The **Honu Half-Ironman Triathlon** (☎ 808/329-0063 🌐 www.honuhalfironman.com) in early June is an Ironman "farm team event." Participants swim at Hāpuna beach, bike the Ironman course, and run on the Mauna Lani resort grounds.

Supermen/women do the Ironman. A few notches down on the difficulty scale, but still extremely challenging, is the **Manna-Man Eco-Biathlon** (☎ 808/989-3655 🌐 www.bigislandraceschedule.com), held the last Sunday in March. The race occurs in and around Kealakeua Bay. You're required to either wear or carry your shoes while swimming (points are given for creative ways to keep 'em with you, and you're penalized for leaving equipment or trash anywhere on the racecourse).

How about racing on an active volcano? No, you're not trying to outrun flowing lava (which is actually not much of a challenge, given the speed at which it usually travels). The **Kīlauea Volcano Wilderness Runs** (☎ 808/985-8725 🌐 www.volcanoartcenter.org) includes a marathon, 10-mi and 5-mi races, and a noncompetitive 5-mi run-walk. This July event is held completely within Hawai'i Volcanoes National Park.

For the most current race information, check out the **Big Island Race Schedule** (🌐 www.bigislandraceschedule.com/RaceLinks.html).

downhill-only rides that end with a swim. Tours, which last from four to eight hours and cover 8 to 55 mi, start at $125 per person. The outfitter also runs deluxe seasonal "Tour de Paradise" vacation packages including hotels, some meals, and all gear for $1,895 and up per person for four to six days of cycling. 📫 *Box 3486, Kailua-Kona 96745* ☎ *808/327-0087 or 800/219-2324* 🌐 *www.orchidislebicycling.com.*

Bike Shops & Clubs

If you want to strike out on your own, there are several rental shops in Kailua-Kona and a couple in Waimea and Hilo. Resorts rent bicycles that can be used around the properties. Most outfitters listed can provide a bicycle rack for your car. All offer reduced rates for rentals longer than one day.

Bike Works. This branch operation of Hawaiian Pedals caters to more advanced bicyclists and Ironman wannabes with its rentals of deluxe road bikes and full-suspension mountain bikes, starting at $40 a day. ✉ *Hale Hana Centre, 74-5583 Luhia St., Kailua-Kona* ☎ *808/326–2453* 🌐 *www.hpbikeworks.com.*

Cycle Station. This shop, which has a variety of bikes to rent, from road sport to racing bikes, hybrids to tandems, will also deliver to and pick up at hotels. They have trailers for toddlers. Daily rentals range from $20 for a hybrid to $35 for a road or mountain bike. ✉ *73-5619 Kauhola St. #105, Kailua-Kona* ☎ *808/327–0087* 🌐 *www.cyclestationhawaii.com.*

Hawaiian Pedals. For those who prefer comfort over speed, Hawaiian Pedals rents seven-speed cruiser, hybrids, and basic mountain bikes starting at $15 for five hours. Full day rental rates begin at $20. ✉ *Kona Inn Shopping Village, 75-5744 Ali'i Dr., Kailua-Kona* ☎ *808/329–2294* 🌐 *www.hpbikeworks.com.*

Mid Pacific Wheels. This bike shop carries a full line of bikes and related accessories. They also rent mountain bikes for exploring the Hilo and east Hawai'i area. Rental rates are $20 per day. They can provide information on best places to go, what to see, do, and experience on a self-guided bike tour. ✉ *1133C Manono St., Hilo 96720* ☎ *808/935–6211.*

GOLF

For golfers, the Big Island is a big deal—starting with Mauna Kea, which opened in 1964 and remains one of the state's top courses. Black lava and deep blue sea are the predominant themes on the island. In the roughly 40 mi from the Kona Country Club out to the Mauna Kea Resort, nine courses are sculpted into sunny seaside lava, with four more in the hills above. Indeed, most of the Big Island's best courses are concentrated along the Kona Coast, statistically the sunniest spot in the Hawaiian archipelago. Vertically speaking, although the majority of courses are seaside or at least at sea level, three are located above 2,000 feet, another at 4,200 feet. This is significant because in Hawai'i temperatures drop by three degrees for every 1,000 feet of elevation gained.

Green Fees: Green fees listed here are the highest course rates per round on weekdays for U.S. residents. Courses with varying weekend rates are noted in the individual listings. (Some courses charge non-U.S. residents higher prices.) ■ TIP→ **Discounts are often available for resort guests and for those who book tee times on the Web. Twilight fees are usually offered, call individual courses for information.**

★ **Big Island Country Club.** Set 2,000 feet above sea level on the slopes of Mauna Kea, the Big Island Country Club is rather out of the way but well worth the drive. Pete and Perry Dye (1997) created a gem that plays through an upland woodlands—more than 2,500 trees line the fairways. On the par-5 15th, a giant tree in the middle of the fairway must be avoided with the second shot. Five lakes and a meandering natural mountain stream mean water comes into play on nine holes. The most dramatic

TIPS FOR THE GREEN

Golf is golf, and Hawai'i is part of the United States, but island golf nevertheless has its own quirks. Here are a few tips to make your golf experience in the Islands more pleasant.

- Sunscreen. Buy it, apply it (minimum 30 SPF). The sub-tropical rays of the sun are intense, even in December. Good advice is to apply sunscreen, at a minimum, on the first and 10th tees.
- Stay hydrated. Spending four-plus hours in the sun and heat means you'll perspire away considerable fluids and energy.
- All resort courses and many daily fee courses provide rental clubs. In many cases, they're the latest lines from Titleist, Ping, Callaway, and the like. This is true for both men and women, as well as lefthanders, which means you don't have to shlep clubs across the Pacific.
- Pro shops at most courses are well-stocked with balls, tees, and other accoutrements, so even if you bring your own bag, it needn't weigh a ton.
- Come spikeless—very few Hawai'i courses still permit metal spikes.
- Resort courses, in particular, offer more than the usual three sets of tees, sometimes four or five. So bite off as much or little challenge as you like. Tee it up from the tips and you'll end up playing a few 600-yard par-5s and see a few 250-yard forced carries.
- In theory, you can play golf in Hawai'i 365 days a year. But there's a reason the Hawaiian islands are so green. Better to bring an umbrella and light jacket and not use them than to not bring them and get soaked.
- Unless you play a muni or certain daily fee courses, plan on taking a cart. Riding carts are mandatory at most courses and are included in the green fees.

is on the par-3 17th, where Dye creates a knockoff of his infamous 17th at the TPC at Sawgrass. ✉ *71-1420 Māmalahoa Hwy., Kailua-Kona* ☎ *808/325–5044* 🌐 *www.intrawest.com* *18 holes. 7034 yds. Par 72. Green Fee: $109* ☞ *Facilities: Driving range, putting green, golf carts, rental clubs, pro shop, lessons.*

Hāmākua Country Club. The typical modern 18-hole golf course requires at least 250 acres. The 9-hole, par-33 public Hāmākua course requires just 19. Compact is the word, and with several holes crisscrossing, this is BYO Hard Hat. A product of Hawai'i's plantation era, holes run up and down a fairly steep slope overlooking the ocean. There is no clubhouse or other amenities, and the 9th green is square, but for $15 bucks, whaddaya want? ✉ *Hwy. 19, 41 mi north of Hilo, Honoka'a* ☎ *808/775–7244* *9 holes. 2520 yds. Par 33. Green Fee: $15* ☞ *Facilities: Putting green, golf carts, pull carts.*

Hilo Municipal Golf Course. Hilo Muni is living proof that you don't need a single sand bunker to create a challenging course. Trees and several

CLOSE UP

In Search of Birdies, Eagles & Whales

BREATHTAKING SCENERY is to be expected on Hawai'i golf courses—as it is everywhere around the tropical archipelago—but many golfers are surprised at the variety of fauna to be seen among the verdant flora during a round.

Fortunately, this being Hawai'i, there are no snakes, no man-eating mammals, not a single critter that poses a golfer any threat. But many do offer oohs and ahhs. The most dramatic by far are humpback whales. From late November through April, these two-ton cetaceans call Hawai'i home. Whether they're spouting, slapping tails on the surface, or leaping completely free of the sea and landing with a tremendous splash, humpbacks are a delightful distraction.

Among the Big Island courses from which golfers have reported sighting whales: Mauna Kea, Hāpuna, Mauna Lani, Waikoloa, and Kona CC.

While whales almost always induce a "wow," dolphins almost always elicit a smile. Make a double-bogey, see a pod of dolphins leaping past, and it's like the double never happened. Dolphins have been spotted from each of the aforementioned courses.

Lucky golfers, and those with good eyes, may also see sea turtles bobbing just outside the shore break or Hawaiian monk seals sunning on a beach. While seeking birdies and eagles on the course, golfers can also do some colorful—and significant—bird-watching. Significant because Hawai'i leads the United States in species extinctions, and several members of the federal endangered species list can be seen on island golf courses. They include the Hawaiian goose (nēnē), Hawaiian duck (koloa), Hawaiian coot, and Hawaiian stilt (as well as the the monk seal). In particular, the nēnē, the state bird, finds a happy home on lakes at Hāpuna.

Feathered friends range from the bright red American cardinal, seen throughout the islands, to the bright yellow saffron finch, seen primarily at Kona CC and at seaside resorts along the Kona Coast. At Hāpuna, wildlife biologists credit the creation of new courses for increasing bird habitat and the number of birds. The number of new species doubled here, including the Hawaiian owl (pueo). The pueo is important in Hawai'i, where it was a totem of the ancient Hawaiian religion and today remains an *'aumakua*, family deity, for some native Hawaiians. The Waimea CC on the Big Island has been certified as an Audubon Cooperative Sanctuary for its resident population of wild turkeys. The golden plover is seen on many courses while it winters over on the Big Island after spending its summer in Alaska. Like the humpback whale, the golden plover migrates back and forth each year between Alaska and Hawai'i.

A final wildlife note: No threats to health and well-being here, but there are some conniving thieves. At many courses, mynah birds, the most human of birds, have been known to steal a sandwich left in a cart while the owner is hitting a shot between bites. Golfers beware and protect your lunch.

meandering creeks are the danger here. Despite the lack of bunkers, the course, which offers views of Hilo Bay from most holes, has produced many of Hawai'i's top players over the years. Taking a divot reminds you that you're playing on a dormant volcano—the soil is dark black crushed lava. ✉ *340 Haihai St., Hilo* ☎ *808/959–7711* *18 holes. 6325 yds. Par 71. Green Fee: $29 weekdays, $34 weekends* ☞ *Facilities: Driving range, putting green, golf carts, pull carts, rental clubs, pro-shop, lessons, restaurant, bar.*

★ **Hualālai Resort.** Named for the volcanic peak that is the target off the first tee, the Nicklaus Course at Hualālai is semiprivate, open only to guests of the adjacent Four Seasons Resort Hualālai. From the forward and resort tees, this is perhaps Jack Nicklaus's most friendly course in Hawai'i, but the back tees play a full mile longer. The par-3 17th plays across convoluted lava to a seaside green, and the view from the tee is so lovely, you may be tempted to just relax on the koa bench and enjoy the scenery. ✉ *100 Ka'ūpūlehu Dr., Kohala Coast* ☎ *808/325–8480* 🌐 *www.fourseasons.com/hualalai* *18 holes. 7117 yds. Par 72. Green Fee: $195* ☞ *Facilities: Driving range, putting green, golf carts, pull carts, rental clubs, pro shop, lessons, restaurant, bar.*

★ **Kona Country Club.** This venerable country club offers two very different tests with the aptly named Ocean and Ali'i Mountain courses. The Ocean Course (William F. Bell, 1967) is a bit like playing through a coconut plantation, with a few remarkable lava features—such as the "blowhole" in front of the par-4 13th, where sea water propelled through a lava tube erupts like a geyser. The Ali'i Mountain Course (front nine, William F. Bell, 1983: back nine, Robin Nelson and Rodney Wright, 1992) plays a couple of strokes tougher than the Ocean and is the most delightful split personality you may ever encounter. Both nines share breathtaking views of Keauhou Bay, and elevation change is a factor in most shots. The most dramatic view on the front nine is from the tee of the par-3 5th hole, one of the best golf vistas in Hawai'i. The green seems perched on the edge of the earth, with what only seems to be a sheer 500-foot drop just beyond the fringe. The back nine is links-style, with less elevation change—except for the par-3 14th, which drops 100 feet from tee to green, over a lake. The routing, the sight lines and framing of greens, and the risk-reward factors on each hole make this one of the single best nines in Hawai'i. ✉ *78-7000 Ali'i Dr., Kailua-Kona* ☎ *808/322–2595* 🌐 *www.konagolf.com* *Ocean Course: 18 holes. 6806 yds. Par 72. Green Fee: $160. Mountain Course: 18 holes. 6673 yds. Par 72. Green Fee: $145* ☞ *Facilities: Driving range, putting green, golf carts, rental clubs, lessons, restaurant, bar.*

Mākālei Country Club. Set on the slopes of Hualālai, at an elevation of 2,900 feet, Mākālei is one of the rare Hawai'i courses with bentgrass putting greens, which means they're quick and without the grain

LAVA HAZARDS

Lava tends to be razor-sharp and not good for the life of golf balls, or golf shoes. If you hit a ball into the black stuff, consider it an offering to Pele, goddess of lava, and drop another one.

5

associated with bermuda greens. Former PGA Tour official Dick Nugent (1994) designed holes that play through thick forest and open to provide wide ocean views. Elevation change is a factor on many holes, especially the par-3 15th, with the tee 80 feet above the green. ✉ *72-3890 Hawai'i Belt Rd., Kailua-Kona* ☎ *808/325–6625* 🏌 *18 holes. 7041 yds. Par 72. Green Fee: $99* ☞ *Facilities: Driving range, putting green, golf carts, rental clubs, pro shop, lessons, restaurant.*

Fodor's Choice ★ **Mauna Kea Beach Resort.** Mauna Kea Golf Course isn't just a golf course, it's a landmark, an icon, a national treasure. Robert Trent Jones Sr., who designed more than 500 courses around the world, rated Mauna Kea among his three best. Built on a 5,000-year-old lava flow, an essential part of Mauna Kea's greatness is the way Jones insinuated holes into the landscape. Only two fairways, holes five and six, are parallel. Mauna Kea is a classic championship design, somewhat forgiving off the tee but quite stern about approach shots. Although No. 3, which plays across a blue bay from rocky promontory to promontory, gets all the photo ops, the toughest par-3 is the 11th. Arnold Palmer and Ed Seay created the resort's second course, Hāpuna, in 1992. Unlike seaside Mauna Kea, Hāpuna is a links-style course that rises to 600 feet elevation, providing views of the ocean and elevation-change challenges. Trees are a factor on most holes at Mauna Kea, but they seldom are at Hāpuna. Palmer-Seay put a premium on accuracy off the tee, and are more forgiving with approaches. The two courses have separate clubhouses. **Hāpuna Golf Course:** ✉ *62-100 Kauna'oa Dr., Kohala Coast* ☎ *808/880–3000* 🌐 *www.hapunabeachprincehotel.com* 🏌 *18 holes. 6534 yds. Par 72. Green Fee: $290* ☞ *Facilities: Driving range, putting green, golf carts, rental clubs, pro shop, lessons, restaurant, bar.* **Mauna Kea Golf Course:** ✉ *62-100 Mauna Kea Beach Dr., Kohala Coast* ☎ *808/882–5400* 🌐 *www.maunakearesort.com* 🏌 *18 holes. 6737 yds. Par 72. Green Fee: $210* ☞ *Facilities: Driving range, putting green, golf carts, rental clubs, pro shop, lessons, restaurant, bar.*

Fodor's Choice ★ **Mauna Lani Resort.** Black lava flows, lush green turf, white sand, and the Pacific's multihues of blue define the 36 holes at Mauna Lani. The South Course includes the par-3 15th across a turquoise bay, one of the most photographed holes in Hawai'i. But it shares "signature hole" honors with the seventh. A long par-3, it plays downhill over convoluted patches of black lava, with the Pacific immediately to the left and a dune to the right. The North Course plays a couple of shots tougher. Its most distinctive hole is the 17th, a par-3 with the green set in a lava pit 50 feet deep. The shot from an elevated tee must carry a pillar of lava that rises from the pit and partially blocks your view of the green. ✉ *68-1310 Mauna Lani Dr., Kohala Coast* ☎ *808/885–6655* 🌐 *www.maunalani.com* 🏌 *North Course: 18 holes. 6601 yds. Par 72. Green Fee: $205. South Course: 18 holes. 6436 yds. Par 72. Green Fee: $205* ☞ *Facilities: Driving range, putting green, golf carts, rental clubs, pro shop, lessons, restaurant, bar.*

Naniloa Country Club. A flat 9-holer set on Hilo's scenic Banyan Drive, Naniloa plays through stands of, what else, banyan trees. The curving par-5 ninth is a terrific closing hole. ✉ *120 Banyan Dr., Hilo* ☎ *808/*

SAVING THE BEST FOR LAST

Among golf's great traditions is the 19th Hole. No matter how the first 18 go, the 19th is sure to offer comfort and cheer, not to mention a chilled beverage. Both courses at the Mauna Kea Resort offer a bit of history with excellent fare. At Mauna Kea, photos and framed scorecards from the "Big Three" match between Arnold Palmer, Jack Nicklaus, and Gary Player line the walls, while at Hāpuna, Arnie's features numerous photos and drawings celebrating Palmer's career. At Mauna Lani, the 19th hole overlooks the South Course's first and 18th holes and the North Course's 18th. At the Kona CC, the restaurant attracts non-golfers for lunch and dinner, offering good fare and views of the Ocean Course and Keauhou Bay. Cheers!

935–3000 ⛳ 9 holes. 2735 yds. Par 35. Green Fee: 9 holes $30, 18 holes $54 ☞ Facilities: driving range, putting green, golf carts, pull carts, rental clubs, lessons.

Volcano Golf & Country Club. Located just outside Volcanoes National Park—and barely a stout drive from Halema'uma'u Crater—Volcano is by far Hawai'i's highest course. At 4,200 feet elevation, shots tend to fly a bit farther than at sea level, even in the often cool, misty air. Because of the elevation and climate, Volcano is one of the few Hawai'i courses with bent-grass putting greens. The course is mostly flat and holes play through stands of Norfolk pines, flowering *lehua* trees, and multitrunk *hau* trees. The uphill par-4 15th doglegs through a tangle of *hau.* ✉ *Pi'i Mauna Dr. off Hwy. 11, Volcanoes National Park* ☎ *808/967–7331* 🌐 *www.volcanogolfshop.com* ⛳ *18 holes. 6106 yds. Par 72. Green Fee: $63 mornings, $51 after noon* ☞ *Facilities: Driving range, putting green, golf carts, rental clubs, restaurant, bar.*

Fodor'sChoice ★ **Waikoloa Beach Resort.** Robert Trent Jones Jr. built the Beach Course at Waikoloa (1981) on an old flow of crinkly *'a'ā* lava, which he used to create holes that are as artful as they are challenging. The third tee, for instance, is set at the base of a towering mound of lava. The par-5 12th plays through a chute of black lava to an ocean-side green, the blue sea on the right coming into play on the second and third shots. At the King's Course at Waikoloa (1990), Tom Weiskopf and Jay Morrish built a very links-esque track. It turns out lava's natural humps and declivities remarkably replicate the contours of seaside Scotland. But there are a few island twists—such as seven lakes. This is "option golf" as Weiskopf and Morrish provide different risk-reward tactics on each hole. Beach and King's have separate clubhouses. **Beach Course:** ✉ *1020 Keana Pl., Waikoloa* ☎ *808/886–6060* 🌐 *www.waikoloagolf.com* ⛳ *18 holes. 6566 yds. Par 70. Green Fee: $195* ☞ *Facilities: Driving range, putting green, golf carts, rental clubs, lessons, restaurant, bar.* **Kings' Course:** ✉ *600 Waikoloa Beach Dr., Waikoloa* ☎ *808/886–7888* 🌐 *www.waikoloagolf.com* ⛳ *18 holes. 6594 yds. Par 72. Green Fee: $195* ☞ *Facilities: Driving range, putting green, golf carts, rental clubs, lessons, restaurant, bar.*

Waikoloa Village Golf Course. A 20-minute drive from Waikoloa Beach Resort, Robert Trent Jones Jr.'s Waikoloa Village (1972) is not affiliated with the resort. It is, however, the site of the annual Waikoloa Open, one of the most prestigious tournaments in Hawai'i. Holes run across rolling hills with sweeping mountain and ocean views. ✉ *68-1792 Melia St., Waikoloa* ☎ *808/883–9621* 🌐 *www.waikoloa.org* *18 holes. 6230 yds. Par 72. Green Fee: $75* ☞ *Facilities: Driving range, putting green, golf carts, rental clubs, lessons, restaurant, bar.*

HIKING

Meteorologists classify the world's weather into 23 climates. Twenty-one are here on the Big Island, and you can experience as many of them as you like. The ancient Hawaiians blazed many trails across their archipelago, and many of these paths can still be used today. Part of the King's Trail at 'Anaeho'omalu winds through a field of lava rocks covered with prehistoric carvings called petroglyphs, meant to communicate stories of births, deaths, marriages, and other family events. Plus, the serenity of remote beaches, such as Papakōlea Beach (Green Sand Beach), is accessible only to hikers.

For information on all Big Island's state parks, contact the **Department of Land and Natural Resources, State Parks Division** (✉ 75 Aupuni St., Hilo 96720 ☎ 808/974–6200 🌐 www.state.hi.us/dlnr/dsp/hawaii.html).

Best Spots

At **Kekaha Kai (Kona Coast) State Park** (✉ Hwy. 19, sign about 2 mi north of Keāhole–Kona International Airport marks rough road), two 1½-mi-long unpaved roads lead to the Mahai'ula Beach and Kua Bay sections of the park. (*See also* Chapter 3, Beaches.) Connecting the two is the 4½-mi Ala Kahakai historic coastal trail. Midway, a hike to the summit of Pu'u Ku'ili, a 342-foot-high cinder cone, offers an excellent view of the coastline. It's dry and hot with no drinking water, so be sure to pack sunscreen and bottled water.

The **Kealakekua Bay and Captain Cook Monument Trail** (✉ Trailhead just off Hwy. 11 at Captain Cook town on Nāpō'opo'o Rd. to Kealakekua Bay) is one of Kona's more popular moderately difficult hikes. About 100 yards from the turnoff, the steep, loose gravel and dirt trail descends several hundred feet across old lava flows. There are some steep switchbacks. Shade along the upper section gives way to sun where the trail opens to lava fields. Nearer to the bay, the trail passes through old Hawaiian village ruins and by the Captain Cook Monument, a tall white obelisk on the spot where the famed navigator was killed in 1779 in a dispute with native Hawaiians. The bay is the site of the Kealakekua Underwater Marine Reserve and is popular with divers and snorkelers. The 2½-mi hike is about a three-hour round trip. The hike back up is steep and tiring, so allow plenty of time. Park along the road. Bring sunscreen, hat, water, and food.

Hawai'i Volcanoes National Park (✉ Near Volcano Village, Hwy. 11, 30 mi south of Hilo ☎ 808/985–6000 🌐 www.hawaii.volcanoes.nationalpark.com) is perhaps the Big Island's premier hiking center. The 150 mi of trails provide closeup views of fern and rain forest environments, cinder cones, steam vents, lava fields, and current lava flow activity. Day hikes range from easy to moderately difficult, and from one or two hours to a full day. For a bigger challenge, consider an overnight or multi-day backcountry hike with a stay in a park cabin. To do so, you must first obtain a free permit at the Kīlauea Visitor Center.

For more on Hawai'i Volcanoes National Park, see page 46.

HIKING HAWAI'I'S TRAILS

- Trails on the eastern or windward sides of the islands are often wet and muddy, making them slippery and unstable, so wear good hiking shoes or boots.
- Do bring along a cell phone, but know that communication signals may be blocked by dead areas, trees, and gulches on the island.
- Though they'll tempt you, don't eat any unknown fruits or plants.
- Darkness comes soon after sunset here. Carry a flashlight if you are out after dark.

Guided Hikes

To get to some of the best trails and places, it's worth going with a skilled guide. Costs range from $95 to $165, and some hikes include picnic meals or refreshments and gear, such as binoculars, ponchos, and walking sticks. The outfitters mentioned here also offer customized adventure tours.

Hawai'i Forest & Trail. Expert naturalist guides take you to 500-foot Kalopa Falls in North Kohala, through the 4,000-year-old craters at Mount Hualālai (the volcano that created all those lava fields along the coast), and on bird-watching expeditions throughout the island. In addition to its other expeditions, the company offers tours in Pinzgauers (Austrian all-terrain vehicles) that are perfect for groups, especially those that include off-road junkies. It offers tours into lava tubes and through normally inaccessible areas of Hawai'i Volcanoes National Park. ☎ *808/331–8505 or 800/464–1993* 🌐 *www.hawaii-forest.com.*

Hawaiian Walkways. Hawaiian Walkways conducts several tours—a Kona Cloud Forest botanical walk, waterfall hikes, coastal adventures, a hike on the "saddle" road between Mauna Kea and Mauna Loa, and jaunts through Hawai'i Volcanoes National Park—as well as custom-designed trips. ☎ *808/775–0372 or 800/457–7759* 🌐 *www.hawaiianwalkways.com.*

HORSEBACK RIDING

With its *paniolo* (cowboy) heritage and the ranches it spawned, the Big Island is a great place for equestrians. Riders can gallop through green pastures, ride to Kealakekua Bay to see the Captain Cook Monument, or saunter into Waipi'o Valley for a taste of old Hawai'i. In addition to the companies listed below, the Mauna Kea Beach Hotel maintains stables in Waimea.

King's Trail Rides. Riders take a 2-hour excursion to the Captain Cook Monument in Kealakekua Bay for snorkeling. All your gear is pro-

Continued on page 126

HAWAI'I'S PLANTS 101

Hawai'i is a bounty of rainbow-colored flowers and plants. The evening air is scented with their fragrance. Just look at the front yard of almost any home, travel any road, or visit any local park and you'll see a spectacular array of colored blossoms and leaves. What most visitors don't know is that the plants they are seeing are not native to Hawai'i; rather, they were introduced during the last two centuries as ornamental plants, or for timber, shade, or fruit.

Hawai'i boasts every climate on the planet, excluding the two most extreme: arctic tundra and arid desert. The Islands have wine-growing regions, cactus-speckled ranchlands, icy mountaintops, and the rainiest forests on earth.

Plants introduced from around the world thrive here. The lush lowland valleys along the windward coasts are predominantly populated by non-native trees including yellow- and red-fruited **guava**, silvery-leafed **kukui**, and orange-flowered **tulip trees**.

The colorful **plumeria flower**, very fragrant and commonly used in lei making, and the giant multicolored **hibiscus flower**, are both used by many women as hair adornments, and are two of the most common plants found around homes and hotels. The umbrella-like **monkey pod tree** from Central America provides shade in many of Hawai'i's parks including Kapiolani Park in Honolulu. Hawai'i's largest tree, found in Lahaina, Maui, is a giant **banyan tree.** Its canopy and massive support roots cover several acres. The native **o'hia tree**, with its brilliant red brush-like flowers, and the **hapu'u,** a giant tree fern, are common in Hawai'i's forests and are also used ornamentally in gardens and around homes.

*endemic to Hawai'i

DID YOU KNOW?

Over 2,200 plant species are found in the Hawaiian Islands, but only about 1,000 are native. Of these, 282 are so rare, they are endangered. Hawai'i's endemic plants evolved from ancestral seeds arriving on the islands over thousands of years as baggage on birds, floating on ocean currents, or drifting on winds from continents thousands of miles away. Once here, these plants evolved in isolation creating many new species known nowhere else in the world.

CLOSE UP

Hawaiian Cowboys?

WHEN BRITISH CAPTAIN George Vancouver gave King Kamehameha a gift of cattle in the 1790s, he probably didn't anticipate the chain of events he would set in motion. The cattle, which were allowed to roam free, multiplied. Within a few years there were thousands of wild cattle on the island. In the early 1800s, when the young sailor John Palmer Parker jumped ship and settled in Hawai'i, he was appointed a wild cattle hunter to control the herds, which were a nuisance to many people. Parker soon began trading the meat, tallow, and hides with visiting ships. He married a high chief's daughter and gradually expanded his lands, eventually establishing Parker Ranch. Thus was born the big country cattle industry.

In the mid-1800s, *vaqueros* (Spanish-Mexican cowboys) were brought to the Big Island to help control the wild cattle. They also taught the fine art of cowboying to the Hawaiians. The *paniolos* (Hawaiian for cowboys) taught the natives how to ride a horse and rope cattle and the other skills a cowboy needed. Today, Hawai'i's *paniolos* are a product of that cross-cultural experience.

vided, except for fins and reef walkers. It costs $135–$150 per person, with lunch. ✉ *81-6420 Mamalahoa Hwy. (Hwy. 11), Kealakekua* ☎ *808/323–2388 or 808/345–0616* 🌐 *www.konacowboy.com.*

Na'alapa Stables. This company is a good bet, especially for novice riders. The horses are well trained, and the stable is well run. Rides through the Waipi'o Valley cross freshwater streams and pass a black-sand beach. Rides depart twice daily, 9:30 AM and 1 PM, from Waipi'o Valley Artworks. Rates for the 2½-hour ride into the valley begin at $89 per person. ✉ *Off Hwy. 240, Kukuihaele* ☎ *808/775–0419* 🌐 *www.naalapastables.com.*

Waipi'o Ridge Stables. Two different rides around the rim of Waipi'o Valley are offered—a 2½-hour trek for $85 and a 5-hour hidden-waterfall adventure (with swimming) for $165. Riders meet at Waipi'o Valley Artworks. ✉ *Off Hwy. 240, Kukuihaele* ☎ *808/775–1007 or 877/757–1414* 🌐 *www.waipioridgestables.com.*

Waipi'o on Horseback. Not many outfits venture into the green jungle of the floor of the Waipi'o Valley. Waipi'o on Horseback takes you to an authentic taro farm. Rides, which depart twice daily from the Last Chance Store, cost $78. ✉ *Last Chance Store, off Hwy. 240, Kukuihaele* ☎ *877/775–7291 or 808/775–7291* 🌐 *www.waipio.homestead.com.*

SKIING

Where else but Hawai'i can you surf, snorkel, and snow ski on the same day? In winter, the 13,796-foot Mauna Kea (Hawaiian for "white mountain") has snow at higher elevations—and along with that, skiing. No lifts, no manicured slopes, no faux-Alpine lodges, no après-ski nightlife—but the chance to ski some of the most remote (and let's face it, unlikely) runs on earth. Some people even have been known to use boogie board as sleds, but we don't recommend it. As long as you're up there, fill your cooler with the white stuff for a snowball fight on the beach with local kids.

Ski Guides Hawai'i. So you're an experienced skier but didn't pack your gear on a tropical Hawaiian vacation? Christopher Langan of Mauna Kea Ski Corporation is the only licensed outfitter providing transportation, guide services, and ski equipment on Mauna Kea. Snow can fall from Thanksgiving through June, but the most likely months are February and March. This isn't Sun Valley; the runs are fairly short, and hidden lava rocks and other dangers abound. Langan charges $450 per person for a daylong experience that includes refreshments, lunch, ski or snowboard equipment, guide service, transportation from Waimea, and four-wheel-drive shuttle back up the mountain after each ski run. He also offers a $250 mountain ski service without the frills and ski or snowboard rentals. *Box 1954, Kamuela 96743 ☎ 808/885–4188, 808/884–5131 off-season ⊕ www.skihawaii.com.*

5

TENNIS

Many of the island's resorts allow nonguests to play for a fee. They also rent rackets, balls, and shoes. On the Kohala Coast, try the Fairmont Orchid Hawai'i, the Mauna Kea Beach Hotel, Hilton Waikoloa Village, and Waikoloa Beach Marriott. In Kailua-Kona there's the Ohana Keauhou Beach Resort, King Kamehameha's Kona Beach Hotel, and the Royal Kona Resort.

Contact the **County of Hawai'i Department of Parks and Recreation** (✉ 25 Aupuni St., Hilo 96720 ☎ 808/961–8311 ⊕ www.hawaii-county.com/directory/dir_parks.htm) for information on all public courts.

In Kailua-Kona, you can play for free at the **Kailua Playground** (✉ 75-5794 Kuakini Hwy., Kailua-Kona ☎ 808/886–1655). Tennis courts are available at **Old Kona Airport State Recreation Area** (✉ North end of Kuakini Hwy., Kailua-Kona ☎ 808/327–4958 or 808/974–6200).

On the Hilo side, there's a small fee to play on the eight courts (three lighted for night play) at **Hilo Tennis Stadium** (✉ Ho'olulu County Park, Pi'ilani and Kalanikoa Sts., Hilo ☎ 808/961–8720).

ON THE SIDELINES

The world's best players compete in January in the **United States Tennis Association Challenger** (☎ 518/274–1674 or 808/886-2222) on the courts of Hilton Waikoloa Village.

Shops & Spas

WORD OF MOUTH

"Go to the farmer's market in Hilo, buy some fresh fruit for the day, head up to Rainbow Falls and Boiling Pots (Pe'epe'e Falls), then head up to the volcano."

–matnikstym

By Amy Westervelt

RESIDENTS LIKE TO COMPLAIN that there isn't a lot of great shopping on the Big Island, but unless you're searching for winter coats or high-tech toys, you can find plenty to deplete your pocketbook. Dozens of shops in Kailua-Kona offer a range of souvenirs from far-flung corners of the globe and plenty of local coffee and foodstuffs to take home to everyone you left behind. Housewares and artworks made from local materials (lava rock, minerals, koa, and milo wood) fill the shelves of small boutiques and galleries throughout the island. Upscale shops in the resorts along the Kohala Coast carry high-quality clothing and accessories, as do a few boutiques scattered around the island. Galleries and gift shops, many showcasing the work of local artists, fill historic buildings in Waimea and North Kohala, and many of the island's former sugar plantation towns have been turned into charming art communities, with local artists selling their wares directly from their studios. Hotel shops generally offer the most attractive and original resort wear but, as with everything else at resorts, the prices run higher than elsewhere on the island.

SHOPS

In general, stores and shopping centers on the Big Island open at 9 or 10 AM and close by 6 PM. Hilo's Prince Kūhiō Shopping Plaza stays open until 9 PM on weekdays. In Kona, most shops in shopping plazas that are geared to tourists also remain open until 9 PM. Big outlets such as KTA Superstore are open until midnight.

Kohala

Shopping Centers

Kawaihae Harbor Center. This harborside shopping plaza houses a dive shop, a bathing-suit store, restaurants, and art galleries, including the Harbor Gallery. ✉ *Hwy. 270, Kawaihae.*

King's Shops at Waikoloa Village. Here you can find fine stores such as Under the Koa Tree, with its upscale gift items crafted by artisans, along with high-end outlets such as DFS Galleria and Louis Vuitton and several other specialty resort shops and boutiques. At the other end of the spectrum, there are also a couple of convenience stores here, but the prices are stiff. ✉ *250 Waikoloa Beach Dr., Waikoloa* ☎ *808/886–8811.*

Books & Maps

Kohala Book Shop. In the historic Old Nanbu Hotel, the state's largest used-book store contains one of the most complete Hawaiian and Pacific collections. There are also some rare first editions. ✉ *54-3885 Akoni Pule Hwy., Kapa'au* ☎ *808/889–6400.*

Clothing

As Hawi Turns. This North Kohala shop, in the historic 1932 Toyama Building, adds a sophisticated touch to resort wear with items made of hand-painted silk. There are vintage and secondhand treasures as well. ✉ *Akoni Pule Hwy., Hāwī* ☎ *808/889–5023.*

Hawaiian Arts & Crafts

■ TIP→ **Remote North Kohala has a remarkable number of galleries in its old restored plantation buildings.**

Ackerman Fine Art Gallery. Painter Gary Ackerman; his wife, Yesan; and their daughter, Camille, have a fine and varied collection of gifts for sale in their side-by-side gallery and gift shop near the King Kamehameha statue. ✉ *54-3878 Akoni Pule Hwy., Kapa'au* ☎ *808/889–5971.*

Elements Jewelry & Fine Crafts. The Old Nanbu Hotel, built in 1898, is a must-see on any stop in North Kohala. While you're there, check out John Flynn's beautiful store. In the front window Flynn creates exquisite jewelry like delicate silver leis and gold waterfalls. The shop also showcases carefully chosen gifts, including unusual ceramics and glass. ✉ *54-3885 Akoni Pule Hwy., Kapa'au* ☎ *808/889–0760.*

Gallery at Bamboo. Inside the Bamboo Restaurant, one of the Island's favorite eateries, this gallery seduces visitors with elegant koa-wood pieces such as rocking chairs and writing desks. It also has a wealth of gift items such as boxes, jewelry, and Hawaiian wrapping paper. ✉ *Hwy. 270, Hāwī* ☎ *808/889–1441.*

Nanbu Gallery. Here you can admire the paintings of owner Patrick Sweeney, along with the work of glass artist Robinson Scott and other island artists. ✉ *54-3885 Akoni Pule Hwy., Kapa'au* ☎ *808/889–0997.*

6

Rankin Gallery. Watercolorist and oil painter Patrick Louis Rankin showcases his own and other local artists' work in his shop in a restored old plantation store (the Wo On Store), next to the Chinese community and social hall, the Tong Wo Society. ✉ *53-4380 Akoni Pule Hwy., Kapa'au* ☎ *808/889–6849.*

Swerdlow Art Gallery. This is a great little gallery with Swerdlow's studio in the back and unique, beautiful paintings and prints in the front. Swerdlow also showcases the work of other local artists, offering everything from paintings to prints and etched glass, plus a range of gift items and interesting home objets d'art. ✉ *54-3862 Akoni Pule Hwy., Kapa'au* ☎ *808/889–0002.*

Tropical Flowers

Na Pua O Kohala. At this popular North Kohala flower shop, you can order lei or let owner Johanna Bard help you create a memorable bouquet. She'll ship your selections for you. ✉ *55-3413 Akoni Pule Hwy., Hāwī* ☎ *808/889–5541 or 877/889–5571.*

Waimea

Shopping Centers

Parker Ranch Center. With a snazzy ranch-style motif, this shopping hub includes a supermarket, coffee shop, natural foods store, and some clothing boutiques. The Parker Ranch Store and Parker Ranch Visitor Center and Museum are also here, and the Kahilu Center next door hosts plays and musical entertainment most nights. ✉ *67-1185 Māmalahoa Hwy., Waimea.*

Parker Square. Browse around boutiques here and in the adjacent **High Country Traders,** where you may find hand-stitched Hawaiian quilts, antiques, or local artworks. ✉ *65-1279 Kawaihae Rd., Waimea* ☎ *808/331–1000.*

Continued on page 134

ALL ABOUT LEIS

Leis brighten every occasion in Hawai'i, from birthdays to bar mitzvahs to baptisms. Creative artisans weave nature's bounty—flowers, ferns, vines, and seeds—into gorgeous creations that convey an array of heartfelt messages: "Welcome," "Congratulations," "Good luck," "Farewell," "Thank you," "I love you." When it's difficult to find the right words, a lei expresses exactly the right sentiments.

WHERE TO BUY THE BEST LEIS

Florists **Na Pua O Kohala** (54-3760 Akoni Pule Hwy., Kapa'au, 808/885-5541); **Honopua Farm** (Waimea, 808/885-4148); **Hawai'i Tropicals** (71 Banyan Dr., Hilo, 808/961-5575); **Elegant Flowers and Gifts** (68-1845 Waikoloa Rd., Waikoloa Village, 808/883-0225). Lei stands at the Kona and Hilo airports sell a surprisingly nice assortment of leis at reasonable prices. KTA, Safeway, and Costco also sell leis, but they tend to stick to "basics" like plumeria, orchid or tuberose.

LEI ETIQUETTE

- To wear a closed lei, drape it over your shoulders, half in front and half in back. Open leis are worn around the neck, with the ends draped over the front in equal lengths.
- Pīkake, ginger, and other sweet, delicate blossoms are "feminine" leis. Men opt for cigar, crown flower, and carnation, which are sturdier and don't emit as much fragrance.
- Leis are always presented with a kiss, a custom that supposedly dates back to World War II when a hula dancer fancied an officer at a U.S.O. show. Taking a dare from members of her troupe, she took off her lei, placed it around his neck, and kissed him on the cheek.
- You shouldn't wear a lei before you give it to someone else. Hawaiians believe the lei absorbs your *mana* (spirit); if you give your lei away, you'll be giving away part of your essence.

	ORCHID
	Growing wild on every continent except Antarctica, orchids—which range in color from yellow to green to purple—comprise the largest family of plants in the world. There are more than 20,000 species of orchids, but only three are native to Hawai'i—and they are very rare. The pretty lavender vanda you see hanging by the dozens at local lei stands has probably been imported from Thailand.
	MAILE
	Maile, an endemic twining vine with a heady aroma, is sacred to Laka, goddess of the hula. In ancient times, dancers wore maile and decorated hula altars with it to honor Laka. Today, "open" maile leis usually are given to men. Instead of ribbon, interwoven lengths of maile are used at dedications of new businesses. The maile is untied, never snipped, for doing so would symbolically "cut" the company's success.
	'ILIMA
	Designated by Hawai'i's Territorial Legislature in 1923 as the official flower of the island of O'ahu, the golden 'ilima is so delicate it lasts for just a day. Five to seven hundred blossoms are needed to make one garland. Queen Emma, wife of King Kamehameha IV, preferred 'ilima over all other leis, which may have led to the incorrect belief that they were reserved only for royalty.
	PLUMERIA
	This ubiquitous flower is named after Charles Plumier, the noted French botanist who discovered it in Central America in the late 1600s. Plumeria ranks among the most popular leis in Hawai'i because it's fragrant, hardy, plentiful, inexpensive, and requires very little care. Although yellow is the most common color, you'll also find plumeria leis in shades of pink, red, orange, and "rainbow" blends.
	PĪKAKE
	Favored for its fragile beauty and sweet scent, pīkake was introduced from India. In lieu of pearls, many brides in Hawai'i adorn themselves with long, multiple strands of white pīkake. Princess Kaiulani enjoyed showing guests her beloved pīkake and peacocks at Āinahau, her Waikīkī home. Interestingly, pīkake is the Hawaiian word for both the bird and the blossom.
	KUKUI
	The kukui (candlenut) is Hawai'i's state tree. Early Hawaiians strung kukui nuts (which are quite oily) together and burned them for light; mixed burned nuts with oil to make an indelible dye; and mashed roasted nuts to consume as a laxative. Kukui nut leis may not have been made until after Western contact, when the Hawaiians saw black beads from Europe and wanted to imitate them.

Waimea Center. This standard strip mall has a handful of fast-food restaurants, a grocery store, video store, gift shop, and a travel agency. It's highly useful if you're passing through Waimea and need to pick up a few things along the way. ✉ *65-1158 Māmalahoa Hwy., Waimea.*

Hawaiian Arts & Crafts

Dan DeLuz's Woods. Master bowl-turner Dan DeLuz creates works of art from 50 types of exotic wood grown on the Big Island. The shop features a variety of items—from picture frames to jewelry boxes—made from koa, monkeypod, mango, kiawe, and other fine local hardwoods. Dan's wife, Mary Lou, operates the Koa Shop Kaffee restaurant next door. There's another branch south of Hilo in Kurtistown. ✉ *64-1013 Māmalahoa Hwy., Waimea* ☎ *808/885–5856* ✉ *Hwy. 19, Kurtistown* ☎ *808/968–6607.*

Gallery of Great Things. It's not just a cleverly named boutique. At this Parker Square shop, you might fall in love with the Ni'ihau shell lei ranging from $150 to $7,000. More affordable are koa mirrors and other high-quality artifacts from around the Pacific basin. ✉ *65-1279 Kawaihae Rd., Waimea* ☎ *808/885–7706.*

Harbor Gallery. For fine art, furniture, and decorative pieces made with koa and other native woods, be sure to stop here. Though it also carries some of the usual ocean scene schlock, Harbor has one of the better and more unique selections of art on the island. The gallery is next to Harbor Grill. ✉ *Kawaihae Harbor Center, Hwy. 270, Kawaihae* ☎ *808/882–1510.*

Mauna Kea Galleries. The specialty here is rare vintage collectibles, including hula dolls, prints, and koa furniture. ✉ *65-1298 Kawaihae Rd., Waimea* ☎ *808/887–2244.*

Kailua-Kona

Shopping Centers

Coconut Grove Marketplace. Just south of Kona Inn Shopping Village, this meandering labyrinth of airy buildings hides coffee shops, boutiques, ethnic restaurants, and an exquisite gallery. At night locals gather here to watch the outdoor sand volleyball games held in the middle of the marketplace or grab a couple of beers at the sports bar. ✉ *75-5795–75-5825 Ali'i Dr.* ☎ *808/326–2555.*

Crossroads Shopping Center. Shopping in Kailua-Kona has begun to go the way of mainland cities at this complex with a Safeway and a Wal-Mart. But this is also where you'll find Kona Natural Foods, one of the best whole foods stores on the island, and Mana Korean BBQ, a cheap, fast, and tasty mixed-plate favorite. Borders, Jamba Juice, and a second location of A'ama Surf & Sports are right across the street. ✉ *75-1000 Henry St.* ☎ *808/329–4822.*

Keauhou Shopping Center. About 5 mi south of Kailua-Kona, the stores and boutiques here include KTA Superstore, Longs Drugs, and Alapaki's Hawaiian Gifts, along with Kenichi Pacific, a killer sushi restaurant; a multiplex movie theater; and Peaberry & Galette, the only hip café on the island. ✉ *78-6831 Ali'i Dr.* ☎ *808/322–3000.*

King Kamehameha Shopping Mall. Just around the corner from the King Kamehameha Hotel, this outdoor mall includes a wine market and bar, a couple of quality clothing stores, and a popular Internet café. ✉ 75-*5626 Kuakini Hwy.*

Kona Marketplace. On the *makai* side of Ali'i Drive in the heart of Kailua-Kona, extending for an entire block along Kailua Bay, the village is crammed with boutiques selling bright beach wraps and knickknacks. The marketplace, whose tenants seem to change almost annually, is across the street from Tacos El Unico, one of the few authentic Mexican food joints on the island. ✉ *75-5744 Ali'i Dr.* ☎ *808/329–6573.*

Makalapua Center. Just north of Kona, off Highway 19, islanders find bargains at Kmart and island-influenced clothing, jewelry, and housewares at the large Macy's, along with one of the island's largest movie theaters. ✉ *Kamakaeha Ave. at Hwy. 19, south of Kailua-Kona.*

Books

Middle Earth Bookshoppe. This is a great independent bookstore with superb maps and an esoteric collection of literary works. ✉ *75-5719 Ali'i Dr., Kailua-Kona* ☎ *808/329–2123.*

Candies & Chocolates

Kailua Candy Company. The chocolate here is made with locally grown cacao beans from the Original Hawaiian Chocolate Factory, and most truffles and candies incorporate other local ingredients as well (passion fruit truffles—yum). Of course, tasting is part of the fun. Through a glass wall you can watch the chocolate artists at work. ✉ *In the Koloko Industrial Area, Kamanu and Kauholo Sts., Kailua-Kona* ☎ *808/329–2522.*

Clothing

'A'ama Surf & Sport. This boutique has some cool button-ups for men, along with cropped pants in a variety of fabrics and unbelievably cute swimsuits for women (many from the Salinas beachwear label). There's a second location on Henry, across the street from the Crossroads Shopping Center. ✉ *75-5741 Kuakini Hwy.* ☎ *808/326–7890* ✉ *75-1002 Henry St.* ☎ *808/326–7890* 🌐 *www.aamasurf.com.*

Coconut Willie. The only shop downtown to shun beachwear in favor of trendier threads for women, Coconut Willie sells mainland standards like Free People tops, Seven jeans, and Juicy sweats. Prepare to pay the same price or more than you would back home. ✉ *Kona Inn Shopping Village, 75-5744 Ali'i Dr.* ☎ *808/329–6573.*

Flamingo's. Stop by this little shop to browse vintage clothing and antique jewelry. ✉ *Kona Inn Shopping Village, 75-5744 Ali'i Dr.* ☎ *808/329–4122.*

★ **Hilo Hattie.** The west coast outlet of the well-known clothier matches his-and-her aloha wear and carries a huge selection of casual clothes, slippers, jewelry, and souvenirs. Call for free transportation from nearby hotels. ✉ *75-5597 Palani Rd., Kopiko Plaza, Kailua-Kona* ☎ *808/329–7200.*

Honolua Surf Company. Surfer chic, compliments of Roxy, Volcom, and the like: This is a great place to look for a bikini or board shorts or to pick up a cool, casual T-shirt. ✉ *Kona Inn Shopping Village* ☎ *808/329–1001.*

Island Salsa. You'll find plenty of tropical toppers and gift items, as well as cute souvenir T-shirts, at this little shop. ✉ *Kona Inn Shopping Village, 75-5744 Ali'i Dr.* ☎ *808/329–9279.*

Paradise Found. In the upcountry town of Kainaliu, as well as in two of Kailua-Kona's shopping centers, this reputable spot carries contemporary silk and rayon clothing. ✉ *Māmalahoa Hwy. 11, Kainaliu* ☎ *808/322–2111* ✉ *Lanihau Center, 75-5595 Palani Rd., Kailua-Kona* ☎ *808/329–2221* ✉ *Keauhou Shopping Center, 78-6831 Ali'i Dr., Kailua-Kona* ☎ *808/324–1177.*

Sirena. Kealakekua is home to the first high-end designer boutique on the Big Island, a prayer answered for locals who had been forever complaining that they couldn't find "cool" clothes anywhere. Sirena carries squeal-worthy contemporary clothing from designers like Carlos Miele, Barbara Bui, and Catherine Malandrino. If these names are familiar, we don't need to tell you to expect high prices. ✉ *79-7491 Māmalahoa Hwy., Kealakekua* ☎ *808/322–3900.*

Food & Wine Specialties

Kona Wine Market. This popular wine market carries both local and imported varietals, along with a selection of fine cheeses and other gourmet food products, Hawaiian gifts and products (macadamia nuts, coffee, etc.), and the best selection of cigars and tobacco products on the island. As an added bonus, they'll deliver wine and any of their gourmet food products to your hotel or condo. Their Mixx bar is a somewhat recent addition to the Kailua-Kona nightlife scene (not that it really qualifies as a "scene"), and with live music and happy hour deals it has become popular fast. ✉ *King Kamehameha Mall, 75-5626 Kuakini Hwy.* ☎ *808/329–9400* 🌐 *www.konawinemarket.com.*

Hawaiian Arts & Crafts

Alapaki's Hawaiian Gifts. For hula instruments, intricate feather headbands, and other original art, look no farther than this popular shop. ✉ *Keauhou Shopping Center, 78-6831 Ali'i Dr.* ☎ *808/322–2007.*

★ **Antiques and Orchids.** Housed in a great old green building with white trim along Highway 11, this shop lives up to its name, offering shoppers a well-selected collection of antiques and Hawaiiana, interspersed with orchids of various colors and varieties. ✉ *King Kamehameha's Kona Beach Hotel, 81-6224 Mamalahoa Hwy.* ☎ *808/323–9851.*

Hōlualoa Gallery. In the little coffee town of Hōlualoa, this is one of several excellent galleries that crowd the narrow street. It carries stunning raku (Japanese lead-glazed pottery). ✉ *76-5921 Māmalahoa Hwy., Hōlualoa* ☎ *808/322–8484.*

★ **Kimura's Lauhala Shop.** Men can pick up an authentic *lau hala* hat here for some stylish sun protection. ✉ *Māmalahoa Hwy., Hōlualoa* ☎ *808/324–0053.*

Kona Arts Center. There's an entire community of artists at work in this complex; feel free to drop in if the doors are open. ✉ *Māmalahoa Hwy., Hōlualoa.*

★ **Made on the Big Island.** This place is geared to cruise-ship passengers with little time on their hands. It's one-stop shopping for traditional island gifts. You can find quite a few treasures here, such as koa boxes and bonsai trees that may be exported. ✉ *King Kamehameha's Kona Beach Hotel, 75-5660 Palani Rd.* ☎ *808/326–4949.*

ISN'T IT GOOD, HAWAIIAN WOOD?

That pretty wood with the tiger's eye grain you see in shops around the island is koa wood, one of the few species native to Hawai'i (even the palm tree was a transplant). It's expensive and you're not likely to find a good deal on it no matter how hard you look. Why? Koa wood is now protected under a moratorium and you must have a permit to harvest it. Supply, demand, you get the drift.

Markets

Ali'i Gardens Marketplace. More a flea market than a farmers' market, this cluster of about 50 vendor stalls has beautiful tropical flowers, jewelry, clothing, produce, coffee, and even 'ukuleles. It's open Wednesday to Sunday, 9 AM until 5 PM. ✉ *75-6129 Ali'i Dr., 1½ mi south of Kona Inn Shopping Village, Kailua-Kona* ☎ *808/334–1381.*

Keauhou Farmers' Market. Less obvious than the others in its location 5 mi south of Kailua-Kona, this market is packed most Saturdays (8 AM–noon) for good reason: live music, plus local produce (much of it organic, some of it experimental), honey, goat cheese, meat, seafood, flowers, coffee, macadamia nuts, and more. ✉ *78-6831 Ali'i Dr.*

Kona Inn Farmers' Market. This low-key farmers' market is filled with produce, coffee, and macadamia nuts from around the region. It's held in the parking lot of the Kona Inn Shopping Village on Wednesday and Saturday from 7 AM until 3 PM. ✉ *75-7544 Ali'i Dr., park at Kona Inn Shopping Village parking lot, Kailua-Kona.*

Kona International Market. The new kid on the block, housed in an open-air facility, has attracted vendors away from a lot of other island markets to sell flowers, local produce, Hawaiian crafts, clothes, and random collectibles. It's open Tuesday through Sunday, from 9 AM to 5 PM. ✉ *On Luhia St., in Kailua-Kona's Old Industrial Area.*

Hilo

Shopping Centers

Hilo Shopping Center. This rather dated shopping plaza has several air-conditioned shops and restaurants. Great cookies, cakes, and baked goodies are at Lanky's Pastries. There's plenty of free parking. ✉ *Kekuanaoa St. at Kīlauea Ave., Hilo.*

Prince Kūhiō Shopping Plaza. Hilo's most comprehensive mall, Prince Kūhiō Shopping Plaza is where you can find Macy's for fashion, Safeway for food, and Longs Drugs for just about everything else, along with several other shops and boutiques. ✉ *111 E. Puainako St., at Hwy. 11, Hilo* ☎ *808/959–3555.*

Waiakea Center. Here you can find a Borders Books & Music, Island Naturals, and a Wal-Mart. If all the shopping makes you hungry, there's also a food court. ✉ *Maka'ala St. and Kanoelehua Ave., across from Prince Kūhiō Shopping Plaza, at Hwy. 11, Hilo* ☎ *808/792–7225.*

Books & Magazines

Basically Books. This shop stocks one of Hawai'i's largest selections of maps and charts, including topographical and relief maps. It also has Hawaiiana books, with great choices for children. ✉ *160 Kamehameha Ave., Hilo* ☎ *808/961–0144 or 800/903–6277.*

Candies & Chocolate

★ **Big Island Candies.** This chocolate factory lets you tour and taste before you buy. ✉ *585 Hinano St., Hilo* ☎ *808/935–8890.*

Clothing

★ **Hilo Hattie.** The east coast outlet of the well-known clothier is slightly smaller than its Kailua-Kona cousin, but still offers plenty of the same his-and-her aloha wear, casual clothes, slippers, jewelry, and souvenirs. ✉ *Prince Kūhiō Shopping Plaza, 111 E. Puainako St., Hilo* ☎ *808/961–3077.*

★ **Sig Zane Designs.** This acclaimed boutique sells distinctive island wearables with bold colors and motifs. ✉ *122 Kamehameha Ave., Hilo* ☎ *808/935–7077.*

Gifts

Dragon Mama. Step into this popular downtown Hilo spot to find authentic Japanese fabrics, futons, and antiques, along with a limited but elegant selection of clothing, sleepwear, and slippers for women. ✉ *266 Kamehameha Ave., Hilo* ☎ *808/934–9081.*

Ets'ko. You'll find Japanese tea sets, exquisite ceramics, and affordable bamboo ware here. ✉ *35 Waiānuenue Ave., Hilo* ☎ *808/961–3778.*

Fuku-Bonsai Cultural Center. In addition to selling and shipping miniature *brassaia lava* plantings and other bonsai plants, this place on the way to Volcano has interesting exhibits of different ethnic styles of pruning. ✉ *Ola'a Rd., Kurtistown* ☎ *808/982–9880.*

Hilo Coffee Mill. In addition to a fantastic coffee farm tour, the Hilo Coffee Mill sells coffee from a variety of local producers, along with locally made baked goods, candies, artwork, and gifts. ✉ *17-995 Volcano Road, between mile markers 12 and 13, Mountain View* ☎ *808/968–1333* 🌐 *www.hilocoffeemill.com.*

Hoaloha. If you're driving north from Hilo, take time to browse through this shop and pick up a colorful *pareu* (beach wrap). ✉ *Last Chance Store, off Hwy. 240, Kukuihaele* ☎ *808/775–0502.*

Most Irresistible Shop. This place lives up to its name by stocking unique gifts from around the Pacific, be it coconut-flavored butter or whimsi-

GROWN WITH ALOHA

The Big Island is home to more farmers' markets than most cities, each offering a different range of goods, but all providing at the very least a good place to pick up fresh produce while you're in town (especially helpful if you're staying in a condo). Not surprisingly, locally grown mango, papaya, pineapple, passion fruit, coconut, and guava are available in abundance at great prices, but you can also find delicious avocados, organic peppers, fantastic goat cheese, and, of course, coffee.

Hawai'i's farmers are experimenting with hundreds of varieties of avocados and citrus, and with exotic fruits such as poha berries, bilimbi, and mamey sapoy. If you come across unfamiliar fruits, try them—particularly the sweet, fluffy pulp inside the yard-long ice cream bean. Because of government restrictions, these fruits generally can't leave the island, so this is your chance to sample them.

The markets located in Kailua-Kona and Hilo are listed under the corresponding shopping sections; the following markets are scattered about the Big Island. You might happily stumble upon them as you explore the coasts.

ON THE KONA SIDE

Hawaiian Homesteaders Assn. Farmers' Market. Check out the crafts sold here in the Kuhio Hale Building before you head to Waimea's more expensive stores. Produce, flowers, plants, and baked goods are also available. Open 7 AM to noon every Saturday.

Ka'u Farmers' Market. On a trip to the South Point, stock up on local produce and handmade baked goods at this market held at the Na'alehu Theater every Saturday, 8 AM to noon.

Under the Banyans Farmers' Market. Fresh produce, seasonal fruit, plants, and craft items are sold at this market way up north in the village of Hāwī. It's open Saturdays from 7:30 AM until 1 PM.

ON THE HILO SIDE

Downtown Honok'a Farmers' Market. This good old-fashioned farmers' market in the midst of a charming old plantation town is a good stop during a drive up the Hāmākua Coast. It begins at 8 AM on Saturdays.

The following markets are all south of Hilo.

Kea'au Village Farmers' Market. Fresh local farm produce featuring super sweet corn and flowers daily from 7 AM to 5 PM; on Fridays, vendors also sell handmade Hawaiian arts and crafts.

Maku'u Farmers' Market. There's food and produce here, but what differentiates it from the rest are the Hawaiian crafts, plants, jewelry, shells, ethnic and recycled clothing, records/CDs, and books. It's along the Kea'au/Pāhoa Highway, Sundays 8 AM to noon.

Pāhoa Village Farmers' Market. A great market, held in a large, covered outdoor space with local produce, prepared foods, coffee, clothing, and live music 9 AM to 3 PM every Sunday.

Volcano Village Farmers Market. A favorite on the east side of the island. Local produce, flowers, prepared foods, baked goods, and an occasional clothing swap, in the Cooper Center, every Sunday 8:30–11 AM.

cal wind chimes. ✉ *256 Kamehameha Ave.* ☎ *808/935–9644* ✉ *Prince Kūhiō Shopping Plaza, 111 E. Puainako St., at Hwy. 11, Hilo* ☎ *808/959–6515.*

Markets

★ **Hilo Farmers' Market.** The farmers here sell a profusion of tropical flowers, high-quality produce, and macadamia nuts. This colorful, open-air market—the most popular in the state—opens for business Wednesday and Saturday from 6:30 AM to 2:30 PM. ✉ *Kamehameha Ave. and Mamo St., Hilo.*

★ **Panaewa Hawaiian Homestead Farmers' Market.** The bonus here is the fresh fish, but there are also the usual farmers' market produce vendors 8 AM–5 PM every day on the sidewalk in front of the Hilo Wal-Mart. ✉ *325 Makaala St., Hilo.*

★ **Rainbow Falls Market Place.** A little less crowded than the main Hilo market, the Rainbow Falls market has the added bonus of a free hula show. Mondays and Thursdays, 8 AM to 4 PM. ✉ *Across from Rainbow Falls, Hilo* ☎ *808/933–9173.*

Hāmākua Coast

Shopping Centers

Kaloko Industrial Park. Developed for local consumers, this shopping plaza has outlets such as Costco Warehouse and Home Depot. It can be useful for practical purchases (food from Costco can be a good deal if you're staying in a condo for a week or more) and the occasional surprise gift item (you don't have to tell them you got it at the Hawai'i Costco). ✉ *Off Hwy. 19 and Hina Lani St., near Kona Airport.*

Gifts

Glass from the Past. The best place to stop for a quirky gift or just to poke around a truly unique store chock full of a colorful assortment of old bottles, plus antiques, vintage clothing, and ephemera. ✉ *28-1672 Old Mamalahoa Hwy. # A, Honomū* ☎ *808/963–6449.*

Kama'aina Woods. A great little shop in charming Honoka'a, and the only place in Hawai'i (possibly in the world) where you can pick up your very own set of "Huli Hands," salad tongs shaped like hula hands and made from koa wood. If the Huli Hands don't get you, their renowned koa wood bowls surely will. ✉ *Off Hwy. 19, Honoka'a* ☎ *808/775–7722* 🌐 *www.hulihands.com.*

Waipi'o Valley Artworks. In this remote gallery you can find finely crafted wooden bowls, koa furniture, paintings, and jewelry—all made by local artists, plus a great little café where you can pick up a sandwich or ice cream before descending into the valley. ✉ *Off Hwy. 240, Kukuihaele* ☎ *808/775–0958.*

Woodshop Gallery. This pleasant surprise in Honomū, run by local artists Peter and Janette McLaren, showcases their woodwork and photography collections along with beautiful ceramics, woodwork, photography, glass, and fine art from other Big Island artists. The McClarens also serve up sandwiches and ice cream to hungry tourists from nearby 'Akaka Falls.

CLOSE UP

Hawaiian Healing

The Hawaiians have held healers in high regard since ancient times, and many of their old traditions still hold sway, even in the fanciest of resort spas. Every spa on the island blends some aspect of local culture and ingredients into its menu, from traditional Hawaiian standbys like *lomi lomi* massage and *kukui* (candlenut) oil to lesser-known ancient rituals like *opu huli* (literally "stomach turn"), an abdominal massage that is great for gastritis, jet lag, or menstrual cramps. There are also Hawaiian versions of popular therapies: imagine a hot stone massage done with lava rocks and warm coconut oil. Following are a few of our favorite Hawaiian healing rituals and the best places to experience them first-hand:

***Lomi lomi* massage:** This traditional form of massage is intended to relieve physical *and* emotional stress. Our favorite is administered by the *kahune* (specialists) of the Spa Without Walls at the Fairmont Orchid, on the beach.

Healing waters: For their healing rituals, the ancient Hawaiians often used Coconut Island, in Hilo, because of the restorative powers of its spring waters. You can visit any time for free. On the Kona side of the island, Mamalahoa Hot Tubs provides a slightly more modern experience with luxurious soaks in beautiful wooden tubs.

La'au Lapa'au: Ancient Hawaiian herbal medicine is utilized to great effect these days in a number of fine skin treatments, like the Alo Lani treatment at the Four Seasons Spa Hualālai, which includes a warm kukui and coconut back and neck massage and a soothing facial massage treatment utilizing noni juice, known throughout the islands for its healing powers.

✉ 28-1692 Old Government Rd., Honomū ☎ 808/963–6363 🌐 www.woodshopgallery.com.

6

SPAS

The Big Island's spa directors have done their homework and produced menus full of "only in Hawai'i" treatments well worth a holiday splurge. Local specialties include *lomi lomi* massages, hot lava stone massages, and scrubs and wraps that incorporate plenty of coconut, orchids, ginger, and macadamia nuts. Expect to also find Swedish and deep tissue massages and, at some spas, Thai massage. And in romantic Hawai'i, couples can be pampered side by side in a variety of offerings. TIP→ ***Lomi lomi* massage can be a little too close to deep tissue massage for some, but most *kahune* (practitioners) are happy to adjust the pressure to your needs.** The only full-service spas on the Big Island are associated with the resorts on the west coast. With the exception of the Four Seasons Spa at Hualālai, the resort spas are open to anyone. In fact, many of the hotels outsource management of their spas, and there is no difference in price for guests and non-guests, although guests have the added bonus of receiving in-room services.

Ho'ōla Spa at the Sheraton Keauhou Bay. The Sheraton Keauhou Bay occupies one of the prettier corners of the island, with an unbeatable view from most parts of the hotel. The Ho'ōla Spa, which opened in 2005, takes full advantage of its location with several windows facing the bay. The spa menu includes a variety of locally influenced treatments. The warm lava-rock massage is a little slice of heaven, and the facials are relaxing and rejuvenating. The packages are an excellent deal, combining several services for far less than you would pay à la carte. For couples, the spa offers an ocean-side massage that takes place on a balcony overlooking the water, followed by a dip in a whirlpool bath. ✉ *78-128 Ehukai St., Kailua-Kona* ☎ *808/930–4900* 🌐 *www.sheratonkeauhou.com* ☞ *$110 50-min lomi lomi massage; $215–$345 half-day packages. Hair salon, hot tub, sauna, steam room. Services: aromatherapy, body scrubs and wraps, facials, massages, waxing.*

Kalona Salon & Spa at the Outrigger Keauhou Beach Resort. This spa is a great place to get a massage or body treatment for much less than you'd likely pay at the big resorts. Though not quite as nice as the bigger facilities, it's simple and clean, on the ocean, and staffed with well-trained therapists. The spa offers facials using its own line of products made from island ingredients. Be careful if you have touchy skin. ✉ *78-6740 Ali'i Dr., Kailua-Kona* ☎ *808/322–3441 or 800/462–6262* 🌐 *www.outrigger.com* ☞ *$85 50-min lomi lomi massage; $115–$220 half-day packages. Services: facials, massage.*

★ **Kohala Sports Club & Spa at the Hilton Waikoloa Village.** The orchids that run riot in the rain forests of the Big Island suffuse the signature treatments at the Kohala Sports Club & Spa. By the end of the Orchid Isle Wrap, you're completely immersed in the scent and in bone-deep relaxation. The island's volcanic character is also expressed in several treatments, as well as in the design of the lava-rock soaking tubs. Locker rooms are outfitted with private changing rooms for the modest and a wealth of beauty and bath products for the adventurous. The extensive hair and nail salon could satisfy even Bridezilla with its updo consultations and luxe pedicure stations. The nearby ocean-side cabanas are the perfect venue for a massage on the beach. The fitness center is well-equipped, but group classes that roam across the beautifully manicured resort grounds—like tai chi on the lawn or walking meditation at Buddha Point—are much more appealing. ✉ *Hilton Waikoloa Village, 425 Waikoloa Beach Dr., Kohala Coast* ☎ *808/886–2828 or 800/445–8667* 🌐 *www.kohalaspa.com* ☞ *$135 50-min lomi lomi massage; $399–$431 half-day packages. Hair salon, hot tubs (indoor and outdoor), sauna, steam room. Gym with: cardiovascular machines, free weights, weight-training equipment. Services: acupuncture, aromatherapy, body scrubs and wraps, facials, hydromassage, massage. Classes and programs: body sculpting, fitness analysis, personal training, Pilates, Spinning, step aerobics, tai chi, yoga.*

★ **Mamalahoa Hot Tubs and Massage.** Tucked into a residential neighborhood above Kealekekua, this little gem is a welcome alternative to the large resort spas. Soaking tubs are made of the finest quality wood, tropical plants and flowers abound, and each tub is enclosed in its own little gazebo, with portholes in the roof for your star-gazing pleasure.

Tastefully laid out and run, there's no seedy "hot tub party" vibe here, just a pleasant soak followed by, if you like, an hour-long massage. Mamalahoa offers *lomi lomi,* Swedish, deep tissue, and a Hawaiian hot stone massage performed with lava rocks collected from around the island. In addition to its secret hideaway ambience, Mamalahoa's prices are lower than any other spa on the island. ✉ *Kealekekua, south of Kailua-Kona* ☎ *808/323–2288* 🌐 *www.mamalahoa-hottubs.com* ☞ *$30 60-min soak; $85 30-min soak plus 60-min lomi lomi, Swedish, or deep tissue massage; $135 30-min soak plus 90-min hot stone massage* ⏲ *By appointment only. Open Wed.–Sat. noon–8 PM.*

★ **Mandara Spa at the Waikoloa Beach Marriott Resort.** A brand spanking new two-story spa overlooking the hotel's main pool with a distant view of the ocean, Mandara offers a very complete if not unique spa menu, with more available facial options than you'll find at the island's other spas. Mandara operates spas throughout the world and on a number of cruise lines, and they are managing this one for Marriott, using Elemis and La Therapie products in spa and salon treatments. The spa menu contains the usual suspects—*lomi lomi,* a variety of facials, scrubs, and wraps—but they do incorporate local ingredients where appropriate (lemon and ginger in the scrubs, warm coconut milk in the wraps), and the new facilities are beautiful. ✉ *69-275 Waikoloa Beach Dr., Kohala Coast* ☎ *808/886–8191* 🌐 *www.mandaraspa.com* ☞ *$115 50-min lomi lomi massage; $215–$400 half-day packages. Hair salon, steam room.*

Mauna Lani Spa. If you're looking for a one-of-a-kind experience, this is your destination. Most treatments take place in outdoor, bamboo-floor *hales* (houses) surrounded by lava rock. Incredible therapists offer a mix of the old standbys (*lomi lomi* massage, moisturizing facials) and innovative treatments, many of which are heavily influenced by ancient traditions and incorporate local products. One exfoliating body treatment is self-administered in one of the outdoor saunas—a great choice for people who aren't too keen on therapists seeing them in their birthday suits. Watsu therapy takes place in an amazing pool filled by the adjacent lava tube. Meant to re-create the feeling of being in a womb, the hour-long therapy is essentially an underwater massage. You feel totally weightless, thanks to some artfully applied weights and the buoyancy of the warm salt water. It's a great treatment for people with disabilities that keep them from enjoying a traditional massage. The aesthetic treatments on the menu incorporate high-end products from Epicuran and Emminence, so a facial will have a real and lasting therapeutic effect on your skin. The spa also offers a full regimen of fitness and yoga classes, as well as more mainland-style procedures like Botox and Restylane injections. ✉ *Mauna Lani Resort, 68-1400 Mauna Lani Dr., Kohala Coast* ☎ *808/885–6622* 🌐 *www.maunalani.com* ☞ *$135 50-min lomi lomi massage; $275–$425 half-day packages. Hair salon, hot tubs (indoor and outdoor), sauna, steam room. Gym with: cardiovascular machines, free weights, weight-training equipment. Services: aquatic therapy, baths, body wraps, Botox, facials, massage, Restylane, scrubs. Classes and programs: aerobics, kickboxing, personal training, Pilates, Spinning, weight training, yoga.*

INDEPENDENT CONTRACTORS

Sometimes all you want is a good massage, preferably on the beach–no high prices, herbal tea, or aromatherapy required. Following are a few of our favorite local practitioners. They work by appointment only.

An Ocean Front Therapeutic Massage. Let the marvelous Bea work out your kinks as you listen to the ocean just a few feet away. This is not on the beach, but it is ocean front, with an ocean view and windows open so it's pretty darn close. ✉ *Kona Inn Shopping Village Suite 250, Kailua-Kona* ☎ *808/329-8912* ☞ *$80 60-min massage.*

Healing Arts Alliance. If you're a deep tissue fan, look no further than Scott Miller. Specializing in rolfing and deep tissue massage, Scott is also a licensed acupuncturist with several years' experience. His colleague, Lynn Vrooman, does gentler *lomi lomi* massages for those who prefer a gentler touch. ✉ *103 Kalakaua St., Hilo* ☎ *808/934-7030* ☞ *Scott: $50 60-min deep tissue massage. Lynn: $50 90-min lomi lomi massage.*

Pilates and Yoga Centre of Kona. Although best paired with a yoga or Pilates session, Laura Crittendon's lomi lomi is tough to beat. ✉ *75-5995 Kuakini Hwy., Suite 900, Kona* ☎ *808/329-3211* 🌐 *www.konapilates.com* ☞ *$75 60-min massage.*

Paul Brown Salon & Spa at the Hāpuna Beach Prince Hotel. It's not unusual for locals to drive an hour each way to get their hair cut here. Paul Brown has been in the business for 30 years, and he now has three locations in Hawai'i. Hair is still the specialty, but it's not just a salon. The full-service spa—nicely designed to let in lots of light—has an extensive menu of massages, facials, and body treatments. The well-run facility also has a trained practitioner who administers expert acupuncture treatments. It's the best place for waxing in case you didn't have time before you left home. You can use the gym at the Hāpuna Golf Course's clubhouse, accessible via a free shuttle. ✉ *62-100 Kauna'oa Dr., Kohala Coast* ☎ *808/880–1111 or 800/882–6060* 🌐 *www.princeresortshawaii.com* ☞ *$115 50-min lomi lomi massage; $240–$380 half-day package. Hair salon, sauna, steam room. Services: acupuncture, body wraps, facials, massage. Classes and programs: aerobics, yoga.*

Spa Without Walls at the Fairmont Orchid Hawai'i. This is possibly the best massage on the island, partially due to having the best setting. Massages at the Spa Without Walls are either facing the ocean or a waterfall. Though most people will probably opt for the ocean, both settings are absolutely peaceful. There are other great treatments as well, including facials, fragrant herbal wraps, and coffee and vanilla scrubs, but the massages are the best thing going. ✉ *Fairmont Orchid Hawai'i, 1 N. Kanikū Dr., Kohala Coast* ☎ *808/885–2000* 🌐 *www.fairmont.com* ☞ *$155 45-min lomi lomi massage; $285–$295 half-day packages. Sauna, steam room.*

Gym with: cardiovascular machines, free weights, weight-training equipment. Services: baths, body wraps, facials, massage, scrubs. Classes and programs: aquaerobics, guided walks, meditation, personal training, yoga.

The Spa at Hualālai. The Spa at Hualālai is for the exclusive use of Four Seasons Resort guests, so you can sign everything to your room and never have a problem booking a treatment. Though it can feel like a New York spa dropped onto a tropical island, the Spa at Hualālai does include outdoor massage *hales*, which affords more of a Hawaiian experience. The therapists are also top-notch, and a real effort has been made to incorporate local traditions and ingredients like honey, kokui nuts, and coconut into spa treatments. ✉ *100 Ka'ūpūlehu Dr., Ka'ūpūlehu/Kona* ☎ *808/325–8000* 🌐 *www.fourseasons.com* ☞ *$120 50-min massage; $145 body scrub; $120 facials. Hair salon, outdoor hot tubs, sauna, steam room. Gym with: cardiovascular machines, free weights, weight-training equipment. Services: body treatments, facials, massage. Classes and programs: personal training, Pilates, Spinning, tai chi, yoga.*

Entertainment & Nightlife

WORD OF MOUTH

"The old town of Kona is pretty funky and simple. It's right on the water and there are many open-air restaurants. But nothing super fancy." –JPJH

"The Big Island is (or at least can be) about Hawaiian history and culture, an experience which has nothing to do with miniature golf courses and extensive nightlife. Both Kailua-Kona and Hilo fold up their sidewalks precisely at ten (well, nine actually) and people who live there are not seen again." –fdecarlo

www.fodors.com/forums

By Amy Westervelt

IF YOU'RE THE SORT OF PERSON who doesn't come alive until after dark, you might be a little lonely on the Big Island. Blame it on the plantation heritage. People did their cane-raising in the morning. Still, there are a few lively bars on the island, a handful of great local playhouses, half a dozen or so movie houses (including those that play foreign and independent films), and plenty of musical entertainment to keep you occupied. And let's not forget the lū'aus. These fantastic dance and musical performances are combined with some of the best meals on the island and are plenty of fun for the whole family.

ENTERTAINMENT

Festivals

There is a festival dedicated to just about everything on the Big Island. Some of them are small community affairs, but a handful of film, food, and music festivals provide quality entertainment for visitors and locals alike. The following is a list of our favorites:

Black & White Night. This lovely annual outdoor party is in downtown Hilo. The stores stay open late, the sidewalks are dotted with live jazz bands, and everyone dresses in black and white, some in shorts and tees and others in gowns and tuxes, to enter the "Best Dressed" contest. ☎ *808/933–9772* ⏲ *Early Nov.*

Chinese New Year. Hilo throws a big free party complete with live music, food, drums, and fireworks downtown to commemorate this holiday every year. There's a smaller celebration along Ali'i Drive in Kona as well. ☎ *808/933–9772* ⏲ *Feb.*

Kona Brewers Festival. At this great annual party, roughly 30 breweries and 25 restaurants offer samples and live music, fire dancers, and fashion shows. ☎ *808/331–3033* 🌐 *www.konabrewersfestival.com* ⏲ *Early Mar.*

Kona Coffee Cultural Festival. The oldest food festival in Hawai'i brings together a variety of events over a ten-day period, but our favorite is the coffee recipe cooking contest. Coffee chili is one of the best things you've never tasted. 🌐 *www.konacoffeefest.com* ⏲ *Early Nov.*

★ **Merrie Monarch Festival.** The mother of all Big Island festivals, the Merrie Monarch celebrates all things hula and completely overtakes Hilo for one fantastic weekend a year. The largest event of its kind in the world honors the legacy of King David Kalākaua, Hawai'i's last king and the man responsible for reviving a lot of the fading Hawaiian traditions including the hula (of which he was a big fan). The festival is staged at the spacious Edith Kanaka'ole Stadium during the first week following Easter Sunday. Hula *hālau* (schools) compete in various classes of ancient and modern dance styles. You need to reserve accommodations and tickets up to a year in advance. If you're planning on being in Hilo during this time of year but not attending the festival, know that most accommodations will be booked about a year out and plan accordingly. ☎ *808/935–9168* 🌐 *www.merriemonarchfestival.org* ⏲ *Apr.*

A Taste of the Hawaiian Range Food and Agricultural Festival. Since 1995, this culinary event has been giving locals and visitors a taste of what

CLOSE UP

Roasted Pigs, Poi & Hula: the Lū'au Explained

LARGE PARTIES HAVE ALWAYS been a part of Hawaiian culture. In ancient times they were referred to as *aha-aina* (gathering for a meal). In the 1800s, King Kamehameha II broke the entrenched *kapu* (a system of social rules and taboos) by dining with women. That single action abolished the kapu system entirely, lifting the ban not only on men and women eating together but also on what types of food women could eat. Subsequent large feasts included everyone in the community sharing the same food, and the word lū'au was chosen to describe these new gatherings.

Lū'au actually referred to the edible leaves of a young taro plant, which were used to wrap various foods before placing them in the *imu* (an oven dug into the ground). Taro is still incorporated into the modern-day lū'au in the form of *poi* (pounded taro root)—usually the one thing left virtually untouched on every guest's plate. Let's just say it's an acquired taste.

If you think the modern-day version of the lū'au is large and extravagant, keep in mind that the Hawaiian royal lū'au blew today's parties out of the water. King Kalakaua, known as the "Merry Monarch" for his love of parties and dance (Hilo's annual hula festival is named after him), invited over 1,500 guests to his 50th birthday lū'au, and fed them in shifts of 500.

7

the Island's best chefs and farms have to offer, from grass-fed beef and bison to organic produce, cheese, chocolates, and coffee. ☎ *808/322-4892* 🌐 *www.ctahr.hawaii.edu/taste* 🕓 *Early Oct.*

Lū'au & Polynesian Revues

KOHALA COAST & WAIKOLOA

Hilton Waikoloa Village. The Hilton seats 400 people outdoors at the Kamehameha Court, where the acclaimed Polynesian group Tihati performs a lively show. A buffet dinner provides samplings of Hawaiian food as well as fish, beef, and chicken to appeal to all tastes. ✉ *425 Waikoloa Beach Dr., Waikoloa* ☎ *808/886-1234* 🌐 *www.hiltonwaikoloavillage.com* 🎫 *$74* 🕓 *Fri. at 6.*

★ **Kona Village Resort.** In its utter isolation, the lū'au here is one of the most authentic and traditional on the Islands. As in other lū'au, activities include the steaming of a whole pig in the *imu* (ground oven). The Wednesday night show focuses solely on Hawaiian traditions and music, while Friday night incorporates Polynesian dancing, music, and traditions as well. The dancing, done on a stage over a lagoon, is magical. ✉ *Queen Ka'ahumanu Hwy., 6 mi north of Kona International Airport, Kailua-Kona* ☎ *808/325-5555 or 808/325-4273* 🌐 *www.konavillage.com* 🎫 *$84, including open bar* 🕓 *Wed. and Fri. from 5; walking tour at 5:30, imu ceremony at 6:30, dinner at 7, show at 8.*

Mauna Kea Beach Hotel. Every Tuesday, on the gracious North Pointe Lū'au Grounds of the Mauna Kea Beach Hotel, you can sample the best of Hawaiian cuisine while listening to the enchanting songs of Nani Lim. Chefs come together here to create a traditional Hawaiian *pa'ina* (din-

Continued on page 153

MORE THAN A FOLK DANCE

Hula has been called "the heartbeat of the Hawaiian people." Also, "the world's best-known, most misunderstood dance." Both true. Hula isn't just dance. It is storytelling. No words, no hula.

Chanter Edith McKinzie calls it "an extension of a piece of poetry." In its adornments, implements, and customs, hula integrates every important Hawaiian cultural practice: poetry, history, genealogy, craft, plant cultivation, martial arts, religion, protocol. So when 19th-century Christian missionaries sought to eradicate a practice they considered depraved, they threatened more than just a folk dance.

With public performance outlawed and private hula practice discouraged, hula went underground for a generation, to rural villages. The fragile verbal link by which culture was transmitted from teacher to student hung by a thread. Even increasing literacy did not help because hula's practitioners were—and, to a degree, still are—a secretive and protected circle.

As if that weren't bad enough, vaudeville, Broadway, and Hollywood got hold of the hula, giving it the glitz treatment in an unbroken line from "Oh, How She Could Wicky Wacky Woo" to "Rock-A-Hula Baby." Hula became shorthand for paradise: fragrant flowers, lazy hours. Ironically, this development assured that hundreds of Hawaiians could make a living performing and teaching hula. Many danced *'auana* (modern form) in performance; but taught *kahiko* (traditional), quietly, at home or in hula schools.

Today, 30 years after the cultural revival known as the Hawaiian Renaissance, language immersion programs have assured a new generation of proficient—and even eloquent—chanters, song-writers, and translators. Visitors can see more, and more authentic, hula than anytime in the last 200 years.

Like the culture of which it is the beating heart, hula has survived.

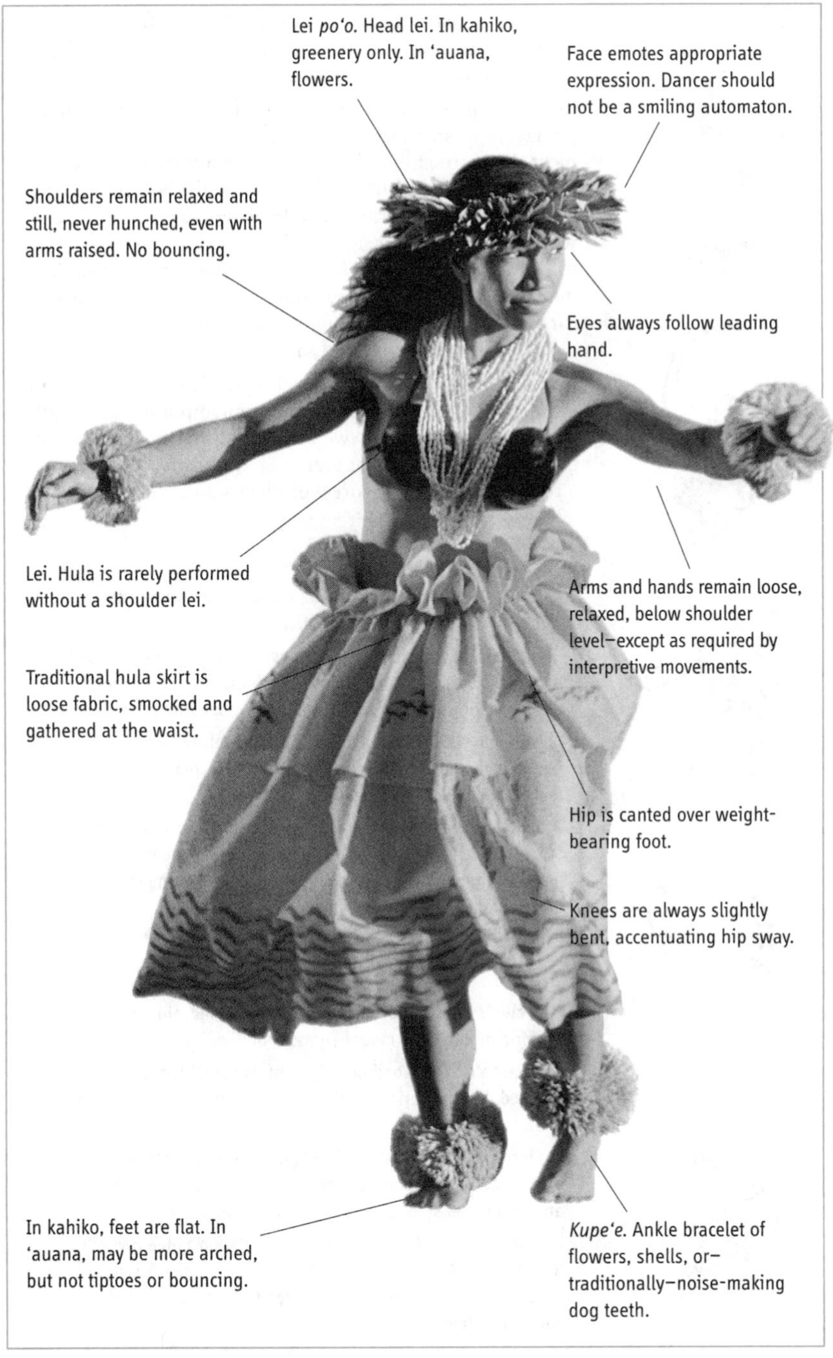

Lei *po'o*. Head lei. In kahiko, greenery only. In 'auana, flowers.

Face emotes appropriate expression. Dancer should not be a smiling automaton.

Shoulders remain relaxed and still, never hunched, even with arms raised. No bouncing.

Eyes always follow leading hand.

Lei. Hula is rarely performed without a shoulder lei.

Arms and hands remain loose, relaxed, below shoulder level—except as required by interpretive movements.

Traditional hula skirt is loose fabric, smocked and gathered at the waist.

Hip is canted over weight-bearing foot.

Knees are always slightly bent, accentuating hip sway.

In kahiko, feet are flat. In 'auana, may be more arched, but not tiptoes or bouncing.

Kupe'e. Ankle bracelet of flowers, shells, or—traditionally—noise-making dog teeth.

BASIC MOTIONS

Speak or Sing

Moon or Sun

Grass Shack or House

Mountains or Heights

Love or Caress

At backyard parties, hula is performed in bare feet and street clothes, but in performance, adornments play a key role, as do rhythm-keeping implements.

In hula kahiko (traditional style), the usual dress is multiple layers of stiff fabric (often with a Pellon lining, which most closely resembles *kapa*, the paper-like bark cloth of the Hawaiians). These wrap tightly around the bosom but flare below the waist to form a skirt. In pre-contact times, dancers wore only kapa skirts. Monarchy-period hula is performed in voluminous Mother Hubbard mu'umu'u or high-necked muslin blouses and gathered skirts. Men wear loincloths or, for monarchy period, white or gingham shirts and black pants—sometimes with red sashes.

In hula 'auana (modern), dress for women can range from grass skirts and strapless tops to contemporary tea-length dresses. Men generally wear aloha shirts, but sometimes grass skirts over pants or even everyday gear. (One group at a recent competition wore wetsuits to do a surfing song!)

SURPRISING HULA FACTS

- Grass skirts are not traditional; workers from Kiribati (the Gilbert Islands) brought this custom to Hawai'i.
- In olden-day Hawai'i, *mele* (songs) for hula were composed for every occasion—name songs for babies, dirges for funerals, welcome songs for visitors, celebrations of favorite pursuits.
- Hula *ma'i* is a traditional hula form in praise of a noble's genitals; the power of the *'ali* (royalty) to procreate gave *mana* (spiritual power) to the entire culture.
- Hula students in old Hawai'i adhered to high standards: scrupulous cleanliness, no sex, daily cleansing rituals, certain food prohibitions, and no contact with the dead. They were fined if they broke the rules.

WHERE TO WATCH

- **Brown's Beach House** at the Fairmont Orchid. Hula dancers perform nightly on a moonlit grassy knoll.
- **Kamaha'o "The Wondrous Myths of Hawai'i."** The island's most talented dancers perform in this weekly lū'au production at the Sheraton Keauhou.
- **Merrie Monarch Festival.** The king of all hula festivals, held annually the first Thursday after Easter Sunday in Hilo. Tickets are hard to get so book as early as possible.
- **Volcano Center & Volcanoes National Park Na Mea Hawai'i Hula Kahiko.** A series of free public performances takes place outdoors facing Halema'uma'u crater, the sacred home of the volcano goddess Pele.

ner feast), which includes the classic *kālua* (roasted in an underground oven) pig. ✉ *62-100 Mauna Kea Beach Dr., Kohala Coast* ☎ *808/882–7222* 🌐 *www.maunakeabeachhotel.com* *$76* ⏲ *Tues. at 6.*

Waikoloa Beach Marriott. At this celebration, entertainment includes a Samoan fire dance as well as songs and dances of various Pacific cultures. Traditional Hawaiian dishes are served alongside more familiar fare. ✉ *69-275 Waikoloa Beach Dr., Waikoloa* ☎ *808/886–6789* 🌐 *www.marriott.com* *$67, including open bar* ⏲ *Wed. and Sun. 5–8:30.*

KAILUA-KONA **King Kamehameha's Kona Beach Hotel.** Witness the royal court arrive by canoe at the Island Breeze Lū'au, a beachfront event, which includes a 22-item buffet, an open bar, and a show. ✉ *75-5660 Palani Rd., Kailua-Kona* ☎ *808/326–4969 or 808/329–8111* 🌐 *www.islandbreezeluau.com* *$62.50* ⏲ *Tues.–Thurs. and Sun. 5:30–8:30.*

Royal Kona Resort. This resort lights lū'au torches for a full Polynesian show and a Hawaiian-style oceanfront buffet three times a week. ✉ *75-5852 Ali'i Dr., Kailua-Kona* ☎ *808/329–3111, Ext. 4* 🌐 *www.konaluau.com* *$62* ⏲ *Mon., Wed., Fri., and Sat. at 5.*

Sheraton Keauhou Bay. The newest addition to the Big Island's lū'au scene, Kamaha'o–The Wondrous Myths of Hawai'i, adds a little Cirque du Soleil to the traditional Hawaiian formula, mixing Hawaiian language, story telling, and traditional hula with modern dance and acrobatics to create a highly entertaining theatrical display. And the open bar doesn't hurt either. ✉ *75-5852 Ali'i Dr., Kailua-Kona* ☎ *808/930–4900* 🌐 *www.sheratonkeauhou.com* *$79.95* ⏲ *Mon., Wed., Fri., and Sat. at 5.*

Sunset Cruises

★ **Captain Beans' Polynesian Dinner Cruise.** Sometimes called "the booze cruise," this is the ever-popular standby in sunset dinner cruises. You can't miss it—as the sun sets, look out over the water and you'll see a big gaudy boat with distinctive orange sails. This cruise is corny, and dinner is nothing special, but it's an experience, with unlimited drinks and a Hawaiian show. This is for adults only. ✉ *Kailua Pier, Kailua-Kona* ☎ *808/329–2955 or 800/831–5541* 🌐 *www.robertshawaii.com* *$60* ⏲ *Tues.–Sun. at 5:15.*

★ **Hawaiian Sunset Pūpū Cruise and Dolphin Adventure.** Blue Sea Cruises offers a classed-up alternative to the booze cruise, with soothing Hawaiian music, elegant pūpūs, tropical juices and cocktails, and a focus on the sunset and the scenery, and the chance to see spinner dolphins (and whales from November to May). ✉ *Kailua Pier, Kailua-Kona* ☎ *808/331–8875* 🌐 *www.blueseacruisesinc.com* *$60* ⏲ *Tues.–Sun., check in at 4:40 PM.*

Film

Aloha Spirit Film Festival. This independent film festival, held in mid-September, screens cutting-edge documentaries, shorts, and feature films from throughout the islands. Screenings and festivities are held at the Aloha Theatre in Kainaliu and the Sheraton Keauhou Bau just south of Kailua-Kona. 🌐 *www.alohafilmfest.com.*

Louis Vuitton Hawai'i International Film Festival. Showing throughout the Islands and in Hilo (Palace Theater) and Kainaliu (Aloha Theatre) on the Big Island, this festival has been blazing trails in the exhibition of Asian and Pacific feature films since 1981. It runs for about 10 days in late October. 🌐 *www.hiff.org.*

KONA SIDE **Keauhou 7 Cinemas.** This is a splendid seven-theater complex, and there are several pre- or post-movie food options in the center. ✉ *Keauhou Shopping Center, 78-6831 Ali'i Dr.* ☎ *808/324–7200.*

Makalapua Stadium Cinemas. The 10-screen theater has stadium seating and digital surround sound. ✉ *Makalapua Ave., next to Kmart* ☎ *808/327–0444.*

HILO First-run films are shown on the nine screens of the state-of-the-art **Prince Kūhiō Stadium Cinemas** (✉ Prince Kūhiō Plaza, 111 E. Puainako St. ☎ 808/959–4595), while **Kress Cinemas** (✉ 174 Kamehameha Ave. ☎ 808/961–3456) and **Honoka'a People's Theater** (✉ Mamane St., Honoka'a ☎ 808/775–0000) screen selected art films (Honoka'a's theater also screens more mainstream films on weekends).

Palace Theatre. After decades of being closed, the 1925 theater has been beautifully restored and now shows not-so-recently released movies. The price is right: the first show of the day is only 50¢. ✉ *38 Haili St., Hilo* ☎ *808/934–7010.*

Theater

Aloha Angel Performing Arts Center. Local talent stages musicals and Broadway plays at this charming old plantation center near Kailua-Kona. ✉ *Aloha Angel Theatre Café, 79-7384 Māmalahoa Hwy., Kainaliu* ☎ *808/322–2122.*

★ **Kahilu Theatre.** For legitimate theater, the little town of Waimea is your best bet. The Kahilu Theater hosts regular internationally acclaimed performances, interspersed with a variety of top-notch music acts. In a recent season, Chick Corea, Laurie Anderson, and Pink Martini shared the calendar with modern dance performances, plays, and traditional Hawaiian dance shows. ✉ *Parker Ranch Center, 67-1185 Māmalahoa Hwy., Waimea* ☎ *808/885–6868* 🌐 *www.kahilutheatre.org.*

University of Hawai'i at Hilo Theater. A full concert series of varied performances, acts, musical groups, and plays is held from September through May each year. ✉ *200 W. Kawili St., Hilo* ☎ *808/974–7310.*

★ **Volcano Art Center.** Annual and special performances of Hawaiian music and dance, as well as theatre performances, are hosted by this local art center. People drive here from all over the island for some of their Hawaiian music concerts. ✉ *Volcano House Hotel, adjacent to the Kīlauea Visitors Center, Hawai'i Volcanoes National Park* ☎ *808/967–8222* 🌐 *www.volcanoartcenter.org.*

NIGHTLIFE

Kohala District

Honu Bar. This elegant spot at the Mauna Lani Bay Hotel & Bungalows has a nice dance floor for weekend revelry. Delicious appetizers, imported cigars, and fine cognacs make this a popular gathering spot on the Kohala Coast. ✉ *68-1400 Mauna Lani Dr., Kohala Coast* ☎ *808/885–6622.*

Malolo Lounge. A favorite after-work spot for employees from the surrounding hotels, this lounge in the Hilton Waikoloa Village offers decent live music (usually jazz), friendly bartenders, and a pool table. ✉ *425 Waikoloa Beach Dr., Waikoloa* ☎ *808/886–1234.*

Polo Bar. This wood-paneled watering hole in the Fairmont Orchid Hawai'i has a huge lānai and a great view. Bartenders are great, service is impeccable. The crowd's not rowdy, so it's a great place for an early evening cocktail or an after-dinner port. ✉ *1 N. Kanikū Dr., Kohala Coast* ☎ *808/885–2000.*

Kailua-Kona

Durty Jake's. In addition to a cheap and reasonably tasty ocean view breakfast, Durty Jake's hosts popular karaoke nights every week and catches the spillover from Lulu's on weekends. ✉ *75-5817 Ali'i Dr., Kailua-Kona* ☎ *808/329–7366.*

BEST SUNSET MAI TAIS

Huggo's on the Rocks (Kailua-Kona). Literally on the rocks with a sand-floored bar, strong drinks, and live music Friday and Saturday.

Kawaihae Harbor Grill (Kohala). Views off the deck of the upstairs Seafood Bar, great food in the restaurant next door, and well-poured drinks.

Kona Inn (Kailua-Kona). Wide, unobstructed view, in the middle of downtown, best mai tais on the island.

Wai'oli Lounge in the Hilo Hawaiian Hotel (Hilo). A nice view of Coconut Island, live music most nights and karaoke others.

Huggo's on the Rocks. Jazz, country, and even rock bands perform at this popular restaurant, so call ahead to find out what's on. Outside, people often dance in the sand to Hawaiian songs. The crowd skews to slightly older and better behaved than Lulu's or Durty Jake's across the street. ✉ *75-5828 Kahakai Rd., at Ali'i Dr., Kailua-Kona* ☎ *808/329–1493.*

Kona Brewing Company. Still very popular, the Kona Brewery has been a local favorite practically since it opened. Good food, good local beer (go for the sampler and try them all), and an outdoor patio with nightly live music acts make sure it stays that way. ✉ *75-5629 Kuakini Hwy.* ☎ *808/334–2739* 🌐 *www.konabrewingco.com.*

Lulu's. On weekends, the young crowd gyrates until late in the evening to hot dance music—hip-hop, R&B, and rock—spun by a professional DJ. ✉ *75-5819 Ali'i Dr., Kailua-Kona* ☎ *808/331–2633.*

Mixx Bar and Bistro. Kailua-Kona's first and only wine bar, adjacent to the Kona Wine Market, Mixx is also the only air-conditioned bar in Kona, but it's got a few other things going for it as well—namely good food, stiff and inventive cocktails, and live music nightly on their outdoor patio. ✉ *King Kamehameha Mall, 75-5626 Kuakini Hwy.* ☎ *808/329–7334* 🌐 *www.konawinemarket.com.*

Oceans Sports Bar & Grill. A somewhat recent addition to Kona, and still a popular gathering place, this sports bar in the back of the Coconut Grove Marketplace has a pool table and an outdoor patio, along with the dozens of TVs you'd expect at a sports bar. This place really gets hopping on the weekends. ✉ *Coconut Grove Marketplace, 75-5811 Ali'i Dr., Kailua-Kona* ☎ *808/327–9494.*

SLACK KEYS & 'UKULELES

It's easy to forget that Hawai'i has its own music until you step off a plane on the Islands and then there's no escaping it. It's a unique blend of the strings and percussion favored by the early settlers and the chants and rituals of the ancient Hawaiians. Hawaiian music today includes Island-devised variations on acoustic guitar—slack key and steel guitar—along with the 'ukulele (a small, four-string guitar about the size of a violin), and vocals that have evolved from ritual chants to more melodic compositions.

This is one of the few folk music traditions in the United States that is fully embraced by the younger generation, with no prodding from their parents or grandparents. More than half the radio stations on the Big Island play solely Hawaiian music, and concerts performed by Island favorites like Makana are filled with fans of all ages.

The best way to get an introduction to the music is to attend one of the annual festivals: The free **Annual Hawai'i Slack Key Guitar Festival** (July) features a handful of greats performing throughout the day at the Sheraton Keauhou Bay; the **Annual 'Ukulele and Slack Key Guitar Institute** (November) at the Kahilu Theatre in Waimea takes it one step further, providing both a variety of concerts and workshops for those interested in learning to play the instruments; and the **Annual Big Island Hawaiian Music Festival** (July) at the UH Hilo Performing Arts Center is a weekend full of slack key, steel guitar, and 'ukulele madness.

Or, you can catch live performances most nights at one of a handful of local bars and clubs, including **Mixx Bar and Bistro, Huggo's on the Rocks,** or the **Kona Brewing Company** in Kailua-Kona, and **Cronie's Bar and Grill,** in Hilo.

Hilo

Cronie's Bar & Grill. A sportsbar and hamburger joint by day, Cronie's is a local favorite when the lights go down, with a packed bar and a steady schedule of live local bands. ✉ *11 Waianuenue Ave, Hilo* ☎ *808/961–9666.*

Flipside Too. The crowd can get a little rowdy here, especially on weekends, but that's sort of the point. With tons of cheap and exotic drinks like the large green Midori-filled "Exorcist," a pool table, free karaoke, electronic darts, and pinball machines, not to mention plenty of friendly locals, Flipside Too has a well-deserved rep as a fun place to grab a drink any night of the week. ✉ *94 Mamo St.* ☎ *808/961–0057.*

Ho'omalimali Lounge. This lounge and dance club at the Hawai'i Naniloa Resort competes with the crashing surf on Friday and Saturday night with live music until midnight. ✉ *93 Banyan Dr., Hilo* ☎ *808/969–3333.*

Shooter's Bar & Grill. Another sportsbar-turned-nightclub: Come for the game, stay for the late-night live music and drunken karaoke. ✉ *121 Banyan Dr., Hilo* ☎ *808/969–7069.*

Where to Eat

WORD OF MOUTH

"I'll second Café 100 in Hilo and the loco moco. Great stuff–not exactly gourmet or health food but real "stick to your ribs" stuff."

–al

"Four Seasons: what a view! So close to the ocean you're practically in it. Soothing breezes. So lovely. So enjoyable. So peaceful . . . if I could only go to one breakfast buffet on the Big Island it would be this one."

–connecticut_lady

www.fodors.com/forums

DINING PLANNER

Reservations

Though it's rare to find a restaurant completely booked on the Big Island, a select few are sticklers about reservations. If you're booking a special occasion dinner, call ahead just in case, or check with your hotel concierge.

Buy Local

Buying local ingredients has become increasingly important to chefs and residents of the Big Island. To figure out whether your food grew here or flew here, keep an eye out for menu items like "Waimea tomatoes," "Kālua pork," and "Kona Kampachi" (a fish that is sustainably farmed by a local aquaculture company).

What to Wear

There isn't a single place on the Big Island that requires formal attire. The general rule is anything goes, although there are a handful of restaurants (Pahu i'a at the Four Seasons, the CanoeHouse at the Mauna Lani, and Batik at Mauna Kea) where you might feel out of place in your beach clothes.

In the Know

Though it might seem at first glance like the Big Island's restaurant scene consists of either very high-end restaurants or divey holes-in-the-wall, there is in fact a fairly large middle ground. The best way to find it is to eat where the locals eat—local families aren't going to splurge on resort restaurants, nor would they bother eating out to see roaches scampering across a dining room. We have included quite a few of these true value restaurants in our Where to Eat reviews, but there are always new places cropping up. Don't be afraid to ask the salesperson in a store or the local folks you bump into on the street where they recommend eating. Locals are generally happy to share their secrets.

A Word About Water

If you're staying at a condo and planning on cooking at home, it's best to use purified water for anything you're not boiling. The water on the Big Island is often chlorinated, which is not only not great for you, but can seriously ruin your morning Kona coffee.

Hours and Prices

Unless we state otherwise, restaurants are open for lunch and dinner daily.

WHAT IT COSTS

	$$$$	$$$	$$	$	¢
Restaurants	over $35	$27–$35	$18–$26	$10–$17	under $10

Restaurant prices are for one main course at dinner.

By Amy Westervelt

BETWEEN STAR CHEFS and a crop (pun intended) of quality new local farms, the Big Island restaurant scene has been heating up in the past couple of years. In the past it used to be a pleasant surprise for visitors to discover a gourmet meal on the island, but now food writers from national magazines are praising the chefs of the Big Island for their ability to turn the local bounty into inventive blends of the island's cultural heritage. Drawn by reviews and the reputations of some world-renowned chefs, the Big Island has become a destination for foodies on vacation.

Hotels along the Kohala Coast have long invested in celebrated chefs who know how to make a meal memorable, from inventive entrées to spot-on wine pairings. But great food on the Big Island doesn't begin and end with the resorts. A handful of cutting-edge chefs have retired from the fast-paced hotel world and opened up their own small bistros closer to the farms in Upcountry Waimea. And, as the old plantation towns transform into youthful arts communities, unique and wonderful restaurants have cropped up in Hāwī, Kainaliu, and on the east side of the island in Hilo. Though the larger, gourmet restaurants (especially those at the resorts) tend to be very pricey, there are still "ono grindz" (Hawaiian slang for tasty local food) to be found at budget prices throughout the island, from greasy plate lunch specials to reasonably priced organic fare at a number of cafés and health food markets. Less populated areas like Ka'ū, the Hāmākua Coast, and Puna offer limited choices for dinner, but usually at least one or two spots that do a decent plate lunch, and a handful of excellent bakeries.

In addition to the individual restaurants, events such as the Great Waikoloa Food, Wine & Music Fest at the Hilton Waikoloa Village, the Kona Coffee Cultural Festival at the Outrigger Keauhou, and Cuisines of the Sun at the Mauna Lani Bay Hotel draw hundreds of guests to starlighted open-air dinners celebrating the bounty of the isle's land and waters. Island tourism bureaus have also made an effort as of late to promote agritourism, and it has turned into a booming new business. Farm tours afford visitors the opportunity to meet with and learn from the local farmers and tour a variety of organic farms. Some tours conclude with a meal comprised of items sourced from the same farms. From goat farms churning creamy, pungent goat cheese to Waimea farms planting row after row of bright tomatoes to small aquaculture operations, visitors can see exactly where their next meal will come from and taste the difference that local, fresh, and organic production can make.

8

Kohala

American–Casual

$–$$$ ✕ **Café Pesto.** This branch of Café Pesto, in the quaint harbor town of Kawaihae, is just as popular as its sibling in Hilo. Exotic pizzas (with chili-grilled shrimp, shiitake mushrooms, and cilantro crème fraîche, for example), Asian-inspired pastas and risottos, and fresh seafood reflect the ethnic diversity of the island. Local microbrews and a full-service bar make this a good place to end the evening. ✉ *Kawaihae Harbor*

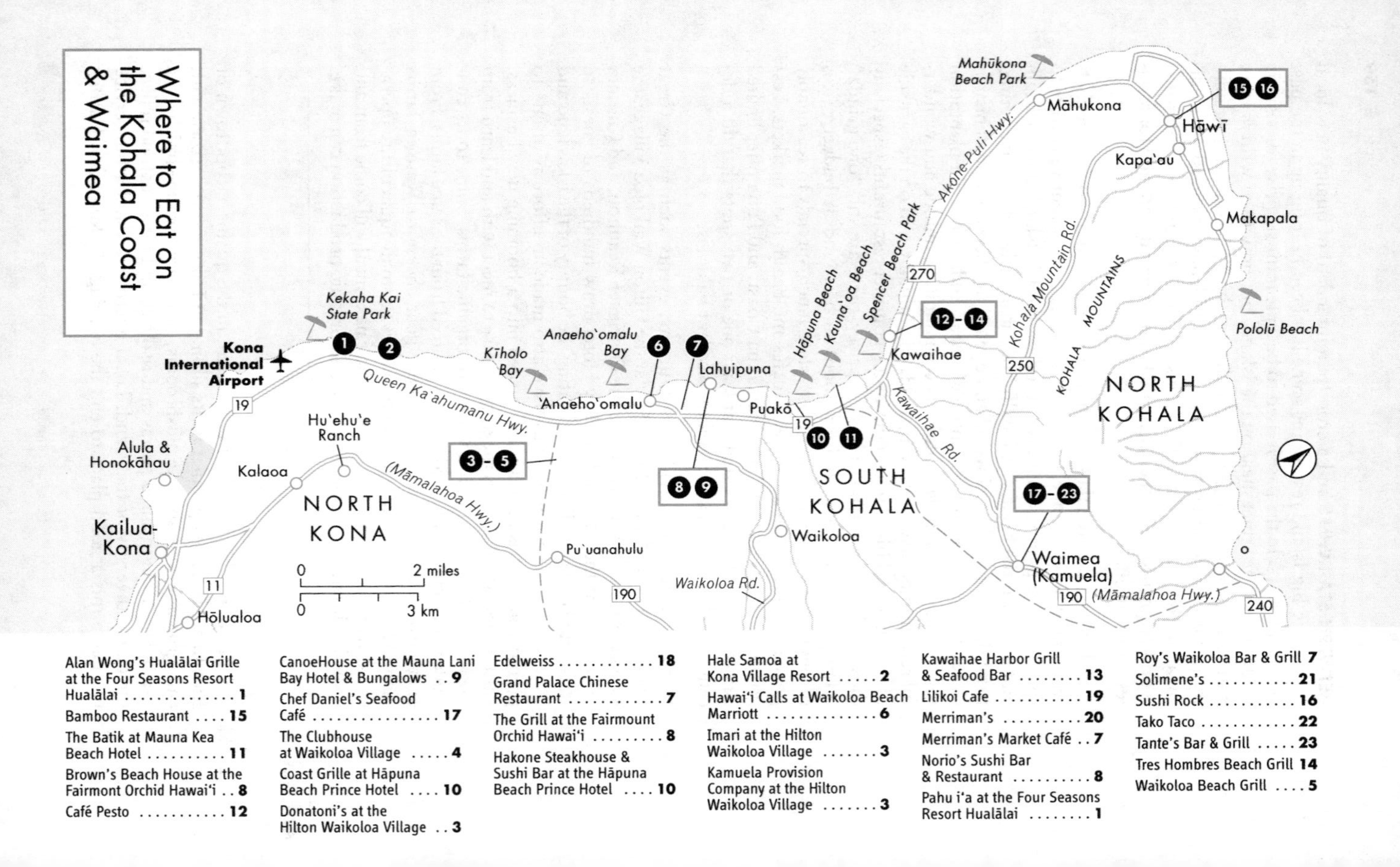

Alan Wong's Hualālai Grille at the Four Seasons Resort Hualālai . . . 1
Bamboo Restaurant 15
The Batik at Mauna Kea Beach Hotel . . . 11
Brown's Beach House at the Fairmont Orchid Hawai'i . . 8
Café Pesto . . . 12
CanoeHouse at the Mauna Lani Bay Hotel & Bungalows . . 9
Chef Daniel's Seafood Café . . . 17
The Clubhouse at Waikoloa Village . . . 4
Coast Grille at Hāpuna Beach Prince Hotel . . . 10
Donatoni's at the Hilton Waikoloa Village . . 3
Edelweiss . . . 18
Grand Palace Chinese Restaurant . . . 7
The Grill at the Fairmount Orchid Hawai'i . . . 8
Hakone Steakhouse & Sushi Bar at the Hāpuna Beach Prince Hotel . . . 10
Hale Samoa at Kona Village Resort . . . 2
Hawai'i Calls at Waikoloa Beach Marriott . . . 6
Imari at the Hilton Waikoloa Village . . . 3
Kamuela Provision Company at the Hilton Waikoloa Village . . . 3
Kawaihae Harbor Grill & Seafood Bar . . . 13
Lilikoi Cafe . . . 19
Merriman's . . . 20
Merriman's Market Café . . 7
Norio's Sushi Bar & Restaurant . . . 8
Pahu i'a at the Four Seasons Resort Hualālai . . . 1
Roy's Waikoloa Bar & Grill 7
Solimene's . . . 21
Sushi Rock . . . 16
Tako Taco . . . 22
Tante's Bar & Grill . . . 23
Tres Hombres Beach Grill 14
Waikoloa Beach Grill . . . 5

Center, Hwy. 270, Kawaihae ☎ 808/882–1071 ▭ AE, D, DC, MC, V. $10–$29.

$$ ✕ **Waikoloa Beach Grill.** Although on resort grounds (the first tee of the Waikoloa Beach golf course, to be exact), the Waikoloa Beach Grill is independently owned and operated by two accomplished chefs, Stephen Tabor (grill master) and David Brown (bread and pastries). The menu comprises well-done classics from the Coquille St. Jacques (a French shellfish casserole baked with cream sauce and sprinkled with browned breadcrumbs) to the grilled rib eye to the best Bloody Mary's on the island. Desserts are delicious and made fresh daily—the pies are outstanding, as is the cheese plate. Lunch includes entrée-size salads and huge sandwiches and burgers served on homemade bread. It's great value, especially given the skyrocketing rates of the surrounding establishments. *✉ 69-1022 Keana Pl., Waikoloa ☎ 808/886–6131 ▭ AE, D, MC, V. $18–$25.*

$–$$ ✕ **Kawaihae Harbor Grill & Seafood Bar.** This little restaurant is always packed—there's something about the crisp green-and-white, 1850s building that draws people in. That and the fact that it smells way too good to pass up if you're hungry. The food is not adventurous but very good; fresh island fish, chicken, and ribs, all served in hearty portions. Inside, it's all vintage Hawaiiana—old records, a surfboard, and hula skirts. The Seafood Bar is upstairs in a separate structure that also dates from the 1850s, and it has been a hot spot since it opened in 2003. The bar is a good place to wait until your table is ready, or to feast from the all-*pūpū* (appetizers) menu. *✉ Kawaihae Harbor, Hwy. 270, Kawaihae ☎ 808/882–1368 ▭ MC, V. $10–$24.*

8

Chinese

$–$$$$ ✕ **Grand Palace Chinese Restaurant.** A reasonably priced alternative in a land of hotel dining, this restaurant offers dishes from most regions, including such standards as egg foo yung, wonton soup, chicken with snow peas, and beef with broccoli. More adventurous dishes include sautéed local seafood, lobster, and sizzling shrimp with garlic sauce. Etched-glass panels are a nice embellishment. *✉ King's Shops at Waikoloa Village, 250 Waikoloa Beach Dr., Kohala Coast ☎ 808/886–6668 ▭ AE, DC, MC, V. $9–$40.*

Contemporary–Hawaiian

$$$$ ✕ **Hale Samoa at Kona Village Resort.** Formal and romantic, this Kona Village restaurant has a magical atmosphere, especially at sunset. In a Samoan setting with screens and candles, you can feast on five-course prix-fixe dinners that change daily. Specialties may include papaya-and-coconut bisque, duck stuffed with andouille sausage, or wok-charred prime strip loin. Reservations can be made only on the day you want to dine. *✉ Kona Village Resort, Hwy. 19, 12 mi north of Kailua-Kona, North Kona Coast ☎ 808/325–5555 ✍ Reservations essential ▭ AE, DC, MC, V ⏲ Closed Wed., Fri., and 1st wk in Dec. $65–$90.*

$$$–$$$$ Fodor'sChoice ★ ✕ **Brown's Beach House at the Fairmont Orchid Hawai'i.** This waterfront wonder is well worth the splurge—the menu is inventive (but not too inventive), and the wine list is excellent. Though you can order steak here, the seafood is really where it's happening. Their crab-crusted ono is a little piece of heaven, sitting on clouds of wasabi mashed potatoes. Leave room for dessert; the sweets change regularly, but they're always worth the indulgence. Local musicians play nightly on the grassy knoll outside. ✉ *Fairmont Orchid Hawai'i, 1 N. Kanikū Dr., Kohala Coast* ☎ *808/885–2000* ▭ *AE, D, DC, MC, V* ⊙ *No lunch. $31–$50.*

$$$–$$$$ ✕ **CanoeHouse at the Mauna Lani Bay Hotel & Bungalows.** Although the open-air, beachfront setting is stunning, the CanoeHouse is starting to lose some ground to the other resort restaurants in the food department. It was among the first on the island to offer Pacific Rim fusion, and it still does it well, but the menu lacks originality—meat or seafood paired with sauces derived from local fruits and vegetables. Shanghai lobster is the standout, but it's not exactly amazing. That said, the wine list is great, and the location could almost make the price tag worth it, if there weren't better restaurants a few miles away. ✉ *Mauna Lani Bay Hotel & Bungalows, 68-1400 Mauna Lani Dr., Kohala Coast* ☎ *808/885–6622* ▭ *AE, D, DC, MC, V. $27–$40.*

$$$–$$$$ ✕ **Kamuela Provision Company at the Hilton Waikoloa Village.** Quiet guitar music, tables set along a breezy lānai, and a sweeping view of the Kohala-Kona coastline are the perfect accompaniments to the elegant yet down-to-earth Hawai'i regional cuisine. Popular are the bouillabaisse with *nori crostini* and the Parker Ranch rib-eye steak with green peppercorn sauce. This is a great place to sip cocktails—the adjacent Wine Bar makes for a romantic evening in itself, with an appetizer menu and more than 40 labels available by the glass. ✉ *Hilton Waikoloa Village, 425 Waikoloa Beach Dr., Kohala Coast* ☎ *808/886–1234* ▭ *AE, D, DC, MC, V* ⊙ *No lunch. $28–$52.*

★ $$–$$$$ ✕ **Alan Wong's Hualālai Grille at the Four Seasons Resort Hualālai.** The menu changes regularly, depending on availability of local produce, fish, and meat, but expect the sort of "fusion" fare you'd find in a top-notch New York or San Francisco restaurant. The added bonus is that you can sit outside and enjoy balmy breezes. The food is surprisingly reasonable for what you get and where you're eating. You could easily make a meal out of a selection of *pūpū*. The wine list is extensive and well-chosen, and servers are extremely well-versed and helpful. ✉ *Four Seasons Resort Hualālai, 100 Ka'ūpūlehu Dr., North Kona Coast* ✍ *Reservations essential* ▭ *AE, DC, MC, V* ⊙ *Closed Wed., Fri., and 1st wk in Dec. $18–$90.*

★ $$–$$$$ ✕ **Coast Grille at Hāpuna Beach Prince Hotel.** This is a beautiful spot, with high ceilings and a lānai overlooking the ocean. It offers perhaps the best seafood menu on the island, including loads of fresh oysters and creative Pacific Rim dishes like pan-seared *opah* (moonfish) in cardamom sauce and, when available, delicate farm-raised moi, in ancient times enjoyed only by chiefs. Don't overlook the appetizer sampler with seared 'ahi and tempura sushi, and save room for warm Valrhona chocolate cake. If you're in the mood for an early dinner (before 6:30 PM), Coast Grille has a selection of very reasonably priced three-course prix-fixe meals. ✉ *Hāpuna Beach Prince Hotel, 62-100 Kauna'oa Dr., Kohala Coast* ☎ *808/880–3192* ▭ *AE, D, DC, MC, V* ⊙ *No lunch. $18–$36.*

$$–$$$$ ✕ **Hawai'i Calls at Waikoloa Beach Marriott.** With its retro art calling to mind the '20s to the '50s, Hawai'i Calls offers a nostalgic taste of the Islands. The menu, however, is contemporary and fresh, changing seasonally, with specialties such as moi, seared crispy and served with coconut rice, pickled ginger, and spicy cucumber salad. Don't miss the macadamia-chocolate tart with vanilla ice cream. The spacious outdoor setting is lovely—ask for a table near the koi pond and waterfall—and a great place to watch the sun set as tiki torches light up the gardens. The adjacent Clipper Lounge serves tropical drinks and features a bistro menu. ✉ *Waikoloa Beach Marriott, 69-275 Waikoloa Beach Dr., Kohala Coast* ☎ *808/886–6789* ▭ *AE, D, DC, MC, V. $20–$42.*

RESORT HOPPING

Don't feel like you have to splurge at your resort restaurant or not at all. If you're staying at one of the Kohala Coast resorts you're within easy driving distance of the rest, so go with the best restaurant even if it's not the closest.

$$–$$$$ Fodor's Choice ★ ✕ **Pahu i'a at the Four Seasons Resort Hualālai.** *Pahu i'a* means "aquarium," so it's fitting that a 9- by 4-foot aquarium in the entrance casts a dreamy light through this exquisite restaurant. Presentation is paramount—tables are beautifully set, with handblown glassware—and the food tastes as good as it looks. Asian-influenced dishes stand out for their layers of flavor. Don't miss the three sashimi and three caviar appetizers, or the crispy whole moi served with Asian slaw, black beans, and sweet chili-lime vinaigrette. Breakfast is also superb; there's a buffet, as well as a menu. Their lemon ricotta pancakes are so good they should be illegal. Reserve a table on the patio and you may be able to spot whales while dining. At sunset, the oceanfront tables in the upstairs Lava Lounge are an excellent spot to take it all in. ✉ *Four Seasons Resort Hualālai, 100 Ka'ūpūlehu Dr., North Kona Coast* ☎ *808/325–8000* ▭ *AE, D, DC, MC, V* ⊗ *No lunch. $25–$48.*

$$–$$$ ✕ **Roy's Waikoloa Bar & Grill.** You can easily fill up on the enormous selection of appetizers at Roy Yamaguchi's cool and classy place overlooking a lake. Roy's restaurants are well known for top-notch seafood entrées prepared with a pan-Asian twist. Some of our favorite examples include the blackened island 'ahi with spicy soy-mustard-butter sauce, or jade-pesto steamed Hawaiian whitefish with cilantro, ginger, and garlic. An extensive wine-by-the-glass list offers good pairing options. Be forewarned that the place tends to get noisy. ✉ *King's Shops at Waikoloa Village, 250 Waikoloa Beach Dr., Kohala Coast* ☎ *808/886–4321* 🌐 *www.roysrestaurant.com* ▭ *AE, D, DC, MC, V. $18–$29.*

$–$$$ ✕ **Bamboo Restaurant.** It's out of the way, but the food at this spot in the heart of Hāwī is good and the service and ambience have a Hawaiian country flair. Creative entrées feature fresh island fish prepared several ways. The Thai-style fish, for example, combines lemongrass, Kaffir lime leaves, and coconut milk—best washed down with a passion-fruit margarita or passion-fruit iced tea. Bamboo finishes, bold artwork, and an old unfinished wooden floor make the restaurant cozy.

8

Local musicians entertain on Friday and Saturday night. ✉ *Hwy. 270, Hāwī* ☎ *808/889–5555* ▭ *MC, V* ⊙ *Closed Mon. No dinner Sun. $15–$28.*

Italian

★ $$–$$$$ ✕ **Donatoni's at the Hilton Waikoloa Village.** This romantic restaurant overlooking the boat canal resembles an Italian villa and serves scrumptious dishes with the subtle sauces of northern Italy. From mahimahi with marinated artichokes to fettuccine with Hawaiian lobster, this intimate place sets out to please. Be sure to look over the Italian wine and champagne list. ✉ *425 Waikoloa Beach Dr., Kohala Coast* ☎ *808/886–1234* ▭ *AE, D, DC, MC, V* ⊙ *No lunch. $18–$46.*

¢–$ ✕ **Merriman's Market Café.** From Peter Merriman, one of Hawai'i's star chefs, comes a more affordable alternative to his upscale Waimea and Maui restaurants. The simple but delicious Mediterranean-influenced menu includes a variety of pasta dishes, tasty appetizers, and some of the island's best salads. Its huge patio has quickly become a favorite for locals and visitors alike, which means you could have a bit of a wait for a table. ✉ *King's Shops at Waikoloa Village, 250 Waikoloa Beach Dr., Kohala Coast* ☎ *808/886–1700* ▭ *AE, MC, V. $9–$16.*

Japanese

$$$–$$$$ ✕ **Hakone Steakhouse & Sushi Bar at the Hāpuna Beach Prince Hotel.** It's hard not to start whispering in this tranquil and graceful restaurant. Choose from exquisite Japanese sukiyaki, *shabu shabu* (thin slices of beef cooked in broth), and the selections at the elaborate sushi bar. The broad selection of sake (try a sakitini, a martini made with sake) is guaranteed to enliven your meal. The best time to visit is on a Friday or Saturday night when the restaurant serves a great dinner buffet. ✉ *Hāpuna Beach Prince Hotel, 62-100 Kauna'oa Dr., Kohala Coast* ☎ *808/880–3192* ▭ *AE, D, DC, MC, V* ⊙ *No lunch. $34–$45.*

$$–$$$$ ✕ **Imari at the Hilton Waikoloa Village.** This elegant restaurant, complete with waterfalls and a teahouse, serves sukiyaki and tempura aimed to please mainland tastes. Beyond the impressive display of Imari porcelain at the entrance, you can find *teppanyaki* (beef or shrimp cooked table-side), shabu shabu (beef and vegetables in broth), and an outstanding sushi bar. Impeccable service by kimono-clad waitresses adds to the quiet refinement. ✉ *425 Waikoloa Beach Dr., Kohala Coast* ☎ *808/886–1234* ▭ *AE, D, DC, MC, V* ⊙ *No lunch. $25–$52.*

$$–$$$ ✕ **Norio's Sushi Bar & Restaurant.** Sashimi and sushi are lovingly prepared with the freshest possible fish (both from the ocean and from the numerous aqua farms on the island). The flounder, 'ahi, and abalone are not to be missed. Some equally delicious hot dishes include baked sea scallops and miso butterfish. The assortment of tropical drinks is tasty, as is the sinfully good chocolate fondue, served with an assortment of tropical fruits. ✉ *Fairmont Orchid Hawai'i, 1 N. Kaniku Dr., Kohala Coast* ☎ *808/885–2000* ▭ *AE, D, DC, MC, V* ⊙ *Closed Tues. and Wed. No lunch. $20–$30.*

$$–$$$ ✕ **Sushi Rock.** In Hāwī's funky Without Boundaries, Sushi Rock offers both the island's freshest raw fish (including lots of new-wave Califor-

Continued on page 168

AUTHENTIC TASTE OF HAWAI'I: LŪ'AU OR LAULAU?

The best place to sample Hawaiian food is at a backyard lū'au. Aunts and uncles are cooking, the pig is from a cousin's farm, and the fish is from a brother's boat.

But even locals have to angle for invitations to those rare occasions. So your choice is most likely between a commercial lū'au and a Hawaiian restaurant.

Most commercial lū'au will offer you little of the authentic diet; they're more about umbrella drinks, laughs, spectacle, and fun. Expect to spend some time and no small amount of cash.

For greater authenticity, folksy experiences, and rock-bottom prices, visit a Hawaiian restaurant (most are in anonymous storefronts in residential neighborhoods). Expect rough edges and some effort negotiating the menu.

In either case, much of what is known today as Hawaiian food would be as foreign to a 16th-century Hawaiian as risotto or chow mein. The pre-contact diet was simple and healthy—mainly raw and steamed seafood and vegetables. Early Hawaiians used earth ovens and heated stones to cook seafood, taro, sweet potatoes, and breadfruit and seasoned their food with sea salt and ground kukui nuts. Seaweed, fern shoots, sweet potato vines, coconut, banana, sugar cane, and select greens and roots rounded out the diet.

Successive waves of immigrants added their favorites to the ti leaf–lined table. So it is that foods as disparate as salt salmon and chicken long rice are now Hawaiian—even though there is no salmon in Hawaiian waters and long rice (cellophane noodles) is Chinese.

AT THE LŪ'AU: KĀLUA PORK

The heart of any lū'au is the *imu*, the earth oven in which a whole pig is roasted. The preparation of an imu is an arduous affair for most families, who tackle it only for special occasions or at Thanksgiving, when many Islanders prefer to imu their turkeys. Commercial lū'au operations have it down to a science, however.

THE ART OF THE STONE

The key to a proper imu is the *pohaku*, the stones. Imu cook by means of long, slow, moist heat released by special stones which can withstand a hot fire without exploding. Many Hawaiian families treasure their imu stones, keeping them in a pile in the back yard and passing them on through generations.

PIT COOKING

The imu makers first dig a pit about the size of a refrigerator, then lay down *kiawe* (mesquite) wood and stones, and build a white-hot fire that is allowed to burn itself out. The ashes are raked away, and the hot stones covered with banana and ti leaves. Well-wrapped in leaves and a net of chicken wire, the pig is lowered onto the leaf-covered stones. *Laulau* may also be placed inside. The whole is topped with more leaves, wet burlap sacks, and a canvas tarp, and left to steam for the better part of a day.

OPENING THE IMU

This is the moment everyone waits for: The imu is unwrapped like a giant present and the imu keepers gingerly wrestle out the steaming pig. When it's unwrapped, the meat falls moist and smoky-flavored from the bone, looking and tasting just like Southern-style pulled pork, but without the barbecue sauce.

WHICH LŪ'AU?

Fairmont Orchid. Blends modern and traditional music with stories of the kings of Hawai'i, Tahiti, Samoa, and New Zealand. Foods from all four cultures are served.

Sheraton Keauhou. Fantastic show blends modern lighting and aesthetic with traditional myths and dances. Open bar and full buffet are bonuses.

Kona Village. The imu ceremony and tradional show make this a long-time island favorite. In addition to the pig, they put fresh fish in the imu—delicious.

MEA 'AI 'ONO. GOOD THINGS TO EAT.

LAULAU

Steamed meats, fish, and taro leaf in ti-leaf bundles: fork-tender, a medley of flavors; the taro resembles spinach.

LOMI LOMI SALMON

Salt salmon in a piquant salad or relish with onions, tomatoes.

POI (DON'T CALL IT LIBRARY PASTE.)

Islanders are beyond tired of jokes about poi, a paste made of pounded taro root.

Consider: The Hawaiian Adam is descended from *kalo* (taro). Young taro plants are called "keiki"—children. Poi is the first food after mother's milk for many Islanders. 'Ai, the word for food, is synonymous with poi in many contexts.

Not only that. We like it. "There is no meat that doesn't taste good with poi," the old Hawaiians said.

But you have to know how to eat it: with something rich or powerfully flavored. "It is salt that makes the poi go in," is another adage. When you're served poi, try it with a mouthful of smoky kālua pork or salty lomi lomi salmon. Its slightly sour blandness cleanses the palate. And if you don't like it, smile and say something polite. (And slide that bowl over to a local.)

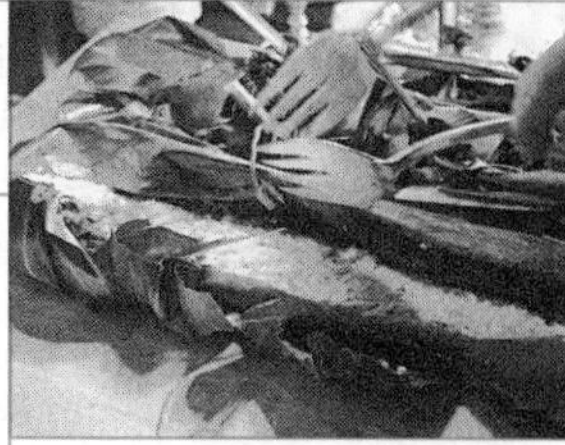

Laulau

Lomi Lomi Salmon

Poi

E HELE MAI 'AI! COME AND EAT!

Hawaiian restaurants tend to be inconveniently located in well-worn storefronts with little or no parking, outfitted with battered tables and clattering Melmac dishes, open odd (and usually limited) hours and days, and often so crowded you have to wait. But they personify aloha, invariably run by local families who welcome tourists who take the trouble to find them.

Many are cash-only operations and combination plates are a standard feature: one or two entrées, a side such as chicken long rice, choice of poi or steamed rice and—if the place is really old-style—a tiny portion of coarse Hawaiian salt and some raw onions for relish.

Most serve some foods that aren't, strictly speaking, Hawaiian, but are beloved of kama'āina, such as salt meat with watercress (preserved meat in a tasty broth), or *akubone* (skipjack tuna fried in a vinegar sauce).

Our two favorites: **Kanaka-Kava and Kūhiō Grille.**

nia-style rolls and a terrific Hawaiian-style ceviche) and a variety of cooked seafood, noodle dishes, and salads. Everything is served beautifully either at the sushi bar, at one of the handful of indoor tables, or on the covered back patio. There's also a full bar. ✉ *55-3435 Akoni Pule Hwy., Hāwī* ☎ *808/889-5900* ▭ *AE, DC, MC, V* ⊗ *No lunch. $20–$30.*

Mexican

$–$$ ✕ **Tres Hombres Beach Grill.** The food is decent, if a bit pricey, but what you come here for are the marvelous margaritas. They're in all sorts of tropical flavors, including *liliko'i* (passion fruit). Lunch is the usual Mexican combination platters (tacos, enchiladas, chiles rellenos) as well as burgers and sandwiches. Dinner entrées include fresh fish, killer fajitas, bean-and-rice combinations, and steaks. ✉ *Kawaihae Harbor Center, Hwy. 270, Kawaihae* ☎ *808/882-1031* ▭ *MC, V. $11–$20.*

Steak Houses

★ **$$$$** ✕ **The Grill at the Fairmont Orchid Hawai'i.** Set back from the beach, the Grill is a martini-and-filet-mignon kind of place. The menu is heavier on meats (leaving the seafood to the nearby Brown's Beach House), and you'd be hard-pressed to find a better steak on the island. The service is impeccable, the wine list superb, and the macadamia-nut pie may be the best dessert we've ever had. Open-air seating is available, and the tables are still close enough to the ocean to catch the breeze. ✉ *Fairmont Orchid Hawai'i, 1 N. Kanikū Dr., Kohala Coast* ☎ *808/885-2000* ✍ *Reservations essential* ▭ *AE, D, DC, MC, V. $36–$59.*

$–$$$ ✕ **The Clubhouse at Waikoloa Village.** Sunset views overlooking the golf course and steaks are the highlights here. Start with *pūpū* like skewered shrimp, crab cakes, or Hawaiian-Chinese mushrooms. Steaks come in all sizes and include filet mignon, New York strip, T-bone, and porterhouse. Other entrées include fresh island fish, chicken with orange sauce, baby back ribs with passion fruit–hoisin sauce, pork chops with pineapple, and curry-coconut prawns. There's a quiet, comfortable clubhouse atmosphere. Reservations are recommended. ✉ *68-1792 Melia St., Waikoloa* ☎ *808/883-9644* ▭ *AE, D, MC, V* ⊗ *Closed Mon. $15–$30.*

Waimea

American–Casual

$$–$$$ ✕ **Tante's Bar & Grill.** You fully expect to see Hawaiian *paniolos* sauntering up to the bar here—and it's not unheard of. Tante's is the John Wayne version of an elegant dining room with plenty of steaks and ribs on the menu to satisfy even the hungriest cowpoke at prices that won't break the bank. And of course, since this is Hawai'i after all, expect to see multicultural dishes rubbing elbows with cowboy classics. Locals flock here for fantastic Filipino dishes like pork *adobo* (slow-cooked pork simmered in garlic, oil, and vinegar) and chicken *lau lau* (ground chicken with spices and taro, wrapped in ti leaf and steamed). ✉ *67-1185 Mamalahoa Hwy., G-138, Parker Ranch Center, Hwy. 19* ☎ *808/885-8942* ▭ *MC, V. $12–$24.*

CLOSE UP

Green Hawai'i: Farm Tours

AS LOCAL INGREDIENTS CONTINUE to play a more prominent role on Big Island menus, chefs and farmers are working together to support a burgeoning ag-tourism industry in Hawai'i. Several local farms have cropped up over the past few years to make specialty items that cater to the island's gourmet restaurants. The **Hawai'i Island Goat Dairy** produces specialty cheese; lone bee-keeper Richard Spiegel of **Volcano Island Honey Co.** produces a rare and delicious honey now available not only in local restaurants but on the shelves of high-end stores like Neiman Marcus; and the **Hāmākua Heritage Farm** has turned mowed down koa forests into a safe haven for gourmet mushrooms. While a handful of farms—like **Mountain Thunder,** which produces 100% organic Kona coffee, and **Hawaiian Vanilla Vineyards,** which is cultivating vanilla from orchids growing wild on the Hāmākua Coast—are open to the public and offer free tours, others have opted instead to offer limited tours through group operators. Chef Peter Merriman has put together a tour with **Hawai'i Forest and Trail** (🌐 www.hawaii-forest.com/adv-farmtour.html for booking information) that includes stops at **Kahua Ranch,** a working cattle ranch at 3,000 feet in the Kohala Mountains, and **Honopua Farm,** where organic vegetables, lavender, and cut flowers are grown. The tour finishes up at Merriman's Restaurant where the group is treated to a five-course dinner prepared from the local ingredients they have just seen growing. The **Big Island Farm Bureau** has also tried to encourage local farming and ag-tourism through the creation of **Hawai'i AgVentures,** a new organization that schedules farm visits (to either a single or multiple farms) for interested parties (see 🌐 www.hawaiiagventures.com for more information).

¢–$ ✕ **Lilikoi Cafe.** This bright and cheerful café on the backside of the Parker Ranch Center serves up healthy, hearty breakfast and lunch items, ranging from homemade breakfast burritos to salads and comforting plates of meatloaf. The word on the street is they'll be staying open for dinner soon, too. ✉ *Off Hwy. 19, Parker Ranch Center, behind the food Ct.* ☎ *808/887–1400* ▭ *No credit cards* ⊗ *Closed Sun. $5–$10.*

Contemporary

$$–$$$$ ✕ **Chef Daniel's Seafood Café.** The building that once held the historic Chock In Store, which catered to the ranching community beginning in 1900, has been transformed into an eatery with five dining areas. The store's redwood countertop now serves as one long community dining table. Collectibles abound, such as antique porcelain pieces. Chef Daniel Thiebaut's French-Asian creations include an amazing appetizer of sweet-corn crab cake with a lemongrass, coconut, and lobster sauce. Other signature dishes include Hunan-style rack of lamb served with eggplant compote, and Big Island goat cheese. ✉ *65-1259 Kawaihae Rd., Waimea* ☎ *808/887–2200* ▭ *AE, D, DC, MC, V. $20–$40.*

★ $$–$$$ ✕ **Merriman's.** This is the signature restaurant of Peter Merriman, one of the pioneers of Hawai'i regional cuisine. Merriman's is the home of the original wok-charred 'ahi, usually served with buttery Wainaku corn. If you prefer meat, try the Kahuā Ranch lamb, raised to the restaurant's specifications, or opt for the prime Kansas City Cut steak, grilled to order. The wine list includes 22 selections poured by the glass, and the staff is refreshingly knowledgeable. For true foodies, Merriman's now offers a farmers' market tour—four hours spent browsing around local ranches and food stands, culminating in a fantastic five-course meal using produce and meat bought throughout the day. ✉ *'Opelo Plaza, 65-1227 'Opelo Rd., Waimea* ☎ *808/885–6822* ✍ *Reservations essential* ▭ *AE, MC, V. $20–$33.*

German

★ $$–$$$$ ✕ **Edelweiss.** An authentic German *gasthaus* right in the middle of Hawai'i, Edelweiss is truly a great place. Fear not if you don't see anything you want on the menu; there are 15 to 20 daily specials that your server will rattle off without batting an eye. No one can figure out how (or why) they do it. The rack of lamb is always good, and anything ending in schnitzel is a safe bet, as are items ending in brat or braten. The chicken Cordon Bleu is large enough and rich enough for two. Soup (almost always what sounds like a weird combination turns out to be a real treat), salad, and coffee or tea are included in dinner prices. The wine list is decent, but c'mon, get the Hefeweizen. You won't have room for dessert with the size of their portions, but you're not missing much. If you're a potato pancake fan, call two days ahead and the kitchen will whip up a batch for you. ✉ *Hwy. 19, Waimea* ☎ *808/885–6800* ✍ *Reservations essential* ▭ *MC, V* ⊗ *Closed Sun. and Mon. and Sept. $21–$56.*

Italian

$ ✕ **Solimene's.** Stick with the tasty thin crust pizzas, and you won't be disappointed by Solimene's. Pasta dishes are underwhelming, although nightly specials ranging from eggplant parmigiana to meatball subs tend to be quite good. For dessert, although you might be tempted by the tiramisu, the chocolate hazelnut ice cream is the way to go. ✉ *65-1158 Mamalahoa Hwy. in the Waimea Shopping Center* ☎ *808/887–1313* ▭ *MC, V* ⊗ *Closed Mon. No dinner Sun. $10–$15.*

Mexican

$–$$ ✕ **Tako Taco.** Everyone in Waimea and beyond is heralding the reopening of Tako Taco, one of the best Mexican restaurants on the island. With a focus on fresh ingredients, Tako Taco whips up awesome tacos, burritos, Mexican salads, enchiladas, rellenos, and seriously *ono* (Hawaiian slang for "tasty") quesadillas fresh to order. The tomatillo pineapple salsa is the bee's knees, and they're also now serving top shelf margaritas, both classic and flavored (strawberry, mango, or lilikoi), along with local beers and wine. ✉ *64-1066A Mamalahoa Hwy.* ☎ *808/887–1717* ▭ *MC, V. $7–$12.*

Kailua-Kona

American–Casual

$$–$$$$ **Kona Inn Restaurant.** This historic open-air restaurant offers some of the best, unobstructed ocean views on the island. It's a great place to have a mai tai and some appetizers while watching the sunset, or to enjoy a tasty calamari or ono sandwich and a salad at lunch. Dinner is also available, but for the prices there are better options once the sun disappears. ✉ *75-5744 Ali'i Dr., Kailua-Kona* ☎ *808/329–4455* ▭ *AE, MC, V. $19–$36.*

$$–$$$ **Jameson's by the Sea.** If you can't get a table outside, Jameson's is not really worth the trip. Make sure to reserve one in advance—the waves actually splash your feet while you eat. The traditional Continental fare is decent but not amazing; fresh fish is always the best bet. ✉ *77-6452 Ali'i Dr., Kailua-Kona* ☎ *808/329–3195* ▭ *AE, D, DC, MC, V* ⊙ *No lunch weekends. $21–$27.*

$–$$ **Jacke Rey's Ohana Grill.** Uphill from downtown Kailua-Kona, this bright green open-air restaurant is a popular lunch destination. The chicken sandwich with avocado and Swiss is an excellent combination of flavors, and the fries are crisped to perfection. For dinner, inventive salads and fresh fish dishes make this place worth the slight detour out of town. ✉ *Pottery Terrace, 75-5995 Kuakini Hwy., Kailua-Kona* ▭ *MC, V. $10–$20.*

¢–$ **Bubba Gump Shrimp Company.** Okay, it's a chain, and a chain that centers around a Tom Hanks movie, no less. Get over it. For starters, it has one of the largest oceanfront patios on the island. And the food's not bad, once you get past the silly names. Anything with popcorn shrimp in it is good, and the "Run Chicken Run" salad (a combination of chicken, Gorgonzola cheese, walnuts, and cranberries) is the perfect size for lunch. The place does a great breakfast, too, with strong coffee and plenty of options, from the cream-cheese stuffed French toast to bacon and eggs. ✉ *75-5776 Ali'i Dr., Kailua-Kona* ☎ *808/331–8442* ▭ *MC, V. $7–$12.*

¢–$ **Harbor House.** The fish here is probably a few hours off the boat—if that. Located at the Honokohau harbor, Harbor House is a local favorite for fresh fish sandwiches and a variety of fried fish and chip combos. The icy schooners of Kona Brewing Company ale don't hurt, either. ✉ *74-425 Kealakehe Pkwy. Ste. 4, Honokohau Harbor* ☎ *808/326–4166* ▭ *MC, V. $6–$10.*

¢–$ **Kona Brewing Company & Brewpub.** One of the better additions to Kailua-Kona's restaurant and bar scene, Kona Brewing Company has an ex-

> **BEST FOR KEIKI (KIDS)**
>
> **Bubba Gump's** (Kailua-Kona). A quirky theme with a great kids' menu and virgin umbrella drinks.
> **Manago Hotel** (Kainaliu). The kids' menu is ridiculously cheap, there's a huge koi pond, and you get to take home cool T-shirts.
> **Seaside** (Hilo). What's not kid-friendly about a restaurant perched above aquaculture ponds surrounded by cranes?
> **Tako Taco** (Waimea). You control the spice level at this colorful, playful restaurant.
> **U-Top-It** (Kailua-Kona). The taro cake is healthy for kids without them realizing it.

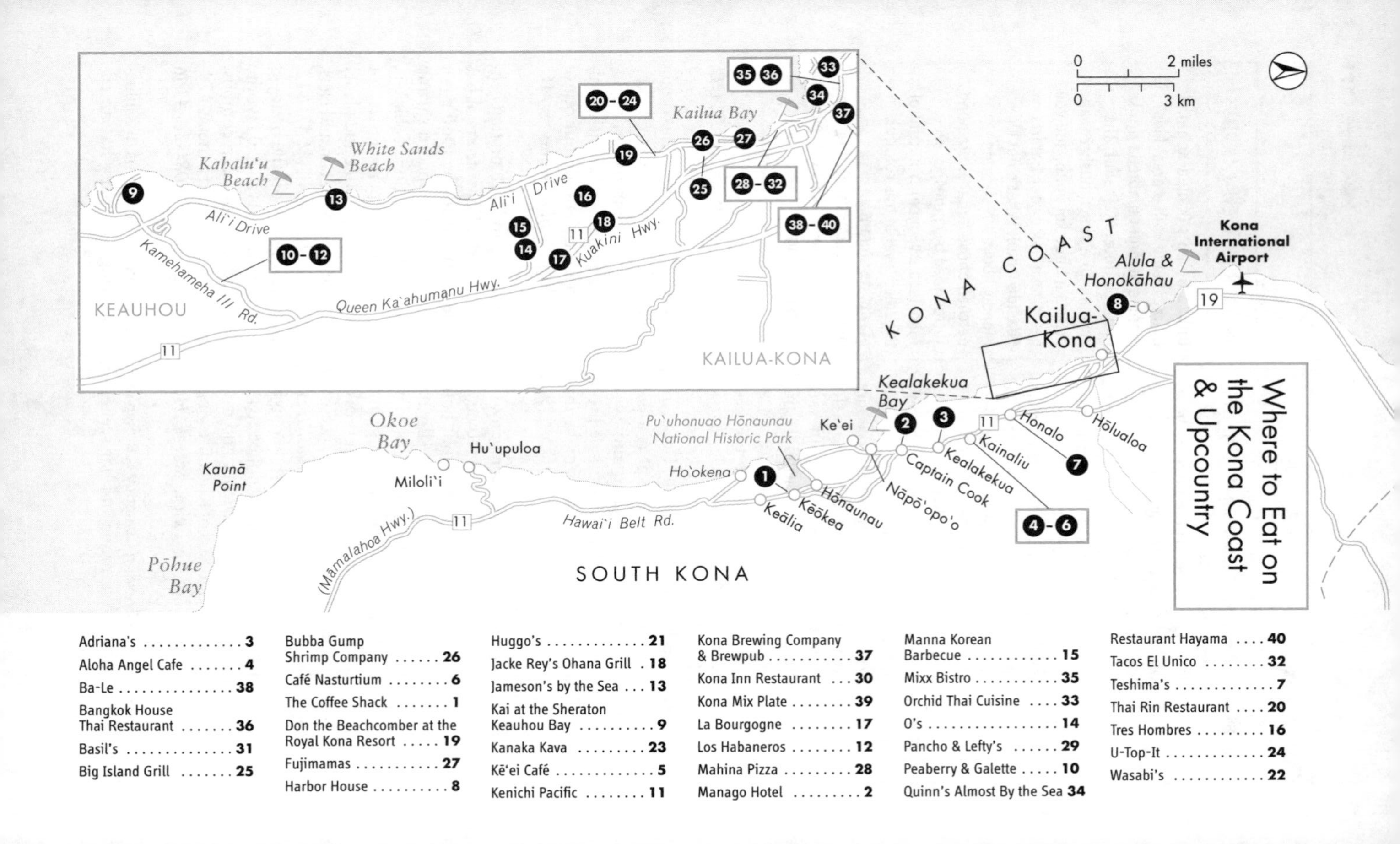

Adriana's **3**	Bubba Gump Shrimp Company **26**	Huggo's **21**	Kona Brewing Company & Brewpub **37**	Manna Korean Barbecue **15**	Restaurant Hayama **40**
Aloha Angel Cafe **4**	Café Nasturtium **6**	Jacke Rey's Ohana Grill . **18**	Kona Inn Restaurant . . . **30**	Mixx Bistro **35**	Tacos El Unico **32**
Ba-Le **38**	The Coffee Shack **1**	Jameson's by the Sea . . . **13**	Kona Mix Plate **39**	Orchid Thai Cuisine **33**	Teshima's **7**
Bangkok House Thai Restaurant **36**	Don the Beachcomber at the Royal Kona Resort **19**	Kai at the Sheraton Keauhou Bay **9**	La Bourgogne **17**	O's **14**	Thai Rin Restaurant **20**
Basil's **31**	Fujimamas **27**	Kanaka Kava **23**	Los Habaneros **12**	Pancho & Lefty's **29**	Tres Hombres **16**
Big Island Grill **25**	Harbor House **8**	Kē'ei Café **5**	Mahina Pizza **28**	Peaberry & Galette **10**	U-Top-It **24**
		Kenichi Pacific **11**	Managō Hotel **2**	Quinn's Almost By the Sea **34**	Wasabi's **22**

cellent and varied menu including pulled-pork quesadillas, gourmet pizzas, and a killer spinach salad with Gorgonzola cheese, macadamia nuts, all topped with strawberry dressing. Go for the beer tasting menu—it's six of the eight microbrews in miniature glasses that are roughly equivalent to two regular-size mugs. ✉ *75-5629 Kuakini Hwy., just past Palani intersection on right, Kailua-Kona* ☎ *808/329–2739* ▭ *MC, V. $9–$15.*

¢–$ ✕ **Quinn's Almost By the Sea.** Okay, Quinn's is a bit of a dive. That said, it does have a few things going for it—the best ono sandwiches on the island, for example. It's open until 11 PM, later than any other restaurant in Kailua-Kona (except Denny's). If time gets away from you on a drive to South Point, Quinn's is awaiting your return with a cheap beer and a basket of excellent calamari. You can also have a beer at the funky bar filled with fishermen. ✉ *75-5655A Palani Rd., Kailua-Kona* ☎ *808/329–3822* ▭ *MC, V. $8–$15.*

¢–$ ✕ **U-Top-It.** Tucked behind the shops and cafés of the Coconut Grove Marketplace, U-Top-It is a local favorite breakfast joint. Opened by a former Kona Village resort chef, all dishes at U-Top-It are built upon the restaurant's terrific taro pan crepes, which guests can choose to top with any combination of over 100 different toppings ranging from straightforward fruit or egg combinations to more unusual toppings. At lunch time, try pairing one of the crepes with beef or chicken teriyaki. ✉ *75-5799 Ali'i Dr., Coconut Grove Market Pl.* ☎ *808/329–0092* ▭ *MC, V* ⏲ *Closed Mon. $7–$12.*

Contemporary

$$–$$$$ ✕ **Fujimamas.** A fantastic new addition to the Kona dining scene, Fujimamas serves up tasty fusion dishes like shiitake sirloin with wasabi mashed potatoes, pan-seared salmon on a curried corn pancake, and a positively addictive "Thai Caesar salad" that is big enough to share. Unless it's a rare chilly night, opt to sit outside on the patio, surrounded by bamboo and colorful artwork, while sipping a passionfruit cocktail. ✉ *75-5719 Ali'i Dr., Kailua-Kona* ☎ *808/327–2125* ▭ *AE, D, MC, V* ⏲ *Closed Mon. $12–$28.*

$$–$$$ ✕ **Don the Beachcomber at the Royal Kona Resort.** The "original home of the Mai Tai," Don the Beachcomber also offers a great oceanfront breakfast buffet. Though dinners may seem a bit pricey for this hotel, the location and surprising quality of the food are worth the mark-up. Try any of the nightly seafood specials or the Huli Huli chicken, and save room for the Molten Lava cake. ✉ *75-5852 Ali'i Dr., in the Royal Kona Resort* ☎ *808/329–3111* ▭ *AE, D, MC, V. $22–$30.*

$–$$$ ✕ **Huggo's.** This is the only restaurant in town with prices and atmosphere comparable to the splurge restaurants at the Kohala-coast resorts. Open windows extend out over the rocks at the ocean's edge, and at night you can almost touch the manta rays drawn to the spotlights. Relax with a cocktail for two and feast on fresh local seafood; the catch changes daily, and the nightly chef's special is always a good bet. **Huggo's on the Rocks,** next door, is a great outdoor bar with a floor of sand; it's become Kailua-Kona's hot spot for drinks and live music on Friday nights. ✉ *75-5828 Kahakai Rd., off Ali'i Dr., Kailua-Kona* ☎ *808/329–1493* ▭ *AE, D, DC, MC, V. $15–$30.*

$–$$ ✕ **Kai at the Sheraton Keauhou Bay.** Aside from the lobby, this restaurant is the best-looking part of the Sheraton Keauhou Bay. Facing Keauhou Bay, Kai has a primo view. The enormous windows are left open most of the time, making it almost feel like an outdoor restaurant. The menu is limited, but each entrée is good, from the fresh local fish to the brined and roasted hormone-free chicken. Everything is prepared with that fusion of Pacific Rim and Continental that makes up Hawaiian cuisine. The seared ʻahi appetizer is not to be missed. Breakfast is a good bet as well; very reasonable, great buffet, and the view during the daytime is just about perfect. ✉ *78-128 Ehukai St., Kailua-Kona* ☎ *808/930–4900* 💳 *AE, MC, V. $13–$25.*

$–$$ ✕ **O's.** Chef Amy Ferguson-Ota combines Southwestern flavors with Hawaiʻi regional cuisine and a touch of French cooking. There are noodles of all types, in all shapes, from all ethnic backgrounds—be they as delicate spring rolls, as a crisp garnish to an exquisite salad, or as orecchiette in Ota's tuna casserole with wok-seared spiced ʻahi and shiitake cream. ✉ *Crossroads Shopping Center, 75-1129 Henry St., Kailua-Kona* ☎ *808/329–9222* 💳 *AE, D, DC, MC, V. $15–$22.*

¢–$$ ✕ **Mixx Bistro.** Kona never knew it needed a wine bar until it got Mixx, but now the town would seem strange without it. In addition to their fantastic wine and cheese delivery service, Mixx serves up a tasty menu of bistro-inspired *pūpū* (tapas or appetizers) ranging from super healthy plates of sautéed veggies and tofu to what they claim are "the Island's best fries." They also offer a handful of entrée options, including steak frites and a whole crab or lobster served with drawn butter. And then of course there's the cheese plate. And the wine. *Sigh*. Live music keeps the patio lively most nights and Sunday afternoons. ✉ *75-5626 Kuakini Hwy., in the King Kamehameha Center* ☎ *808/329–7334* 🌐 *www.konawinemarket.com* 💳 *MC, V. $5–$15.*

French

$$–$$$ ✕ **La Bourgogne.** A genial husband-and-wife team owns this relaxing, country-style bistro with dark-wood walls and private, romantic booths. The traditional French menu has classics such as escargots, beef with a cabernet sauvignon sauce, rack of lamb with roasted garlic and rosemary, and a less-traditional venison with a pomegranate glaze. Call well in advance for reservations. ✉ *77-6400 Nālani St., Kailua-Kona* ☎ *808/329–6711* ✍ *Reservations essential* 💳 *AE, D, DC, MC, V* ⏲ *Closed Sun. and Mon. No lunch. $20–$32.*

$ ✕ **Peaberry & Galette.** This little creperie is a welcome addition to the neighborhood. It serves Illy espresso, excellent sweet and savory crepes, and rich desserts like lemon cheesecake and chocolate mousse that are made fresh daily. It's got a cool, urban-café vibe, and is a nice place to hang for a bit if you're waiting for a film at the theater next door, or just feel like taking a break from paradise to sip a decent espresso and flip through the latest *W.* ✉ *Keauhou Shopping Center, 78-6740 Makolea St., Kailua-Kona* ☎ *808/322–6020* 💳 *MC, V. $10–$15.*

Hawaiian

¢–$ ✕ **Big Island Grill.** Huge portions of local favorites including pork chops, chicken *katsu,* and an assortment of grilled or pan-seared fish specialties at very reasonable prices. This place has been popular with locals since it opened a few years back, so there's usually a wait for a table. "Biggie's" also serves a great breakfast—the prices and portions make this a great place to take large groups or families. ✉ *75-5702 Kuakini Hwy.* ☎ *808/326–1153* ▭ *MC, V* ⊙ *Closed Sun. $7–$15.*

¢–$ ✕ **Kanaka Kava.** A popular local hang out, and not just because da kava makes you mellow. Their *pūpū* rock! Fresh poke, smoky, tender bowls of pulled kālua pork, and healthy sautéed veggies are available in fairly large portions for less than you'll pay anywhere else on the island. Seating tends to be at a premium, but don't be afraid to share a table and make friends. ✉ *75-5803 Ali'i Dr., Space B6, in the Coconut Grove Market Pl.* ☎ *808/883–6260* ▭ *MC, V. $3–$4 per dish.*

¢ ✕ **Ba-Le.** Comparable to Kona Mix Plate in terms of prices, food quality, and street cred, Ba-Le serves a great plate lunch. It also has tasty Vietnamese-influenced food, such as their popular croissant sandwiches stuffed with mint, lemongrass, sprouts, and your choice from a variety of Vietnamese-style meats. *Pho* (Vietnamese noodle soup) is another great option, especially if you have the misfortune of catching an island cold. There are 20 other shops throughout the state, but it's Hawaiian-owned and operated, so the place doesn't feel like a chain. ✉ *Kona Coast Shopping Center, 74-5588 Palani Rd., Kailua-Kona* ☎ *808/327–1212* ▭ *No credit cards. $5–$7.*

¢ ✕ **Kona Mix Plate.** Don't be surprised if you find yourself rubbing elbows with lots of hungry locals at this inconspicuous Kona lunch spot. The antithesis of a tourist trap, this casual island favorite with fluorescent lighting and wooden tables is all about the food. Try the teriyaki chicken, shrimp tempura, or *katsu*—a chicken breast fried with bread crumbs and served with a sweet sauce. ✉ *341 Palani St., Kailua-Kona* ☎ *808/329–8104* ▭ *No credit cards* ⊙ *Closed Sun. $5–$7.*

Italian

$–$$$ ✕ **Basil's.** This tiny traditional trattoria is nothing special, really—the tablecloths are checkered, the candles are in chianti bottles, there's spaghetti on the menu, and it always feels a little hot and greasy inside. That said, the pizza is decent, the beer's cheap, and you can't beat the location. It's on Ali'i Drive in downtown Kailua-Kona, right across the street from the ocean. ✉ *75-5707 Ali'i Dr., Kailua-Kona* ☎ *808/326–7836* ▭ *MC, V. $12–$30.*

$ ✕ **Mahina Pizza.** Locals are ecstatic to see Mahina's, a favorite pizza joint in town a few years back, reopen in the Kona Inn Shopping Village. Upstairs, above the shops,

[CON]FUSION

What is referred to as "Hawai'i cuisine" is most often a blend of several Pacific Rim and Asian cuisines, along with a few European influences. The Islands are home to large populations of Japanese, Chinese, Portuguese, Thai, Vietnamese, Korean, and Filipino immigrants, and each group has brought a little bit of home with them. This explains why a "traditional Hawaiian" restaurant will include everything from teriyaki to chicken katsu to pork adobo and Portuguese sausage on the menu. We still can't figure out how Spam got involved.

Mahina's serves up some of the tastiest pies on the island (from the usual pepperoni, sausage, and mushroom combos to a great "Garden of Eden" vegetarian option) accompanied by cool ocean breezes and pleasant "downtown" Kona views. It is not uncommon for the owner to close up shop to go paddling, so call ahead to make sure they're open. ✉ *75-5744 Ali'i Dr., in the Kona Inn Shopping Village* ☎ *808/326-1577* ▭ *MC, V. $5–$12.*

Japanese

$–$$$ ✕ **Kenichi Pacific.** With its black-lacquer tables and lipstick-red banquettes, Kenichi's seems a little out of place in this small strip mall. The location keeps many tourists from finding it, even though it's been open for several years now. This is where everyone in Kailua-Kona goes when they feel like splurging on top-notch sushi. It's a little on the spendy side, but it's worth it. The sashimi is so fresh it melts in your mouth, and the signature rolls are inventive and tasty. For vegetarians, the Austin roll—tempura asparagus—is fish-free and delicious. ✉ *Keauhou Shopping Center, 78-6831 Ali'i Dr., Kailua-Kona* ☎ *808/322-9140* ▭ *No credit cards. $17–$30.*

$–$$ ✕ **Restaurant Hayama.** Tucked into Kopiko Plaza, just below Long's, this local favorite for quality Japanese fare goes beyond sushi. Hayama serves traditional Japanese specialties like sukiyaki, teriyaki, shabu shabu, and udon, all made from quality local ingredients. Sushi is available as well, but only traditional nigiri and sashimi. Lunch specials are a great deal, and dinner specials provide a three-course dinner for two for $40. Despite its strip mall location, Hayama manages to pull off a Zen vibe that matches the quiet and attentive, albeit slow, service. ✉ *75-5660 Kopiko St., D1* ☎ *808/331-8888* ▭ *MC, V. $12–$20.*

$–$$ ✕ **Wasabi's.** A tiny little place tucked into the back of the Coconut Plaza on Ali'i, Wasabi's five little tables tend to be occupied by the west side's Japanese population, here for some of the best sashimi on the island. Prices may seem steep, but the fish is of the highest quality. Fans of Americanized sushi rolls will find the familiar California and spicy tuna rolls here, along with a few unique inventions. And for those who will never be hip to the raw fish thing, teriyaki, udon, and sukiyaki options abound. ✉ *75-5803 Ali'i Dr., Coconut Grove Market Pl.* ☎ *808/326-2352* ▭ *MC, V. $13–$22.*

Korean

¢–$ ✕ **Manna Korean Barbecue.** This little hole in the wall next to Safeway serves up shockingly good Korean food for very low prices. The chicken *katsu* is fantastic, as is the Korean spicy pork—each meal comes with your choice of four sides, including perfectly spiced *kimchee.* ✉ *75-1027 Henry St. # 104, Kailua-Kona* ☎ *808/334-0880* ▭ *No credit cards. $6–$12.*

Mexican

$–$$ ✕ **Pancho & Lefty's.** Across the street from the Kona Village Shopping Center, Pancho & Lefty's is a typical Tex-Mex place—great for nachos and margaritas (watch out, they pour 'em strong) on a lazy afternoon. Some of the items on the menu are expensive, and some of the combos are described exactly the same way in other sections of the menu for less, so read carefully. ✉ *75-5719 Ali'i Dr., Kailua-Kona* ☎ *808/326–2171* ▭ *MC, V. $12–$18.*

$–$$ ✕ **Tres Hombres.** The food's good, if a little overpriced for Mexican. Fajitas are always solid, but the real reason to come here is the assortment of margaritas, many mixed with fresh local fruit juice. There's also a location in Kawaihae. ✉ *75-5864 Walua Rd., Kailua-Kona* ☎ *808/329–1292* ▭ *MC, V. $11–$20.*

¢ ✕ **Los Habaneros.** A surprising find in the corner of this shopping mall, next to the movie theater, Habaneros serves up tasty, fresh, and fast Mexican food for low low prices. Our favorites are usually the day's specials, which can be anything from enchilada plates to homemade sopes and chiles rellenos. Their giant burritos are also a solid pick, stuffed with meat, beans, cheese, and all the fixings. ✉ *Phase II, Keauhou Shopping Center* ☎ *808/324–4688* ▭ *MC, V* ⊙ *Closed Sun. $5–$9.*

¢ ✕ **Tacos El Unico.** An array of soft-taco choices (beef and chicken, among others), burritos, quesadillas, and great homemade tamales. Order at the counter, take a seat outside at one of a dozen yellow tables with blue umbrellas, and enjoy all the good flavors served up in those red plastic baskets. ✉ *Kona Marketplace, 75-5729 Ali'i Dr., Kailua-Kona* ☎ *808/326–4033* ▭ *No credit cards. $3–$7.*

BEST BREAKFAST

Bubba Gump's (Kailua-Kona). A chain with the best ocean-front seating in Kailua-Kona and cinnamon-raisin French toast.
Café 100 (Hilo). Local destination for *loco moco* on the Hilo side.
Coffee Shack (Captain Cook). Spectacular view, homemade bread and pastries, and killer eggs Benedict and coffee.
Ken's House of Pancakes (Hilo). Like IHOP, but with Spam.
Pahu i'a at the Four Seasons Hualālai (Kohala). Hands-down the best fancy brunch on the island.

Thai

¢–$$ ✕ **Bangkok House Thai Restaurant.** It may not look like much, but Bangkok House is the local go-to for good Thai food. One of few Thai restaurants on the island to add enough spice to their sauces, Bangkok serves up tasty curries, satays, and soups, along with a random assortment of Chinese entrées. ✉ *75-5626 Kuakini Hwy., in the King Kamehameha Mall* ☎ *808/329–7764* ▭ *MC, V. $9–$18.*

¢–$ ✕ **Orchid Thai Cuisine.** This reasonably priced, family-run restaurant is off the beaten track in a small strip mall. It's cheerfully decorated with purple-and-gold fabrics, and orchids (real and fake) abound. Entrées range from basic curries (red, green, yellow, and "evil") to barbecued hen with lemongrass and garlic. Don't miss the tasty summer rolls. Top off your meal with a dessert of mango and sticky rice. ✉ *77-5563 Kaiwi St., Suite B 27–28, Kailua-Kona* ☎ *808/327–9437* ▭ *MC, V* ⊙ *Closed Sun. $7–$14.*

¢–$ ✕ **Thai Rin Restaurant.** The Thai owner at this old-timer in Ali'i Sunset Plaza is likely to take your order, cook it, and bring it to your table himself. The menu includes five curries, a green-papaya salad, and a popular platter that combines spring rolls, satay, beef salad, and *tom yum*

MOST ROMANTIC

Brown's Beach House (Kohala). For the more laid-back romantic, dine steps away from the beach, with live music and balmy ocean breezes.

Fujimama's (Kailua-Kona). The quiet bamboo patio pleasantly lit with tiki torches is the perfect spot for couples to enjoy a tropical drink and a delicious meal.

Ke'ei Cafe (Kainaliu). Tropical breezes waft into a beautiful koa wood dining room through huge open windows. Diners enjoy views of the treetops and a blend of local fish and meats and Asian and South American influences.

Pahu i'a at the Four Seasons Hualālai (Kohala). Perfect food meets its match in a stunning view from an intimate, well-designed space.

Restaurant Kaikodo (Hilo). Beautiful dining room: check. Elegant dishes: check. Candlelight and lush fabrics: check, check.

(lemongrass soup). ✉ *75-5799 Ali'i Dr., Kailua-Kona* ☎ *808/329–2929* ▭ *AE, D, DC, MC, V. $9–$17.*

South Kona

American–Casual

¢–$$ ✕ **Aloha Angel Cafe.** With an emphasis on healthy, organic fare, this friendly café adjacent to the Aloha Theatre serves tasty, mostly good-for-you options on a lānai overlooking Kealakekua Bay and the orchards above it. Choose from an assortment of egg dishes and pastries in the morning, burgers, fish sandwiches, and salads for lunch, and pasta, grilled fish, or steak for dinner, all at very reasonable prices. For dessert, save room to sample selections from the café's killer pastry case. ✉ *79-7384 Mamalahoa Hwy., Kainaliu* ☎ *808/322–3383* ▭ *MC, V. $8–$18.*

¢–$$ ✕ **Ke'ei Café.** This beautiful restaurant is in a plantation-style building 15 minutes south of Kona. Delicious dinners with Brazilian, Asian, and European flavors utilize fresh ingredients provided by local farmers. Try the Thai red curry or wok-seared 'ahi accompanied by a selection from the extensive wine list. ✉ *Hwy. 11, ½ mi south of Kainaliu, Hōnaunau* ☎ *808/328–8451* ✍ *Reservations essential* ▭ *No credit cards* ⊙ *Closed Sun. and Mon. $9–$19.*

¢–$ ✕ **Café Nasturtium.** This café is tucked into a cheerful little red-orange house in Kainaliu, about 10 minutes from Kailua-Kona. They've planted signs before and after the restaurant, so you'll know when it's coming up and when you've passed it. They serve only organic food here, some of it vegan and all of it very good, from soups made fresh daily to 'ahi tuna sandwiches to homemade *liliko'i* (passion fruit) sorbet. The back patio is sunny and green, with flowers and vines climbing the walls. The downside: service is painfully slow, and the hours are erratic. Call ahead to make sure it's open. ✉ *Hwy. 11, Kainaliu* ☎ *808/322–5083* ▭ *MC, V* ⊙ *Closed weekends. $9–$15.*

¢–$ ✕ **The Coffee Shack.** There's really no flaw to this place. The view is stunning, the service is excellent even when it's busy (which is most of the time), and the eggs Benedict and hot Reuben sandwich are the best on the island. Breads and pastries are all homemade, and the coffee is strong and tasty. On your way to nowhere in particular, stop by for a Hawaiian smoothie, an iced honey mocha latte, or homemade lūʻau bread—all worth a detour. In the evening, enjoy gourmet pizza and an amazing sunset view. ✉ *83-5799 Mamalahoa Hwy.* ☎ *808/328–9555* ▭ *MC, V. $8–$15.*

★ ¢–$ ✕ **Manago Hotel.** About 20 minutes south of Kailua-Kona, Manago is a time-warp experience. A vintage neon sign identifies the hotel, and Formica tables, ceiling fans, and venetian blinds add to the flavor of this film-noir spot. The T-shirts (which are great if you need to bring back a gift for anyone) brag that the place has the best pork chops in town, and it's not false advertising. The fresh fish is excellent as well, especially ono and butterfish. Unless you request otherwise, the fish is all sautéed with a special butter-soy sauce concoction (always good, don't worry). Meals come with rice for the table (served family style, of course) and an assortment of side dishes that changes from time to time. ✉ *82-6155 Māmalahoa Hwy., Captain Cook* ☎ *808/323–2642* ▭ *D, DC, MC, V* ⏲ *Closed Mon. $7–$12.*

Japanese

¢–$ ✕ **Teshima's.** Locals show up at Teshima's whenever they're in the mood for fresh sashimi, puffy shrimp tempura, or *hekka* (beef and vegetables cooked in an iron pot) at a reasonable price. You might also want to try a *teishoku* (tray) of assorted Japanese delicacies. The service is laid-back and friendly. The restaurant is 15 minutes south of Kailua-Kona. ✉ *Māmalahoa Hwy., Honalo* ☎ *808/322–9140* ▭ *No credit cards. $8–$16.*

8

Mexican

¢ ✕ **Adriana's.** The restaurant's owner and namesake serves up home-cooked El Salvadoran food—generally very similar to Mexican food, except with slightly fewer chiles. Adriana's handmade tamales are incredible, and no other spot on the island beats the salsa bar here. ✉ *Kealakekua Ranch Center* ☎ *808/217–7405* ▭ *No credit cards* ⏲ *Closed weekends. $6–$8.*

Volcano

American–Casual

¢–$$ ✕ **Lava Rock Café.** This is a decent place to grab a sandwich or a coffee and check your e-mail before heading to the Volcano. (Lava Rock also serves dinner, but service tends to be less than stellar, especially for tourists.) Dishes range from chicken salad to New York steak, beverages from cappuccino to wine. Though it's not perfect, Lava Rock is a good place to stop if you want to take a picnic into the park: once inside, the park's concessionaires sell bland, overpriced food, and within Volcano Village there are no other fast and tasty deli options. ✉ *Old Volcano Hwy., behind Kīlauea General Store, Volcano* ☎ *808/967–8526* ⏲ *No dinner Sun.* ▭ *MC, V. $7–$18.*

¢–$ ✕ **Volcano Golf & Country Club.** A local favorite for its large portions and classic, greasy breakfasts: ordering the breakfast burger (with fried egg, cheese, and your choice of meat) and a cup of local coffee is the way to

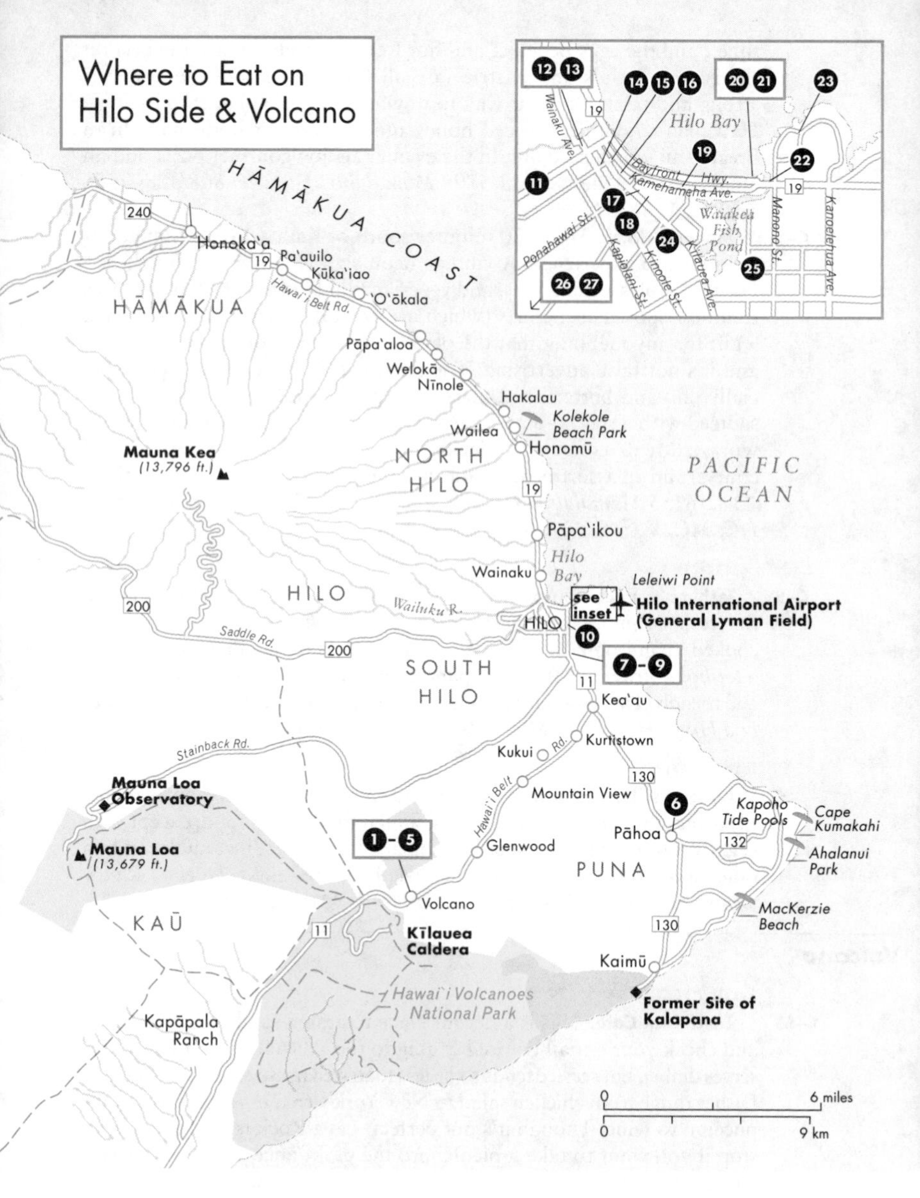

Ba-Le 9	Hilo Bay Café 7	Miyo's 25	Royal Siam 26
Bears' Coffee 13	Ken's House of Pancakes 10	Naung Mai 18	The Seaside 20
Big Island Pizza 16	Kiawe Kitchen 4	Nihon Restaurant 23	Sombat's Fresh Thai Cuisine 27
Blane's Drive-In 11	Kīlauea Lodge 3	Pescatore 14	Thai Thai Restaurant 5
Café 100 17	Kūhiō Grille 8	Queen's Court at the Hilo Hawaiian Hotel ... 19	Uncle Billy's 19
Café Pesto 15	Lava Rock Café 1	Restaurant Kaikodo ... 12	Volcano Golf & Country Club 2
Happy Valley Seafood Restaurant ... 24	Luquin's Mexican Restaurant 6	Reuben's Mexican Restaurant 22	
Harrington's 21			

go. If it's lunchtime, you can't beat the burgers. ✉ *Pi'i Mauna Dr., off Hwy. 11, Volcano* ☎ *808/967–8228* ⊙ *No dinner* ▭ *MC, V. $5–$12.*

Contemporary

$–$$$$ ✕ **Kīlauea Lodge.** Chef Albert Jeyte combines contemporary trends with traditional cooking styles from the mainland, France, and his native Hamburg, Germany. Entrées include venison, duck à l'orange with an apricot-mustard glaze, and authentic *hasenpfeffer* (braised rabbit) served with Jeyte's signature sauerbraten. Built in 1937 as a YMCA camp, the restaurant still has the original "Friendship Fireplace" made from stones from around the world. The roaring fire, koa-wood tables, and warm lighting make the sunny main building feel like a lodge. ✉ *Old Volcano Hwy., Volcano* ☎ *808/967–7366* ▭ *AE, MC, V* ⊙ *No lunch. $17–$38.*

Italian

$–$$ ✕ **Kiawe Kitchen.** Everyone around here says the same thing: "Kiawe has awesome pizza, but it's a little expensive for pizza." And it's true—the wood-fired pizza has a perfect thin crust and an authentic Italian taste, but you have to be prepared to spend around $15 on a typical pie. Food options are limited in this area, though. Go for it. ✉ *19-4005 Old Volcano Rd., Volcano* ☎ *808/967–7711* ▭ *MC, V* ⊙ *Closed Wed. $15–$25.*

Thai

¢–$ ✕ **Thai Thai Restaurant.** The food is authentic, and the prices are reasonable at this little Volcano Village find. A steaming-hot plate of curry or a dish of pad thai noodles is the perfect antidote to a chilly day on the volcano. The chicken satay is excellent—the peanut dipping sauce the perfect match of sweet and spicy. Be careful when you order, as "medium" is more than spicy enough even for hard-core chili addicts. The service is warm and friendly. ✉ *19-4084 Old Volcano Rd., Volcano* ☎ *808/967–7969* ⊙ *No lunch* ▭ *MC, V. $9–$16.*

Hilo & Puna

American-Casual

$–$$$ ✕ **The Seaside.** The Nakagawa family has been running this eatery since the early 1920s. The latest son to manage the place has spruced it up a bit with tablecloths and candles, but the decor is still bare-bones. No matter, since it serves some of the freshest fish on the island. (Not a surprise, as the fish come from the restaurant's own aqua farm.) Islanders travel great distances for the fried *āholehole* (young Hawaiian flagtail). Not a fish eater? Try the grilled lamb chops, chicken, or prime rib. Arrive before sunset and request a table on the patio for a view of the egrets roosting around the fish ponds. ✉ *1790 Kalaniana'ole Ave., Hilo* ☎ *808/935–8825* ▭ *AE, DC, MC, V* ⊙ *Closed Mon. No lunch. $11–$27.*

$–$$ ✕ **Harrington's.** A great view and a daily happy hour make this steak-and-seafood restaurant on Reed's Bay a popular place. You can't go wrong with either the catch of the day served in a tangy citrus-wasabi beurre blanc or the peppercorn steak. The garlic-laced Slavic steak is a specialty of the house. For lunch try the Harrington's burger, served with cream-cheese aioli. ✉ *135 Kalaniana'ole Ave., Hilo* ☎ *808/961–4966* ▭ *MC, V. $16–$25.*

$–$$ ✕ **Queen's Court at the Hilo Hawaiian Hotel.** Queen's Court is known for one thing: buffets. On the weekends the spread includes seafood (Friday and Saturday) and Hawaiian fare (Sunday), but during the week it's prime rib every night. The prime rib's not great, but the seafood specialties are. ✉ *1730 Kamehameha Ave., Hilo* ☎ *808/935–8711* ▭ *AE, D, DC, MC, V. $16–$25.*

¢–$$ ✕ **Hilo Bay Café.** Not the greatest setting (in a strip mall that contains Office Max and Wal-Mart), but fantastic food. When in season, the out-of-this-world heirloom tomato salad puts any mainland variation to shame. The vegan offerings, which range from garlic fries to potpie, are good enough to seduce meat-eaters. Other excellent options include cheese fondue, pepper steak, roasted chicken breast stuffed with pine nuts and garlic cream cheese, and any of the salads (the beet salad is a stand-out). Prices are exceedingly reasonable given the quality of the food. ✉ *315 Makaala St., Hilo* ☎ *808/935–4939* ▭ *AE, DC, MC, V. $7–$20.*

¢–$$ ✕ **Uncle Billy's.** Uncle Billy's is pure Hawaiian kitsch—right out of 1930s Hollywood—but the thatch roofs, tinkling capiz-shell wind chimes, and Tahitian-print curtains add to the fun, as does a free nightly hula show. The show and the ambience are the reasons to visit; the food is so-so. Choose from mahimahi meunière, teriyaki chicken, and local specialties. ✉ *Hilo Bay Hotel, 87 Banyan Dr., Hilo* ☎ *808/935–0861* ▭ *AE, D, DC, MC, V* ⏲ *No lunch. $9–$25.*

¢–$ ✕ **Bears' Coffee.** A favorite Hilo breakfast spot, much loved for their fresh fruit waffles and tasty morning coffee. Service can be a little slow, but where are you running off to anyway? For lunch they serve up huge deli sandwiches and decent entrée-size salads. In keeping with its name, the little diner is full of stuffed bears, ceramic bears, even bear wallpaper—it's a little much, but the kids will like it. ✉ *106 Keawe St.* ☎ *808/935–0708* ▭ *No credit cards. $7–$10.*

¢–$ ✕ **Ken's House of Pancakes.** For years this 24-hour coffee shop between the airport and the hotels along Banyan Drive has been a gathering place for Hilo residents. As its name implies, Ken's serves good pancakes, but there are about 180 other tasty local specialties and American diner–inspired items from which to choose. Wednesday is prime rib night. ✉ *1730 Kamehameha Ave., Hilo* ☎ *808/935–8711* ▭ *AE, D, DC, MC, V. $8–$15.*

Chinese

$$ ✕ **Happy Valley Seafood Restaurant.** Don't let the name fool you. Though Hilo's best Chinese restaurant does specialize in seafood (the salt and pepper prawns are fantastic), they also offer a wide range of other Cantonese treats, including the sizzling lamb platter, salt and pepper pork, mongolian beef or chicken, and vegetarian specialties like garlic eggplant and crispy green beans. The food is good, portions are large, and the price is right. ✉ *1263 Kilauea Ave., Ste. 320* ☎ *808/933–1083* ▭ *MC, V. $10–$16.*

Contemporary

★ **$–$$$** ✕ **Restaurant Kaikodo.** Now that the service has improved and the menu has gone through a couple of revisions, Kaikodo is back on top of its game. The salmon sautéed in miso butter and served with crab on buckwheat soba noodles is excellent, but most nights the best bet is the seafood special. It's always something caught locally and prepared in an inven-

CLOSE UP

The Plate Lunch Tradition

TO EXPERIENCE ISLAND HISTORY FIRST-HAND, take a seat at one of Hawai'i's ubiquitous "plate lunch" eateries, and order a segmented Styrofoam plate piled with rice, macaroni salad, and maybe some fiery pickled vegetable condiment. On the sugar plantations, native Hawaiians and immigrant workers from many different countries ate together in the fields, sharing food from their kaukau kits, the utilitarian version of the Japanese *bento* lunchbox. From this melting pot came the vibrant language of pidgin and its equivalent in food: the plate lunch.

At beaches and events, you can probably see a few tiny kitchens-on-wheels, another excellent venue for sampling plate lunch. These portable restaurants are descendants of lunch wagons that began selling food to plantation workers in the 1930s. Try the deep-fried chicken *katsu* (rolled in Japanese panko flour and spices). The marinated beef teriyaki is another good choice, as is miso butterfish. The noodle soup, *saimin,* with its Japanese fish stock and Chinese red-tinted barbecue pork, is a distinctly local medley. Koreans have contributed spicy barbecue *kal-bi* ribs, often served with chili-laden *kimchee* (pickled cabbage). Portuguese bean soup and tangy Filipino *adobo* stew are also favorites. The most popular Hawaiian contribution to the plate lunch is the *laulau,* a mix of meat and fish and young taro leaves, wrapped in more taro leaves and steamed.

8

tive way. The lamb and steak dishes are also excellent. Desserts are good, too. ✉ *60 Keawe St., Hilo* ☎ *808/961–2558* ▭ *AE, D, DC, MC, V. $16–$35.*

Hawaiian Fast Food

¢–$ ✕ **Café 100.** This popular local restaurant is famous for its tasty *loco moco,* prepared in more than a dozen ways, and its dirt-cheap breakfast and lunch specials. (You can stuff yourself for $3 if you order right.) If you're looking for a salad, keep walking. ✉ *969 Kīlauea Ave., Hilo* ☎ *808/935–8683* ▭ *No credit cards. $5–$10.*

¢–$ ✕ **Kūhiō Grille.** There's no ambience to speak of, and water is served in unbreakable plastic, but if you're searching for local fare—that eclectic and undefinable fusion of ethnic cuisines—Kūhiō Grille is a must. Sam Araki serves a 1-pound *laulau* (a steamed bundle of taro leaves and pork) that is worth the trip. This diner at the edge of Hilo's largest mall opens at 6 AM. ✉ *Prince Kūhiō Shopping Plaza, 111 E. Puainako St., at Hwy. 11* ☎ *808/959–2336* ▭ *AE, MC, V. $5–$14.*

¢ ✕ **Ba-Le.** This place serves a great plate lunch, but people come here for the tasty sandwiches—mixtures of mint, lemongrass, sprouts, and your choice of Vietnamese-style meats served on a croissant or crusty French bread. ✉ *111 E. Puainako, Hilo* ☎ *808/959–1300* ▭ *No credit cards. $5–$7.*

¢ ✕ **Blane's Drive-In.** With a vast menu second only to Ken's House of Pancakes, Blane's serves up everything from standard hamburgers to chicken *katsu*. There's a mean plate lunch with tons of fresh fish for only $7. The slow-cooked homemade chili and sticky white rice is a meal in itself, and costs less than $3. ✉ *217 Wainuenue Ave., Hilo* ☎ *808/969–9494* ▭ *No credit cards. $2–$7.*

Italian

$–$$$ ✕ **Café Pesto.** Both branches of Café Pesto—here and in Kawaihae—are equally popular. Fresh local seafood is one of the best reasons to stop by for dinner, but their pizzas are also among the best on the island. Local microbrews and a full-service bar make this a good place to end the evening. ✉ *308 Kamehameha Ave., Hilo* ☎ *808/969–6640* ▭ *AE, D, DC, MC, V. $10–$29.*

$–$$$ ✕ **Pescatore.** With dim lights, stately high-back chairs, and dark-wood paneling, Pescatore conjures up an Italian trattoria. The surprisingly authentic Italian cuisine includes items like lasagne, chicken marsala, and chicken or veal parmigiana. Lunch consists of Italian-style sandwiches; breakfast, served on weekends only, features omelets and crepes. Families love the pastas made to please choosy children. ✉ *235 Keawe St., at Haili St., Hilo* ☎ *808/969–9090* ▭ *AE, D, DC, MC, V. $15–$29.*

$–$$$ ✕ **Big Island Pizza.** If spending a twenty on a large pizza is something you just can't come to grips with, steer clear of Big Island Pizza. If, on the other hand, you can rationalize paying more for a pie that's topped with things like Black Tiger shrimp, scallops, and chunks of crab meat (the "Ali'i Feast"), then order up and get ready for a little slice of heaven. They also deliver to the eastern side of the island. ✉ *760 Kilauea Ave.* ☎ *808/934–8000* 🌐 *www.bigislandpizza.com* ▭ *AE, D, MC, V. $8–$20.*

Japanese

$–$$$ ✕ **Nihon Restaurant.** This open, airy dining room has a great view of Hilo Bay. Servers are dressed in colorful kimonos, and Japanese art and music add to the ambience. The menu offers a wide choice of authentic Japanese cuisine including beef, pork, chicken, and seafood dishes. Try the soba noodles, the teriyaki steak, and the grilled butterfish marinated in a rich miso-soy sauce. A sushi bar provides a full range of wonderful and varied sushi and sashimi. The restaurant is adjacent to the Lili'uokalani Gardens. ✉ *123 Lihiwai St., Hilo* ☎ *808/969–1133* ▭ *AE, MC, V* ⏲ *Closed Sun. $12–$30.*

¢–$ ✕ **Miyo's.** Tucked behind a karaoke bar at the Waiakea Villas Hotel, Miyo's large open dining room overlooks a beautiful pond. The menu focuses on fresh and delicious sashimi, complemented by fluffy tempura and not-too-sweet teriyaki. Each dish is served on a platter with salad, miso soup, and rice. Most meals are under $10, making Miyo's a terrific find. ✉ *400 Hualani St., Hilo* ☎ *808/935–2273* ▭ *MC, V* ⏲ *Closed Sun. $8–$15.*

Mexican

$–$$ ✕ **Luquin's Mexican Restaurant.** Long an island favorite for tasty, albeit greasy, Mexican grub, Luquin's is still going strong in the funky town of Pahoa. Tacos are great here (go for crispy), especially when stuffed with grilled, seasoned local fish. Chips are warm and salty, the salsa's got some kick, and the beans are thick with lard and topped with melted

NEW & NOTABLE RESTAURANTS

At this writing, a handful of restaurants had just opened. We weren't able to completely vet them in time for publication, but they looked pretty cool so we thought we'd at least mention them:

Tommy Bahama's Steakhouse (The Shops at Mauna Lani, Mauna Lani Resort, Kohala Coast). An upscale tropical-style steakhouse decked out in the tasteful vintage Hawaiiana the Tommy Bahama brand is known for. Dinner prices are high, but comparable to those at surrounding restaurants. The bar has already become popular with Kohala Coast employees and residents looking for a happy hour watering hole.

Fish Hopper Restaurant (Ali'i Drive, downtown Kailua-Kona). The new Hawaiian outpost of a popular Monterey, California seafood restaurant. The Big Island version will focus on local fish specialties (seared 'ahi, macadamia-crusted Mahi Mahi), along with the restaurant's popular clam chowder and fish 'n' chips.

Ruth's Chris Steakhouse (The Shops at Mauna Lani, Mauna Lani Resort, Kohala Coast). They claim to have vegetarian options, but the Big Island location of the popular Louisiana steakhouse is for meat-lovers only. Steaks come sizzling, with tasty, unhealthy classic sides like creamed spinach, broccoli with cheddar cheese, and au gratin potatoes. All menu items are à la carte so be prepared for a large bill.

8

cheese. Not something you'd eat before a long swim, but perfect after a long day of exploring. ✉ *Main St., Pahoa* ☎ *808/965–9990* ▭ *MC, V. $9–$15.*

$–$$ ✕ **Reuben's Mexican Restaurant.** It's not the best Mexican food you've ever had, but if you're in Hilo and you're jonesing for some chile verde, Reuben's has got you pretty well covered. You could make a meal out of their warm chips and salsa alone, and they're known for pouring a stiff margarita. Fancy? No. Authentic? *Mas o menos* (more or less). Sometimes you just want a greasy plate of nachos and a margarita. ✉ *336 Kamehameha Ave., Hilo* ☎ *808/961–2552* ▭ *No credit cards. $10–$20.*

Thai

¢–$ ✕ **Naung Mai.** There's not much to this downtown eatery: five tables, three booths, and owner Alisa Rung Khongnok hard at work in the kitchen. It's a bit hard to find, but fresh, reasonably priced meals make it worth seeking out. It may be the best Thai food on the island. For those who like to pair spicy curry with cold beer, feel free to pick up a six-pack at the grocery store up the street. Naung Mai charges $2 for glasses. ✉ *86 Kīlauea Ave., Hilo* ☎ *808/934–7540* ▭ *MC, V* ⏲ *Closed Sun. No lunch Wed. or Sat. $8–$11.*

¢–$ ✕ **Royal Siam.** A downtown Hilo fixture, this authentic Thai eatery offers little ambience. But you don't need a dramatic view when you can choose from a menu that includes five kinds of curries and plenty of stir-fried meals. The tangy stir-fried garlic shrimp with coconut milk and wild mushrooms is particularly good. ✉ *70 Mamo St., Hilo* ☎ *808/961–6100* 💳 *AE, D, DC, MC, V* ⏲ *Closed Sun. $7–$12.*

¢–$ ✕ **Sombat's Fresh Thai Cuisine.** The name says it all. Sombat Parente uses only the freshest local ingredients to prepare authentic and tasty Thai treats like pumpkin curry, spring rolls with lime sauce, and green papaya salad. In fact, many of the items on the menu come directly from Sombat's own garden. Their weekday lunch plate special is a steal ($6 for an entrée plus rice and salad, $7 for two entrée choices, and $8 for three). And if you can't leave the island without it, Sombat's infamous pad thai sauce is available to take home in jars. ✉ *88 Kanoelehue Ave., Waiakea Kai Plaza* ☎ *808/969–9336* 🌐 *www.sombats.com* 💳 *MC, V* ⏲ *Closed Sun. $8–$15.*

Where to Stay

WORD OF MOUTH

"Before designating a 'central location' for the BI you first need to decide what you want to see and do. If proximity to white sand beaches and good weather are priorities, Kohala is the best choice."
–fdecarlo

" I recommend staying as close as possible to Volcanoes National Park so that you have less driving to do and you don't worry too much about staying late to see the lava flow at night."
–mrkindallas

www.fodors.com/forums

LODGING PLANNER

Resorts

The resorts—all clustered on the Kohala Coast—are expensive, there are no two ways about it. That said, many offer free nights with longer stays (5th or 7th night free) and often team up with airlines or consolidators to offer great package deals that may include a rental car, meals, spa treatments, golf, and other activities. Children under 17 can sometimes stay for free. Ask about specials when you book, and check their Web site as well—many resorts have Internet-only deals.

Condos & Vacation Rentals

Condos and vacation homes are the best deal going on the island. There are hundreds to choose from in and around Kailua-Kona, and dozens more dotted around the island. More and more are being built every day, which keeps driving rates down. You can get more space and save some money by eating in (although it's easy to amass a huge bill at the grocery store, so you still have to be careful).

B&Bs

B&Bs are a nice halfway point between the resorts and condos, offering breakfast and maid service, but without the extras that drive up rates at resorts. Be sure to check the association Web sites as well as property Web sites and call to ask questions. There are still a few "B&B"s that are really just a dumpy room in someone's house and you don't want to end up there.

Reservations

You'll almost always be able to find a room on the Big Island, but you might not get your first choice if you wait until the last minute. Make reservations six months to a year in advance if you're visiting during the winter season (December 15 through April 15). The week after Easter Sunday, when the Merrie Monarch Festival is in full swing, all of Hilo's rooms are booked. Kailua-Kona is packed in mid-October during the Ironman World Triathlon Championship. (Even tougher than trying to find a room at these times is trying to find a rental car.)

Keep in Mind

Most of the resorts now charge "resort fees" for things like parking, daily newspaper service and activities—the charges run from $20 a day to $40 for the duration of your stay. Some condos and vacation rentals charge an additional cleaning fee.

What It Costs

All rates quoted here are rack rates given by the properties at this writing. Always ask about specials and discounts when you book, and look online for great package deals. Generally, the farther you are from the beach, the less you'll pay. If you're willing to drive 10 to 30 minutes to get to the beach, you can find great deals. At the beach, you can get a slight rate reduction if you opt for a garden view instead of the ocean view. High season is usually considered December to February and June to August.

WHAT IT COSTS

	$$$$	$$$	$$	$	¢
Hotels	over 340	261–340	181–260	100–180	under 100

Prices are for two people in a standard double room in high season. Condo price categories reflect rates for a studio, one-bedroom or the smallest unit available.

By Amy Westervelt

EVEN AMONG LOCALS, there is an ongoing debate about which side of the Big Island is "better," so don't worry if you're having a tough time deciding where to stay. Our recommendation? Do both. Each side of the island offers a totally different range of accommodations, restaurants, and activities. Consider staying at one of the resorts or in a condo in Kailua-Kona or along the Kohala Coast for half of your trip. Then, shift gears and check into a romantic B&B on the Hāmākua Coast or in Hilo. If you've got keiki in tow, opt for a vacation home or one of Hilo's family-friendly hotels. On the west coast, lounge on the pristine beaches and try some of the fine-dining restaurants; on the east, hike through rain forests, frolic in waterfalls, and go for a plate lunch.

If you choose a B&B, inn, or an out-of-the-way hotel, explain your expectations fully and ask plenty of questions before booking. Be clear about your travel and location needs. Some places require stays of two or three days. When booking, ask about car-rental arrangements, as many B&B networks offer discounted rates. No matter where you stay, you'll want to rent a car—preferably one with four-wheel drive. This is imperative for getting to some of the best beaches and really seeing the island.

Members of the Big Island–based **Hawai'i Island Bed & Breakfast Association** (www.stayhawaii.com) are listed with phone numbers and rates in a comprehensive online brochure. In order to join this network, B&Bs must be evaluated and meet fairly stringent minimum requirements, including a yearly walk-through by Association officers to maintain their membership.

Other B&B associations include **Bed & Breakfast Honolulu (Statewide)** (☏ 800/288–4666 🖷 808/595–7533 🌐 www.hawaiibnb.com) and **Hawai'i's Best Bed & Breakfasts** (☏ 808/985–7488 or 800/262–9912 🖷 808/967–8610 🌐 www.bestbnb.com).

For information on camping at county parks, including Spencer Beach Park, contact the **Department of Parks and Recreation** (✉ 25 Aupuni St., Hilo 96720 ☏ 808/961–8311 🌐 www.hawaii-county.com).

9

Kohala Coast

The Kohala Coast is home to all of the Big Island's resorts. One after the other, manicured lawns and golf courses, luxurious hotels, and white sand beaches break up the long expanse of black lava rock along the northwest coast. Many visitors to the Big Island check in here and rarely leave, except to try the restaurants, spas, or golf courses at neighboring resorts. If you're looking to be pampered (for a price!) and lounge on the beach or by the pool all day with an umbrella drink in hand, this is where you need to be. That's not to say that staying in Kohala makes it difficult to see the rest of the island. On the contrary, most of the hiking and adventure tour companies on the island offer pick-ups at the Kohala resorts, and many of the hotels have deals with various rental car agencies so you can be as active or lazy as you like.

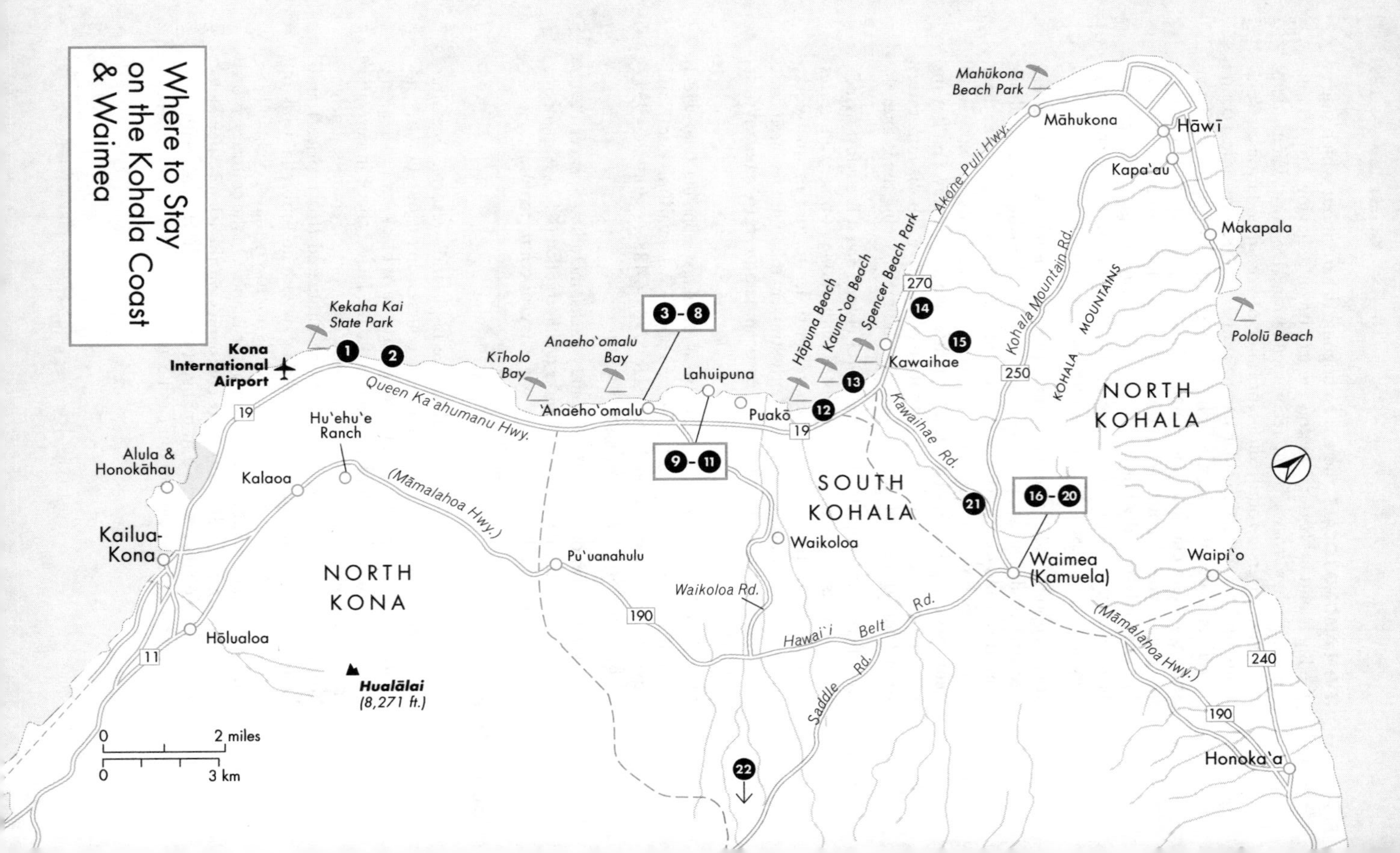
Where to Stay on the Kohala Coast & Waimea
Kona International Airport
Kekaha Kai State Park
Kīholo Bay
Anaeho`omalu Bay
`Anaeho`omalu
Lahuipuna
Puakō
Hāpuna Beach
Kauna`oa Beach
Spencer Beach Park
Kawaihae
Mahūkona Beach Park
Māhukona
Hāwī
Kapa'au
Makapala
Pololū Beach
Akone Puli Hwy.
Kohala Mountain Rd.
KOHALA MOUNTAINS
NORTH KOHALA
SOUTH KOHALA
Kawaihae Rd.
Waimea (Kamuela)
Waipi`o
Honoka`a
(Māmalahoa Hwy.)
Hawai`i Belt Rd.
Saddle Rd.
Waikoloa
Waikoloa Rd.
Pu`uanahulu
Queen Ka`ahumanu Hwy.
Hu`ehu`e Ranch
Kalaoa
Alula & Honokāhau
Kailua-Kona
Hōlualoa
NORTH KONA
Hualālai (8,271 ft.)
19
190
250
270
240
11
0
2 miles
3 km

WHERE TO STAY ON THE KOHALA COAST & WAIMEA

HOTEL NAME	Worth Noting	Cost $	Pools	On the Beach	Golf Courses	Tennis Courts	Gym	Spa	Children's Programs	Rooms or Units	Restaurants	Other	Location
Hotels & Resorts													
★ 9 Fairmont Orchid Hawai'i	*Massages on the beach*	*309–559*	*1*	*yes*	*yes*	*10*	*yes*	*yes*	*5–12*	*540*	*4*	*shops*	*South Kohala*
★ 1 Four Seasons Hualālai	*King's Pond snorkeling*	*560–775*	*5*	*yes*	*yes*	*8*	*yes*	*yes*	*5–12*	*274*	*3*		*North Kona*
12 Hāpuna Beach Prince	*Fantastic beach*	*360–650*	*1*	*yes*	*yes*	*13*	*yes*	*yes*	*5–12*	*350*	*5*		*South Kohala*
★ 3 Hilton Waikoloa Village	*Dolphin Quest program*	*199–649*	*3*	*yes*	*yes*	*8*	*yes*	*yes*	*5–12*	*1297*	*10*	*shops*	*Waikoloa*
★ 2 Kona Village Resort	*2 lū'au options*	*530–940*	*2*	*yes*		*3*	*yes*	*yes*	*6–17*	*125*	*2*	*no A/C*	*North Kona*
13 Mauna Kea Beach Hotel	*Impressive art collection*	*370–650*	*1*	*yes*	*yes*	*13*	*yes*	*yes*	*5–12*	*310*	*5*		*South Kohala*
★ 10 Mauna Lani Bay	*Renowned golf & spa*	*395–850*	*1*	*yes*	*yes*	*16*	*yes*	*yes*	*5–12*	*350*	*8*		*South Kohala*
4 Waikoloa Beach Marriott	*Great deal for location*	*254–445*	*1*	*yes*	*yes*	*6*	*yes*	*yes*	*5–12*	*545*	*1*		*Waikoloa*
20 Waimea Country Lodge	*Includes breakfast*	*101–127*								*21*		*no A/C*	*Waimea*
Condos & Vacation Rentals													
16 Aloha Vacation Cottages	*Private, close to beach*	*135–145*								*2*		*no A/C*	*Waimea*
14 Kohala Ranch	*Beautiful views*	*150*								*varies*		*kitchens*	*Kawaihae*
★ 11 Mauna Lani Point, Terrace	*Waterfall pool*	*326–415*	*1*		*priv.*					*61*		*kitchens*	*South Kohala*
5 Outrigger Fairway Villas	*Infinity pool, gym*	*215–239*	*1*				*yes*			*80*		*kitchens*	*Waikoloa*
6 Outrigger Kolea	*Infinity pool, kids pool*	*450*	*2*				*yes*			*70*		*kitchens*	*Waikoloa*
7 ResortQuest Shores	*Great package deals*	*224–345*	*1*			*2*	*yes*			*75*		*kitchens*	*Waikoloa*
8 Vista Waikoloa	*2 lānais per unit*	*180–250*	*1*			*1*	*yes*			*70*		*kitchens*	*Waikoloa*
★ 17 Waimea Gardens Cottage	*Mountainside stream*	*150–160*								*3*		*kitchens*	*Waimea*
B&Bs													
21 Aaah, The Views!	*Streamside, those views*	*80–155*								*4*		*kitchens*	*Waimea*
15 Hale Ho'onanea	*Great deal*	*100–130*								*3*		*no A/C*	*Kawaihae*
★ 18 Jacaranda Inn	*Good breakfast, big rooms*	*159–225, cottage 350*								*9*		*no A/C*	*Waimea*
19 Kamuela Inn	*Reasonable prices*	*60–85*					*yes*			*31*		*no A/C*	*Waimea*
22 Mana Ranch	*Mauna Kea views*	*75–125*								*3*			*Waimea*

Hotels & Resorts

★ $$$$ **Four Seasons Resort Hualālai.** Beautiful views everywhere, polished wood floors, brand new furnishings and linens in warm earth and cool white tones, and Hawaiian artwork make Hualālai a peaceful retreat. Ground-level rooms have outdoor garden showers. Bungalows are large and cozy, with down comforters and spacious slate-floor bathrooms. One of the five pools, called King's Pond, is a brackish water pond with loads of fish and two manta rays that guests have the opportunity to feed daily. The main infinity pool looks like something out of an ad for an expensive liquor—it's long and peaceful, surrounded by cabanas and palm trees with a clear view to the ocean beyond. The on-site Hawaiian Cultural Center honors the grounds' spiritual heritage, and the sports club and spa offer top-rate health and fitness options. Hualālai's golf course hosts the Senior PGA Tournament of Champions. Despite its quiet luxury, the resort is also super kid-friendly, with a great activities program, and a few pool options for families. The downside is this: despite valiant efforts to the contrary, the Four Seasons doesn't feel much like Hawai'i; add to that the number of guests who will be squawking on their cell phones next to you at the pool (despite the sign reading NO CELL PHONES), and you can see why some folks avoid this place. Still, it is beautiful, the restaurants are fantastic (the infamous Alan Wong operates the Hualālai Grill and Pahui'a serves up the best beachfront Sunday brunch on the island), the rooms are more than comfortable, and the service is definitely of Four Seasons quality. *100 Ka'ūpūlehu Dr. Box 1269, Kailua-Kona 96745 808/325–8000, 800/819–5053, or 888/340–5662 808/325–8200 www.fourseasons.com 243 rooms, 31 suites 3 restaurants, A/C, in-room broadband, in-room safes, cable TV with movies, in-room DVD players, 18-hole golf course, 8 tennis courts, 5 pools, health club, spa, beach, 2 bars, recreation room, babysitting, children's programs (ages 5–12), laundry service, business services, airport shuttle, no-smoking rooms AE, DC, MC, V. $560–$775.*

$$$$ **Hāpuna Beach Prince Hotel.** Often more reasonable than its neighbors, thanks to a variety of ongoing discount options, the Hāpuna Beach Prince is no less luxurious and happens to be sitting on a corner of the best beach on the island. Very much a business hotel, rooms at the Hāpuna are spacious, with marble bathrooms, private lānai, and at least partial views of the ocean. Meandering pathways lead to restaurants, beach facilities, and a spectacular golf course. A hiking trail and a frequent shuttle connect Hāpuna with its sister hotel, the Mauna Kea Beach Hotel. The golf course, designed by Arnold Palmer and Ed Seay, has topped many a "best courses" list and was recently named one of the most women-friendly courses in the world (what that means, we're still trying to figure out). A fully loaded gym is attached to the golf clubhouse, where you can munch on one of the best burgers on the island. After your workout, of course. *62-100 Kauna'oa Dr., Kohala Coast 96743 808/880–1111 or 800/882–6060 808/880–3112 www.princeresortshawaii.com 314 rooms, 36 suites 5 restaurants, A/C, in-room broadband, refrigerators, cable TV with movies, 18-hole golf course, 13 tennis courts, pool, health club, hair salon, hot tub, spa, beach,*

2 bars, children's programs (ages 5–12), business services, no-smoking rooms ▭ *AE, D, DC, MC, V. $360–$650.*

$$$$ Fodor's Choice ★ **Kona Village Resort.** The most Hawaiian of the Kohala Coast resorts, Kona Village was one of the first, and it makes a real effort to keep modern life at bay. Without phones, televisions, or radios, the Kona Village is in a time warp—the perfect place for couples or families to get away from it all in their own thatch-roof *hale* (house) near the resort's sandy beach. Built on the grounds of an ancient Hawaiian village, the modern bungalows reflect styles of South Seas cultures—Tahitian, Samoan, Maori, Fijian, or Hawaiian. The extra-large Royal rooms have private hot tubs. Rates include all meals, an authentic Polynesian Wednesday- or Friday-night lū'au, grounds tours, tennis, sports activities, and rides in the resort's glass-bottom boat. The resort's ocean program has recently been expanded to include sea kayaking, scuba diving on a new boat that can accommodate up to six divers, and snorkeling excursions. Children's programs are not available in May or September, which are designated "adults-only" months. ■ TIP→ **If you're planning a honeymoon to Hawai'i and want to stay at Kona Village, May or September is a good choice.** ✉ *Queen Ka'ahumanu Hwy., Box 1299, Kailua-Kona 96745* ☎ *808/325–5555 or 800/367–5290* 📠 *808/325–5124* 🌐 *www.konavillage.com* *125 bungalows* *2 restaurants, fans, 3 tennis courts, 2 pools, health club, spa, hot tub, beach, boating, 3 bars, children's programs (ages 6–17), business services, airport shuttle; no A/C, no room phones, no room TVs* ▭ *AE, DC, MC, V. $530–$940.*

★ **$$$$** **Mauna Kea Beach Hotel.** The grande dame of Kohala Coast, the Mauna Kea Beach Hotel was designed by Laurance S. Rockefeller in the early 1960s and opened in 1965. It has long been regarded as one of the world's premier vacation resort hotels, and it borders one of the island's finest white-sand beaches, Kauna'oa. The Mauna Kea was damaged in the earthquake of October 2006, and, at this writing, the hotel is closed to overnight guests and expected to remain so for at least a year. Contact the hotel directly for the latest information. You can still enjoy this lovely property, however. The golf course, pro shop, Hau Tree Restaurant, lū'au, and clam bake are still operating. And that beautiful beach is still open. ✉ *62-100 Mauna Kea Beach Dr., Kohala Coast 96743* ☎ *808/882–7222 or 800/882–6060* 📠 *808/880–3112* 🌐 *www.princeresortshawaii.com* *300 rooms, 10 suites* *5 restaurants, A/C, in-room broadband, in-room safes, refrigerators, cable TV, 2 18-hole golf courses, 13 tennis courts, pool, health club, hair salon, spa, beach, children's programs (age 5–12), business services, no-smoking rooms* ▭ *AE, D, DC, MC, V. $370–$650.*

★ **$$$$** **Mauna Lani Bay Hotel & Bungalows.** Another Kohala Coast classic, this is still one of the most beautiful resorts on the island. The open-air lobby has ceilings near the stratosphere, ocean views, and a constant, pleasant breeze. The vast majority of the recently renovated rooms have ocean views, and all have a large lānai. The resort is known for its two spectacular golf courses and award-winning spa. Though the resort's Canoe House restaurant has been highly acclaimed for years and makes for a beautiful dining experience (open air, right on the beach, tons of beautiful koa wood and candlelight), none of the Mauna Lani restaurants really qualify as phenomenal—but not to worry, Tommy Bahama's and Ruth's Chris Steakhouse have opened up in The Shops at Mauna Lani, the Fairmont's restaurants are right next door, and several others await within a 10-mi radius of the hotel. ✉ *68-1400 Mauna Lani Dr., Kohala Coast 96743* ☎ *808/885–6622 or 800/367–2323* 📠 *808/885–1484* 🌐 *www.maunalani.com* *335 rooms, 10 suites, 5 bungalows* *8 restaurants, A/C, in-room broadband, Wi-Fi, in-room safes, minibars, refrigerators, cable TV, in-room VCRs, 2 18-hole golf courses, 16 tennis courts, pool, gym, spa, beach, 5 bars, children's programs (ages 5–12), business services, no-smoking rooms* *AE, D, DC, MC, V. $395–$850.*

$$$–$$$$ Fodor's Choice ★ **Fairmont Orchid Hawai'i.** The Fairmont is an elegant, old-school hotel—rooms are tasteful, if a bit flowery for those with more modern sensibilities, the lobby is enormous with lots of marble and sweeping ocean views, service is impeccable, and the restaurants are all top-notch. The grounds are expansive, lush, and well maintained. This is one of the island's largest resorts, and its romantic botanical gardens and waterfall ponds stretch along 32 beachfront acres. A $40 activity pass good for your entire stay gets you access to all sorts of classes, equipment rentals, and various other amenities. The resort also offers 2½-hour voyages aboard an authentic Polynesian double-hull sailing canoe, the *Hahalua Lele,* or "Flying Manta Ray." The "Gold Floor" includes free breakfast and a daily wine and hors d'oeuvres hour. This can be especially useful for breakfast, as there's nearly always a wait for a table at the restaurant. ✉ *1 N. Kanikū Dr., Kohala Coast 96743* ☎ *808/885–2000 or 800/845–9905* 📠 *808/885–8886* 🌐 *www.fairmont.com* *486 rooms, 54 suites* *4 restaurants, A/C, in-room safes, minibars, cable TV with movies and video games, in-room broadband, 2 18-hole golf courses, 10 tennis courts, pool, health club, hair salon, spa, beach, snorkeling, boating, basketball, volleyball, 4 bars, shops, children's programs (ages 5–12), business services; no smoking* *AE, D, DC, MC, V. $309–$559.*

$$–$$$$ Fodor's Choice ★ **Hilton Waikoloa Village.** Dolphins chirp in the lagoon; a pint-size daredevil zooms down the 175-foot waterslide; a bride poses on the grand staircase; a fire-bearing runner lights the torches along the seaside path at sunset—these are the scenes that greet you at this 62-acre playground of a resort. Shaded pathways lined with a multimillion-dollar Pacific Island art collection connect the three tall buildings; Swiss-made trams and Disney-engineered boats shuttle those weary of the long hallways and meandering paths. In another nod to Disney, employees access the various areas of the resort via underground tunnels. The stars of **Dolphin Quest** (☎ 800/248–3316 🌐 www.dolphinquest.org) are the resort's pride and joy; reserve in advance for an interactive learning session. Though there's no ocean beach, there is a seaside trail to 'Anaeho'omalu Bay, aka A-Bay, one of the island's most pleasant beaches. An artificial sand beach borders the 4-acre resort lagoon. Large, modern rooms in neutral tones have private lānai. Be sure to leave your room with plenty of time before any appointment, or you'll learn to appreciate the size of this place as you sprint past the tram. TIP→ **Brides-to-be take note: this is one-stop shopping; the resort has a wedding-planning office, cakes, flowers, photography, and even fireworks and a "Just Married" boat ride.**

✉ 425 Waikoloa Beach Dr., Waikoloa 96738 ☎ 808/886–1234 or 800/445–8667 🖷 808/886–2900 🌐 www.hiltonwaikoloavillage.com ⇨ 1,240 rooms, 57 suites ♁ 10 restaurants, A/C, room service, in-room broadband, in-room safes, minibars, cable TV with movies, 2 18-hole golf courses, 8 tennis courts, 3 pools, health club, spa, beach, snorkeling, bike rentals, racquetball, volleyball, 9 bars, shops, babysitting, children's programs (ages 5–12), laundry facilities, laundry service, business services, car rental, no-smoking rooms 💳 AE, D, DC, MC, V. $199–$649.

$$–$$$$ **Waikoloa Beach Marriott.** The most affordable resort on the Kohala Coast, the Waikoloa Beach Marriott covers 15 acres and encompasses ancient fishponds, historic trails, and petroglyph fields. All rooms have Hawaiian art and bamboo-type furnishings—the resort is in the process of adding new rooms throughout 2007 and early 2008, so be sure to ask for a room as far away from construction noise as possible. The oversize cabana rooms overlook the lagoon. Reliable dining is available at the Hawai'i Calls restaurant, and the newly opened Mandara Spa offers a full range of treatments. Bordering the white-sand beach of 'Anaeho'omalu Bay, the hotel has a range of ocean activities, including wedding-vow renewals on a catamaran. *✉ 69-275 Waikoloa Beach Dr., Waikoloa 96738 ☎ 808/886–6789 or 800/688–7444 🖷 808/886–1554 🌐 www.marriott.com ⇨ 523 rooms, 22 suites ♁ Restaurant, A/C, in-room broadband, refrigerators, cable TV with movies and video games, 2 18-hole golf courses, 6 tennis courts, pool, health club, hair salon, spa, beach, 2 bars, children's programs (ages 5–12), laundry facilities, business services, no-smoking rooms 💳 AE, D, DC, MC, V. $254–$445.*

BEST FOR KEIKI

Casa de Emdeko (Kailua-Kona). Two large pools, one of salt water and perched at the ocean's edge.
Dolphin Bay Hotel (Hilo). Adjacent to a huge, clean, safe park, walking distance to downtown Hilo, very reasonable prices.
Hilton Waikoloa Village (Kohala Coast). Disneyland meets Polynesia, with plenty of entertainment options for teens and adults, too.
Nāmakani Paio Cabins (Volcano). Camping in a birdhouse cabin next to an active volcanic crater. It doesn't get much better.
Sheraton Keauhou (Kailua-Kona). The best pool on the island.

Condos & Vacation Rentals

Along the Kohala Coast, most of the available condos are associated with the resorts and can be booked through the resort reservations desk. There are, however, a couple of nearby housing developments that have vacation homes for rent. Most owners let a local property management company do the work, but some prefer to handle it themselves, through Web sites like Vacation Rental By Owner 🌐 www.vrbo.com. Nothing in this area will be bad in terms of proximity to the beach, restaurants, airport, and good weather, but double check that the home is located on the coast and not in North Kohala (North Kohala is beautiful, but wetter and more rainforest-like than the coast). Be sure to ask about things like parking, pools, and cleaning deposits.

$$$$ **Outrigger Kolea at Waikoloa.** The latest upscale condo development to join the Waikoloa Beach Resort, Kolea is aiming to capture the very high-end crowd dominated by the condos associated with the Mauna Lani and Four Seasons. These brand new condos are impeccably furnished and turned out, views from each unit's lānai are spectacular, and it's closer to the beach than any of the other complexes in this area. Kolea complex also offers far more amenities than the average condo complex, with both an infinity pool and a kids' pool at their oceanside Beach Club, a fitness center, and a lava rock hot tub. *Waikoloa Beach Resort, 69-289 Waikoloa Beach Dr., 96738 808/886–0036 808/886–0040 www.outrigger.com, www.koleavacations.com, www.waikoloarentals.com 70 units BBQs, A/C, fans, kitchens, cable TV, 2 pools, gym, hot tub, shop AE, D, DC, MC, V. 2-bedroom $450, 3-bedroom $550.*

★ $$$–$$$$ **Mauna Lani Point and Mauna Lani Terrace Condominiums.** Surrounded by the emerald greens of a world-class ocean-side golf course, spacious two-story suites at Mauna Lani Point offer a private, independent home away from home. The privately owned units, individually decorated according to the owners' tastes, have European cabinets and oversize soaking tubs in the main bedrooms. The pool has a little waterfall. The Mauna Lani Terrace Condominiums are closer to the beach, which means they're priced a little higher, but that extra dough pays for an ocean view from the lānai of most units. Whether you choose to stay closer to the golf course at Mauna Lani Point, or to the beach at Mauna Lani Terrace, you're just a few steps away from the Mauna Lani Bay Hotel and Bungalows, where you have access to golf, tennis, spa facilities, and restaurants. *68-1050 Mauna Lani Point Dr., Kohala Coast 96743 808/885–5022 or 800/642–6284 808/885–5015 www.classicresorts.com 61 units BBQs, A/C, fans, some kitchens, some kitchenettes, golf privileges, pool, hot tub, sauna AE, DC, MC, V. 1-bedroom $326–$415, 2-bedroom $426–$555.*

$$–$$$$ **Outrigger Fairway Villas at Waikoloa.** Large and comfy town houses just off the fairway of the Hilton Waikoloa golf course are a short walk from 'Anaeho'omalu Bay. The Fairway Villas, designed to mimic plantation-era homes, are decorated with rattan furniture and cozy earth tones. Unlike most of the other condominium complexes, there is a uniformity to the Fairway Villas—units are individually owned, but all are managed by Outrigger, which means they are all decorated and laid out similarly. The villas have their own infinity pool and hot tub and a small gym right next to the pool. Guests do not have access to the fitness or pool facilities at the

FOR MEMBERS ONLY

A handful of members-only clubs offer discounts on lodging, activities, and meals on the Big Island. **American Automobile Association** (www.aaa.com) discounts are available at most hotels. **Hideaways** (www.hideaways.com) offers stellar deals on condo rentals at Mauna Lani Terrace, ResortQuest Shores at Waikoloa, and Vista Waikoloa. Their annual fee of $185 entitles members to free travel-planning services, room upgrades, discounts on lodging and meals, and special perks at locations throughout the world.

neighboring Hilton Waikoloa Village, but they are welcome at the spa, restaurants, shops, and grounds. ✉ *Waikoloa Beach Resort, 69-200 Pohakulana Pl., 96738* ☎ *808/886-0036* 📠 *808/886-0040* 🌐 *www.outrigger.com* 80 units BBQs, A/C, kitchens, cable TV, pool, gym, hot tub, laundry facilities AE, D, DC, MC, V. 2-bedroom $215–$239, 3-bedroom $339–$500.*

CONDO COMFORTS

There are fewer stores and takeout options on the Kohala Coast, but, as the condos are all associated with resorts, most of your needs will be met. If you require anything not provided by the management, the **King's Shops at Waikoloa Village** (✉ 250 Waikoloa Beach Dr., Waikoloa ☎ 808/886-8811) is the place to go. There are a small grocery store, a liquor store, and a couple of decent takeout options. It's not exactly cheap, but you're paying for the convenience of not having to drive into town.

$$–$$$$ **ResortQuest Shores at Waikoloa.** These red-tile-roof villas are set amid landscaped lagoons and waterfalls at the edge of the championship Waikoloa Village Golf Course. The spacious villas and condo units—the ground floor and upper floor are available separately—are privately owned, so all furnishings are different. Sliding glass doors open onto large lānai. Picture windows look out on rolling green fairways. All have complete kitchens with washer-dryer units and come with maid service. Check the Web site for deals; separate rates are quoted for online booking, and they often advertise specials exclusively on their Web site. ResortQuest also offers a variety of air-inclusive packages, which can be a great deal. ✉ *69-1035 Keana Pl., Waikoloa 96738* ☎ *808/886-5001 or 800/922-7866* 📠 *808/922-8785* 🌐 *www.resortquesthawaii.com* *75 units* *BBQs, A/C, fans, in-room broadband (fee), kitchen, cable TV, 2 tennis courts, pool, gym, hot tub, putting green, laundry facilities, shop* *AE, D, DC, MC, V. 1-bedroom $224–$345, 2-bedroom $272–$400.*

$–$$$$ **Kohala Ranch.** Several homes in this upscale gated community do double duty as vacation rentals. Prices range greatly, from $150 a night for a small house with an ocean view to more than $1,000 a night for a huge mansion on a hill with a private tennis court and pool. This is a fantastic location—close to the island's best beaches, to the resorts, and to the airport. ✉ *Kohala Ranch, Hwy. 19, north of Waikoloa, Kohala Coast* 🌐 *www.vrbo.com or www.hawaiianbeachrentals.com* *Number of units varies* *A/C, kitchens, cable TV* *AE, MC, V. $150–$1,130.*

$–$$ **Vista Waikoloa.** Older and more reasonable than most of the condo complexes along the Kohala Coast, the two-bedroom, two-bath Vista condos offer ocean views and a great value for this part of the island. All are large and well appointed, with lānai, plus they are walking distance to A-Bay, the King's Shops at Waikoloa, and the restaurants and amenities of the Hilton Waikoloa, and within short driving distance of the airport, other resorts, and a variety of Big Island sights. ✉ *Waikoloa Beach Resort, 69-1010 Keana Pl., 96738* ☎ *808/886-3594* 📠 *808/886-1199* 🌐 *www.waikoloarentals.com* *70 units* *BBQ, A/C, kitchens, tennis court, pool, gym, hot tub, laundry facilities* *AE, MC, V. $180–$250.*

B&Bs

$ **Hale Ho'onanea.** The Hawaiian translation of this comfortable home's name is "House of Relaxation." It sits on 3 acres in the Kohala Estates hills, above the ocean. From here you can watch the sun rise over Mauna Kea and set over the Pacific, and view the sparkling beauty of Hawai'i's night sky. It's minutes away from dining and shopping at Waimea and the attractions of the Kohala Coast. The rooms are comfortable and spacious, if not terribly beautiful; the views and grounds make up for what the rooms lack, as does the price in this neck of the woods (less than half the nightly rate of the Kohala Coast resorts). Continental breakfast is included. There's a two-night minimum if you book less than a week in advance; a $25 fee applies to single-night bookings made within seven days of arrival. ✉ *Kohala Estates, 59-513 Ala Kahua Dr., Kawaihae 96743* ☎ *808/882–1653 or 877/882–1653* 📠 *808/882–1653* 🌐 *www.houseofrelaxation.com* *3 suites* *Kitchenettes, cable TV, library; no A/C* 💳 *MC, V. $100–$130.*

Waimea

Though it seems a world away, Waimea is only about a 30- to 40-minute drive from the Kohala Coast resorts, which means it takes roughly the same amount of time to get to the Island's best beaches from Waimea as it does from Kailua-Kona. Yet, few visitors think to book lodging in this pleasant upcountry village, where cool mornings and evenings are enjoyable after a day spent bathing in the sun. To the delight of residents and visitors, a few retired resort chefs have opened up their own little projects in Waimea. Sightseeing is easy: Mauna Kea is a short drive away, and Hilo and Kailua-Kona can be reached in about an hour. Because Waimea doesn't attract as many visitors as the coasts, you won't find as many condos and hotels, but the B&Bs in the area are superb. They also offer some of the island's best lodging deals, especially when you consider that their vantage point up in the hills affords some pretty spectacular views.

Hotels & Resorts

$ **Waimea Country Lodge.** In the heart of cowboy country, this modest lodge offers views of the green, rolling slopes of Mauna Kea. It's so quiet you forget you're close to busy Waimea. The rooms are adequate and clean, with Hawaiian quilts lending an authentic touch. A Continental breakfast is included in the rate, and you can charge meals at Merriman's and Paniolo Country Inn to your room. A handful of studios with kitchenettes are also available, and there are plenty of grocery stores in Waimea to stock up on provisions for the week. ✉ *65-1210 Lindsey Rd., Waimea* 📫 *Box 2559, Kamuela 96743* ☎ *808/885–4100 or 800/367–5004* 📠 *808/885–6711* 🌐 *www.castleresorts.com* *21 rooms* *In-room data ports, some kitchenettes, cable TV with movies, no-smoking rooms; no A/C* 💳 *AE, D, DC, MC, V. $101–$127.*

Condos & Vacation Rentals

$ **Aloha Vacation Cottages.** These two rental cottages—one larger than the other—are clean, comfortable, and well stocked with beach toys, towels and mats, books, cable TV, videos, you name it. The price is right, and they are just a 10-minute drive from the Kohala Coast. To fully relax during your stay, book a massage when you reserve a cottage. *Box 1395, Waimea 96743 877/875–1722 or 808/885–6535 www.alohacottages.net 2 units Kitchens, in-room broadband, cable TV, in-room DVD/VCR players; no A/C MC, V. $135–$145.*

★ $ **Waimea Gardens Cottage.** These sweet cottages look like they just leapt out of a painting and into your dream vacation. One (Kohala) includes a full kitchen and the other (Waimea) a kitchenette, both of which are stocked with provisions for a self-serve Continental breakfast. Both have their own private gardens, beautiful hardwood floors, and lovely furnishings. The grounds are full of birds and plantlife that will make you want to move in for good. *Box 520, Kamuela 96743 808/885–8550 www.waimeagardens.com 2 cottages, 1 studio BBQs, kitchen or kitchenette, in-room VCR No credit cards. $150–$160.*

B&Bs

★ $–$$ **Jacaranda Inn.** You can spot the lavender Jacaranda Inn miles away, but don't let the color keep you away: this place is a great deal, and recently renovated rooms are very comfortable. Built in 1897, the sprawling estate was once the home of the manager of Parker Ranch. Charming inside and out, it's been redecorated in hues of raspberry and lavender, with lots of koa wood accents. Most of the rooms have hot tubs. The units are booked under two separate plans. Plan A includes daily maid service, full breakfasts, and a bottle of wine; Plan B is simpler, with Continental breakfast and less service. *65-1444 Kawaihae Rd., Waimea 96743 808/885–8813 808/885–6096 www.jacarandainn.com 8 suites, 1 cottage Hot tubs, billiards, recreation room; no A/C, no room phones, no room TVs, no smoking MC, V. $159–$225, cottage $350.*

¢–$ **Aaah, The Views!** This tranquil and pretty stream-side mountain home in upcountry Waimea is lovingly tended by owners Erika and Derek Stuart. Rooms are clean and bright, with lots of windows to enjoy the views. The Dream Room is actually an apartment, with a full kitchen, private deck, and hot tub. The house has a sauna and a yoga room (private lessons available), and there's even wireless Internet access. *66-1773 Alaneo St., off Akulani, just past mile marker 60 on Hwy. 19, Waimea 96743 808/885–3455 www.aaahtheviews.com 4 rooms Wi-Fi, some kitchens, microwaves, refrigerators, cable TV, sauna, no-smoking rooms No credit cards. $80–$155.*

¢–$ **Mana Ranch.** A quiet and removed mountainside ranch in the shadows of Mauna Kea, Mana Ranch is an idyllic retreat. There are two rooms available in the main house and a separate "paniolo cottage" with a kitchenette, which sleeps four. Rooms are clean and comfortable with a pleasant blend of modern decor and Hawaiian accents. The spa room is a nice touch, especially with its views of Mauna Kea, and its private shower and bath come in handy if your neighbors across the hall in the main house are bathroom hogs—the two bedrooms share a bathroom. *64-5163 Mana Rd., 96743 866/399–5842 www.manaranch.com 3 rooms Wi-Fi, cable TV, in-room DVD player MC, V. $75–$125.*

¢ **Kamuela Inn.** The rooms at this unpretentious, peaceful inn, just 20 minutes from the beaches, are clean and comfortable. Small lānai look out over the inn's gardens. Depending on your needs, you can choose anything from a no-nonsense single bedroom to two connecting penthouse suites with a lānai and full kitchen. The owners also have a five-bedroom log cabin for rent, nestled below the hills in Ahualoa on the Hāmākua Coast near Honoko'a; the cabin is a bit more swanky than the inn, with a full kitchen, large rooms, and a hot tub outside in its own gazebo. ✉ *65-1300 Kawaihae Rd., Box 1994, Waimea 96743* ☎ *808/885–4243 or 800/555–8968* 🖷 *808/885–8857* 🌐 *www.hawaiibnb.com/kamuela.html* *20 rooms, 11 suites* *Some kitchenettes, cable TV; no A/C, no phones in some rooms* 💳 *AE, D, DC, MC, V. Inn $60–$85, log cabin $375.*

Kailua-Kona

Kailua-Kona, a bustling little village full of restaurants, shops, and entertainment options, has a zillion lodging options. In addition to half a dozen hotels, oceanfront Ali'i Drive is crammed with condo complexes and homes on both sides of the street, and there are several grocery stores for those who choose to go the condo or vacation home route. Kailua-Kona has three beaches—White Sands, Kahalu'u, and King Kamehameha—each has its selling point: Kahalu'u is renowned for its snorkeling, White Sands is a local favorite that's great for body surfing (but the beach is small), and King Kamehameha is a small beach next to a calm marina, which makes it great for kids. The downside is that you'll have to drive 30–45 minutes up the road to the Kohala Coast to get Hawai'i's signature long white sand beaches. That said, you'll also pay about half what you would at any of the beachfront resorts, and Kailua-Kona has a bit more local charm.

Hotels & Resorts

★ $$$–$$$$ **Sheraton Keauhou Bay Resort & Spa.** Long-time Big Island visitors might remember it as the old Kona Surf. Left empty for several years, this hotel on the edge of Keauhou Bay has been restored to its former glory. The lobby is particularly stunning, and the well-designed restaurant Kai serves a limited but excellent menu. Rooms are bright, modern, and comfortable; many have great views of the bay. The pool, which can only be described as massive, is one of the coolest on the island, with a slide, waterfalls, and an ocean view. They also have a full-service, oceanfront spa (Ho'ola), a highly acclaimed new lū'au, an oceanfront wedding area, and the Manta Ray Experience, which allows guests to view manta rays nearly every night (provided the rays cooperate). ✉ *78-128 Ehukai St., Kailua-Kona 96740* ☎ *808/930–4900* 🖷 *808/930–4800* 🌐 *www.sheratonkeauhou.com* *511 rooms, 10 suites* *Restaurant, A/C, in-room data ports, Wi-Fi, in-room safes, refrigerators, cable TV with movies, 2 tennis courts, pool, health club, spa, beach, volleyball, bar, playground, business services, no-smoking rooms* 💳 *AE, D, DC, MC, V. $325–$460.*

$$–$$$$ **Royal Kona Resort.** This is a great option if you're on a budget. The resort has seen better days, but the owners are finally doing a bit of renovation. The location is great, the lobby, pool, and restaurant are right

on the water, and lānai-front rooms are decked out in Hawaiian kitsch. The resort is within walking distance of Kailua-Kona and across the street from numerous shops and restaurants. The weekly lū'au with Polynesian entertainment is fun and quite popular. Their restaurant leaves something to be desired, so you're better off walking a few blocks and spending your money more wisely at one of the better restaurants in town. Make sure to book online, where the rates can be 50% less than the rack rates. ✉ *75-5852 Ali'i Dr., Kailua-Kona 96740* ☎ *808/329–3111 or 800/222–5642* 🖷 *808/329–9532* 🌐 *www.royalkona.com* *452 rooms, 8 suites* *Restaurant, A/C, in-room safes, refrigerators, cable TV with movies, in-room data ports, 4 tennis courts, pool, health club, hair salon, spa, beach, bar, laundry facilities, Internet room, no-smoking rooms* 💳 *AE, D, DC, MC, V. $210–$385.*

HAWAI'I ON A BUDGET

Kona Tiki Hotel (Kailua-Kona). Oceanfront, 1950s Hawai'i motif, all rooms have ocean views, walking distance to downtown.

Manago Hotel (South Kona). Historic, Japanese theme, clean, some oceanfront rooms, super reasonable, excellent restaurant.

Nāmakani Paio Cabins (Volcano Village). Close to the Volcano, cheap, clean, recently renovated.

Royal Kona Resort (Kailua-Kona). Old-school Hawai'i, oceanfront, great bar, good package deals, close to downtown Kailua-Kona.

$–$$ **King Kamehameha's Kona Beach Hotel.** Rooms here are not particularly special (the fifth- and sixth-floor oceanfront rooms are best), and the hotel itself is not aging gracefully. What you get instead of the luxury of the upscale resorts is a bit of local history, a reasonable rate, and a great central location. It's on a small white-sand beach with a calm swimming bay next to Kailua Pier. You can explore the lush grounds and historic Ahu'ena Heiau, which King Kamehameha I had reconstructed in the early 1800s. The hotel serves an ample champagne brunch every Sunday and hosts a fabulous beachfront Polynesian lū'au several nights a week. ✉ *75-5660 Palani Rd., Kailua-Kona 96740* ☎ *808/329–2911 or 800/367–6060* 🖷 *808/329–4602* 🌐 *www.konabeachhotel.com* *455 rooms* *2 restaurants, A/C, in-room data ports, in-room safes, cable TV with movies, tennis courts, pool, hair salon, hot tub, sauna, beach, 2 bars, shops, laundry facilities, laundry service, travel services* 💳 *AE, D, DC, MC, V. $170–$250.*

$–$$ **Outrigger Keauhou Beach Resort.** Although it has won awards for preserving its unique history (the grounds include a *heiau*, a sacred fishpond, and a replica of the summer home of King David Kalākaua), the Outrigger Keauhou Beach Resort is not doing such a hot job at preserving the guest accommodations. That said, if you can find a good rate, this is still a decent place to stay, mainly for its proximity to Kahalu'u, one of the best snorkeling beaches on the island, and its surprisingly good restaurant. ✉ *78-6740 Ali'i Dr., Kailua-Kona 96740* ☎ *808/322–3441 or 800/462–6262* 🖷 *808/322–3117* 🌐 *www.outrigger.com* *311 rooms, 6 suites* *Restaurant, A/C, cable TV with movies and video games, 6 tennis courts, pool, health club, beach, bar, laundry facilities, laundry service, no-smoking rooms* 💳 *AE, D, DC, MC, V. $119–$250.*

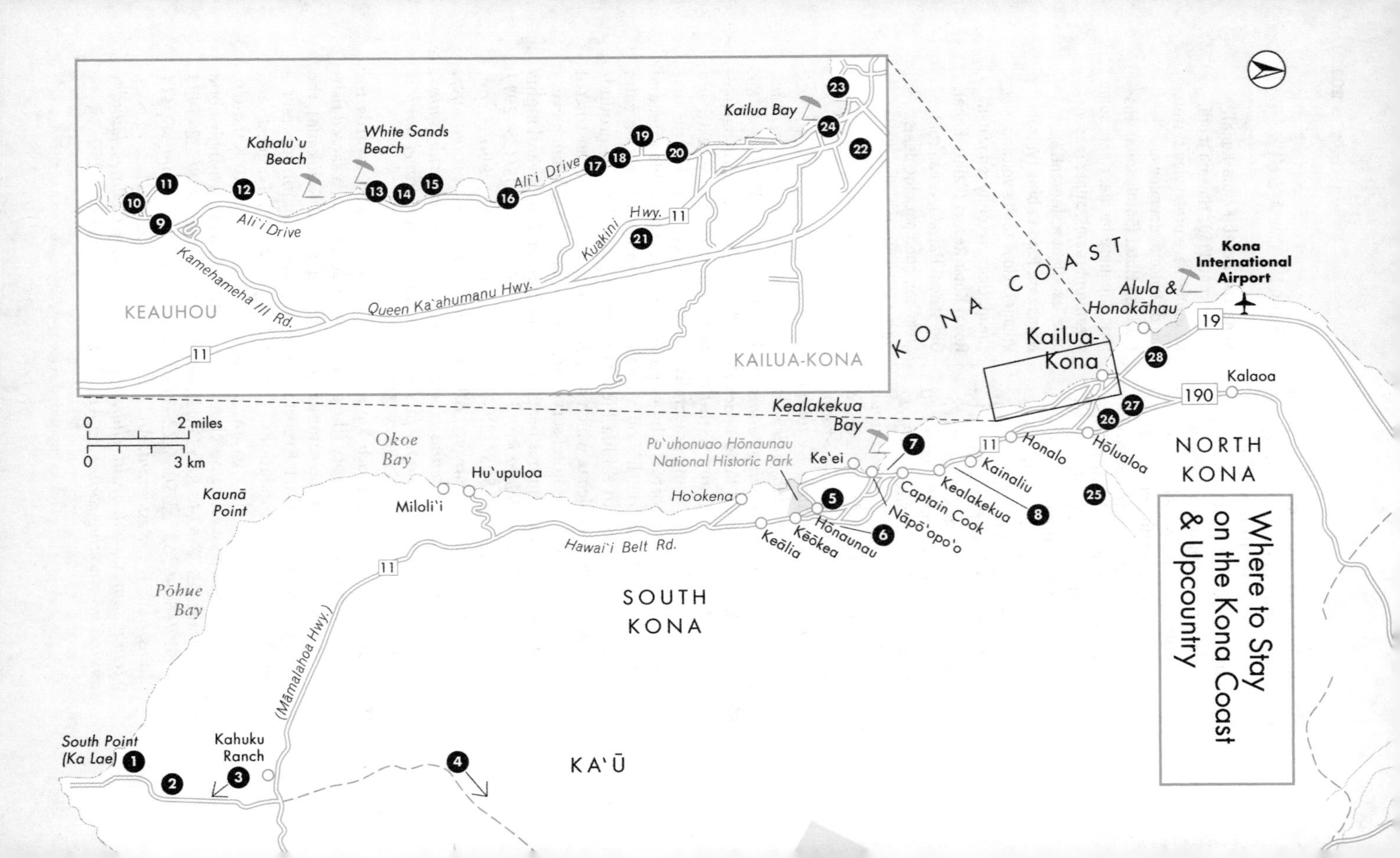

Where to Stay
on the Kona Coast
& Upcountry
NORTH KONA
SOUTH KONA
KA'Ū
KONA COAST
Kona International Airport
Alula & Honokāhau
Kalaoa
Kailua-Kona
Hōlualoa
Honalo
Kainaliu
Kealakekua
Captain Cook
Nāpō'opo'o
Kealakekua Bay
Ke'ei
Hōnaunau
Kēōkea
Keālia
Pu'uhonuao Hōnaunau National Historic Park
Ho'okena
Hawai'i Belt Rd.
Hu'upuloa
Miloli'i
Okoe Bay
Kaunā Point
Pōhue Bay
(Māmalahoa Hwy.)
Kahuku Ranch
South Point (Ka Lae)
2 miles
3 km
KAILUA-KONA
KEAUHOU
Kailua Bay
White Sands Beach
Kahalu'u Beach
Ali'i Drive
Kuakini Hwy.
Queen Ka'ahumanu Hwy.
Kamehameha III Rd.

WHERE TO STAY ON THE KONA COAST & UPCOUNTRY

HOTEL NAME	Worth Noting	Cost	Pools	On the Beach	Golf Courses	Tennis Courts	Gym	Spa	Children's Programs	Rooms or Units	Restaurants	Other	Location
Hotels & Resorts													
23 King Kamehameha's	*Hawaiian history, calm bay*	*170–250*	*1*	*yes*						*455*	*2*	*shops*	*Kailua-Kona*
22 Kona Seaside Hotel	*Budget prices*	*60–120*	*2*				*yes*			*225*			*Kailua-Kona*
20 Kona Tiki Hotel	*Oceanfront lānai*	*61–84*	*1*							*15*		*no A/C*	*Kailua-Kona*
7 Manago Hotel		*31–70*								*106*	*1*	*no A/C*	*Captian Cook*
12 Outrigger Keauhou	*Close to Kahulu'u Beach*	*119–250*	*1*	*yes*		*6*	*yes*			*317*	*1*		*Kailua-Kona*
24 Royal Kona Resort	*Good rates for oceanfront*	*210–385*	*1*	*yes*		*4*	*yes*	*yes*		*460*	*1*		*Kailua-Kona*
★ 9 Sheraton Keauhou Bay	*Cool pool with slide*	*325–460*	*1*	*yes*		*2*	*yes*	*yes*		*521*	*1*		*Kailua-Kona*
Condos & Vacation Rentals													
15 Casa de Emdeko	*Oceanfront saltwater pool*	*95–135*	*2*							*85*		*kitchens*	*Kailua-Kona*
3 Colony One Sea Mountain	*Close to Black Sand Beach*	*50–95*	*1*		*yes*	*1*				*74*		*kitchens*	*Ka'u*
4 Hale O'Luna	*Peaceful, quiet, remote*	*85–125*								*2*		*no A/C*	*Ka'u*
19 Hale Puhako	*All units oceanfront*	*210–235*		*yes*						*6*		*kitchens*	*Kailua-Kona*
11 Keauhou Kona Club	*Tennis courts, big pool*	*175*	*1*			*3*				*188*		*kitchens*	*Kailua-Kona*
16 Kona Bali Kai	*View of White Sands Beach*	*75–125*	*1*							*62*		*kitchens*	*Kailua-Kona*
13 Kona Magic Sands	*Ocean view from all units*	*85–135*	*1*							*37*	*1*	*kitchens*	*Kailua-Kona*
★ 18 Kona Nalu	*Huge lānai, ocean views*	*190–250*	*1*	*yes*						*15*		*kitchens*	*Kailua-Kona*
★ 21 Kona Pacific	*Ocean view from pool, BBQ*	*73–135*	*1*							*80*		*kitchens*	*Kailua-Kona*
17 Kona Riviera Villa	*Quiet oceanfront hideaway*	*80–135*	*1*							*9*		*kitchens*	*Kailua-Kona*
10 Outrigger Kanaloa at Kona	*Oceanfront restaurant*	*169–265*	*3*			*2*				*166*		*kitchens*	*Kailua-Kona*
14 ResortQuest Kona by Sea	*Oceanfront pool*	*270–385*	*1*					*yes*		*78*		*kitchens*	*Kailua-Kona*
28 Silver Oaks Guest Ranch	*Working ranch location*	*175*	*1*							*2*		*no A/C*	*Kailua-Kona*
1 South Point Banyan	*Deck with hot tub*	*185*								*1*		*no A/C*	*Ka'u*
B&Bs													
5 Aloha Guesthouse	*Almost 100% organic*	*140–250*								*5*			*South Kona*
6 Dragonfly Ranch	*Exotic island treehouse*	*100–250*					*yes*	*yes*		*6*			*South Kona*
27 Hale Hualalai	*Outstanding breakfast*	*135,*								*6*		*no A/C*	*Hōlualoa*
★ 26 Hōlualoa Inn	*Beautiful interior design*	*175–205*	*1*							*6*		*no A/C*	*Hōlualoa*
8 Horizon Guest House	*Infinity pool*	*250*	*1*							*4*		*no A/C*	*South Kona*
2 Kalaekilohana	*Hot breakfast, cozy linens*	*139–159*								*4*		*no A/C*	*Ka'u*
25 Nancy's Hideaway	*Lots of privacy for guests*	*115–135*								*6*		*no A/C*	*Kailua-Kona*

¢–$ **Kona Seaside Hotel.** If you're on a budget, desire a central location, and don't need a spacious room or lavish bath, you'll feel at home in this casual hotel. It's on a busy intersection, right across the street from Kailua Bay. Rooms have been recently renovated and those nearest the street are built around a private pool. The staff is very friendly. ✉ *75-5646 Palani Rd., Kailua-Kona 96740* ☎ *808/329–2455 or 800/560–5558* 🖷 *808/329–6157* 🌐 *www.konaseasidehotel.com* *224 rooms, 1 suite* *A/C, fans, refrigerators, cable TV, 2 pools, gym, bar, laundry facilities, no-smoking rooms* 💳 *AE, D, DC, MC, V. $60–$120.*

¢ **Kona Tiki Hotel.** The best thing about this three-story walk-up budget hotel, about a mile south of Kailua-Kona, is that all the units have lānai right next to the ocean. The rooms are modest but pleasantly decorated. You can sunbathe by the seaside pool, where a complimentary Continental breakfast is served. Some would call this place old-fashioned; others would say it's local, has a certain kitschy charm, and is the best deal in town, with glorious sunsets no different from those at the resorts. ✉ *75-5968 Ali'i Dr., Kailua-Kona 96745* ☎ *808/329–1425* 🖷 *808/327–9402* *15 rooms* *BBQs, fans, refrigerators, pool; no A/C, no room phones, no room TVs* 💳 *No credit cards. $61–$84.*

Condos & Vacation Rentals

$$$–$$$$ **ResortQuest Kona by the Sea.** Complete modern kitchens, tile lānai, and washer-dryer units can be found in every suite of this comfortable oceanfront condo complex. Despite being near the bustling town of Kailua-Kona, this four-story place is quiet and relaxing. The nearest sandy beach is 2 mi away, but the pool is next to the ocean. Be sure to check the Web site for specials: they usually offer a fourth or fifth night free and often advertise deals only on their own Web site. ✉ *75-6106 Ali'i Dr., Kailua-Kona 96740* ☎ *808/327–2300 or 800/922–7866* 🖷 *808/922–8785* 🌐 *www.resortquesthawaii.com* *37 1-bedroom units, 41 2-bedroom units* *A/C, kitchens, cable TV, pool, hot tub, spa, laundry facilities, no-smoking rooms* 💳 *AE, D, DC, MC, V. 1-bedroom $270–$385, 2-bedroom $335–$445.*

$–$$$ **Keauhou Kona Surf & Racquet Club.** This large gated complex sits right along the ocean, offering prime views from oceanfront units and the pool. Condos are large, comfortable, and very well maintained. Unlike many other complexes, Keauhou Kona has tennis courts and a very large pool. The two-story town houses are ideal for larger groups, although these are a bit more dated than the rest of the complex. ✉ *78-6800 Ali'i Dr., 96740 Kailua-Kona* ☎ *800/799–5662 or 808/322–6696* 🌐 *www.konarentals.com or www.konahawaii.com* *188 units* *BBQ, A/C, kitchens, 3 tennis courts, pool, laundry facilities* 💳 *MC, V. 1-bedroom $175, 2-bedroom $195–$295, 3-bedroom $300–$325.*

$–$$$ **Outrigger Kanaloa at Kona.** The 16-acre grounds provide a peaceful and verdant background for this low-rise condominium complex bordering the Keauhou-Kona Country Club. It's walking distance from the golf course but within a five-minute drive of the nearest beaches (Kahalu'u and White Sands). Large one-, two-, and three-bedroom apartments have koa-wood cabinetwork and washer-dryers; oceanfront villas have private hot tubs. A restaurant, The Bar and Grill at Kanaloa, serves up New

A TEMPORARY HOME IN HAWAI'I

Renting a condo or vacation house gives you much more room than the average hotel, the chance to meet more people (neighbors are usually friendly, kids always hang together at the pool), lower nightly rates, and the option of cooking or barbecuing some nights rather than eating out. When booking, remember that most are individually owned and most owners outsource the rental process to property management companies. A handful of property management and rental agencies handle the bulk of condo and vacation home rentals on the Big Island, and their Web sites are the best places to look for rentals. Following is a list of our favorites for various lodging types throughout the island. Be sure to call and ask questions before booking, even if the pictures online are *real purdy.*

Abbey Vacation Rentals (🌐 www.waikoloarentals.com) has luxury condos on the Kohala Coast.

Big Island Villas (🌐 www.bigislandvillas.com) lists a variety of condos attached to the Four Seasons Hualālai, Mauna Kea, and Mauna Lani resorts.

CJ Kimberly Realty (🌐 www.cjkimberly.com) offers fantastic deals on some oceanfront homes and condos.

Hawaiian Beach Rentals (🌐 www.hawaiianbeachrentals.com) and **Tropical Villa Vacations** (🌐 www.tropicalvillavacations.com) are excellent for high-end, ocean- or beach-front homes.

Hawai'i Vacation Rentals (🌐 www.vacationbigisland.com) lists several properties on the beach in Puako, a sleepy beach settlement just up the road from the Kohala coast resorts.

Keauohou Property Management (🌐 www.konacondo.net) has condos along the Kona coast, just south of Kailua-Kona around Keauhou Bay.

Kolea Vacations (🌐 www.koleavacations.com) lists dozens of condos at the Kolea at Waikoloa complex as well as a stunning oceanfront home on Ali'i in Kailua-Kona.

Kona Hawai'i Vacation Rentals (🌐 www.konahawaii.com) offers very affordable condos in Kailua-Kona.

Knutson and Associates (🌐 www.konahawaiirentals.com) handles rentals for a wide variety of Kailua-Kona condos and oceanfront vacation homes.

Property Network (☎ 808/329-7977 🌐 www.hawaii-kona.com) lists and manages dozens of condo rentals in and around Kailua-Kona.

Rent Hawai'i Home (🌐 www.renthawaiihome.com) offers several affordable cottage and beach house rentals, ideal for those who are staying for a while and want some room/privacy, but don't want to spend half a year's salary on a beachfront palace.

South Kohala Management (🌐 www.southkohala.com) lists a wide variety of luxury Kohala Coast condos.

Vacation Rental By Owner (🌐 www.vrbo.com) has homes and condos for rent all over the island.

American cuisine on a lovely covered outdoor patio. ✉ *78-261 Manukai St., Kailua-Kona 96740* ☎ *808/322–9625, 808/322–2272, or 800/688–7444* 🖷 *808/322–3818* 🌐 *www.outrigger.com* *166 units* *A/C in some rooms, in-room safes, kitchenettes, 2 tennis courts, 3 pools, hot tub, bar, laundry facilities* 💳 *AE, D, DC, MC, V. 1-bedroom $169–$265, 2-bedroom $185–$315.*

$$ **Hale Puhako.** A tiny complex with just six 2-bedroom, 2-bathroom units tucked off Ali'i Drive and right next to the ocean, Hale Puhako is a great find. Only a few of the units are available as vacation rentals, but all are ocean front with lānai, and it's the only complex with its own little beach. Units are large and nicely furnished. ✉ *76-6194 Ali'i Dr., 96740* ☎ *888/311–6020 or 808/329–6020* 🌐 *www.konacondo.com* *6 2-bedroom units* *A/C, kitchens, cable TV, in-room VCR, beach paddle tennis, laundry facilities. $210–$235.*

★ $$ **Kona Nalu.** One of the nicest complexes on the ocean side of Ali'i, Kona Nalu units are large and beautifully furnished with super-sized lānai, and ocean views from all units. The pool is tiny, but they have a small sandy beach for lying in the sun, and the complex itself is small so you won't be fighting for pool room. ✉ *76-6212 Ali'i Dr, 96740* ☎ *808/329–6438* 🌐 *www.konarentals.net or www.sunquest-hawaii.com* *15 units* *BBQs, A/C, kitchens, pool, beach, laundry facilities* 💳 *MC, V. $190–$250.*

$ **Silver Oaks Guest Ranch.** These two private cottages set on a 10-acre working ranch are one of the best deals going on the west side of the island. Five miles from the airport and from Kailua-Kona, the cottages afford total privacy, with a few more amenities than a vacation house or condo. Owners Mark and Amy drop off a welcome basket with breakfast goodies your first day, there's a washer and dryer in each unit, an outdoor pool and hot tub, great ocean views from your private deck, and the ranch is like a little petting zoo with horses, goats, and chickens throughout. Each cottage is stocked with a library of books and videos, various beach toys, backpacks, coolers, beach towels, binoculars, robes, hair dryers, and even snorkeling equipment. The only hitch: There's a five-night minimum stay. ✉ *73-4570 Mamalahoa Hwy., just before (or after, if you're coming from Kailua-Kona) Kaloko Dr., 96740* ☎ *877/325–2300 or 808/325–2000* 🖷 *808/325–2200* 🌐 *www.silveroaksranch.com* *2 cottages* *BBQs, kitchens, Wi-Fi, in-room VCRs, pool, hot tub, laundry facilities; no A/C* 💳 *MC, V. $175 (5-night minimum).*

¢–$ **Casa de Emdeko.** A large and pretty complex on the *makai* (oceanfront) side of Ali'i Drive, Casa de Emdeko offers a few more amenities than most condo complexes, including an on-site convenience store that makes great sandwiches, a sandy oceanfront area for sunbathing, and both fresh and salt water pools. As with any complex, decor and maintenance of units varies depending on the owner, so be sure to view photos of the specific unit you're renting. All units have lānai, with either garden or ocean views (ocean view is a bit more expensive). ✉ *75-6082 Ali'i Dr., 96740* ☎ *808/329–2160* 🌐 *www.konahawaiirentals.com or www.konaawesomecondo.com* *85 units* *BBQs, A/C, kitchens, cable TV in some units, 2 pools, shops* 💳 *AE, MC, V. Garden $95–$110, ocean $110–$135.*

¢–$ **Kona Bali Kai.** These slightly older condominium units, spread out through three low-rises on the ocean side of Ali'i Drive, have a pretty good location. They're just a couple of minutes from Kailua-Kona and walking-distance to popular White Sands beach. And they're great for families. Kitchens are fully equipped, and there's a little convenience store. If you can afford it, choose an oceanfront unit for the luxury of quiet sunsets. ✉ *76-6246 Ali'i Dr., Kailua-Kona 96740* ☎ *808/329–9381 or 800/535–0085* 📠 *808/326–6056* 🌐 *www.marcresorts.com* *62 units* *BBQs, A/C in some rooms, fans, kitchens, in-room VCRs, pool, hair salon, hot tub, shop, laundry facilities* 💳 *AE, D, DC, MC, V. Studios $75–$95, 1-bedroom $100–$125, 2-bedroom $135–$167.*

¢–$ **Kona Magic Sands.** Cradled between two small beaches, this condo complex is great for swimmers and sunbathers in summer (the sand at Magic Sands washes away in winter). Units vary because they're individually owned, but all the studios are oceanfront, spacious, and light. Some units have enclosed lānai, and all have an ocean view. ✉ *77-6452 Ali'i Dr., Kailua-Kona 96740* ☎ *808/329–9393 or 800/622–5348* 📠 *808/326–4137* 🌐 *www.konahawaii.com* *37 units* *Restaurant, A/C in some rooms, kitchens, pool, bar* 💳 *MC, V. $85–$135.*

★ ¢–$ **Kona Pacific.** Once a hotel, the Kona Pacific gives you plenty of space. The one-bedroom units, which comfortably sleep four, are the size of two large hotel rooms, with a full kitchen and usually two bathrooms. There are ocean views from the lānai of most units and the pool. This large and well-maintained complex is just at the edge of Kailua-Kona, within walking distance of shops and restaurants. If you don't feel like cooking or barbecuing by the pool, a great Mexican food restaurant is waiting across the street with margaritas and fajitas. Note that the acceptance of credit cards varies with the unit owners. ✉ *75-5865 Walua Rd., 96740* ☎ *808/329–6140* 🌐 *www.marylvacations.com* *80 units* *BBQs, A/C, kitchens, pool. Studios $73–$95, 1-bedroom $80–$135, 2-bedroom $135–$175.*

¢–$ **Kona Riviera Villa.** A small and charming pink complex with white trim, set back from the road on the *makai* (ocean) side of Ali'i Drive, the Kona Riviera feels like a secret hideaway. All units are one-bedroom, the pool juts out over the ocean, and the complex is very well maintained. From oceanfront units you can practically feel the spray off the waves. A convenience store is one block away. Note that the acceptance of credit cards varies with the unit owners. ✉ *75-6124 Ali'i Dr., 96740* ☎ *808/329–1996* 🌐 *www.*

CONDO COMFORTS

Crossroads Shopping Center. The **Safeway** here is the cleanest, largest, and best-stocked store on the island. It's right next to **Kona Natural Foods,** so you can supplement with local organic produce and other tasty treats. There's also a **Coldstone Creamery** in this shopping center, so dessert is taken care of, too. ✉ *75-1000 Henry St., Kailua-Kona.*

Blockbuster. ✉ *Kona Coast Shopping Center, 74-5588 Palani Rd., Kailua-Kona* ☎ *808/326-7694.*

Pizza-wise, **Kona Brewing Company** is best if you're willing to go pick it up. Otherwise, **Domino's** (☎ 808/329–9500) is actually good here.

konahawaiirentals.com 9 *units* *BBQs, fans, kitchens, pool, laundry facilities. $80–$135.*

B&Bs

★ $–$$ **Hōlualoa Inn.** Six spacious rooms are available in this beautiful cedar home on a 40-acre coffee country estate, 4 mi above Kailua Bay and steps away from the artists' town of Hōlualoa. The Balinese suite, one of the nicest here, has wraparound windows with stunning views. A lavish breakfast includes estate-grown coffee as well as homemade breads and macadamia-nut butter. Rooftop gazebos inspire quiet, relaxing moments, and for stargazers there's a telescope. *76-5932 Māmalahoa Hwy., Box 222, Hōlualoa 96725* *808/324–1121 or 800/392–1812* *808/322–2472* *www.holualoainn.com* *6 rooms* *Fans, pool, hot tub, billiards; no A/C, no room TVs, no kids under 13, no smoking* *AE, D, DC, MC, V. $175–$205.*

$ **Hale Hualalai.** Near the artsy village of Hōlualoa, Hale Hualalai has four suites with exposed beams, hardwood floors, hot tubs, and private lānai. Perhaps the most memorable aspect of Hale Hualalai is the food—owner Lonn Armour was a professional chef for 20 years, and cooks up a breakfast that puts other B&B offerings to shame. *74-4968 Māmalahoa Hwy., Hōlualoa 96725* *808/326–2909* *www.halehualalai.com* *6 rooms* *Refrigerators, hot tub; no A/C, no room phones* *No credit cards. $135.*

$ **Nancy's Hideaway.** A few miles up the hill from Kailua-Kona, this charming cottage and studio offer modern comforts and ocean views. Each has its own entrance, a lānai, and a wet bar. The cottage stands alone; the studio is attached to the main house, but is very private. Breakfast is served in the rooms to give guests their privacy. This place is ideal for couples, but not for families with kids. *73-1530 Uanani Pl., Kailua-Kona 96740* *808/325–3132 or 866/325–3132* *808/325–3132* *www.nancyshideaway.com* *6 rooms* *Cable TV, in-room VCRs; no A/C, no kids under 13, no smoking* *MC, V. $115–$135.*

South Kona & Ka'u

There are no resorts in this area, but there are plenty of fantastic B&Bs around Kealakekua Bay and some great deals to be had on vacation condos and homes in the hills above the bay. The main attraction here *is* the bay, where kayaking and snorkeling are superb. The towns of Captain Cook and Kainaliu provide some excellent dining and shopping options, and there are dozens of coffee farms open for tours as well. You can get to the Volcano in about an hour. It's a nice place to stay if you want to be out of the fray, but there's one drawback: There are no beaches in this area. The "beach" by Kealakekua Bay is all rocks, although the bay is great for a swim; Kailua-Kona area beaches are a 15- to 30-minute drive, and the sandy Kohala Coast is an hour or more away.

Hotels

¢ **Manago Hotel.** This historic hotel is a good option if you want to escape the touristy thing but still be close to everything on the island. Don't let the front TV room creep you out—you have not checked into an old folks' home. The place has an authentic Hawai'i vibe, and the restaurant is one of the best on the island. Dwight Manago—whose grandparents, Kinzo and Osame Manago, built the main building in 1917—has maintained one Japanese-style room with tatami mats and a *furo*, a traditional Japanese bath. The other rooms are nothing special, but those in the newer wing have great views high above the Kona Coast. ✉ *81-6155 Māmalahoa Hwy., Box 145, Captain Cook 96704* ☎ *808/323–2642* 📠 *808/323–3451* 🌐 *www.managohotel.com* *64 rooms, 42 with bath* *Restaurant, bar; no A/C, no room TVs* 💳 *D, MC, V. $31–$70.*

Condos & Vacation Rentals

$$ **South Point Banyan Tree House.** Ideal for romance, this charming little tree cottage is built into a Chinese banyan tree. The partially transparent roof is the world's greatest skylight, letting in lots of light and offering views of the beautiful tree canopy above. A wraparound deck with a hot tub provides one of the best places on the island to watch the sunset. ✉ *Hwy. 11 at Pinao St., in Waiohinu (near South Point), 96742* ☎ *715/302–8180* 🌐 *www.southpointbth.com* *1 cottage* *BBQ, fans, kitchen, cable TV, in-room VCR, hot tub, laundry facilities; no A/C* 💳 *MC, V. $185 (2-night minimum).*

¢–$ **Hale O'Luna.** At this vacation house in the old plantation village of Pahala, you can rent just a room or the whole place, depending on the size of your group. The pretty, quiet house has a full kitchen for the use of all guests. The house has hardwood floors, authentic antiques, and a fully stocked library. Pahala is not an exciting place, but you are close to the black-sand beach of Punalu'u Beach Park, Hawai'i Volcanoes National Park, and some of the lesser-known sights of the area, like Wood Temple. ✉ *96-3181 Pikake St., Pahala* ☎ *808/928–8144* 🌐 *www.pahala.info* *2 rooms* *Library; no A/C, no room TVs* 💳 *No credit cards. $85–$125.*

¢ **Colony One at Sea Mountain.** Near the Punalu'u black sand beach, these condos have been recently renovated, and the grounds have been much improved. Though not beachfront, they are close to the beach, near enough to hear the ocean, and just a short trip (30 minutes or less) from the Volcano. Their prices are lower than anything else on the island apart from camping. ✉ *95-789 Ninole Loop Rd., 96742* ☎ *800/359–6089 or 808/939–7368* 🌐 *www.landofficehawaii.com* *74 units* *BBQs, kitchens, cable TV, some in-room VCRs, tennis court, 18-hole golf course, pool, exercise equipment, laundry facilities* 💳 *MC, V. $50–$95.*

B&Bs

$$ **Horizon Guest House.** Four suites with private entrances and lānai are perched on the rolling hills of the McCandless Ranch, just south of Kona, overlooking Kealakekua Bay. The 360-degree views from both the private lānai and the Guest House's awesome infinity-edge pool make this one of the more beautiful places to stay on the island. Coffeemakers in each room make it easy for guests to have a little morning privacy before joining the other guests for a lavish breakfast buffet in the dining room. ✉ *86-3992 Hwy. 11, McCandless Ranch, on the left, just past mile marker 101, 96726* ☎ *808/328–2540 or 888/328–8301* 📠 *808/328–8707* 🌐 *www.horizonguesthouse.com* *4 suites* *Fans, refrigerator, pool, hot tub; no A/C* 💳 *MC, V. $250.*

$–$$ **Aloha Guesthouse.** In the hills above Kealakekua Bay, Aloha Guesthouse offers quiet elegance, complete privacy, and ocean views from every room. With a focus on nature, the house is furnished in earth tones. The bath products are 100% organic, and the yummy full breakfasts are as close to organic as they can muster. Common areas include a kitchenette for guests who want to cook their own meals, as well as a high-definition television, a DVD library, and a computer with high-speed Internet. ✉ *Old Tobacco Rd., off Hwy. 11 near mile marker 104, Captain Cook* ☎ *808/328–8955* 🌐 *www.alohaguesthouse.com* *5 rooms* *Wi-Fi, refrigerators, cable TV, some in-room DVD players, hot tub, Internet room* *AE, MC, V. $140–$250.*

$–$$ **Dragonfly Ranch.** A unique hideaway built into the trees of Honaunau (about 10 mi south of Kealakekua Bay), the Dragonfly is not for everyone but for some it is paradise. Dubbed an eco-retreat, this remarkable jungle treehouse brings the outside in, with windows everywhere, lots of open-air sitting areas, and plants and flowers galore. The ranch doubles as a Healing Arts Center: food is prepared from the ranch's organic garden, a labyrinth walk and *lomi lomi* massages are available, as are dolphin swims (they take you to the bay to "play respectfully with dolphins," and they keep a variety of musical instruments in the front room for anyone to play. ✉ *Box 675, Honaunau off Hwy. 160, 96726* ☎ *808/328–2159* 🌐 *www.dragonflyranch.com* *3 rooms, 2 suites, 1 cottage* *Wi-Fi, cable TV, gym, sauna, spa (with massages), DVD library* *MC, V. Rooms and suites $100–$250; detached 3 bed–2 bath Dragonfly Cottage $300.*

$ **Kalaekilohana.** You wouldn't really expect to find a top-notch B&B in Ka'u, but just up the road from South Point, this charming yellow house offers large, comfortable private suites with beautifully restored hardwood floors, private lānai with ocean and mountain views, and big, comfy beds decked out with high threadcount sheets and fluffy down comforters. Breakfast is entirely up to the guest; choose between a full hot breakfast or a Continental breakfast of local fruits and baked goods. For those anxious to get an early start on exploring the area's green and black sand beaches or Volcanoes National Park (a half hour drive away), hosts Kenny Joyce and Kilohana Domingo are happy to pack a bento box to go. Guests can also look forward to a nightly cocktail hour and plenty of great advice from their hosts. ✉ *94-2152 South Point Rd., Na'alehu 96772* ☎ *808/939–8052* 🌐 *www.kau-hawaii.com* *4* *In-room broadband, laundry facilities; no A/C* *MC, V. $139–$159.*

Volcano

If you are going to visit Volcanoes National Park, and we highly recommend that you do if you haven't before, stay the night in Volcano Village. This allows you to do the late-night lava hike—the best way to see lava—without worrying about driving an hour or more back to your condo, hotel, or B&B. Lucky for you, there are plenty of lodging options in the area, and many of them are both charming and reasonable. Volcano Village has just enough restaurant and shop options to satisfy you for a day or two. From here you are also close to Hilo, the Puna region, and Punalu'u's black sand beach, should you decide to make Volcano your home base for more than a day or two.

Hotels & Resorts

$–$$ **Inn at Volcano.** At this high-end boutique resort, afternoon tea is served before a fireplace. A candlelit breakfast under a glittering chandelier adds a touch of elegance. The Inn's two-story Treehouse Suite ($299), with wraparound windows, a marble wet bar, and a fireplace, gives one the impression of floating on the tops of the trees. ✉ *Wright Rd., Volcano Village 96785* ☎ *808/967–7786 or 800/937–7786* 🖷 *808/967–8660* 🌐 *www.volcano-hawaii.com* *6 rooms* *Cable TV, in-room VCRs, hot tubs* 💳 *AE, D, DC, MC, V. Rooms $170–$185, suites $200–$400.*

★ **$–$$** **Kīlauea Lodge.** A mile from the entrance of Hawai'i Volcanoes National Park, this lodge was initially built as a YMCA camp in the 1930s. Now it is a pleasant inn, tastefully furnished with European antiques. Rooms have rich quilts and Hawaiian photographs, and some have their own wood-burning fireplaces. A charming two-bedroom cottage with a gas fireplace and a private balcony is perfect for romance. Cottages off the main property include Pi'i Mauna House, on the fairway of the Volcano Golf Course. Rates include a full gourmet breakfast at the Lodge's restaurant. ✉ *Old Volcano Hwy., 1 mi northeast of Volcano Store* *Box 116, Volcano Village 96785* ☎ *808/967–7366* 🖷 *808/967–7367* 🌐 *www.kilauealodge.com* *11 rooms, 3 cottages* *Restaurant, dining room, hot tub, shop; no A/C, no TV in some rooms, no smoking* 💳 *AE, MC, V. $150–$190.*

¢–$$ **Volcano House.** On the very rim of a volcano, this place has knockout views of Kīlauea Caldera that make it worth a visit even if you're not staying here. It's the only lodging option (except for cabins and campsites) within Hawai'i Volcanoes National Park. Book a crater-view room as far from the busy dining room area as possible. Alas, the 1941 hotel is looking a bit worn, with tired carpeting and '50s-era furnishings. ✉ *Crater Rim Dr., Box 53, Hawai'i Volcanoes National Park, 96718* ☎ *808/967–7321* 🖷 *808/967–8429* *42 rooms* *Restaurant, shop; no A/C* 💳 *AE, D, DC, MC, V. $95–$225.*

B&Bs and Vacation Rentals

¢–$$$$ **Chalet Kīlauea Collection.** The Collection comprises five inns and lodges and five vacation houses in and around Volcano Village; the theme rooms, suites, and vacation homes range from no-frills dorm-style bedrooms in a funky old house to a plantation mansion with its own six-person hot tub. Among its reasonably priced offerings is the **Volcano Bed & Breakfast** ($49–$69 double-occupancy room), which has a communal kitchen and fireplace. ✉ *Wright Rd., Volcano Village 96785* ☎ *808/967–7786 or 800/937–7786* 🖷 *808/967–8660* 🌐 *www.volcano-hawaii.com* *11 rooms, 9 suites, 5 houses* *Some kitchens, some microwaves, cable TV with movies; no A/C, no phones in some rooms, no smoking* 💳 *AE, D, DC, MC, V. $49–$399.*

¢–$$ **Volcano Places.** A collection of lovely vacation homes, the accommodations range from a simple cottage in the rain forest to a stunning Craftsman-style house with its own spa room. Many can accommodate up to

9

eight people comfortably. All come equipped with full kitchens. *Box 159, Volcano 96785 808/967–7990 www.volcanoplaces.com 3 cottages A/C, kitchens, refrigerators, some in-room VCRs, hot tubs MC, V. $95–$250.*

$ **Carson's Volcano Cottage.** New owners (the Winslows) have taken over from the Carsons and are doing a bang-up job of bringing these guest rooms and cottage back to life. The handful of guest rooms plus one private cottage (Nick's Cabin) are decorated in Hawaiian and Asian themes with comfy Hawaiian quilts and antiques. The cottage also has its own woodburning stove and kitchen. A large covered hot tub is set up in the middle of the rainforest outside—perfect on a clear, starry night. A huge buffet breakfast is served in the dining room every morning for all guests. *501 Sixth St., at Jade Ave., 96785 800/845–5282 or 808/967–7683 808/967–8094 www.carsonsvolcanocottage.com 4 rooms, 1 cabin Some kitchens, some room TVs, hot tub; no A/C, no phones in some rooms AE, D, MC, V. $115–$130.*

$ **Hydrangea Cottage & Mountain House.** You'll find this landscaped estate about a mile from Hawai'i Volcanoes National Park. The one-bedroom cottage has a wraparound porch and floor-to-ceiling windows looking out over giant tree ferns. The Mountain House has two living rooms and three bedrooms filled with antique furnishings. Each bedroom has its own bath. Both units have kitchens, and breakfast fixings are provided. *Box 563, Waimea 96743 808/262–8133 1 house, 1 cottage Kitchen, cable TV, in-room VCRs, laundry facilities; no A/C No credit cards. 1-bedroom cottage $125–$150, 3-bedroom house $375–$450.*

★ $ **Volcano Teapot Cottage.** A near-perfect spot for couples seeking a romantic getaway, this cute red-and-white cottage is completely private. The claw-foot bathtub, hot tub, and fireplace add to the general coziness. Breakfast is included, and the restaurants in Volcano Village are nearby. *19-3820 Old Volcano Hwy., Volcano Village Box 511, Volcano 96785 808/967–7112 www.volcanoteapot.com 1 cottage Kitchen, in-room VCR, hot tub No credit cards. $175.*

¢–$ **Hale Ohia Cottages.** A stately and comfortable Queen Anne–style mansion, Hale Ohia was built in the 1930s as a summer place for a wealthy Scotsman. The namesake Ohia cottage, large enough for a family, has a full kitchen. The 'Ihilani cottage is the cushiest of the group; built into an old water tank, it's naturally lighted, beautifully designed, and completely private. Breakfast (including homemade bread made with bananas, macadamia nuts, and cranberries) is left in your refrigerator while you're away in the afternoon so that you can enjoy it at your leisure in the morning. This place does everything possible to make you feel at home. *Hale Ohia Rd., off Hwy. 11 808/967–7986 www.haleohia.com 4 rooms, 3 cottages, 1 suite Some kitchenettes, some microwaves, some refrigerators, hot tub, no-smoking rooms; no A/C, no room phones MC, V. $95–$159.*

¢–$ **My Island Bed & Breakfast Inn.** Gordon and Joann Morse, along with their daughter Ki'i, opened their historic home and 7-acre botanical estate to visitors in 1985. The oldest in Volcano, it was built in 1886 by the Lyman missionary family. Three rooms, sharing two baths, are in the main house. Scattered around the area are three garden apartments

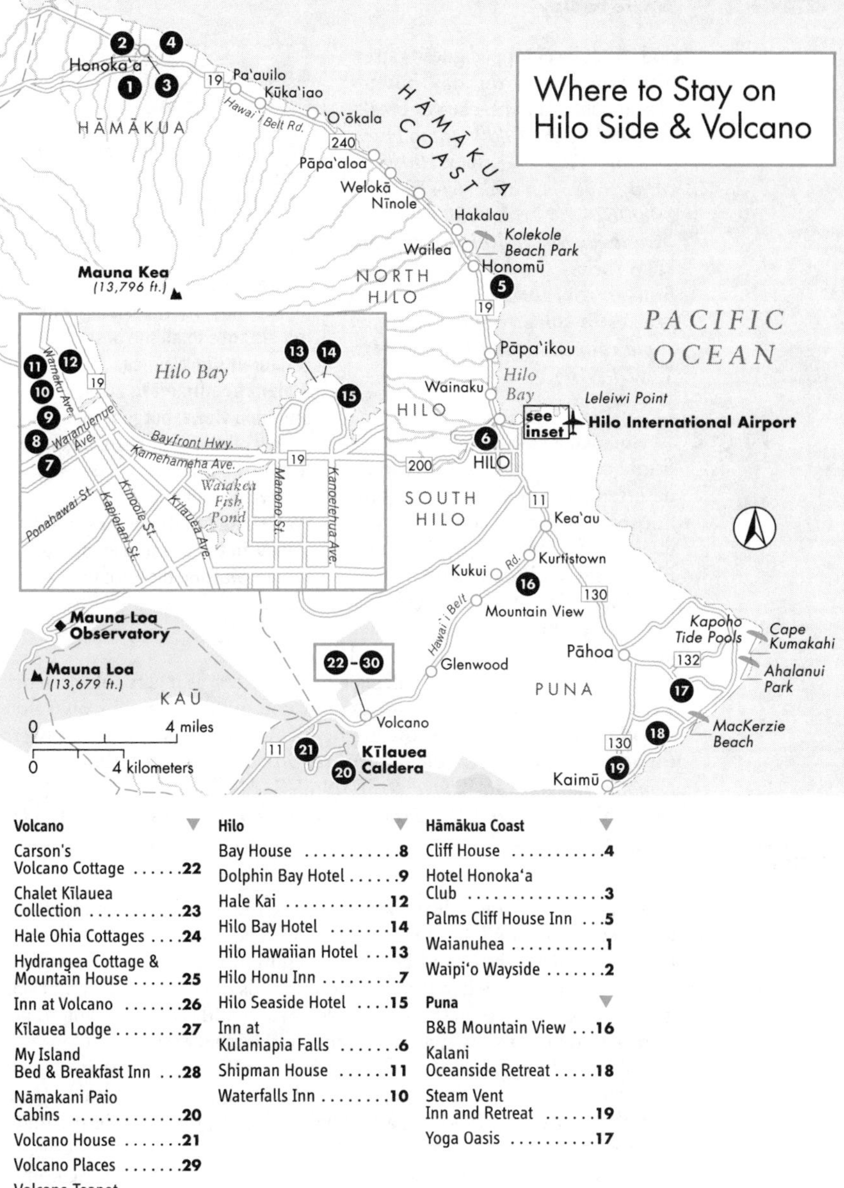

Volcano	
Carson's Volcano Cottage	22
Chalet Kīlauea Collection	23
Hale Ohia Cottages	24
Hydrangea Cottage & Mountain House	25
Inn at Volcano	26
Kīlauea Lodge	27
My Island Bed & Breakfast Inn	28
Nāmakani Paio Cabins	20
Volcano House	21
Volcano Places	29
Volcano Teapot Cottage	30

Hilo	
Bay House	8
Dolphin Bay Hotel	9
Hale Kai	12
Hilo Bay Hotel	14
Hilo Hawaiian Hotel	13
Hilo Honu Inn	7
Hilo Seaside Hotel	15
Inn at Kulaniapia Falls	6
Shipman House	11
Waterfalls Inn	10

Hāmākua Coast	
Cliff House	4
Hotel Honoka'a Club	3
Palms Cliff House Inn	5
Waianuhea	1
Waipi'o Wayside	2

Puna	
B&B Mountain View	16
Kalani Oceanside Retreat	18
Steam Vent Inn and Retreat	19
Yoga Oasis	17

and five fully equipped guesthouses. You won't start the day hungry after a deluxe all-you-can-eat breakfast. ✉ *19-3896 Old Volcano Hwy., Volcano Village* ⓟ *Box 100, Volcano 96785* ☎ *808/967-7216 or 808/967-7110* 🖷 *808/967-7719* 🌐 *www.myislandinnhawaii.com* ⇨ *6 rooms, 3 with bath; 5 guesthouses* ♨ *Library; no A/C, no phones in some rooms, no TV in some rooms, no smoking* ▭ *MC, V. $70–$105.*

Cabins

¢ **Nāmakani Paio Cabins.** These A-frame cabins at the end of a long, deserted road, look like little bird houses. Though recently remodeled, and managed by Volcano House, the cabins are definitely for those who are into roughing it. Inexpensive and clean, each has a double bed, two bunk beds, and electric lights, but no outlets. Bring extra blankets, as it gets cold at night. Each cabin also has a grill outside, but you must bring your own firewood. A communal bathroom facility provides toilets and hot showers for all cabin guests. ✉ *Volcano House, Box 53, Hawai'i Volcanoes National Park, Volcano Village* ☎ *808/967-7321* 🖷 *808/967-8429* ⇨ *10 cabins* ♨ *BBQs; no A/C, no room phones, no room TVs* ▭ *MC, V. $45.*

> **BED & BREAKFAST, HAWAIIAN-STYLE**
>
> **Hōlualoa Inn** (Kailua-Kona). Gorgeous wood floors, quiet location, beautiful coffee-country views, close to the quaint artist's community of Hōlualoa.
> **Jacaranda Inn** (Waimea). Charming, country-style, Jacuzzis, walking distance to all the best restaurants in Waimea.
> **Waianuhea** (Hāmākua Coast). Stunning views, hot tub, completely off the grid, beautiful architecture, delicious hors d'oeuvres and wine tasting nightly.
> **Waterfalls Inn** (Hilo). Quiet and stately, in the nicest neighborhood in Hilo, walking distance to downtown.

Hilo

Hilo is the wetter, more lush eastern side of the Big Island, which means if you stay here you'll be close to waterfalls and rainforest hikes, but not to a warm, dry, white sand beach. Though Hilo had the wind knocked out of its sails a bit when sugar left the islands over a decade ago, it has gotten back on its feet in the last couple of years and is experiencing something of a revival. Locals, driven farther and farther east by development in the west, have taken a greater interest in Hilo; signs of that interest are showing in new restaurants, restored buildings, and a handful of clean and pleasant parks. Hilo has a few decent hotels, but none of the high-end resorts that are the domain of the west. So, get into the groove at one of Hilo's fantastic B&Bs. Most have taken over lovely historic homes and serve breakfast comprised of ingredients from their backyard gardens. The Volcano is only a 30- to 40-minute drive, as are the sights of the Puna region. The beaches, unfortunately, are at least an hour's drive.

Hotels & Resorts

$–$$ **Hilo Hawaiian Hotel.** Though it does show its age and some of the rooms are in dire need of a refresh, this older hotel, with large bay-front rooms offering spectacular views of Mauna Kea and Coconut Island, is one of the most pleasant lodgings on Hilo Bay. Streetside rooms overlook the golf course. Most accommodations have private lānai, and kitchenettes are available in some one-bedroom suites. Views of the bay are showcased in the Queen's Court dining room, and the Wai'oli Lounge has entertainment Thursday through Saturday. ✉ *71 Banyan Dr., Hilo 96720* ☎ *808/935–9361, 800/367–5004 from mainland, 800/272–5275 interisland* 🖷 *808/961–9642* 🌐 *www.hilohawaiian.com* ⇒ *286 rooms, 6 suites* ♨ *Restaurant, A/C, in-room data ports, some kitchenettes, refrigerators, cable TV, pool, bar, laundry facilities, no-smoking rooms* ▭ *AE, D, DC, MC, V. Rooms $135–$247, suites $385.*

¢–$ **Hilo Seaside Hotel.** Like some of its neighbors, the Hilo Seaside Hotel is showing its age. It's also a bit noisy due to its proximity to the airport. That said, it is a friendly, laid-back, and otherwise peaceful place, with tropical rooms that have private lānai. The nicest ones overlook the koi-filled lagoon, or are around the pool. The staff is friendly, the restaurant serves local fare, and the tropical foliage around you gives you a sense of old Hawai'i. ✉ *126 Banyan Way, Hilo 96720* ☎ *808/935–0821 or 800/560–5557* 🖷 *808/969–9195* 🌐 *www.hiloseasidehotel.com* ⇒ *135 rooms* ♨ *Restaurant, A/C, fans, some kitchenettes, refrigerators, cable TV, pool, laundry facilities, no-smoking rooms* ▭ *AE, D, DC, MC, V. $55–$110.*

★ ¢ **Dolphin Bay Hotel.** A glowing lava flow sign marks the office and bespeaks owner John Alexander's passion for the volcano. Stunning lava pictures adorn the common area, and Alexander is a great source of information for visiting the park and for exploring the back roads of Hilo. Units in the 1950s-style motor lodge are modest, but they are clean and inexpensive. Coffee and fresh fruit are offered daily. Four blocks from Hilo Bay, in a residential area called Pu'ue'o, the hotel borders a verdant 2-acre Hawaiian garden with jungle trails and shady places to rest. Guests of the hotel return repeatedly, and it's ideal for families who seek a home base. ✉ *333 'Iliahi St., Hilo 96720* ☎ *808/935–1466* 🖷 *808/935–1523* 🌐 *www.dolphinbayhotel.com* ⇒ *13 rooms, 4 1-bedroom units, 1 2-bedroom unit* ♨ *Fans, kitchens, kitchenettes, microwaves; no A/C, no room phones, no room TVs* ▭ *MC, V. $66–$99.*

¢ **Hilo Bay Hotel.** Funky and cheap—enough said. This is a popular stopover for those who enjoy proprietor Uncle Billy Kimo's Hawaiian hospitality. A nightly hula show and entertainment during dinner at Uncle Billy's restaurant are part of the fun. ✉ *87 Banyan Dr., Hilo 96720* ☎ *808/935–0861, 800/367–5102 from the mainland, 800/442–5841 interisland* 🖷 *808/935–7903* 🌐 *www.unclebilly.com* ⇒ *145 rooms* ♨ *Restaurant, A/C, some kitchenettes, refrigerators, pool, bar, laundry facilities, Internet room, no-smoking rooms* ▭ *AE, D, DC, MC, V. $84–$94.*

B&Bs & Vacation Rentals

★ $$ **Shipman House Bed & Breakfast Inn.** You'll have a choice between three rooms in the "castle"—the turreted main house dating from 1899—or two rooms in a separate cottage. The B&B is on 5½ verdant acres on Reed's Island; the house is furnished with antique koa and period pieces, some dating from the days when Queen Lili'uokalani came to tea. On

9

Tuesday night, an authentic hula school practices Hawai'i's ancient dances in the house. Barbara (part of the Shipman family) and her husband Gary are friendly hosts with a vast knowledge of the area and the rest of the island; they're also excellent cooks, which means you should try absolutely everything at breakfast. ✉ *131 Ka'iulani St., Hilo 96720* ☎ *808/934–8002 or 800/627–8447* 🖷 *808/934–8002* 🌐 *www.hilohawaii.com* *3 rooms, 2 cottage rooms* *Fans, refrigerators, library; no A/C, no room phones, no room TVs, no kids, no smoking* *AE, MC, V. $199–$219.*

★ $–$$ **Hilo Honu Inn.** A charming old craftsman home lovingly restored by a friendly and hospitable couple from North Carolina, the Hilo Honu offers quite a bit of variety. Its three rooms range from the small and reasonably priced Honu's Nest to the large and luxurious Samurai Suite. The Honu's Nest provides fantastic views of the sunrise over Hilo Bay from the comforts of a large, comfy bed. The larger Bali Hai Suite has a sitting room and a window seat that looks out on tree ferns, orchids, and anthuriums. Upstairs, the entire second floor is the Samurai Suite, furnished with traditional tatami mats and beautiful antiques imported from Japan. The suite also includes a large stone soaking tub for two and a beautiful sun porch that looks out over all of Hilo and the bay beyond. Breakfast is delicious and usually includes a variety of homemade baked goods. ✉ *465 Haili St., Hilo 96720* ☎ *808/935–4325* 🌐 *www.hilohonu.com* *3 rooms* *Refrigerators, Wi-Fi, cable TV, in-room DVD/VCR players; no A/C, no kids under 6* *AE, MC, V. $140–$250.*

$ **The Bay House.** Overlooking Hilo Bay and just steps away from the "Singing Bridge" into Hilo's historic downtown area, this small, quiet B&B is pleasantly decorated, with comfy beds and private lānai. An outdoor hot tub on the cliff offers excellent views of the bay below. A Continental breakfast buffet is provided with fresh fruits, breads, and coffee from the area—guests are invited to take what they want from the buffet back to their lānai for a more private breakfast. ✉ *42 Pukihae St, Hilo 96720* ☎ *888/235–8195 or 808/961–6311* 🌐 *www.bayhousehawaii.com* *3 rooms* *Fans, Wi-Fi, cable TV, hot tub; no A/C* *AE, MC, V. $125.*

$ **Hale Kai.** On a bluff above Hilo Bay, this 5,400-square-foot modern home is 2 mi from downtown Hilo. Four impeccable rooms with patios have been freshly painted and spruced up by new owners Maria Macias and Ricardo Zepeda, as has the private loft, which is ideal for families. All rooms have grand ocean views and are within earshot of lapping waves. Fresh flowers add a warm, European touch. Maria and Ricardo serve a full hot breakfast every morning on an outdoor deck or in the kitchen's bay-window dining area. ✉ *111 Honoli'i Pali St., Hilo 96720* ☎ *808/935–6330* 🖷 *808/935–8439* 🌐 *www.halekaihawaii.com* *4 rooms, 1 suite* *A/C, fans, cable TV, pool, hot tub, laundry service; no kids, no smoking* *No credit cards. $115–$140.*

$ **The Inn at Kulaniapia Falls.** The Inn at Kulaniapia has wonderful views both of Hilo Bay and a magnificent 120-foot waterfall that tumbles into a 300-foot-wide swimming pond. The Pagoda, a private guesthouse with a kitchen and living room, sleeps four adults and two children for $175 a night. The only drawbacks are the slightly tacky decor and less than amazing service. The spa has a menu of eight different massages. All in all, this place is a good deal for those who aren't expecting four-star accommodations. *Box 11338, Hilo 96721 808/935–8088 or 888/838–6373 808/935–8088 www.waterfall.net 4 rooms No A/C, no smoking AE, MC, V. $109.*

★ $ **Waterfalls Inn Bed & Breakfast.** This elegant old family home is in the exclusive Reed's Bay neighborhood, just a few blocks from downtown Hilo. Relaxation is the key here. Bounded on two sides by tropical streams and forest, there's no noise except the gentle gurgle of the stream. The 1916-era home has been carefully restored, retaining the original light fixtures, fine 'ōhi'a wood flooring, antique furniture, and some original bath fixtures; some of the rooms include large whirlpool tubs. You'll find lots of room to unwind in the expansive glassed-in lānai. Breakfast (George always whips up a warm and wonderful treat) is served in the large dining room. Business travelers enjoy easy access to town, government offices, and the University of Hawai'i at Hilo. There's a $20 additional fee for one-night stays. *240 Ka'iulani St., Hilo 96720 808/969–3407 www.waterfallsinn.com 4 suites Refrigerators, Wi-Fi, cable TV, in-room DVD/VCR players; no A/C, no kids under 6 AE, MC, V. $130–$175.*

Hāmākua Coast

One of the most beautiful stretches of coastline in the world, the Hāmākua Coast is an ideal spot for those seeking peace, tranquility, and beautiful views, which is why it tends to be a favorite with honeymooners. A half dozen or so über-romantic B&Bs dot the coast, each with its own personality and views. As with Hilo, the beaches are an hour's drive away or more, so most visitors spend a few nights here and a few closer to the beaches on the west coast. A handful of vacation homes provide an extra level of privacy for couples, groups, or families, but the nearest grocery store is 15 mi up the road in either Hilo or Waimea.

$$–$$$$ **The Palms Cliff House Inn.** This handsome Victorian-style mansion, 15 mi north of Hilo, is perched on the sea cliffs 150 feet above the crashing surf of the tropical Hāmākua Coast. You can pick tropical fruit and macadamia nuts from the gardens of the 3½-acre estate. Individually decorated rooms have private lānai. Suites include double hot tubs (the one in Room 8 is in the window with a stunning view of the coast), but there's also a communal hot tub in the garden. A husband-and-wife team serves breakfast with pride on the veranda overlooking the cliffs; meals generally include fresh-baked muffins, locally grown fruit, a warm egg or meat dish (they always ask about food allergies or dietary restrictions ahead of time), and, of course, fantastic local coffee. Dinner is available on request. They can help you plan activities, including hula lessons. *28-3514 Māmalahoa Hwy., Honomū 96728 808/963–6076 808/963–6316 www.palmscliffhouse.com 2 rooms, 6 suites A/C in some rooms, fans, in-room data ports, in-room safes, cable TV, in-room DVD players, hot tub; no kids under 12, no smoking AE, D, DC, MC, V. $250–$375.*

9

$$–$$$ **Waianuhea.** Waianuhea defines Hawaiian country elegance. Fully self-contained, this gorgeous country home sits in a forested area on the Hāmākua Coast. The four guest rooms and large suite have tasteful color schemes and lavish furnishings, and there is contemporary artwork throughout. The large common room with its stunning ocean views and lava-rock fireplace is a big attraction, especially at the wine tasting and hors d'oeuvres hour each evening. Stroll the flower garden and fruit orchards. The house has solar-electric power. *45-3503 Kahana Dr., Honoka'a 96727 888/775–2577 or 808/775–1118 888/296–6302 www.waianuhea.com 4 rooms, 1 suite Cable TV, in-room DVD players, Internet room; no A/C, no smoking AE, D, MC, V. Rooms $190–$310, suite $400.*

Fodor'sChoice ★

MOST ROMANTIC

Palms Cliff House Inn (Hāmākua Coast). Stunning views, private in-room hot tubs.

Kona Village Resort (Kohala Coast). Totally removed from modern life; beautiful setting, completely private *hales.*

South Point Banyan Treehouse (Ka'u). Total privacy; it's tucked into a banyan tree with a hot tub for two on the deck.

Volcano Teapot Cottage (Volcano). Unbelievably charming, from the fireplace to the antiques to the hot tub in the back.

Waianuhea (Hāmākua Coast). Gorgeous house, and a great wine and hors d'oeuvres hour.

$$ **The Cliff House.** A private two-bedroom home, the Cliff House sits on rolling pasture lands and looks out over an incredible view of the coast. Owner Richard Mastronardo also owns Waipi'o Valley Artworks in nearby Honoka'a and has decorated the house with items from the store—beautiful locally made furniture, art, and crafts—and stocked it with pleasant extras like a chess set, telescope, binoculars for whale watching, and an answering machine for the phone. The large deck is a fantastic place to spend the afternoon, hypnotized by the view. *Box 5045, Kukuihaele 96727 808/775–0005 or 800/492–4746 www.cliffhousehawaii.com 2-bedroom house BBQ, fans, in-room data ports, kitchen, 2 TVs with premium satellite package (HBO), laundry facilities; no A/C MC, V. $195 (2-night minimum).*

¢–$ **Waipi'o Wayside.** Nestled amid the avocado, mango, and kukui trees of a plantation estate, this serene inn provides a retreat close to the Waipi'o Valley. Jacqueline Horne has given each room its own character with, for example, rare Chinese antiques or patchwork quilts. A sprawling garden has an orchid-covered deck and a little gazebo has hammocks to help you indulge your lazy side. Many of the rooms have ocean views and some also have skylights. Breakfast includes fresh fruit from the estate, locally grown coffee, granola, yogurt, and muffins. *Waipi'o Valley Rd., Hwy. 240, Honoka'a 96727 808/775–0275 or 800/833–8849 808/775–0275 www.waipiowayside.com 5 rooms In-room data ports; no A/C, no room phones, no room TVs, no smoking MC, V. $95–$170.*

¢ **Hotel Honoka'a Club.** This bargain hotel is 45 minutes from Hilo and close to Waipi'o Valley. Rustic rooms range from lower-level dormitory-style units—bring your own sleeping bag—to upper-story rooms with private baths, ocean views, and a complimentary Continental breakfast. ✉ *45-3480 Māmane St., Box 247, Honoka'a 96727* ☎ *808/775–0678 or 800/808–0678* 🌐 *www.hotelhonokaa.com* *13 rooms, 5 dorm-style rooms* *Restaurant, Wi-Fi; no A/C, no room phones, no TV in some rooms, no smoking* 💳 *MC, V. Dorm rooms $18–$38, standard rooms $50–$75.*

Puna

Puna is a world apart—wild jungles, volcanically heated hot springs, and not a resort for miles around. There are, however, a handful of vacation homes and bed-and-breakfasts, most of which are a great deal due to the fact that Puna doesn't attract nearly as many visitors as other regions on the island. This is not a typical vacation spot: There are a few black sand beaches (some of them clothing-optional), very few dining or entertainment options, and quite a few, er, interesting locals. That said, for those who want to have a unique experience, get away from everything, and like the thought of rubbing shoulders with the locals, this is the place to do it. The Volcano, Hilo, and the Hāmākua Coast are all within easy driving distance, and nearby Pahoa has a few restaurants.

$–$$ **Kalani Oceanside Retreat.** This lodging sponsors numerous meditation and yoga classes in addition to programs on Hawaiian culture, healing, and gay relationships. Accommodations include campsites, shared rooms, cottage units with shared kitchens, lodge rooms, and private, luxurious tree-house units. Bathing suits are optional both on the nearby beach and at the Olympic-size pool. There's a thermal spring nearby. Even the driveway is beautiful, and the grounds are lush and well kept. The food is good, too, but a bit pricey considering it's served cafeteria style. Full meal plans are available at an additional charge. ✉ *Pāhoa-Beach Rd., Hwy. 137, R.R. 2, Box 4500, Pāhoa 96778* ☎ *808/965–7828 or 800/800–6886* 📠 *808/965–0527* 🌐 *www.kalani.com* *24 rooms with shared bath, 9 cottages, 4 tree-house units, 3 guesthouse rooms* *Fans, some refrigerators, tennis court, pool, hair salon, hot tub, sauna, laundry facilities, laundry service, no-smoking rooms; no A/C, no room TVs* 💳 *AE, D, MC, V. $110–$240.*

¢–$ **Bed & Breakfast Mountain View.** This modern home is surrounded by rolling forest and farmland. The secluded 4-acre estate has extensive floral gardens and a fishpond. Owners Linus and Jane Chao are longtime Big Island art educators and have an art studio on the lower level where they teach classes. Some special packages include art lessons. The house itself is a virtual art gallery with varied displays in oil, acrylic, watercolor, and Oriental brush paintings. ✉ *South Kulani Rd., Kurtistown 96760* ☎ *808/968–6868 or 888/698–9896* 📠 *808/968–7017* 🌐 *www.bbmtview.com* *4 rooms, 2 with shared bath* *Fishing, billiards, laundry facilities; no A/C, no TV in some rooms, no kids under 5* 💳 *MC, V. $55–$110.*

¢–$ **Yoga Oasis.** This center, on 26 tropical acres, has a bit of a commune feel. With its exposed redwood beams, Balinese doorways, and imported art, Yoga Oasis draws those who seek relaxation and rejuvena-

9

LODGING ALTERNATIVES

HOME EXCHANGES

If you would like to exchange your home for someone else's, join a home-exchange organization, which will send you its updated listings of available exchanges for a year and will include your own listing in at least one of them. It's up to you to make specific arrangements.

Exchange Clubs **HomeLink USA** ✉ 2937 NW 9th Terrace, Wilton Manors, FL 33311 ☎ 954/566-2687 or 800/638-3841 🖷 954/566-2783 🌐 www.homelink.org; $75 yearly for a listing and online access; $45 additional to receive directories. **Intervac U.S.** ✉ 30 Corte San Fernando, Tiburon, CA 94920 ☎ 800/756-4663 🖷 415/435-7440 🌐 www.intervacus.com; $128 yearly for a listing, online access, and a catalog; $68 without catalog.

HOSTELS

No matter what your age, you can save on lodging costs by staying at hostels. In some 4,500 locations in more than 70 countries around the world, Hostelling International (HI), the umbrella group for a number of national youth-hostel associations, offers single-sex, dorm-style beds and, at many hostels, rooms for couples and family accommodations. Membership in any HI national hostel association, open to travelers of all ages, allows you to stay in HI-affiliated hostels at member rates; one-year membership is about $28 for adults (C$35 for a two-year minimum membership in Canada, £15 in the U.K., A$52 in Australia, and NZ$40 in New Zealand); hostels charge about $10–$30 per night. Members have priority if the hostel is full; they're also eligible for discounts around the world, even on rail and bus travel in some countries.

Organizations **Hostelling International–USA** ✉ 8401 Colesville Rd., Suite 600, Silver Spring, MD 20910 ☎ 301/495-1240 🖷 301/495-6697 🌐 www.hiusa.org.

Local Resources **Hilo Bay Hostel** ✉ 101 Waianuenue Ave., 96720 ☎ 808/933-2771 🌐 www.hawaiihostel.net. **Holo Holo Inn** ✉ 19-4036 Kalani Honua Rd., Volcano Village 96785 ☎ 808/967-7950 🌐 www.enable.org/holoholo/. **Hotel Honoka'a Club** ✉ 45-3480 Māmane St., Box 247, Honoka'a 96727 ☎ 808/775-0678 or 800/808-0678 🌐 www.hotelhonokaa.com. **Koa Wood Hale Inn** ✉ 75-184 Ala Ona Ona St., Kailua-Kona 96740 ☎ 808/329-9663 🌐 www.alternative-hawaii.com/affordable/kona.htm.

tion, and perhaps a free yoga lesson or two. A 1,600-square-foot state-of-the-art yoga and gymnastics space, with 18-foot ceilings, crowns this friendly retreat. You're close to hot springs and black-sand beaches, and the volcano is a 45-minute drive away. Bathrooms are shared. ✉ *Pohoiki Rd., Box 1935, Pāhoa 96778* ☎ *808/965–8460 or 800/274–4446* 🌐 *www.yogaoasis.org* *5 rooms with shared bath, 4 bungalows, 1 cottage* *Some fans, massage, laundry service; no A/C, no room phones, no room TVs, no smoking* *MC, V. $35–$145.*

¢ **Steam Vent Inn and Retreat.** Not at all luxurious, but the Steam Vent is comfortable and clean, and equipped with volcanically heated showers, hot tubs, and a pond. Massage and reflexology are also available, and a clothing-optional black sand beach is five minutes away. For those on a budget, single-person huts with small kitchenettes are available for only $25 a night. Nicer rooms in the main house are a bit more, but still very reasonable. ✉ *13-3775 Kalapana Hwy., 96778* ☎ *808/965–8800* *10 rooms* *Some kitchenettes, hot tubs, massage available; no A/C, no TV, no phones in rooms* *No credit cards. $25–$75.*

9

UNDERSTANDING THE BIG ISLAND

HAWAI'I AT A GLANCE

A SNAPSHOT OF HAWAI'I

HAWAIIAN VOCABULARY

HAWAI'I AT A GLANCE

Fast Facts

Nickname: Aloha State
Capital: Honolulu
State song: "Hawai'i Pono'i"
State bird: The nēnē, an endangered land bird and variety of goose
State flower: Yellow Hibiscus Brackenridgii
State tree: Kukui (or candlenut), a Polynesian-introduced tree
Administrative divisions: There are four counties with mayors and councils: City and County of Honolulu (island of O'ahu), Hawai'i County (Hawai'i Island), Maui County (islands of Maui, Moloka'i, Lāna'i, and Kaho'olawe), and Kaua'i County (islands of Kaua'i and Ni'ihau)
Entered the Union: August 21, 1959, as the 50th state
Population: 1,334,023
Life expectancy: Female 82, male 76
Literacy: 81%
Ethnic groups: Hawaiian/part Hawaiian 22.1%, Caucasian 20.5%, Japanese 18.3%, Filipino 12.3%, Chinese 4.1%
Religion: Roman Catholic 22%; Buddhist, Shinto and other East Asian religions 15%; Mormon 10%; United Church of Christ 8%; Assembly of God and Baptist 6% each; Episcopal, Jehovah's Witness, and Methodist 5% each
Language: English is the first language of the majority of residents; Hawaiian is the native language of the indigenous Hawaiian people and an official language of the state; other languages spoken include Samoan, Chinese, Japanese, Korean, Spanish, Portuguese, Filipino, and Vietnamese

The loveliest fleet of islands that lies anchored in any ocean.

Mark Twain

Geography & Environment

Land area: An archipelago of 137 islands encompassing a land area of 6,422.6 square mi in the north-central Pacific Ocean (about 2,400 mi from the west coast of the continental U.S.).
Coastline: 750 mi.
Terrain: Volcanic mountains, tropical rain forests, verdant valleys, sea cliffs, canyons, deserts, coral reefs, sand dunes, sandy beaches.
Natural resources: Dimension limestone, crushed stone, sand and gravel, gemstones.
Natural hazards: Hurricanes, earthquakes, tsunamis.
Flora: More than 2,500 species of native and introduced plants throughout the islands.
Fauna: Native mammals include the hoary bat, Hawaiian monk seal, and Polynesian rat. The humpback whale migrates to Hawaiian waters every winter to mate and calve. More than 650 fish and 40 different species of shark live in Hawaiian waters. Freshwater streams are home to hundreds of native and alien species. The humuhumunukunukuāpua'a (Hawaiian triggerfish) is the unofficial state fish.
Environmental issues: Plant and animal species threatened and endangered due to hunting, overfishing, overgrazing by wild and introduced animals, and invasive alien plants.

Hawai'i is not a state of mind, but a state of grace.

Paul Theroux

Economy

Tourism and federal defense spending continue to drive the state's economy. Efforts to diversify in the areas of science and technology, film and television production, sports, ocean research and development, health and education, tourism, agriculture, and floral and specialty food products are ongoing.

GSP: $40.1 billion
Per capita income: $30,000
Inflation: 1%
Unemployment: 4.3%
Work force: 595,450
Debt: $7.3 billion
Major industries: Tourism, federal government (defense and other agencies)
Agricultural products: Sugar, pineapple, papayas, guavas, flower and nursery products, asparagus, alfalfa hay, macadamia nuts, coffee, milk, cattle, eggs, shellfish, algae
Exports: $616 million
Major export products: Aircraft and parts, naphthas, medical equipment and supplies, fruit, steel scrap, electronic components, unleaded gasoline, artwork, cocoa, coffee, flowers, macadamia nuts
Imports: $2.6 billion
Major import products: Crude oil, electronic and digital equipment, coal, passenger motor vehicles

In what other land save this one is the commonest form of greeting not "Good day," or How d'ye do," but "Love"? That greeting is "Aloha"–love, I love, my love to you. . . .It is a positive affirmation of the warmth of one's own heart, giving.

Jack London

Debate has waxed and waned for more than a century over how and when to return to native Hawaiians more than 1 million acres of land and other assets seized when American business interests overthrew the island monarchy in 1893. Certain native factions still advocate a return to independent nationhood. Sovereignty gained new momentum in the 1990s with the passage of a federal law formally apologizing for the overthrow and urging reconciliation. Momentum has since fizzled. Hawai'i's current governor has renewed efforts to have Congress recognize Hawaiians as an indigenous people, much like Native Americans and Alaskans. The governor also has pledged to support continued funding of health care, language, and other cultural programs, and to achieve state and federal obligations to distribute homestead lands to qualified Hawaiians.

Did You Know?

- Hawai'i is home to the world's most active volcano: Kīlauea, on the Big Island.
- 'Iolani Palace had electricity and telephones installed several years before the White House, and is the only palace on U.S. soil.
- Hawai'i has about 12% of all endangered plants and animals in the U.S.; 75% of the country's extinct plants and birds were Hawaiian.
- The Royal Hawaiian Band is the only intact organization from the time of Hawaiian monarchy that is fully functional and still preserves Hawai'i's musical history.

A SNAPSHOT OF HAWAI'I

Any description of Hawai'i's beauty is a cliché by now—we've all seen the postcards and the movies, heard stories from friends, and read the guidebooks. Still, when you experience Hawai'i first hand, it's hard not to gush about the long perfect beaches, dramatic cliffs, greener than green rain forests, and that unbelievable plumeria perfume that hangs over it all. Add to that the fresh pineapple, the amazing marine life, the fascinating culture and history of the Hawaiian people, the location (at nearly 1,900 mi from the next continent, the Hawaiian islands are the most isolated in the world—talk about getting away from it all), and the fact that Hawai'i is one of the few places on Earth where you can watch an active volcano create new land, and it's easy to see why these islands have been such a popular destination for so long.

Know Your Islands

O'ahu. The state's capital, Honolulu, is on O'ahu; this is the center of Hawai'i's economy and by far the most populated island in the chain—875,000 residents adds up to 75% of the state's population. At 597 square mi, O'ahu is the third largest island in the chain; the majority of residents live in or around Honolulu, so the rest of the island still fits neatly into the tropical, untouched vision of Hawai'i. Surfing contests on the legendary North Shore, Pearl Harbor, and iconic Waikīkī Beach are all here.

Maui. The second largest island in the chain, Maui's 727 square mi are home to only 118,000 people but host approximately 2 million tourists every year. Both Lāna'i and Moloka'i are just off the coast of Maui (west and north coasts, respectively), making day trips to either island easy and popular. With its restaurants and lively nightlife, Maui is the only island that competes with O'ahu in terms of entertainment; its charm lies in the fact that while entertainment is available, Maui's towns still feel like island villages.

Hawai'i (The Big Island). Once home to the state's capital, the Big Island has the second largest population of the islands (159,000) but feels sparsely settled due to its size. It's 4,038 square mi and growing—all of the other islands could fit onto the Big Island and there would still be room left over. The southernmost island in the chain, the Big Island is home to Kīleau, the most active volcano on the planet.

Kaua'i. The northernmost island in the chain, Kaua'i is, at approximately 540 square mi, the fourth largest of all the islands and the least populated of the larger islands, with just under 55,000 residents. Known as the Garden Isle, Kaua'i claims the title "wettest spot on Earth" with an annual average rainfall of 460 inches. Lush and peaceful, it's the perfect escape from the modern world.

Moloka'i. Moloka'i is Hawai'i's fifth largest island, encompassing 380 square mi. Moloka'i is very sparsely populated, with just under 7,000 residents, the majority of whom are native Hawaiians. Most of Moloka'i's 450,000 annual visitors travel from Maui or O'ahu to spend the day exploring its beaches, cliffs, and former leper colony.

Lāna'i. Lying just off Maui's western coast, Lāna'i looks nothing like its sister islands, with pine trees and deserts in place of palm trees and beaches. Still, the tiny 140-square-mi island is home to nearly 2,500 residents and draws an average of 70,000 visitors each year to two resorts (one in the mountains and one at the shore), both now operated by the Four Seasons.

Geology

The Hawaiian Islands comprise more than just the islands inhabited and visited by humans. A total of 19 islands and atolls constitute the State of Hawai'i, with a total landmass of 6,423.4 square mi. The islands are actually exposed peaks of a submersed mountain range called the Hawaiian-Emperor seamount chain. The range was formed as the Pacific plate moved very slowly (around 32 mi every million years) over a "hotspot" in the Earth's mantle. Because the plate moved northwestwardly, the islands in the northwest portion of the archipelago (chain) are older, which is also why they're smaller—they have been eroding longer.

The Big Island is the youngest, and thus the largest, island in the chain. It is built from seven different volcanoes, including Mauna Loa, the largest shield volcano on the planet. Mauna Loa and Kīlauea are the only Hawaiian volcanoes still erupting with any sort of frequency. Mauna Loa last erupted in 1984, and Kīlauea has been continuously erupting since 1983. Mauna Kea (Big Island), Hualālai (Big Island), and Haleakalā (Maui) are all in what's called the Post Shield stage of volcanic development—eruptions decrease steadily for up to 250,000 years before ceasing entirely. Kohala (Big Island), Lāna'i (Lāna'i), and Wai'anae (O'ahu) are considered extinct volcanoes, in the erosional stage of development; Ko'olau (O'ahu) and West Maui (Maui) volcanoes are extinct volcanoes in the rejuvenation stage—after lying dormant for hundreds of thousands of years, they began erupting again, but only once every several thousand years. There is currently an active undersea volcano called Lo'ihi that has been erupting regularly. If it continues its current pattern, it should breach the ocean's surface in tens of thousands of years.

Flora & Fauna

Though much of the plant life associated with Hawai'i today (pineapple, hibiscus, orchid, plumeria) was brought there by Tahitian, Samoan, or European visitors, Hawai'i is also home to several endemic species, like the koa tree and the yellow hibiscus. Long dormant volcanic craters are perfect hiding places for rare plants (like the silversword, a rare cousin of the sunflower, which grows on Hawai'i's three tallest peaks and nowhere else on Earth). Many of these endemic species are now threatened by the encroachment of introduced plants and animals. Hawai'i is also home to a handful of plants that have evolved into uniquely Hawaiian versions of their original selves. Mint, for example, develops its unique taste to keep would-be predators from eating its leaves. As there were no such predators in Hawai'i for hundreds of years, a mintless mint evolved; similar stories exist for the islands' nettle-less nettles, thorn-less briars.

Hawai'i's climate is well suited to growing several types of flowers, most of which are introduced species. Plumeria creeps over all of the islands; orchids run rampant on the Big Island; bright orange 'ilima light up the mountains of O'ahu. These flowers give the Hawaiian leis their color and fragrance.

As with the plant life, the majority of the animals in Hawai'i today were brought here by visitors. Axis deer from India roam the mountains of Lāna'i. The Islands are home to dozens of rat species, all stowaways on long boat rides over from Tahiti, England, and Samoa; the mongoose was brought to keep the rats out of the sugar plantations. Most of Hawai'i's birds, like the *nēnē* (Hawai'i's state bird) and the *pu'eo* (Hawaiian owl) are endemic; unfortunately, about 80% are also endangered.

The ocean surrounding the Islands teems with animal life. Once scarce manta rays have made their way back to the Big Island; spinner dolphins and sea turtles can be found off the coast of all the Islands; and every year from December to May, the humpback whales migrate past Hawai'i in droves.

History

Anthropologists believe that the Hawaiian Islands were initially settled by Polynesians from the Marquesas and Society Islands in approximately AD 300. They were followed not long after by Tahitian settlers. For whatever reason, exploration in this part of the world ceased for hundreds of years, and there are very few documented stories of any visitors to Hawai'i from the 300s to the arrival of British explorer Captain James Cook in 1778.

What Cook found was a deeply religious, agrarian society governed by numerous *ali'i,* or chiefs. Though Cook and his compatriots are vilified now in Hawaiian history, they were revered as gods upon their arrival, and the natives bought guns and ammunition from the newcomers. With these, the Big Island chief Kamehameha gained a significant advantage over the other Hawaiian *ali'i.* He united Hawai'i into one kingdom in 1810, bringing an end to the frequent interisland battles that had previously dominated Hawaiian life.

Under Kamehameha (from 1810 to 1819), the kingdom was relatively peaceful, despite the arrival of settlers from both Europe and America. Foreigners were accepted into the society, and they even participated in high levels of government. After the last of King Kamehameha's family died without an heir, Kalakaua was appointed ruler (a great lover of hula, King Kalakaua was also known as the Merrie Monarch, which is where Hawai'i's yearly hula festival gets its name). Unfortunately, Kalakaua was coerced into signing the Bayonet Constitution, which rendered the monarchy powerless. In 1893 Queen Lili'uokalani (Kalakaua's sister and heir to the throne) threatened to repeal the Bayonet Constitution and was subsequently overthrown by a group of American and European businessmen and government officials, aided by an armed militia. This led to the creation of the Republic of Hawai'i, which quickly became a Territory of the United States through resolutions passed by Congress (rather than through treaties). Hawai'i remained a territory for 60 years; Pearl Harbor was attacked as part of the United States in 1941 during World War II. It wasn't until 1959, however, that Hawai'i was officially admitted as the 50th State.

Legends & Mythology

Ancient deities play a huge role in Hawaiian life today—not just in daily rituals, but in the Hawaiians' reverence for their land. Gods and goddesses tend to be associated with particular parts of the land, and most of them are connected with many parts thanks to the body of stories built up around each. The goddess Pele lives in Kīlauea Volcano and rules over the Big Island. She is a feisty goddess known for turning enemies into trees or destroying the homes of adversaries with fire. She also has a penchant for gin, which is why you'll see gin bottles circling some of the craters at Volcanoes National Park. It's not the litter it appears to be, but rather an offering to placate the Volcano goddess. The Valley Isle's namesake, the demigod Maui, is a well-known Polynesian trickster. When his mother Hina complained that there were too few hours in the day, Maui promised to slow the sun. Upon hearing this, the god Moemoe teased Maui for boasting, but undeterred, the demigod wove a strong cord and lassoed the sun. Angry, the sun scorched the fields until an agreement was reached: during summer, the sun would travel more slowly. In winter, it would return to its quick pace. For ridiculing Maui, Moemoe was turned into a large rock that still juts from the water near Kahakualoa.

One of the most important ways the ancient Hawaiians showed respect for their gods and goddesses was through the hula. Various forms of the hula were performed as prayers to the gods and as praise to the chiefs. Performances were taken very seriously, as a mistake was thought to invalidate the prayer, or even to offend the god or chief in question. Hula is still performed both as entertainment and as prayer; it is not uncommon for a hula performance to be included in an official government ceremony.

Hawai'i Today

After a long period of suppression, Hawaiian culture and traditions have experienced a renaissance over the last few decades. There is a real effort to revive traditions and to respect history as the Islands go through major changes and welcome more and more newcomers every day. New developments often have a Hawaiian cultural expert on staff to ensure cultural sensitivity and to educate newcomers.

Nonetheless, development remains a huge issue for all Islanders—land prices are skyrocketing, putting many areas out of reach for the native population. Traffic is becoming a problem on roads that were not designed to accommodate all the new drivers, and the Islands' limited natural resources are being seriously tapped. The government, though sluggish to respond at first, is trying to make development in Hawai'i as sustainable as possible. Rules for new developments protect natural as well as cultural resources, and local governments have set ambitious conservation goals. Despite all efforts to ease its effect on the land and its people, large-scale, rapid development is not anyone's ideal, and Islanders are understandably less than thrilled with the prospect of a million more tourists visiting every year or buying up property that residents themselves can't afford.

That said, the aloha spirit is alive and well. Though you may encounter the occasional "haole hater" (haole—pronounced "howlie"—is Hawaiian for foreigner), the majority of Islanders are warm, a welcoming people who are proud that their home draws so many visitors and who are eager to share their culture with those who respect it.

HAWAIIAN VOCABULARY

Although an understanding of Hawaiian is by no means required on a trip to the Aloha State, a *malihini,* or newcomer, will find plenty of opportunities to pick up a few of the local words and phrases. Traditional names and expressions are widely used in the Islands, thanks in part to legislation enacted in the early '90s to encourage the use of the Hawaiian language. You're likely to read or hear at least a few words each day of your stay. Such exposure enriches a trip to Hawai'i.

With a basic understanding and some uninhibited practice, anyone can have enough command of the local tongue to ask for directions and to order from a restaurant menu. One visitor announced she would not leave until she could pronounce the name of the state fish, the *humuhumunukunukuāpua'a.* Luckily, she had scheduled a nine-day stay.

Simplifying the learning process is the fact that the Hawaiian language contains only eight consonants—*H, K, L, M, N, P, W,* and the silent *'okina,* or glottal stop, written '—plus the five vowels. All syllables, and therefore all words, end in a vowel. Each vowel, with the exception of a few diphthongized double vowels such as *au* (pronounced "ow") or *ai* (pronounced "eye"), is pronounced separately. Thus *'Iolani* is four syllables (ee-oh-la-nee), not three (yo-la-nee). Although some Hawaiian words have only vowels, most also contain some consonants, but consonants are never doubled.

Pronunciation is simple. Pronounce *A* "ah" as in father; *E* "ay" as in weigh; *I* "ee" as in marine; *O* "oh" as in no; *U* "oo" as in true.

Consonants mirror their English equivalents, with the exception of *W.* When the letter begins any syllable other than the first one in a word, it is usually pronounced as a *V. 'Awa,* the Polynesian drink, is pronounced "ava," *'ewa* is pronounced "eva."

Nearly all long Hawaiian words are combinations of shorter words; they are not difficult to pronounce if you segment them into shorter words. *Kalaniana'ole,* the highway running east from Honolulu, is easily understood as *Kalani ana 'ole.* Apply the standard pronunciation rules—the stress falls on the next-to-last syllable of most two- or three-syllable Hawaiian words—and Kalaniana'ole Highway is as easy to say as Main Street.

Now about that fish. Try *humu-humu nuku-nuku āpu a'a.*

The other unusual element in Hawaiian language is the *kahakō,* or macron, written as a short line (¯) placed over a vowel. Like the accent (´) in Spanish, the kahakō puts emphasis on a syllable that would normally not be stressed. The most familiar example is probably *Waikīkī.* With no macrons, the stress would fall on the middle syllable; with only one macron, on the last syllable, the stress would fall on the first and last syllables. Some words become plural with the addition of a macron, often on a syllable that would have been stressed anyway. No Hawaiian word becomes plural with the addition of an *S,* since that letter does not exist in the *'ōlelo Hawai'i* (which is Hawaiian for "Hawaiian language").

What follows is a glossary of some of the most commonly used Hawaiian words. Don't be afraid to give them a try. Hawaiian residents appreciate visitors who at least try to pick up the local language.

'a'ā: rough, crumbling lava, contrasting with *pāhoehoe,* which is smooth.
'ae: yes.
aikane: friend.
āina: land.
akamai: smart, clever, possessing savoir faire.
akua: god.
ala: a road, path, or trail.

ali'i: a Hawaiian chief, a member of the chiefly class.
aloha: love, affection, kindness; also a salutation meaning both greetings and farewell.
'ānuenue: rainbow.
'a'ole: no.
'apōpō: tomorrow.
'auwai: a ditch.
auwē: alas, woe is me!
'ehu: a red-haired Hawaiian.
'ewa: in the direction of 'Ewa plantation, west of Honolulu.
hala: the pandanus tree, whose leaves (*lau hala*) are used to make baskets and plaited mats.
hālau: school.
hale: a house.
hale pule: church, house of worship.
ha mea iki or **ha mea 'ole:** you're welcome.
hana: to work.
haole: ghost. Since the first foreigners were Caucasian, *haole* now means a Caucasian person.
hapa: a part, sometimes a half; often used as a short form of *hapa haole,* to mean a person who is part-Caucasian; thus, the name of a popular local band, whose members represent a variety of ethnicities.
hau'oli: to rejoice. *Hau'oli Makahiki Hou* means Happy New Year. *Hau'oli lā hānau* means Happy Birthday.
heiau: an outdoor stone platform; an ancient Hawaiian place of worship.
holo: to run.
holoholo: to go for a walk, ride, or sail.
holokū: a long Hawaiian dress, somewhat fitted, with a yoke and a train. Influenced by European fashion, it was worn at court, and at least one local translates the word as "expensive mu'umu'u."
holomū: a post–World War II cross between a *holokū* and a mu'umu'u, less fitted than the former but less voluminous than the latter, and having no train.
honi: to kiss; a kiss. A phrase that some tourists may find useful, quoted from a popular hula, is *Honi Ka'ua Wikiwiki:* Kiss me quick!
honu: turtle.
ho'omalimali: flattery, a deceptive "line," bunk, baloney, hooey.
huhū: angry.
hui: a group, club, or assembly. A church may refer to its congregation as a *hui* and a social club may be called a *hui.*
hukilau: a seine; a communal fishing party in which everyone helps to drive the fish into a huge net, pull it in, and divide the catch.
hula: the dance of Hawai'i.
iki: little.
ipo: sweetheart.
ka: the. This is the definite article for most singular words; for plural nouns, the definite article is usually *nā.* Since there is no *S* in Hawaiian, the article may be your only clue that a noun is plural.
kahuna: a priest, doctor, or other trained person of old Hawai'i, endowed with special professional skills that often included the gift of prophecy or other supernatural powers; the plural form is kāhuna.
kai: the sea, saltwater.
kalo: the taro plant from whose root poi is made.
kama'āina: literally, a child of the soil; it refers to people who were born in the Islands or have lived there for a long time.
kanaka: originally a man or humanity in general, it is now used to denote a male Hawaiian or part-Hawaiian, but is occasionally taken as a slur when used by non-Hawaiians. *Kanaka maoli,* originally a full-blooded Hawaiian person, is used by some native Hawaiian rights activists to embrace part-Hawaiians as well.
kāne: a man, a husband. If you see this word on a door, it's the men's room. If you see *kane* on a door, it's probably a misspelling; that is the Hawaiian name for the skin fungus tinea.
kapa: also called by its Tahitian name, *tapa,* a cloth made of beaten bark and usually dyed and stamped with a repeat design.
kapakahi: crooked, cockeyed, uneven. You've got your hat on *kapakahi.*

kapu: keep out, prohibited. This is the Hawaiian version of the more widely known Tongan word *tabu* (taboo).
kapuna: grandparent; elder.
kēia lā: today.
keiki: a child; *keikikāne* is a boy, *keikiwahine* a girl.
kona: the leeward side of the Islands, the direction (south) from which the *kona* wind and *kona* rain come.
kula: upland.
kuleana: a homestead or small plot of ground on which a family has been installed for some generations without necessarily owning it. By extension, *kuleana* is used to denote any area or department in which one has a special interest or prerogative. You'll hear it used this way: If you want to hire a surfboard, see Moki; that's his *kuleana.* And conversely: I can't help you with that; that's not my *kuleana.*
lā: sun.
lamalama: to fish with a torch.
lānai: a porch, a balcony, an outdoor living room. Almost every house in Hawai'i has one. Don't confuse this two-syllable word with the three-syllable name of the island, Lāna'i.
lani: heaven, the sky.
lau hala: the leaf of the *hala,* or pandanus tree, widely used in Hawaiian handicrafts.
lei: a garland of flowers.
limu: sun.
lolo: stupid.
luna: a plantation overseer or foreman.
mahalo: thank you.
makai: toward the ocean.
malihini: a newcomer to the Islands.
mana: the spiritual power that the Hawaiian believed inhabited all things and creatures.
manō: shark.
manuwahi: free, gratis.
mauka: toward the mountains.
mauna: mountain.
mele: a Hawaiian song or chant, often of epic proportions.
Mele Kalikimaka: Merry Christmas (a transliteration from the English phrase).
Menehune: a Hawaiian pixie. The *Menehune* were a legendary race of little people who accomplished prodigious work, such as building fishponds and temples in the course of a single night.
moana: the ocean.
mu'umu'u: the voluminous dress in which the missionaries enveloped Hawaiian women. Now made in bright printed cottons and silks, it is an indispensable garment in a Hawaiian woman's wardrobe. Culturally sensitive locals have embraced the Hawaiian spelling but often shorten the spoken word to "mu'u." Most English dictionaries include the spelling "muumuu," and that version is a part of many apparel companies' names.
nani: beautiful.
nui: big.
ohana: family.
'ono: delicious.
pāhoehoe: smooth, unbroken, satiny lava.
Pākē: Chinese. This *Pākē* carver makes beautiful things.
palapala: document, printed matter.
pali: a cliff, precipice.
pānini: prickly pear cactus.
paniolo: a Hawaiian cowboy, a rough transliteration of *español,* the language of the Islands' earliest cowboys.
pau: finished, done.
pilikia: trouble. The Hawaiian word is much more widely used here than its English equivalent.
puka: a hole.
pupule: crazy, like the celebrated Princess Pupule. This word has replaced its English equivalent in local usage.
pu'u: volcanic cinder cone.
waha: mouth.
wahine: a female, a woman, a wife, and a sign on the ladies' room door; the plural form is *wāhine.*
wai: freshwater, as opposed to saltwater, which is *kai.*
wailele: waterfall.
wikiwiki: to hurry, hurry up (since this is a reduplication of *wiki,* quick, neither *W* is pronounced as a *V*).

Note: Pidgin is the unofficial language of Hawai'i. It is a Creole language, with its own grammar, evolved from the mixture of English, Hawaiian, Japanese, Portuguese, and other languages spoken in 19th-century Hawai'i, and it is heard everywhere: on ranches, in warehouses, on beaches, and in the hallowed halls (and occasionally in the classrooms) of the University of Hawai'i.

Big Island Essentials

PLANNING TOOLS, EXPERT INSIGHT, GREAT CONTACTS

There are planners, and there are those who fly by the seat of their pants. We happily place ourselves among the planners. Our writers and editors try to anticipate all the issues you may face before and during any journey, and then they do their research. This section is the product of their efforts. Use it to get excited about your trip to Hawai'i, to inform your travel planning, or to guide you on the road should the seat of your pants start to feel threadbare.

www.fodors.com/forums

GETTING STARTED

We're really proud of our Web site: Fodors.com is a great place to begin any journey. Scan Travel Wire for suggested itineraries, travel deals, restaurant and hotel openings, and other up-to-the-minute info. Check out Booking to research prices and book plane tickets, hotel rooms, rental cars, and vacation packages. Head to Talk for on-the-ground pointers from travelers who frequent our message boards. You can also link to loads of other travel-related resources.

RESOURCES

ONLINE TRAVEL TOOLS

For more information on the Big Island of Hawai'i, visit 🌐 www.bigisland.org, the Web site of the Big Island Visitors Bureau. Other sites to check out include: 🌐 www.kohalacoastresorts.com, the Kohala Coast Resort Association Web site which provides information on accommodations and activities for this 20-mi stretch; 🌐 www.downtownhilo.com, for information on the historical town of Hilo including a self-guided walking tour; 🌐 www.gohawaii.com, the official Web site of the Hawai'i Visitors & Convention Bureau; 🌐 www.bestplaceshawaii.com for the Hawai'i State Vacation Planner; and 🌐 www.hawaii.gov, the state's official Web site, for all information on the destination, including camping.

Safety **Transportation Security Administration** (TSA) 🌐 www.tsa.gov

Time Zones **Timeanddate.com** 🌐 www.timeanddate.com/worldclock can help you figure out the correct time anywhere in the world.

Weather **Accuweather.com** 🌐 www.accuweather.com is an independent weather-forecasting service with especially good coverage of hurricanes. **Weather.com** 🌐 www.weather.com is the Web site for the Weather Channel.

Other Resources **CIA World Factbook** 🌐 www.odci.gov/cia/publications/factbook/index.html has profiles of every country in the world. It's a good source if you need some quick facts and figures.

VISITOR INFORMATION

Before you go, contact the Big Island Visitors Bureau to request a free official vacation planner with information on accommodations, transportation, sports and activities, dining, arts and entertainment, and culture. Take a virtual visit to the Big Island on the Web, which can be most helpful in planning many aspects of your vacation. The site also has a calendar section that allows you to see what local events are in place during the time of your stay. You can also sign up to receive all-island and golf express e-newsletters.

Big Island Visitors Bureau ☎ 808/961-5797, 800/648-2441 for vacation planner and brochures 🌐 www.bigisland.org.

THINGS TO CONSIDER

GEAR

Hawai'i is casual: sandals, bathing suits, and comfortable, informal clothing are the norm. In summer synthetic slacks and shirts, although easy to care for, can be uncomfortably warm.

Probably the most important thing to tuck into your suitcase is sunscreen. This is the tropics, and the ultraviolet rays are powerful, even on overcast days. Doctors advise putting on sunscreen when you get up in the morning, whether it's cloudy or sunny. Don't forget to reapply sunscreen periodically during the day, since perspiration can wash it away. Consider using sunscreens with a sun protection factor (SPF) of 15 or higher. There are many tanning oils on the market in Hawai'i, including coconut and *kukui* (the nut from a local tree) oils, but they can cause severe burns. Too many Hawaiian vacations have been spoiled by sunburn and even sun poisoning. Hats and sunglasses offer important sun protection,

WORD OF MOUTH

After your trip, be sure to rate the places you visited and share your experiences and travel tips with us and other Fodorites in Travel Ratings and Talk on 🌐 www.fodors.com.

too. Both are easy to find in island shops, but if you already have a favorite packable hat or sun visor, bring it with you, and don't forget to wear it. All major hotels in Hawai'i provide beach towels.

As for clothing in the Hawaiian Islands, there's a saying that when a man wears a suit during the day, he's either going for a loan or he's a lawyer trying a case. Only a few upscale restaurants require a jacket for dinner. The aloha shirt is accepted dress in Hawai'i for business and most social occasions. Shorts are acceptable daytime attire, along with a T-shirt or polo shirt. There's no need to buy expensive sandals on the mainland—here you can get flip-flops for a couple of dollars and off-brand sandals for $20. Golfers should remember that many courses have dress codes requiring a collared shirt; call courses you're interested in for details. If you're not prepared, you can pick up appropriate clothing at resort pro shops. If you're visiting in winter, bring a sweater or light- to medium-weight jacket. A polar fleece pullover is ideal, and makes a great impromptu pillow.

If your vacation plans include Hilo, especially during the spring and winter months, you'll want to pack a folding umbrella and light raincoat. And if you'll be exploring Hawai'i Volcanoes National Park, make sure you pack appropriately as weather ranges from hot and dry along the shore to cool and rainy at the summit. Good boots are recommended if you'll be hiking or camping in the Park.

SHIPPING LUGGAGE AHEAD

Imagine globetrotting with only a carry-on in tow. Shipping your luggage in advance via an air-freight service is a great way to cut down on backaches, hassles, and stress—especially if your packing list includes strollers, car-seats, etc. There are some things to be aware of, though. First, research carry-on restrictions; if you absolutely need something that isn't practical to ship and isn't allowed in carry-ons, this strategy isn't for you.

Second, allow two to three business days to send your bags to the Big Island. Third, plan to spend some money: it will cost at least $100 to send a small piece of luggage, golf bag, or pair of skis to the Big Island. Some people use Federal Express to ship their bags, but this can cost even more than air-freight services. All these services insure your bag (for most, the limit is $1,000, but you should verify that amount); you can, however, purchase additional insurance for $0.50–$1 per $100 of value.

Luggage Concierge ☎ 800/288-9818 🌐 www.luggageconcierge.com. **Luggage Express** ☎ 866/744-7224 🌐 www.usxpluggageexpress.com. **Luggage Free** ☎ 800/361-6871 🌐 www.luggagefree.com. **Sports Express** ☎ 800/357-4174 🌐 www.sportsexpress.com specializes in shipping golf clubs and other sports equipment. **Virtual Bellhop** ☎ 877/235-5467 🌐 www.virtualbellhop.com.

TRIP INSURANCE

What kind of coverage do you honestly need? Do you even need trip insurance at all? Take a deep breath and read on.

We believe that comprehensive trip insurance is especially valuable if you're booking a very expensive or complicated trip (particularly to an isolated region) or if you're booking far in advance. Who knows what could happen six months down the road? But whether or not you get insurance has more to do with how comfortable you are assuming all that risk yourself.

Comprehensive travel policies typically cover trip-cancellation and interruption, letting you cancel or cut your trip short because of a personal emergency, illness, or,

PACKING 101

Why do some people travel with a convoy of huge suitcases yet never have a thing to wear? How do others pack a duffle with a week's worth of outfits *and* supplies for every contingency? We realize that packing is a matter of style, but there's a lot to be said for traveling light. These tips help fight the battle of the bulging bag.

MAKE A LIST. In a recent Fodor's survey, 29% of respondents said they make lists (and often pack) a week before a trip. You can use your list to pack and to repack at the end of your trip. It can also serve as record of the contents of your suitcase—in case it disappears in transit.

THINK IT THROUGH. What's the weather like? Is this a business trip? A cruise? On the Big Island, the style of dress may be less conservative than you're used to. As you create your itinerary, note outfits next to each activity (don't forget accessories).

EDIT YOUR WARDROBE. Plan to wear everything twice (better yet, thrice) and to do laundry along the way. Stick to one basic look—urban chic, sporty casual, etc. Build around one or two neutrals and an accent (e.g., black, white, and olive green). Women can freshen looks by changing scarves or jewelry. For a week's trip, you can look smashing with three bottoms, four or five tops, a sweater, and a jacket.

BE PRACTICAL. Put comfortable shoes atop your list. (Did we need to say this?) Pack lightweight, wrinkle-resistent, compact, washable items. (Or this?) Stack and roll clothes, so they'll wrinkle less. Unless you're on a guided tour or a cruise, select luggage you can readily carry. Porters, like good butlers, are hard to find these days.

CHECK WEIGHT AND SIZE LIMITATIONS. In the United States you may be charged extra for checked bags weighing more than 50 pounds. Abroad some airlines don't allow you to check bags over 60 to 70 pounds, or they charge outrageous fees for every excess pound—or bag. Carry-on size limitations can be stringent, too.

CHECK CARRY-ON RESTRICTIONS. Research restrictions with the TSA. Rules vary abroad, so check them with your airline if you're traveling overseas on a foreign carrier. Consider packing all but essentials (travel documents, prescription meds, wallet) in checked luggage. This leads to a "pack only what you can afford to lose" approach that might help you streamline.

RETHINK VALUABLES. On U.S. flights, airlines are liable for only about $2,800 per person for bags. On international flights, the liability limit is around $635 per bag. But items like computers, cameras, and jewelry aren't covered, and as gadgetry can go on and off the list of carry-on no-no's, you can't count on keeping things safe by keeping them close. Although comprehensive travel policies may cover luggage, the liability limit is often a pittance. Your home-owner's policy may cover you sufficiently when you travel—or not.

LOCK IT UP. If you must pack valuables, use TSA-approved locks (about $10) that can be unlocked by all U.S. security personnel.

TAG IT. Always tag your luggage; use your business address if you don't want people to know your home address. Put the same information (and a copy of your itinerary) inside your luggage, too.

REPORT PROBLEMS IMMEDIATELY. If your bags—or things inside them—are damaged or go astray, file a written claim with your airline *before leaving the airport.* If the airline is at fault, it may give you money for essentials until your luggage arrives. Most lost bags are found within 48 hours, so alert the airline to your whereabouts for two or three days. If your bag was opened for security reasons in the United States and something is missing, file a claim with the TSA.

Insurance Comparison Sites

Insure My Trip.com		www.insuremytrip.com
SquareMouth.com		www.squaremouth.com
COMPREHENSIVE TRAVEL INSURERS		
Access America	866/807-3982	www.accessamerica.com
CSA Travel Protection	800/873-9855	www.csatravelprotection.com
HTH Worldwide	610/254-8700 or 888/243-2358	www.hthworldwide.com
Travelex Insurance	888/457-4602	www.travelex-insurance.com
Travel Guard International	715/345-0505 or 800/826-4919	www.travelguard.com
Travel Insured International	800/243-3174	www.travelinsured.com
MEDICAL-ONLY INSURERS		
International Medical Group	800/628-4664	www.imglobal.com
International SOS	215/942-8000 or 713/521-7611	www.internationalsos.com
Wallach & Company	800/237-6615 or 504/687-3166	www.wallach.com

in some cases, acts of terrorism in your destination. Such policies also cover evacuation and medical care. Some also cover you for trip delays because of bad weather or mechanical problems as well as for lost or delayed baggage. Another type of coverage to look for is financial default—that is, when your trip is disrupted because a tour operator, airline, or cruise line goes out of business. Generally you must buy this when you book your trip or shortly thereafter, and it's only available to you if your operator isn't on a list of excluded companies.

If you're going abroad, consider buying medical-only coverage at the very least. Neither Medicare nor some private insurers cover medical expenses anywhere outside of the United States besides Mexico and Canada (including time aboard a cruise ship, even if it leaves from a U.S. port). Medical-only policies typically reimburse you for medical care (excluding that related to pre-existing conditions) and hospitalization abroad, and provide for evacuation. You still have to pay the bills and await reimbursement from the insurer, though.

Expect comprehensive travel insurance policies to cost about 4% to 7% of the total price of your trip (it's more like 12% if you're over age 70). A medical-only policy may or may not be cheaper than a comprehensive policy. Always read the fine print of your policy to make sure that you are covered for the risks that are of most concern to you. Compare several policies to make sure you're getting the best price and range of coverage available.

■ TIP→ OK. You know you can save a bundle on trips to warm-weather destinations by traveling in rainy season. But there's also a chance that a severe storm will disrupt your plans. The solution? Look for hotels and resorts that offer storm/hurricane guarantees. Although they rarely allow refunds, most guarantees do let you rebook later if a storm strikes.

BOOKING YOUR TRIP

Unless your cousin is a travel agent, you're probably among the millions of people who make most of their travel arrangements online. But have you ever wondered just what the differences are between an online travel agent (a Web site through which you make reservations instead of going directly to the airline, hotel, or car-rental company), a discounter (a firm that does a high volume of business with a hotel chain or airline and accordingly gets good prices), a wholesaler (one that makes cheap reservations in bulk and then re-sells them to people like you), and an aggregator (one that compares all the offerings so you don't have to)? Is it truly better to book directly on an airline or hotel Web site? And when does a real live travel agent come in handy?

ONLINE

You really have to shop around. A travel wholesaler such as Hotels.com or HotelClub.net can be a source of good rates, as can discounters such as Hotwire or Priceline, particularly if you can bid for your hotel room or airfare. Indeed, such sites sometimes have deals that are unavailable elsewhere. They do, however, tend to work only with hotel chains (which makes them just plain useless for getting hotel reservations outside of major cities) or big airlines. Also, with discounters and wholesalers you must generally prepay, and everything is nonrefundable. And before you fork over the dough, be sure to check the terms and conditions, so you know what a given company will do for you if there's a problem and what you'll have to deal with on your own.

■ TIP→ **To be absolutely sure everything was processed correctly, confirm reservations made through online travel agents, discounters, and wholesalers directly with your hotel before leaving home.**

Booking engines like Expedia, Travelocity, and Orbitz are actually travel agents, albeit high-volume, online ones. And airline travel packagers like American Airlines Vacations and Virgin Vacations—well, they're travel agents, too. But they may still not work with all the world's hotels.

An aggregator site will search many sites and pull the best prices for airfares, hotels, and rental cars from them. Most aggregators compare the major travel-booking sites such as Expedia, Travelocity, and Orbitz; some also look at airline Web sites, though rarely the sites of smaller budget airlines. Some aggregators also compare other travel products, including complex packages—a good thing, as you can sometimes get the best overall deal by booking an air-and-hotel package.

WITH A TRAVEL AGENT

If you use an agent—brick-and-mortar or virtual—you'll pay a fee for the service. And know that the service you get from some online agents isn't comprehensive. For example Expedia and Travelocity don't search for prices on budget airlines like jetBlue, Southwest, or small foreign carriers. That said, some agents (online or not) *do* have access to fares that are difficult to find otherwise, and the savings can more than make up for any surcharge.

A knowledgeable brick-and-mortar travel agent can be a godsend if you're booking a cruise, a package trip that's not available to you directly, an air pass, or a complicated itinerary including several overseas flights. What's more, travel agents that specialize in a destination may have exclusive access to certain deals and insider information on things such as charter flights. Agents who specialize in types of travelers (senior citizens, gays and lesbians, naturists) or types of trips (cruises, luxury travel, safaris) can also be invaluable.

A top-notch agent planning your trip may get you a room upgrade or a resort food and beverage credit; the one booking your cruise may arrange to have a bottle of

Online Booking Resources

AGGREGATORS		
Kayak	www.kayak.com	looks at cruises and vacation packages.
Mobissimo	www.mobissimo.com	compares airfare and hotel rates.
Qixo	www.qixo.com	compares cruises, vacation packages, and even travel insurance.
Sidestep	www.sidestep.com	compares vacation packages and lists travel deals.
Travelgrove	www.travelgrove.com	compares cruises and packages.
BOOKING ENGINES		
Cheap Tickets	www.cheaptickets.com	discounter.
Expedia	www.expedia.com	large online agency that charges a booking fee for airline tickets.
Hotwire	www.hotwire.com	discounter.
lastminute.com	www.lastminute.com	specializes in last-minute travel; the main site is for the U.K., but it has a link to a U.S. site.
Luxury Link	www.luxurylink.com	auctions (surprisingly good deals) as well as offers on the high-end side of travel.
Onetravel.com	www.onetravel.com	discounter for hotels, car rentals, airfares, and packages.
Orbitz	www.orbitz.com	charges a booking fee for airline tickets, but gives a clear breakdown of fees and taxes before you book.
Priceline.com	www.priceline.com	discounter that also allows bidding.
Travel.com	www.travel.com	allows you to compare its rates with those of other booking engines.
Travelocity	www.travelocity.com	charges a booking fee for airline tickets, but promises good problem resolution.
ONLINE ACCOMMODATIONS		
Hotelbook.com	www.hotelbook.com	focuses on independent hotels worldwide.
Hotel Club	www.hotelclub.net	good for major cities worldwide.
Hotels.com	www.hotels.com	big Expedia-owned wholesaler that offers rooms in hotels all over the world.
Quikbook	www.quikbook.com	offers "pay when you stay" reservations that let you settle your bill at check out, not when you book.
OTHER RESOURCES		
Bidding For Travel	www.biddingfortravel.com	good place to figure out what you can get and for how much before bidding on, say, Priceline.

champagne chilling in your cabin when you embark. And complain about the surcharges all you like, but when things don't work out the way you'd hoped, it's nice to have an agent to put things right.

TIP→ **Remember that Expedia, Travelocity, and Orbitz are travel agents, not just booking engines. To resolve any problems with a reservation made through these companies, contact them first.**

If this is your first visit to the Big Island, a travel agent or vacation packager specializing in Hawai'i can be extremely helpful in planning a memorable vacation. Not only do they have the knowledge of the destination, but they can save you money by packaging the costs of airfare, hotel, activities, and car rental. In addition, many of the Hawai'i travel agents may offer added values or special deals (i.e., resort food and beverage credit, a free night's stay, etc.) when you book a package with them. The Hawai'i Visitors & Convention Bureau provides a list of member travel agencies and tour operators.

Agent Resources **American Society of Travel Agents** ☎ 703/739-2782 🌐 www.travelsense.org.

Hawai'i Travel Agents **AA Vacations** ☎ 800/321-2121 🌐 www.aavacations.com. **AAA Travel** ☎ 800/436-4222 🌐 www.aaa.com. **All About Hawaii** ☎ 800/274-8687 🌐 www.allabouthawaii.com. **Delta Vacations** ☎ 800/654-6559 🌐 www.deltavacations.com. **Funjet Vacations** ☎ 888/558-6654 🌐 www.funjet.com. **United Vacations** ☎ 800/699-6122 🌐 www.unitedvacations.com.

ACCOMMODATIONS

Whether your ideal vacation is spent sleeping under the stars in a treehouse, relaxing in a private cottage situated alongside a stream, or luxuriating in an oceanfront villa, the Big Island offers a range of accommodations as varied as its topography. And as such, prices vary. You can spend $150 per night at the historic Kīlauea Lodge in the quaint village of Volcano—or up to $1,800 per night for an ocean-

10 WAYS TO SAVE

1. Join "frequent guest" programs. You may get preferential treatment in room choice and/or upgrades in your favorite chains.

2. Call direct. You can sometimes get a better price if you call a hotel's local toll-free number (if available) rather than a central reservations number. And don't be afraid to ask to speak to a manager to inquire about getting a better rate.

3. Check online. Check hotel Web sites, as not all chains are represented on all travel sites.

4. Look for specials. Always inquire about packages and corporate rates.

5. Be flexible. Although one hotel in your desired resort area might be booked, check others nearby.

6. Think about your room view. Ocean-view rooms tend to be much more expensive than garden view rooms. If the hotel isn't fully booked when you arrive, sometimes you can get an upgrade just by asking.

7. Ask about taxes. Verify whether local hotel taxes are included in quoted rates. Currently, the hotel tax in Hawai'i is 11.42% and that's usually added to the bill.

8. Read the fine print. Watch for add-ons, including resort fees, energy surcharges, and "convenience" fees for such things as unlimited local phone service you won't use, valet parking, or newspaper delivery.

9. Know when to go. In Hawai'i, rates can be higher during holidays and from December through April. If you're trying to book, say, in late April, you might save money by changing your dates by a week or two. Ask when rates go down, though: if your dates straddle peak and off-peak seasons, a property may still charge peak-season rates for the entire stay.

10. Weigh your options (we can't say this enough). Weigh transportation times and costs against the savings of staying in a hotel that's cheaper because it's out of the way.

front suite at the Mauna Lani Bay Hotel and Bungalows on the Kohala Coast. The Big Island Visitors Bureau provides a comprehensive listing of accommodation choices including B&Bs, inns, campsites, condominiums, hotels, resorts, and vacation rentals.

Most hotels and other lodgings require you to give your credit-card details before they will confirm your reservation. If you don't feel comfortable e-mailing this information, ask if you can fax it (some places even prefer faxes). However you book, get confirmation in writing and have a copy of it handy when you check in.

Be sure you understand the hotel's cancellation policy. Some places allow you to cancel without any kind of penalty—even if you prepaid to secure a discounted rate—if you cancel at least 24 hours in advance. Others require you to cancel a week in advance or penalize you the cost of one night. Small inns and B&Bs are most likely to require you to cancel far in advance. Most hotels allow children under a certain age to stay in their parents' room at no extra charge, but others charge for them as extra adults; find out the cutoff age for discounts.

■ TIP→ **Assume that hotels operate on the European Plan (EP, no meals) unless we specify that they use the Breakfast Plan (BP, with full breakfast), Continental Plan (CP, Continental breakfast), Full American Plan (FAP, all meals), Modified American Plan (MAP, breakfast and dinner) or are all-inclusive (AI, all meals and most activities).**

BED & BREAKFASTS

For many travelers, nothing compares to the personal service and guest interaction offered at bed-and-breakfasts. There are dozens of B&Bs throughout the Big Island that offer charming accommodations in country and oceanfront settings; breakfasts include everything from tropical fruits and juices, Kona coffee, French toast with macadamia nuts and lilikoi syrup, and even the local favorites of rice and *poi*. A handful of the B&Bs invite their guests to enjoy complimentary wine tastings and activities such as lei making and basket weaving. The Hawai'i Island B&B Association is a member-based organization with 40 properties on the island, many of which offer spectacular views.

Reservation Services **Bed & Breakfast.com** ☎ 512/322-2710 or 800/462-2632 🌐 www.bedandbreakfast.com also sends out an online newsletter. **Bed & Breakfast Honolulu (Statewide)** ☎ 808/595-7533 or 800/288-4666 🌐 www.hawaiibnb.com. **Bed & Breakfast Inns Online** ☎ 615/868-1946 or 800/215-7365 🌐 www.bbonline.com. **BnB Finder.com** ☎ 212/432-7693 or 888/547-8226 🌐 www.bnbfinder.com. **Better Bed and Breakfasts** 🌐 www.betterbedandbreakfasts.com. **Hawaii Island B&B Association** 🌐 www.stayhawaii.com.

CONDOMINIUM & HOUSE RENTALS

Vacation rentals are perfect for couples, families, and friends traveling together who like the convenience of staying at a home away from home. Whether you are seeking a condominium for a week or a large house for a month, you should be able to find the perfect getaway on the Big Island. Properties managed by individual owners can be found on online vacation rental listing directories such as CyberRentals and Vacation Rentals By Owners, as well as on the Big Island Visitors Bureau's Web site. There also are several Big Island-based management companies with vacation rentals.

Though there are rentals throughout the island, there is quite a bit more inventory on the west side of the island. Compare companies, as some offer Internet specials and free night stays when booking. Policies vary, but most require a minimum stay, usually greater during peak travel seasons.

Aloha Hawaii Vacations ☎ 800/662-5642 🌐 www.alohahawaiivacations.com. **CyberRentals Vacation Properties** ☎ 512/684-1098 🌐 www.cyberrentals.com. **Hawaii Holiday Vacation Rentals** ☎ 808/965-0400 www.bigislandvacationrentals.com. **Hawaii Vacation Rentals** 800/332-7081 www.vacationbigisland.com. **Interhome** 954/791-8282 or 800/882-6864 www.interhome.us. **Keauhou Property Management** 800/745-5662 www.konacondo.net. **Kona Hawaii Vacation Rentals** 800/244-4752 www.konahawaii.com. **Mauna Kea Resort** 808/880-3491 www.MaunaKeaResortRentals.com. **Vacation Home Rentals Worldwide** 201/767-9393 or 800/633-3284 www.vhrww.com. **Vacation Rentals By Owner** www.vrbo.com. **Villas International** 415/499-9490 or 800/221-2260 www.villasintl.com. **West Hawaii Property Services** 800/799-5662 www.konarentals.com.

HOME EXCHANGES

With a direct home exchange you stay in someone else's home while they stay in yours. Some outfits also deal with vacation homes, so you're not actually staying in someone's full-time residence, just their vacant weekend place.

Exchange Clubs **Home Exchange.com** 800/877-8723 www.homeexchange.com; $59.95 for a 1-year online listing. **HomeLink International** 800/638-3841 www.homelink.org; $80 yearly for Web-only membership; $125 includes Web access and two catalogs. **Intervac U.S.** 800/756-4663 www.intervacus.com; $78.88 for Web-only membership; $126 includes Web access and a catalog.

> **WORD OF MOUTH**
>
> Did the resort look as good in real life as it did in the photos? Did you sleep like a baby, or were the walls paper thin? Did you get your money's worth? Rate hotels and write your own reviews in Travel Ratings or start a discussion about your favorite places in Travel Talk on www.fodors.com. Your comments might even appear in our books. Yes, you, too, can be a correspondent!

HOSTELS

Hostels offer bare-bones lodging at low, low prices—often in shared dorm rooms with shared baths—to people of all ages, though the primary market is young travelers, especially students. Many hostels provide shared cooking facilities. In some hostels you aren't allowed to be in your room during the day, and there may be a curfew at night. Nevertheless, hostels provide a sense of community, with public rooms where travelers often gather to share stories.

There are a handful of hostels on the Big Island that cater primarily to a lively, international crowd of backpackers and hikers. (Those seeking intimacy or privacy should seek out a B&B.) Arnott's Lodge and Hiking Adventures in Hilo is a popular no-frills spot which offers a camping area for those willing to pitch their own tent; there are also shared bunk rooms, semi-private and private rooms, and suites. There's coin laundry, an entertainment area, bicycle rentals ($2 per day), and free airport shuttles.

Arnott's Lodge and Hiking Adventures 808/969-7097 www.arnottslodge.com.

AIRLINE TICKETS

Most domestic airline tickets are electronic; international tickets may be either electronic or paper. With an e-ticket the only thing you receive is an e-mail receipt citing your itinerary and reservation and ticket numbers. The greatest advantage of an e-ticket is that if you lose your receipt, you can simply print out another copy or ask the airline to do it for you at check-in. You usually pay a surcharge (up to $50) to get a paper ticket, if you can get one at all. The sole advantage of a paper ticket is that it may be easier to endorse over to another airline if your flight is canceled and the airline with which you booked can't accommodate you on another flight.

Check local and community newspapers when you're on the Big Island for deals and coupons on interisland flights, should you

11 WAYS TO SAVE

1. **Nonrefundable is best.** If saving money is more important than flexibility, then nonrefundable tickets work. Just remember that you'll pay dearly (as much as $100) if you change your plans.

2. **Comparison shop.** Web sites and travel agents can have different arrangements with the airlines and offer different prices for exactly the same flights.

3. **Beware those prices.** Many airline Web sites—and most ads—show prices *without* taxes and surcharges. Don't buy until you know the full price.

4. **Stay loyal.** Stick with one or two frequent-flier programs. You'll rack up free trips faster and you'll accumulate more quickly the perks that make trips easier. On some airlines these include a special reservations number, early boarding, access to upgrades, and more roomy economy-class seating.

5. **Watch those ticketing fees.** Surcharges are usually added when you buy your ticket anywhere but on an airline Web site. (That includes by phone—even if you call the airline directly—and paper tickets regardless of how you book.)

6. **Check early and often.** Start looking for cheap fares up to a year in advance, and keep checking back.

7. **Don't work alone.** Some Web sites have tracking features that will e-mail you immediately when good deals are posted.

8. **Jump on the good deals.** Waiting even a few minutes might mean paying more.

10. **Fly mid-week.** Look for departures on Tuesday, Wednesday, and Thursday, typically the cheapest days to travel.

11. **Be flexible.** Check on prices for departures at different times and alternative airports.

wish to visit neighboring islands. Aloha Airlines, go! Airlines, Hawaiian Airlines, and IslandAir offer regular service between the islands. In addition to offering very competitive rates and online specials, all have free frequent flyer programs which will entitle you to rewards and upgrades the more you fly. Be sure to compare prices offered by all of the interisland carriers. If you are somewhat flexible with your dates and times for island-hopping, you should have no problem getting a very affordable roundtrip ticket.

Inter-island Carriers **Aloha Airlines** ☎ 800/367-5250 🌐 www.alohaairlines.com. **go! Airlines** ☎ 888/435-9462 🌐 www.iflygo.com. **Hawaiian Airlines** ☎ 800/367-5320 🌐 www.hawaiianair.com. **IslandAir** ☎ 800/323-3345 🌐 www.islandair.com.

CHARTER FLIGHTS

Pacific Wings offers a variety of charter options at the Hilo, Kamuela, and Kona airports and also serves Lāna'i, Maui, Moloka'i, and O'ahu. Services include premiere (same-day departures on short notice), premium (24-hour notice), priority (48-hour notice), group, and cargo/courier. The company also has a frequent flyer program. The cost of a round-trip between Honolulu and Kamuela purchased in advance through the company's Web site is about $200.

Paragon Air offers 24-hour private charter service to and from the Hilo, Kamuela, and Kona airports. In business since 1981, the company prides itself on its perfect safety record and has served a number of celebrities including Bill Gates, Michael Douglas, and Kevin Costner, among others. You can arrange a customized tour of the Big Island or neighboring islands, as well as air service from any airport in Hawai'i. Charter prices start at $475.

Charter Companies **Pacific Wings** ☎ 888/575-4546 🌐 www.pacificwings.com. **Paragon Air** ☎ 800/428-1231 🌐 www.paragon-air.com.

RENTAL CARS

Should you plan to do any sightseeing on the Big Island, it is best to rent a car due to the size of the island. With more than 260 mi of coastline—and attractions as varied as the Hawai'i Volcanoes National Park, 'Akaka Falls State Park, and Pu'ukoholā Heiau National Historic Site—ideally you should split up your stay between the east and west coasts of the island. Even if all you want to do is relax at your resort, you may want to hop in the car to check out one of the island's popular restaurants.

While on the Big Island, you can rent anything from an econobox to a Ferrari to a motor home. Rates are usually better if you reserve though a rental agency's Web site. It's wise to make reservations far in advance and make sure that a confirmed reservation guarantees you a car, especially if visiting during peak seasons or for major conventions or sporting events. It's not uncommon to find several car categories sold out during major events on the island like the Merrie Monarch Festival in Hilo in April or the Ironman Triathlon World Championship in Kailua-Kona in October. If you're planning on driving to the 13,796-foot summit of Mauna Kea for stargazing, you'll need a four-wheel drive vehicle. Harper Car and Truck Rental, with offices in Hilo and Kona, is a good source for 4x4 vehicles. For some, renting an RV or motor home might be an appealing way to see the island. Harper's has motor homes available and Imua Camper Company rents out Volkswagon Westfalia camping vans.

Rates begin at about $25 to $35 a day for an economy car with air-conditioning, automatic transmission, and unlimited mileage, depending on your pickup location. This does not include the airport concession fee, general excise tax, rental

AUTOMOBILE ASSOCIATIONS		
U.S.: American Automobile Association (AAA)	315/797-5000	www.aaa.com; most contact with the organization is through state and regional members
National Automobile Club	650/294-7000	www.thenac.com; membership for California residents only
LOCAL AGENCIES		
AA Aloha Cars-R-Us	800/655-7989	www.hawaiicarrental.com
Discount Hawai Car Rentals	888/292-3307	www.discounthawaiicarrental.com.
Harper Car and Truck Rental (Big Island)	800/852-9993	www.harpershawaii.com
Imua Camper Company		www.imua-tour.com
MAJOR AGENCIES		
Alamo	800/462-5266	www.alamo.com
Avis	800/230-4898	www.avis.com
Budget	800/527-0700	www.budget.com
Dollar	800/800-4000	www.dollar.com
Enterprise	800/261-7331	www.enterprise.com
Hertz	800/654-3131	www.hertz.com
National Car Rental	800/227-7368	www.nationalcar.com
Thrifty	800/847-4389	www.thrifty.com

10 WAYS TO SAVE

1. **Beware of cheap rates.** Those great rates aren't so great when you add in taxes, surcharges, and insurance. Such extras can double or triple the initial quote.

2. **Rent weekly.** Weekly rates are usually better than daily ones. Even if you only want to rent for five or six days, ask for the weekly rate; it may very well be cheaper than the daily rate for that period of time.

3. **Don't forget the locals.** Price local car-rental companies as well as the majors.

4. **Airport rentals can cost more.** Airports often add surcharges, which you can sometimes avoid by renting from an agency whose office is just off airport property.

5. **Wholesalers can help.** Investigate wholesalers, which don't own fleets but rent in bulk from firms that do, and which frequently offer better rates (note that you must usually pay for such rentals before leaving home).

6. **Look for rate guarantees.** With your rate locked in, you won't pay more, even if the price goes up in the local currency.

7. **Fill up farther away.** Avoid hefty refueling fees by filling the tank at a station well away from where you plan to turn in the car.

8. **Pump it yourself.** Don't buy the tank of gas that's in the car when you rent it unless you plan to do a lot of driving.

9. **Get all your discounts.** Find out whether a credit card you carry or organization or frequent-renter program to which you belong has a discount program. And confirm that such discounts really are a deal. You can often do better with special weekend or weekly rates offered by a rental agency.

10. **Check out package rates.** Adding a car rental onto your air/hotel vacation package may be cheaper than renting a car separately on your own.

vehicle surcharge, or vehicle license fee. When you reserve a car, ask about cancellation penalties and drop-off charges should you plan to pick up the car in one location and return it to another. Many rental companies in Hawai'i offer coupons for discounts at various attractions that could save you money later on in your trip.

In Hawai'i you must be 21 years of age to rent a car and you must have a valid driver's license and a major credit card. Those under 25 will pay a daily surcharge of $15–$25. Request car seats and extras such as GPS when you book. Hawai'i's Child Restraint Law requires that all children three years and younger be in an approved child safety seat in the backseat of a vehicle. Children ages 4–7 must be seated in a rear booster seat or child restraint such as a lap and shoulder belt. Car seats and boosters range from $5 to $8 per day.

In Hawai'i, your unexpired mainland driver's license is valid for rental for up to 90 days.

Since the road circling the Big Island is mostly two lanes, be sure to allow plenty of time to return your vehicle so that you can make your flight. Traffic can be bad during morning and afternoon rush hour, especially in the Kona area. Give yourself about 3½ hours before departure time to return your vehicle.

CAR-RENTAL INSURANCE

Everyone who rents a car wonders whether the insurance that the rental companies offer is worth the expense. No one—including us—has a simple answer. It all depends on how much regular insurance you have, how comfortable you are with risk, and whether or not money is an issue.

If you own a car and carry comprehensive car insurance for both collision and liability, your personal auto insurance will probably cover a rental, but read your policy's fine print to be sure. If you don't have auto insurance, then you should probably buy the collision- or loss-damage waiver (CDW or LDW) from the rental company. This eliminates your liability for damage to the car. Some credit cards offer CDW coverage, but it's usually supplemental to your own insurance and rarely covers SUVs, minivans, luxury models, and the like. If your coverage is secondary, you may still be liable for loss-of-use costs from the car-rental company (again, read the fine print). But no credit-card insurance is valid unless you use that card for *all* transactions, from reserving to paying the final bill.

■ TIP→ **Diners Club offers primary CDW coverage on all rentals reserved and paid for with the card. This means that Diners Club's company—not your own car insurance—pays in case of an accident. It *doesn't* mean that your car-insurance company won't raise your rates once it discovers you had an accident.**

You may also be offered supplemental liability coverage; the car-rental company is required to carry a minimal level of liability coverage insuring all renters, but it's rarely enough to cover claims in a really serious accident if you're at fault. Your own auto-insurance policy will protect you if you own a car; if you don't, you have to decide whether you are willing to take the risk.

U.S. rental companies sell CDWs and LDWs for about $15 to $25 a day; supplemental liability is usually more than $10 a day. The car-rental company may offer you all sorts of other policies, but they're rarely worth the cost. Personal accident insurance, which is basic hospitalization coverage, is an especially egregious rip-off if you already have health insurance.

■ TIP→ **You can decline the insurance from the rental company and purchase it through a third-party provider such as Travel Guard (🌐 www.travelguard.com)—$9 per day for $35,000 of coverage. That's sometimes just under half the price of the CDW offered by some car-rental companies.**

VACATION PACKAGES

Packages *are not* guided excursions. Packages combine airfare, accommodations, and perhaps a rental car or other extras (theater tickets, guided excursions, boat trips, reserved entry to popular museums, transit passes), but they let you do your own thing. During busy periods packages may be your only option, as flights and rooms may be sold out otherwise. Packages will definitely save you time. They can also save you money, particularly in peak seasons, but—and this is a really big "but"—you should price each part of the package separately to be sure. And be aware that prices advertised on Web sites and in newspapers rarely include service charges or taxes, which can up your costs by hundreds of dollars.

■ TIP→ **Some packages and cruises are sold only through travel agents. Don't always assume that you can get the best deal by booking everything yourself.**

Each year consumers are stranded or lose their money when packagers—even large ones with excellent reputations—go out of business. How can you protect yourself? First, always pay with a credit card; if you have a problem, your credit-card company may help you resolve it. Second, buy trip insurance that covers default. Third, choose a company that belongs to the United States Tour Operators Association, whose members must set aside funds to cover defaults. Finally, choose a company that also participates in the Tour Operator Program of the American Society of Travel Agents (ASTA), which will act as mediator in any disputes. You can also check on the tour operator's reputation among travelers by posting an inquiry on one of the Fodors.com forums.

About half of the visitors to the Big Island travel on package tours. All of the wholesalers specializing in Hawai'i offer a range of packages from the low to the high end. Because of the volume of business they do, wholesalers typically have great deals. Combine that with their knowledge of the destination and wholesale packages to the Big Island make a lot of sense. However, shop around and compare before you book to make sure you are getting a good deal.

Organizations **American Society of Travel Agents** (ASTA) ☎ 703/739–2782 or 800/965–2782 🌐 www.astanet.com. **United States Tour Operators Association** (USTOA) ☎ 212/599–6599 🌐 www.ustoa.com.

Hawai'i Tour Operators **American Express Vacations** ☎ 800/528–4800 🌐 www.americanexpressvacations.com. **Apple Vacations** 🌐 www.applevacations.com. **Classic Vacations** ☎ 866/230–2540 🌐 www.classicvacations.com. **Creative Leisure** ☎ 800/413–1000 🌐 www.creativeleisure.com. **Pleasant Holidays** ☎ 800/742–9244 🌐 www.pleasantholidays.com.

TIP→ **Local tourism boards can provide information about lesser-known and small-niche operators that sell packages to only a few destinations.**

GUIDED TOURS

Guided tours are a good option when you don't want to do it all yourself. You travel along with a group (sometimes large, sometimes small), stay in prebooked hotels, eat with your fellow travelers (the cost of meals sometimes included in the price of your tour, sometimes not), and follow a schedule. But not all guided tours are an if-it's-Tuesday-this-must-be-Belgium experience. A knowledgeable guide can take you places that you might never discover on your own, and you may be pushed to see more than you would have otherwise.

Tours aren't for everyone, but they can be just the thing for first-time travelers to the Big Island or those who enjoy the group traveling experience. Whenever you book a guided tour, find out what's included and what isn't. A "land-only" tour includes all your travel (by bus, in most cases) in the destination, but not necessarily your flights to and from or even within it. Also, in most cases prices in tour brochures don't include fees and taxes. And remember that you'll be expected to tip your guide (in cash) at the end of the tour.

Globus has three Hawai'i itineraries that include the Big Island, one of which is an escorted cruise on Norwegian Cruise Lines' *Pride of Aloha* that includes one day each in Kona and Hilo. Tauck Travel and Trafalgar offer several land-based Hawai'i itineraries that include two to three nights on the Big Island, depending on the tour. Both companies offer similar itineraries. Tauck offers 7- and 11-night multi-island tours with two and three nights on the Big Island, respectively, including a "Magical Hawai'i" trip for families. Trafalgar has 7-, 9-, 10-, and 12-night multi-island tours with two nights on the Big Island. In all cases, visits to Hawai'i Volcanoes National Park are included.

EscortedHawaiiTours.com, owned and operated by Atlas Cruises & Tours, sells more than a dozen Hawai'i trips ranging from 7 to 12 nights operated by various guided tour companies including Globus, Tauck, and Trafalgar.

Recommended Companies **Atlas Cruises & Tours** ☎ 800/942–3301 🌐 www.EscortedHawaiiTours.com. **Globus** ☎ 866/755–8581 🌐 www.globusjourneys.com. **Tauck Travel** ☎ 800/788–7885 🌐 www.tauck.com. **Trafalgar** ☎ 866/544–4434 🌐 www.trafalgar.com.

SPECIAL-INTEREST TOURS

BIKING

If you're a bicycling enthusiast, you've got lots of exciting options on the Big Island. Bicycle Adventures has a seven-day Hawai'i tour and a six-day budget tour. You'll ride about 45 mi per day. Priced at about $2,700 per person, the Hawai'i tour incorporates biking, hiking, snorkeling, sailing, and whale watching. The budget tour is priced at about $1,900 per person, and accommodations are in moderately priced hotels; only biking, hiking, and snorkeling are included. Both tour prices include accommodations, meals, snacks, maps, van support, guide, activity fees and park admissions, taxes, and gratuities. Bicycle rental, pre- or post-lodging, and singles supplements are extra.

VBT Bicycling Vacations offers 8- and 9-day escorted bike tours of the island. The land-only tour includes accommodations in Hilo, Kīlauea, Keauhou, and the Kohala Coast, as well as 14 meals (including a welcome lū'au), bike and helmet, two leaders, van support, and sightseeing and cultural excursions. You'll ride 12–30 mi per day with 14–20 other bikers and enjoy visits to Hawai'i Volcanoes National Park (cycling the perimeter of Kīlauea Iki and hiking into the crater), Mauna Loa Macadamia Nut Factory, Parker Ranch, and Pu'uhonua O Hōnaunau National Historic Park, among others. Highlights also include a hike to three waterfalls, a picnic on Kealakekua Bay, and exploration of Puakō Petroglyphs. Prices start at about $2,000 per person.

WomanTours has a seven-night bike tour for women only that circumnavigates the entire island. Included in the $2,099 per person price is seven nights' accommodations (some triple occupancy rooms), some meals (five breakfasts, a picnic lunch, five dinners, and snacks), van support, and trained guides. Rental bikes and upgrades to single or double rooms are available for an additional cost.

Airfare must be purchased separately for all of these bike tours.

TIP→ **Most airlines accommodate bikes as luggage, provided they're dismantled and boxed.**

Bicycle Adventures ☎ 800/443-6060 🌐 www.bicycleadventures.com. **VBT Bicycling Vacations** ☎ 800/245-3868 🌐 www.vbt.com. **WomanTours** ☎ 800/247-1444 🌐 www.womantours.com.

BIRD-WATCHING

Hawai'i boasts more than 150 species of birds that live in the Hawaiian Islands. Offered in association with the University of Hawai'i at Hilo, *A Birder's Paradise: Kaua'i and Hawai'i* is a seven-night land-only Elderhostel tour with three of those nights spent at Hawai'i Volcanoes National Park. There are daily field lectures to bird-watching sites, discussions of Hawai'i's plant and animal species and geologic wonders, as well as a presentation by a world-renowned birder and photographer. Included in the tour are accommodations, meals, ground transportation, and inter-island airfare between Kaua'i and the Big Island. Travelers must purchase their own airfare if coming from out of Hawai'i. Prices start at around $1,740 per person. Elderhostel, a non-profit educational travel organization, has been leading all-inclusive learning adventures around the world for more than 20 years.

Elderhostel ☎ 800/454-5768 🌐 www.elderhostel.org.

CULTURE

Elderhostel also offers several land-only cultural and educational tours. *Big Island of Hawai'i: History, Volcanoes and Marine Life* is a 15-night tour presented in association with Volcano Art Center and Lyman Mission House and Museum. You'll spend five nights in Hilo, five nights at Hawai'i Volcanoes National Park, and four nights in Kona learning about Hawaiian history, geology, star navigation, language, arts and crafts, and medicine from local cultural historians. You'll visit Rainbow and 'Akaka Falls, Waipi'o, orchid and macadamia nut factories, Pu'uhonua O Hōnaunau National Historic Park, Hulihe'e Palace, and Moku'aikaua Church—and you'll walk through rain forests, lava, and petroglyph fields. Visits to beaches and free time also are included. The cost of this tour starts at $2,540 per person and includes accommodations, meals, ground transportation, and admission fees.

Big Island of Hawai'i Odyssey: Earth, Sky and Sea is an 11-night tour designed for children ages 9–12 accompanied by an adult. Highlights include Hawaiian storytelling, an astronomy presentation at the Onizuka Visitor Center at Mauna Kea, horseback riding in Waimea, and a hike to a black sand beach, among others. Prices start at $1,832 per person.

The Big Island also is included in several multi-island tours: a five-island, 15-night

Islands of Life in the Pacific (three nights at Kīlauea Military Camp at Hawai'i Volcanoes National Park and two nights in Kona); *Tropical Splendor,* a four-island, 10-night adventure afloat study cruise onboard Norwegian Cruise Lines' *Pride of Aloha* with ports of call in Kona and Hilo; the 21-night, four-island *Hawai'i: Spectacular Beauty & Vibrant History* (five nights in Hilo and three nights in Kona); a 10-night *Nature, History and Culture on Kaua'i and Hawai'i* with five of those nights in Hilo; the nine-night *O'ahu's North Shore and Kona: Marine Studies and Snorkeling* tour presented in association with Hawai'i Pacific University, where travelers can immerse themselves in Hawai'i's fascinating marine life; *Wellness and Healthy Living: Hawaiian and Asian Practices for the Body, Mind and Spirit,* five nights on *O'ahu* and three nights in Kona featuring tai chi, reiki, acupressure, *lomi lomi* massage, yoga, beach walks, and more; *Submarines, Volcanoes and Tropical Forests: Intergenerational Hawai'i,* a multi-island cruise tour designed for grandparents and their grandchildren; and the O'ahu and Kona (three nights) *Hawaiian Water Adventure: An Intergenerational Marine Exploration* tour for children ages 10–13 accompanied by an adult. Check out the Elderhostel Web site for price information on these tours. **Elderhostel** ☎ 800/454-5768 🌐 www.elderhostel.org.

CULINARY

A Taste of Paradise: Hawaiian Style to the Big Island (three nights each in Kīlauea and Kona) and Maui is another land-only Elderhostel tour. Travelers will wander the stalls of the Hilo Farmers Market where they'll find exotic fresh fruit like rambutan, soursop, jackfruit, and jaboticaba; vegetables such as hydroponic lettuce, organic spinach, eggplant and baby ginger; anthuriums, protea, bonsai plants, herbs, and orchids; locally made crafts and gift items including Hawaiian hardwood bowls, clothing, and shell jewelry; and specialty food items such as dried fish, breads and pastries, jams, and jellies (including the incredibly delicious 'ōhi'a berry jam). There are visits to banana, papaya, coffee, cocoa, salad greens, vanilla, and anthurium farms, as well as the macadamia nut factory. **Elderhostel** ☎ 800/454-5768 🌐 www.elderhostel.org.

ECO TOURS

Buzzard Brand Ecotours offers a swimming, hiking, and exploring tour for families led by a husband-and-wife biologist team. Groups of about 10–15 stay in rustic lodgings and cook and eat together. The first five days are spent in the quiet fishing village of Miloli'i during which time families will explore the Kona coast and Hawai'i Volcanoes National Park. The second half of the trip is spent in the historic Wai'aka Homestead in Waimea. Lodging, food, and a car rental are included in the cost: $1,350 per adult, slightly less for children under 18.

Want to hike and paddle on the Big Island? Since 1992, Betsy Morrigan has been guiding multisport adventure tours on the Big Island. The Hawai'i Pack and Paddle camping trips showcase the entire island and are billed as "low-key and relaxing." All guides are lifeguards and certified in first aid and CPR. There is a guided four-day kayak/hiking trip suitable for beginners to advanced hikers that includes two nights camping on a black sand beach in south Kona, followed by two nights in a B&B in Hawai'i Volcanoes National Park. Included in the price ($265 per day per person, for four days; children ages 6–12 are half price) are kayak and group camping equipment, lightweight sleeping gear, food, tents, snorkel gear, and guide services. A seven-day adventure to explore the island by kayak, foot, and van is slightly higher and includes two nights camping and four nights in a B&B. Airfare is extra with both tours. **Buzzard Brand Ecotours** ☎ 541/926-1230 🌐 www.buzzardbrand.com. **Hawai'i Pack and Paddle** ☎ 808/328-8911 🌐 www.hawaiipackandpaddle.com.

TRANSPORTATION

BY AIR

Flying time to the Big Island is about 10 hours from New York, 8 hours from Chicago, 5 hours from Los Angeles, and 15 hours from London, not including layovers.

Hawai'i is a major destination link for flights traveling to and from the U.S. mainland, Asia, Australia, New Zealand, and the South Pacific. Some of the major airline carriers serving Hawai'i fly direct to the Big Island, allowing you to bypass connecting flights out of Honolulu. For the more spontaneous traveler, island-hopping is easy, with flights departing every 20 to 30 minutes daily until mid-evening. International travelers also have options: O'ahu and the Big Island are gateways to the United States.

Although the Big Island's airports are smaller and more casual than Honolulu International, during peak times they can also be quite busy. Allot extra travel time to all airports during morning and afternoon rush-hour traffic periods.

Plan to arrive at the airport 45 to 60 minutes before departure for interisland flights.

Plants and plant products are subject to regulation by the Department of Agriculture, both on entering and leaving Hawai'i. Upon leaving the Islands, you'll have to have your bags X-rayed and tagged at one of the airport's agricultural inspection stations before you proceed to check-in. Pineapples and coconuts with the packer's agricultural inspection stamp pass freely; papayas must be treated, inspected, and stamped. All other fruits are banned for export to the U.S. mainland. Flowers pass except for gardenia, rose leaves, jade vine, and mauna loa. Also banned are insects, snails, soil, cotton, cacti, sugarcane, and all berry plants.

You'll have to leave dogs and other pets at home. A 120-day quarantine is imposed to keep out rabies, which is nonexistent in Hawai'i. If specific pre- and post-arrival requirements are met, animals may qualify for a 30-day or 5-day-or-less quarantine.

Airlines & Airports **Airline and Airport Links.com** www.airlineandairportlinks.com has links to many of the world's airlines and airports.

Airline Security Issues **Transportation Security Administration** www.tsa.gov has answers for almost every question that might come up.

Air Travel Resources in Hawai'i **State of Hawai'i Airports Division Offices** 808/836-6417 www.hawaii.gov/dot/airports.

AIRPORTS

Honolulu International Airport (HNL) is the main stopover for most domestic and international flights. From Honolulu, there are departing interisland flights to the Big Island departing regularly from early morning until evening. In addition, some carriers now offer nonstop service directly from the Mainland to the Kona International Airport at Keāhole (KOA) and Hilo International Airport (ITO) on a limited basis. Like all of Hawai'i's airports, the two Big Island airports are "open-air," meaning you can enjoy those tradewind breezes until the moment you step on the plane.

HONOLULU/O'AHU AIRPORT

Hawai'i's major airport is Honolulu International, on O'ahu, 20 minutes (9 mi) west of Waikīkī. To travel to the Big Island from Honolulu, you can depart from either the inter-island terminal or the commuter-airline terminal, located in two separate structures adjacent to the main overseas terminal building. A free bus service, the Wiki Wiki Shuttle, operates between terminals.

Honolulu International Airport (HNL) 808/836-6413 www.hawaii.gov/dot/airports.

FLYING 101

Flying may not be as carefree as it once was, but there are some things you can do to make your trip smoother.

MINIMIZE THE TIME SPENT STANDING IN LINE. Buy an e-ticket, check in at an electronic kiosk, or—even better—check in on your airline's Web site before leaving home. Pack light, and limit carry-on items to only the essentials.

ARRIVE WHEN YOU NEED TO. Research your airline's policy. It's usually at least an hour before domestic flights and two to three hours before international flights. But airlines at some busy airports have more stringent requirements. Check the TSA Web site for estimated security waiting times at major airports.

GET TO THE GATE. If you aren't at the gate at least 10 minutes before your flight is scheduled to take off (sometimes earlier), you won't be allowed to board.

DOUBLE-CHECK YOUR FLIGHT TIMES. Do this especially if you reserved far in advance. Schedules change, and alerts may not reach you.

DON'T GO HUNGRY. Ask whether your airline offers anything to eat; even when it does, be prepared to pay.

GET THE SEAT YOU WANT. Often you can pick a seat when you buy your ticket on an airline Web site. But it's not guaranteed; the airline could change the plane after you book, so double-check. You can also select a seat if you check in electronically. Avoid seats on the aisle directly across from the lavatories. Frequent fliers say those are even worse than back-row seats that don't recline.

GOT KIDS? Get info. Ask the airline about its children's menus, activities, and fares. Sometimes infants and toddlers fly free if they sit on a parent's lap, and older children fly for half price in their own seats. Also inquire about policies involving car seats; having one may limit seating options. Also ask about seat-belt extenders for car seats. And note that you can't count on a flight attendant to produce an extender; you may have to ask for one when you board.

CHECK YOUR SCHEDULING. Don't buy a ticket if there's less than an hour between connecting flights. Although schedules are padded, if anything goes wrong you might miss your connection. If you're traveling to an important function, depart a day early.

BRING PAPER. Even when using an e-ticket, always carry a hard copy of your receipt; you may need it to get your boarding pass, which most airports require to get past security.

COMPLAIN AT THE AIRPORT. If your baggage goes astray or your flight goes awry, complain before leaving the airport. Most carriers require that you file a claim immediately.

BEWARE OF OVERBOOKED FLIGHTS. If a flight is oversold, the gate agent will usually ask for volunteers and offer some sort of compensation for taking a different flight. If you're bumped from a flight *involuntarily*, the airline must give you some kind of compensation if an alternate flight can't be found within one hour.

KNOW YOUR RIGHTS. If your flight is delayed because of something within the airline's control (bad weather doesn't count), the airline must get you to your destination on the same day, even if they have to book you on another airline and in an upgraded class. Read the Contract of Carriage, which is usually buried on the airline's Web site.

BE PREPARED. The Boy Scout motto is especially important if you're traveling during a stormy season. To quickly adjust your plans, program a few numbers into your cell: your airline, an airport hotel or two, your destination hotel, your car service, and/or your travel agent.

BIG ISLAND AIRPORTS

Those flying to the Big Island of Hawai'i regularly land at one of two fields. Kona International Airport at Keāhole, on the west side, best serves Kailua-Kona, Keauhou, and the Kohala Coast. There are two Visitor Information Program (VIP) booths located at baggage claims A and B to assist travelers at the Kona International Airport. Additionally, there are news and lei stands, Maxwell's Landing restaurant and a gift shop.

Hilo International Airport is more appropriate for those going to the east side of the island. Here, visitors will find VIP booths across from the Centerplate Coffee Shop & Lounge near the departure lobby and in the arrival areas at each end of the terminal. In addition to the coffee shop, services include a Bank of Hawai'i automatic teller machine, gift shop, and news and lei stands. Waimea-Kohala Airport, called Kamuela Airport by residents, is used primarily for commuting among the Islands.

Hilo International Airport (ITO) ☎ 808/934-5838. **Kona International Airport at Keāhole (KOA)** ☎ 808/329-3423. **Waimea-Kohala Airport (MUE)** ☎ 808/887-8126.

GROUND TRANSPORTATION

Only Arnott's Lodge and the Hawai'i Naniloa Hotel provide airport shuttles to and from the Hilo International Airport. If you're not renting a car, you'll need to take a taxi. There are 13 taxi companies serving the Hilo Airport. The approximate taxi rate is $3 flip, plus $.30 every ⅛ mile, with surcharges for waiting time at $.30 per minute and $1 per bag. Cab fares to locations around the island are estimated as follows: Banyan Drive hotels $11, Hilo town $12, Hilo Pier $13, Volcano $75, Kea'au $22, Pahoa $50, Honoka'a $105, Kamuela/Waimea $148, Waikoloa $188, and Kailua town $240.

At the Kona International Airport, SpeediShuttle offers transportation between the airport and hotels, resorts, and condominium complexes from Waimea to Keauhou. There is an online reservation and fare quote system for information and bookings.

SpeediShuttle ☎ 877/242-5777 🌐 www.speedishuttle.com.

FLIGHTS

Airline Contacts **Aloha Airlines** ☎ 800/367-5250 🌐 www.alohaairlines.com. **America West** ☎ 800/327-7810 🌐 www.americawest.com. **American Airlines** ☎ 800/433-7300 🌐 www.aa.com. **ATA** ☎ 800/435-9282 or 317/282-8308 🌐 www.ata.com. **Continental Airlines** ☎ 800/523-3273 for U.S. and Mexico reservations, 800/231-0856 for international reservations 🌐 www.continental.com. **Delta Airlines** ☎ 800/221-1212 for U.S. reservations 🌐 www.delta.com. **Hawaiian Airlines** ☎ 800/367-5320 🌐 www.hawaiianair.com. **Northwest Airlines** ☎ 800/225-2525 🌐 www.nwa.com. **Southwest Airlines** ☎ 800/435-9792 🌐 www.southwest.com. **United Airlines** ☎ 800/864-8331 for U.S. reservations, 800/538-2929 for international reservations 🌐 www.united.com.

Interisland Flights **Aloha Airlines** ☎ 800/367-5250 🌐 www.alohaairlines.com. **go! Airlines** ☎ 888/434-5946 🌐 www.iflygo.com. **Hawaiian Airlines** ☎ 800/367-5320 🌐 www.hawaiianair.com. **Island Air** ☎ 800/323-3345 🌐 www.islandair.com. **Pacific Wings** ☎ 888/575-4546 🌐 www.pacificwings.com. **Paragon Airlines** ☎ 800/428-1231 🌐 www.paragon-air.com.

BY BOAT

At this writing, a high-speed ferry service that will run between O'ahu (Honolulu), Maui, and Kaua'i is scheduled to begin in July 2007. Daily service to the Big Island is expected to begin sometime in 2009.

BY BUS

Travelers can take advantage of the Hawai'i County Mass Transit Agency's free Hele-On Bus, which travels several routes throughout the island. A one-way journey between Hilo and Kona will take about four hours. There's regular service in and around downtown Hilo, Kailua-Kona, Waimea, North and South Kohala, Honoka'a, and Pāhoa. There is a charge of $1 per piece for bicycles, luggage, and large backpacks that can't fit under a seat. Visitors staying in Hilo can take advantage of the Transit Agency's Shared Ride Taxi program which provides door to door transportation in the area. A one-way fare is $2 and a book of 15 coupons can be purchased for $30.

Hele-On Bus ☎ 808/961-8744 🌐 www.co.hawaii.hi.us/mass_transit/transit_main.htm.

BY CAR

Technically, the Big Island of Hawai'i is the only island you can completely circle by car, the best way to enjoy the sightseeing opportunities afforded by the miles of scenic roadway.

Instead of using compass directions, remember that Hawai'i residents refer to places as being either *mauka* (toward the mountains) or *makai* (toward the ocean) from one another. Hawai'i has a strict seat belt law. Those riding in the front seat must wear a seat belt and children under the age of 17 in the back seats must be belted. The fine for not wearing a seat belt is $92. Jaywalking is also very common in the islands so please pay careful attention to the roads, especially while driving in downtown Hilo, Kailua-Kona, and the smaller towns around the island.

GASOLINE

You can count on having to pay more at the pump for gasoline on the Big Island than on the U.S. mainland.

PARKING

Parking can be a challenge in downtown Kona. If you're willing to walk several blocks, you should be able to find free parking off Ali'i Drive on some of the residential streets. Otherwise, there are municipal lots just off Ali'i Drive with an honor system. You will be ticketed if you don't pay. In Hilo, there is a good availability of free parking.

ROAD CONDITIONS

It's difficult to get lost in most of Hawai'i. Roads and streets, although they may challenge the visitor's tongue, are well marked. Free publications containing good-quality road maps can be found on all Islands.

Roads on the Big Island are generally well-maintained and can be easily negotiated. Most of the roads are two-lane highways with limited shoulders—and yes, even in paradise, there is traffic, especially during the morning and afternoon rush hour. Unless you have a four-wheel drive vehicle, do not attempt Saddle Road between Hilo and Waimea; it's narrow, windy, and poor in many areas. Most rental car agencies do not allow driving on Saddle Road, and several companies make you sign a statement that you won't, even if you rent a four-wheel-drive vehicle.

Gas stations are fairly far apart and in rural areas it's not unusual for the stations to close early. If you see that your tank is getting low, don't take any chances; fill up when you see a station. In Hawai'i, turning right on a red light is legal, except where noted. Use caution during heavy downpours, especially if you see signs warning of falling rocks. The road to Ka Lae, the southernmost tip of the U.S., provides gorgeous views, but is narrow: if you're enjoying the views, pull over to the side.

ROADSIDE EMERGENCIES

If you find yourself in an emergency or accident while driving on the Big Island, pull over if you can. If you have a cell phone with you, call the roadside assistance number on your rental car contract or AAA Help. If you find that your car has been broken into or stolen, report it immediately to your rental car company and they can assist you. If it's an emergency and someone is hurt, call 911 immediately and stay there until medical personnel arrive.

Emergency Services **AAA Help** ☎ 800/222-4357.

ON THE GROUND

COMMUNICATIONS

INTERNET

If you've brought your laptop with you to the Big Island, you should have no problem checking e-mail or connecting to the Internet. Most of the major hotels and resorts offer high-speed access in rooms and/or lobbies. You should check with your hotel in advance to confirm that access is wireless; if not, ask whether in-room cables are provided. In some cases there will be an hourly charge posted to your room that averages about $15 per hour. If you're staying at a small inn or B&B without Internet access, ask the proprietor for the nearest café or coffee shop with wireless access.

Cybercafes www.cybercafes.com lists over 4,000 Internet cafés worldwide.

EATING OUT

Whether it's a romantic candlelit dinner for two or a hole-in-the-wall with the island's best *saimin* (noodle soup), the Big Island has something for every taste bud and every budget. Kailua-Kona has the greatest concentration of restaurants, but each area on the island has a number of delightful spots for couples and families. With chefs using abundant locally grown fruits and vegetables, vegetarians often have many exciting choices for their meals. And because the Big Island is popular among families, restaurants almost always have a kids menu. When you're booking your accommodations or making a reservation at a hotel dining establishment, ask if they have free or reduced meals for children with paying adults.

MEALS & MEALTIMES

Food in Hawai'i is a reflection of the state's diverse cultural makeup and tropical location. Fresh seafood, organic fruits and vegetables, free-range poultry and meat, and locally grown products such as cocoa and macadamia nuts are the hallmarks of Hawai'i regional cuisine. Its preparations are drawn from across the Pacific Rim, including Japan, the Philippines, Korea, and Thailand—and now, Hawaiian food is a cuisine in its own right. (Visit any restaurant run by Peter Merriman, Alan Wong, Sam Choy, Amy Ferguson, or Roy Yamaguchi for proof of that.) Even more exciting, there are dozens of up and coming new chefs who are stretching the culinary boundaries by creating innovative and tasteful fusions for visitors and residents alike.

Whether you're eating at a free-standing or hotel restaurant, breakfast is usually served from 6 or 7 AM to 9:30 or 10 AM, and will often feature à la carte and/or buffet options. Enjoy tropical fresh fruit and juices; banana, mango or coconut breads; Kona coffee; and specialties like island-style French toast made with Portuguese sweet bread or *mochi* waffles made with sweet rice flour.

Of the thousands of McDonald's restaurants across the country, only in Hawai'i will you find menu items created for the local community. If you happen to visit a McDonald's for breakfast while you are on the Big Island, you may want to try the egg, rice, and Portuguese sausage breakfast meal or the *saimin* bowl with its hot broth, noodles, Spam, and fish cake.

Lunch typically runs from 11:30 AM to around 1:30 or 2 PM, and will include salads, sandwiches, and lighter fare. The "plate lunch" is a favorite of many local residents, and usually consists of grilled teriyaki chicken, beef, or fish, served with two scoops of white rice and two side salads, with a big ladle of gravy over the meat and rice. The phrase "broke da mouth" is often used to describe these plates which refers not only to its size, but also its tastiness.

Dinner typically is served from 5 to 9 PM and, depending on the restaurant, can be

LOCAL DO'S & TABOOS

GREETINGS

Hawai'i is a very friendly place and this is reflected in the day-to-day encounters with friends, family, and even business associates. Women will often hug and kiss one another on the cheek and men will shake hands and sometimes combine that with a friendly hug. When a man and woman are greeting each other and are good friends, it is not unusual for them to hug and kiss on the cheek. Children are taught to call any elders "auntie" or "uncle," even if they aren't related. It's a way to show respect and can result in a local Hawai'i child having dozens of aunties or uncles. It's also reflective of the strong sense of family that exists in the Islands.

When you walk off a long flight, perhaps a bit groggy and stiff, nothing quite compares with a Hawaiian lei greeting. The casual ceremony ranks as one of the fastest ways to make the transition from the worries of home to the joys of your vacation. Though the tradition has created an expectation that everyone receives this floral garland when they step off the plane, the state of Hawai'i cannot greet each of its nearly 7 million annual visitors.

If you've booked a vacation with a wholesaler or tour company, a lei greeting might be included in your package, so check before you leave. If not, it's easy to arrange a lei greeting for yourself or for your companions before you arrive. Contact Kama'āina Leis, Flowers & Greeters if you're arriving into Kona International Airport. To be really wowed by the experience, request a lei of plumeria, some of the most divine-smelling blossoms on the planet. A plumeria or dendrobium orchid lei are considered standard and cost $16.50/person. Hilo International Airport does not allow companies to provide lei greeting services, but there are lei vendors at the airport should you wish to purchase leis upon arrival.

Kama'āina Leis, Flowers & Greeters
☏ 800/367-5183 or 808/836-3246 📠 808/836-1814 🌐 www.alohaleigreetings.com.

LANGUAGE

Hawai'i was admitted to the Union in 1959, so residents can be sensitive when visitors refer to their own hometowns as "back in the States." Remember, when in Hawai'i, refer to the contiguous 48 states as "the mainland" and not as the United States. When you do, you won't appear to be such a *malahini* (newcomer).

English is the primary language on the Islands. Making the effort to learn some Hawaiian words can be rewarding, however. Despite the length of many Hawaiian words, the Hawaiian alphabet is actually one of the world's shortest, with only 12 letters: the five vowels, *a, e, i, o, u,* and seven consonants, *h, k, l, m, n, p, w.* Hawaiian words you're most likely to encounter during your visit to the Islands are *aloha, mahalo* (thank you), *keiki* (child), *haole* (Caucasian or foreigner), *mauka* (toward the mountains), *makai* (toward the ocean), and *pau* (finished, all done). Hawaiian history includes waves of immigrants, each bringing their own languages. To communicate with each other, they developed a sort of slang known as "pidgin." If you listen closely, you'll know what is being said by the inflections and by the extensive use of body language. For example, when you know what you want to say but don't know how to say it, just say "you know, da kine." For an informative and somewhat-hilarious view of things Hawaiian, check out Jerry Hopkins's series of books titled *Pidgin to the Max* and *Fax to the Max*, available at most local bookstores in the Hawaiiana sections.

a simple or lavish affair. Stick to the chef specials if you can because they usually represent the best of the season. *Poke* (marinated raw tuna) is a local hallmark and can often be found on *pūpū* menus.

Unless otherwise noted, the restaurants listed in this guide are open daily for lunch and dinner.

PAYING

Credit cards are widely accepted throughout the island, with the exception of smaller restaurants in some of the more rural areas where only cash and checks are the accepted mode of payment. It's best to confirm when you make the reservation if you're unsure.

For guidelines on tipping *see* Tipping *below.*

RESERVATIONS & DRESS

Hawai'i is decidedly casual. Aloha shirts and shorts or long pants for men and island-style dresses or casual resort wear for women are standard attire for evenings in most hotel restaurants and local eateries. T-shirts and shorts will do the trick for breakfast and lunch.

Regardless of where you are, it's a good idea to make a reservation if you can. We only mention them specifically when reservations are essential (there's no other way you'll ever get a table) or when they are not accepted. For popular restaurants, book as far ahead as you can (often 30 days), and reconfirm as soon as you arrive. (Large parties should always call ahead to check the reservations policy.) We mention dress only when men are required to wear a jacket or a jacket and tie.

Online reservation services make it easy to book a table before you even leave home. OpenTable covers most states, including 20 major cities, and has limited listings in Canada, Mexico, the United Kingdom, and elsewhere. DinnerBroker has restaurants throughout the United States as well as a few in Canada.

OpenTable www.opentable.com. **DinnerBroker** www.dinnerbroker.com.

CON OR CONCIERGE?

Good hotel concierges are invaluable—for arranging transportation, getting reservations at the hottest restaurant, and scoring tickets for a sold-out show or entrée to an exclusive nightclub. They're in the know and well connected. That said, sometimes you have to take their advice with a grain of salt.

It's not uncommon for restaurants to ply concierges with free food and drink in exchange for steering diners their way. Indeed, European concierges often receive referral *fees*. Hotel chains usually have guidelines about what their concierges can accept. The best concierges, however, are above reproach. This is particularly true of those who belong to the prestigious international society of Les Clefs d'Or.

What can you expect of a concierge? At a typical tourist-class hotel you can expect him or her to give you the basics: to show you something on a map, make a standard restaurant reservation (particularly if you don't speak the language), or help you book a tour or airport transportation. In Asia concierges perform the vital service of writing out the name or address of your destination for you to give to a cab driver.

Savvy concierges at the finest hotels and resorts can arrange for just about any good or service imaginable—and do so quickly. You should compensate them appropriately. A $10 tip is enough to show appreciation for a table at a hot restaurant. But the reward should really be much greater for tickets to that U2 concert that's been sold out for months or for those last-minute sixth-row-center seats for *The Lion King*.

FOR INTERNATIONAL TRAVELERS

CURRENCY

The dollar is the basic unit of U.S. currency. It has 100 cents. Coins are the penny (1¢); the nickel (5¢), dime (10¢), quarter (25¢), half-dollar (50¢), and the very rare golden $1 coin and even rarer silver $1. Bills are denominated $1, $5, $10, $20, $50, and $100, all mostly green and identical in size; designs and background tints vary. You may come across a $2 bill, but the chances are slim.

CUSTOMS

U.S. Customs and Border Protection 🌐 www.cbp.gov.

DRIVING

Gas costs range from $2.50 to $3.50 a gallon. Driving in the United States is on the right. Speed limits are posted in miles per hour (usually between 55 mph and 70 mph). Watch for lower limits in small towns and on back roads (usually 30 mph to 40 mph). Most states require front-seat passengers to wear seat belts; many states require children to sit in the back seat and to wear seat belts. In major cities rush hour is between 7 and 10 AM; afternoon rush hour is between 4 and 7 PM. To encourage carpooling, some freeways have special lanes, ordinarily marked with a diamond, for high-occupancy vehicles (HOV)—cars carrying two people or more.

Highways are well paved. Interstates—limited-access, multilane highways designated with an "I-" before the number—are fastest. Interstates with three-digit numbers circle urban areas, which may also have other limited-access expressways, freeways, and parkways. Tolls may be levied on limited-access highways. U.S. and state highways aren't necessarily limited-access, but may have several lanes.

Gas stations are plentiful. Most stay open late (24 hours along major highways and in big cities) except in rural areas, where Sunday hours are limited and where you may drive for long stretches without a refueling opportunity. Along larger highways, roadside stops with restrooms, fast-food restaurants, and sundries stores are well spaced. State police and tow trucks patrol major highways. If your car breaks down on an interstate, pull onto the shoulder and wait for help, or have your passengers wait while you walk to an emergency phone (available in most states). If you carry a cell phone, dial *55, noting your location on the small green roadside mileage marker.

ELECTRICITY

The U.S. standard is AC, 110 volts/60 cycles. Plugs have two flat pins set parallel to each other.

EMBASSIES

Australia ☎ 202/797-3000 🌐 www.austemb.org. **Canada** ☎ 202/682-1740 🌐 www.canadianembassy.org. **United Kingdom** ☎ 202/588-7800 🌐 www.britainusa.com.

EMERGENCIES

For police, fire, or ambulance, dial 911 (0 in rural areas).

HOLIDAYS

New Year's Day (Jan. 1); Martin Luther King Day (3rd Mon. in Jan.); Presidents' Day (3rd Mon. in Feb.); Memorial Day (last Mon. in May); Independence Day (July 4); Labor Day (1st Mon. in Sept.); Columbus Day (2nd Mon. in Oct.); Thanksgiving Day (4th Thurs. in Nov.); Christmas Eve and Christmas Day (Dec. 24 and 25); and New Year's Eve (Dec. 31).

MAIL

You can buy stamps and aerograms and send letters and parcels in post offices. Stamp-dispensing machines can occasionally be found in airports, bus and train stations, office buildings, drugstores, and convenience stores. U.S. mail boxes are stout, dark blue steel bins; pickup schedules are posted inside the bin (pull down the handle to see them). Parcels weighing more than a pound must be mailed at a post office or at a private mailing center.

Within the United States a first-class letter weighing 1 ounce or less costs 39¢; each additional ounce costs 24¢. Postcards cost 24¢. A 1-ounce airmail letter to most countries costs 84¢, an airmail postcard costs 75¢; a 1-ounce letter to Canada or Mexico costs 63¢, a postcard 55¢.

To receive mail on the road, have it sent c/o General Delivery at your destination's main post office (use the correct five-digit ZIP code). You must pick up mail in person within 30 days, with a driver's license or passport for identification.

DHL ☎ 800/225-5345 🌐 www.dhl.com. **Federal Express** ☎ 800/463-3339 🌐 www.fedex.com. **Mail Boxes, Etc./The UPS Store** ☎ 800/789-4623 🌐 www.mbe.com. **United States Postal Service** 🌐 www.usps.com.

PASSPORTS & VISAS

Visitor visas aren't necessary for citizens of Australia, Canada, the United Kingdom, or most citizens of European Union countries coming for tourism and staying for fewer than 90 days. If you require a visa, the cost is $100, and waiting time can be substantial, depending on where you live. Apply for a visa at the U.S. consulate in your place of residence; check the U.S. State Department's special Visa Web site for further information.

Visa Information **Destination USA** 🌐 www.unitedstatesvisas.gov.

PHONES

Numbers consist of a three-digit area code and a seven-digit local number. The area code for all calls within the state of Hawai'i is 808. Within many local calling areas you dial only the seven digits; in others you dial "1" first and all 10 digits—just as you would for calls between area-code regions. The same is true for calls to numbers prefixed by "800," "888," "866," and "877"—all toll free. For calls to numbers prefixed by "900" you must pay—usually dearly.

For international calls, dial "011" followed by the country code and the local number. For help, dial "0" and ask for an overseas operator. Most phone books list country codes and U.S. area codes. The country code for Australia is 61, for New Zealand 64, for the United Kingdom 44. Calling Canada is the same as calling within the United States, whose country code, by the way, is 1.

For operator assistance, dial "0." For directory assistance, call 555-1212 or occasionally 411 (free at many public phones). You can reverse long-distance charges by calling "collect"; dial "0" instead of "1" before the 10-digit number.

Instructions are generally posted on pay phones. Usually you insert coins in a slot (usually 25¢–50¢ for local calls) and wait for a steady tone before dialing. On long-distance calls the operator tells you how much to insert; prepaid phone cards, widely available in various denominations, can be used from any phone. Follow the directions to activate the card (there's usually an access number, then an activation code), then dial your number.

CELL PHONES

The United States has several GSM (Global System for Mobile Communications) networks, so multiband mobiles from most countries (except for Japan) work here. Unfortunately, it's almost impossible to buy a pay-as-you-go mobile SIM card in the U.S.—which allows you to avoid roaming charges—without also buying a phone. That said, cell phones with pay-as-you-go plans are available for well under $100. The cheapest ones with decent national coverage are the GoPhone from Cingular and Virgin Mobile, which only offers pay-as-you-go service.

If you're taking your cell phone on vacation with you, make sure roaming is included, otherwise your minutes and bill will quickly add up. Prepaid phone cards are convenient and cost-effective.

Cingular ☎ 888/333-6651 🌐 www.cingular.com. **Virgin Mobile** ☎ No phone 🌐 www.virginmobileusa.com.

WINES, BEER & SPIRITS

Hawai'i has a new generation of microbreweries, including on-site microbreweries at many restaurants. The drinking age in Hawai'i is 21 years of age, and a photo ID must be presented to purchase alcoholic beverages. Bars are open until 2 AM; venues with a cabaret license can stay open until 4 AM. No matter what you might see in the local parks, drinking alcohol in public parks or on the beaches is illegal. It's also illegal to have open containers of alcohol in motor vehicles.

HEALTH

Hawai'i is known as the Health State. The life expectancy here is 79 years, the longest in the nation. Balmy weather makes it easy to remain active year-round, and the low-stress aloha attitude certainly contributes to general well-being. When visiting the Islands, however, there are a few health issues to keep in mind.

The Hawai'i State Department of Health recommends that you drink 16 ounces of water per hour to avoid dehydration when hiking or spending time in the sun. Use sunblock, wear UV-reflective sunglasses, and protect your head with a visor or hat for shade. If you're not acclimated to warm, humid weather you should allow plenty of time for rest stops and refreshments. When visiting freshwater streams, be aware of the tropical disease leptospirosis, which is spread by animal urine and carried into streams and mud. Symptoms include fever, headache, nausea, and red eyes. If left untreated it can cause liver and kidney damage, respiratory failure, internal bleeding, and even death. To avoid this, don't swim or wade in freshwater streams or ponds if you have open sores and don't drink from any freshwater streams or ponds.

On the Islands, fog is a rare occurrence, but there can often be "vog," an airborne haze of gases released from volcanic vents at Kilauea Island. During certain weather conditions such as "Kona Winds," the vog can settle over the Islands and wreak havoc with respiratory and other health conditions, especially asthma or emphysema. If susceptible, stay indoors and get emergency assistance if needed.

The Islands have their share of bugs and insects that enjoy the tropical climate as much as visitors do. Most are harmless but annoying. When planning to spend time outdoors in hiking areas, wear long-sleeve clothing and pants and use mosquito repellent containing DEET. In very damp places you may encounter the dreaded local centipede. On the Islands they usually come in two colors, brown and blue, and they range from the size of a worm to an 8-inch cigar. Their sting is very painful, and the reaction is similar to bee- and wasp-sting reactions. When camping, shake out your sleeping bag before climbing in, and check your shoes in the morning, as the centipedes like cozy places. If planning on hiking or traveling in remote areas, always carry a first-aid kit and appropriate medications for sting reactions.

WORD OF MOUTH

Was the service stellar or not up to snuff? Did the food give you shivers of delight or leave you cold? Did the prices and portions make you happy or sad? Rate restaurants and write your own reviews in Travel Ratings or start a discussion about your favorite places in Travel Talk on www.fodors.com. Your comments might even appear in our books. Yes, you, too, can be a correspondent!

HOURS OF OPERATION

Even people in paradise have to work. Generally local business hours are weekdays 8–5. Banks are usually open Monday–Thursday 8:30–3 and until 6 on Friday. Some banks have Saturday-morning hours.

Many self-serve gas stations stay open around-the-clock, with full-service stations usually open from around 7 AM until

WORST-CASE SCENARIO

All your money and credit cards have just been stolen. In these days of real-time transactions, this isn't a predicament that should destroy your vacation. First, report the theft of the credit cards. Then get any traveler's checks you were carrying replaced. This can usually be done almost immediately, provided that you kept a record of the serial numbers separate from the checks themselves. If you bank at a large international bank like Citibank or HSBC, go to the closest branch; if you know your account number, chances are you can get a new ATM card and withdraw money right away. **Western Union** (☎ 800/325-6000 🌐 www.westernunion.com) sends money almost anywhere. Have someone back home order a transfer online, over the phone, or at one of the company's offices, which is the cheapest option.

9 PM. U.S. post offices are open weekdays 8:30 AM–4:30 PM and Saturday 8:30–noon.

Most museums generally open their doors between 9 AM and 10 AM and stay open until 5 PM Tuesday–Saturday. Many museums operate with afternoon hours only on Sunday and close on Monday. Visitor-attraction hours vary throughout the state, but most sights are open daily with the exception of major holidays such as Christmas. Check local newspapers upon arrival for attraction hours and schedules if visiting over holiday periods. The local dailies carry a listing of "What's Open/What's Not" for those time periods.

Stores in resort areas sometimes open as early as 8, with shopping-center opening hours varying from 9:30 to 10 on weekdays and Saturday, a bit later on Sunday. Bigger malls stay open until 9 weekdays and Saturday and close at 5 on Sunday. Boutiques in resort areas may stay open as late as 11.

ATMS & BANKS

Automatic teller machines for easy access to cash are everywhere on the Islands. ATMs can be found in shopping centers, small convenience and grocery stores, inside hotels and resorts, as well as outside most bank branches. For a directory of locations, call 800/424–7787 for the MasterCard/Cirrus/Maestro network or 800/843–7587 for the Visa/Plus network.

CREDIT CARDS

Throughout this guide, the following abbreviations are used: **AE,** American Express; **D,** Discover; **DC,** Diners Club; **MC,** MasterCard; and **V,** Visa.

It's a good idea to inform your credit-card company before you travel, especially if you're going abroad and don't travel internationally very often. Otherwise, the credit-card company might put a hold on your card owing to unusual activity—not a good thing halfway through your trip. Record all your credit-card numbers—as well as the phone numbers to call if your cards are lost or stolen—in a safe place, so you're prepared should something go wrong. Both MasterCard and Visa have general numbers you can call (collect if you're abroad) if your card is lost, but you're better off calling the number of your issuing bank, since MasterCard and Visa usually just transfer you to your bank; your bank's number is usually printed on your card.

Reporting Lost Cards **American Express** ☎ 800/992-3404 in the U.S. or 336/393-1111 collect from abroad 🌐 www.americanexpress.com. **Diners Club** ☎ 800/234-6377 in the U.S. or 303/799-1504 collect from abroad 🌐 www.dinersclub.com. **Discover** ☎ 800/347-2683 in the U.S. or 801/902-3100 collect from abroad 🌐 www.discovercard.com. **MasterCard** ☎ 800/622-7747 in the U.S. or 636/722-7111 collect from abroad 🌐 www.mastercard.com. **Visa** ☎ 800/847-2911 in the U.S. or 410/581-9994 collect from abroad 🌐 www.visa.com.

TRAVELER'S CHECKS & CARDS

Some consider this the currency of the cave man, and it's true that fewer establishments accept traveler's checks these days. Nevertheless, they're a cheap and secure way to carry extra money, particularly on trips to urban areas. Both Citibank (under the Visa brand) and American Express issue traveler's checks in the United States, but Amex is better known and more widely accepted; you can also avoid hefty surcharges by cashing Amex checks at Amex offices. Whatever you do, keep track of all the serial numbers in case the checks are lost or stolen.

American Express now offers a stored-value card called a Travelers Cheque Card, which you can use wherever American Express credit cards are accepted, including ATMs. The card can carry a minimum of $300 and a maximum of $2,700, and it's a very safe way to carry your funds. Although you can get replacement funds in 24 hours if your card is lost or stolen, it doesn't really strike us as a very good deal. In addition to a high initial cost ($14.95 to set up the card, plus $5 each time you "reload"), you still have to pay a 2% fee for each purchase in a foreign currency (similar to that of any credit card). Further, each time you use the card in an ATM you pay a transaction fee of $2.50 on top of the 2% transaction fee for the conversion—add it all up and it can be considerably more than you would pay when simply using your own ATM card. Regular traveler's checks are just as secure and cost less.

American Express ☎ 888/412-6945 in the U.S., 801/945-9450 collect outside of the U.S. to add value or speak to customer service 🌐 www.americanexpress.com.

SAFETY

Hawai'i is generally a safe tourist destination, but it's still wise to follow the same common sense safety precautions you would normally follow in your own hometown. Hotel and visitor-center staff can provide information should you decide to head out on your own to more remote areas. Rental cars are magnets for break-ins, so don't leave any valuables in the car, not even in a locked trunk. Avoid poorly lighted areas, beach parks, and isolated areas after dark as a precaution. When hiking, stay on marked trails, no matter how alluring the temptation might be to stray. Weather conditions can cause landscapes to become muddy, slippery, and tenuous, so staying on marked trails will lessen the possibility of a fall or getting lost. Ocean safety is of the utmost importance when visiting an island destination. Don't swim alone, and follow the international signage posted at beaches that alerts swimmers to strong currents, man-of-war jellyfish, sharp coral, high surf, sharks, and dangerous shore breaks. At coastal lookouts along cliff tops, heed the signs indicating that waves can climb over the ledges. Check with lifeguards at each beach for current conditions, and if the red flags are up, indicating swimming and surfing are not allowed, don't go in. Waters that look calm on the surface can harbor strong currents and undertows, and not a few people who were just wading have been dragged out to sea.

Be wary of those hawking "too good to be true" prices on everything from car rentals to attractions. Many of these offers are just a lure to get you in the door for time-share presentations. When handed a flyer, read the fine print before you make your decision to participate.

Women traveling alone are generally safe on the Islands, but always follow the safety precautions you would use in any major destination. When booking hotels, request rooms closest to the elevator, and always keep your hotel-room door and balcony doors locked. Stay away from isolated areas after dark; camping and hiking solo are not advised. If you stay out late visiting nightclubs and bars, use caution when exiting night spots and returning to your lodging.

EFFECTIVE COMPLAINING

Things don't always go right when you're traveling, and when you encounter a problem or service that isn't up to snuff, you should complain. But there are good and bad ways to do so.

TAKE A DEEP BREATH. This is always a good strategy, especially when you are aggravated about something. Just inhale, and exhale, and remember that you're on vacation. We know it's hard for Type A people to leave it all behind, but for your own peace of mind, it's worth a try.

COMPLAIN IN PERSON WHEN IT'S SERIOUS. In a hotel, serious problems are usually better dealt with in person, at the front desk; if it's something quick, you can phone.

COMPLAIN EARLY RATHER THAN LATE. Whenever you don't get what you paid for (the type of hotel room you booked or the airline seat you pre-reserved) or when it's something timely (the people next door are making too much noise), try to resolve the problem sooner rather than later. It's always going to be harder to deal with a problem or get something taken off your bill after the fact.

BE WILLING TO ESCALATE, BUT DON'T BE HASTY. Try to deal with the person at the front desk of your hotel or with your waiter in a restaurant before asking to speak to a supervisor or manager. Not only is this polite, but when the person directly serving you can fix the problem, you'll more likely get what you want quicker.

SAY WHAT YOU WANT, AND BE REASONABLE. When things fall apart, be clear about what kind of compensation you expect. Don't leave it to the hotel or restaurant or airline to suggest what they're willing to do for you. That said, the compensation you request must be in line with the problem. You're unlikely to get a free meal because your steak was undercooked or a free hotel stay if your bathroom was dirty.

CHOOSE YOUR BATTLES. You're more likely to get what you want if you limit your complaints to one or two specific things that really matter rather than a litany of wrongs.

DON'T BE OBNOXIOUS. There's nothing that will stop your progress dead in its tracks as readily as an insistent "Don't you know who I am?" or "So what are you going to do about it?" Raising your voice will rarely get a better result.

NICE COUNTS. This doesn't mean you shouldn't be clear that you are displeased. Passive isn't good, either. When it comes right down to it, though, you'll attract more flies with sugar than with vinegar.

DO IT IN WRITING. If you discover a billing error or some other problem after the fact, write a concise letter to the appropriate customer-service representative. Keep it to one page, and as with any complaint, state clearly and reasonably what you want them to do about the problem. Don't give a detailed trip report or list a litany of problems.

TIP→ Distribute your cash, credit cards, IDs, and other valuables between a deep front pocket, an inside jacket or vest pocket, and a hidden money pouch. Don't reach for the money pouch once you're in public.

TAXES

There's a 4.16% state sales tax on all purchases, including food. A hotel room tax of 7.25%, combined with the sales tax of 4%, equals an 11.41% rate added onto your hotel bill. A $3-per-day road tax is also assessed on each rental vehicle.

TIME

Hawai'i is on Hawaiian Standard Time, 5 hours behind New York, 2 hours behind Los Angeles, and 10 hours behind London.

When the U.S. mainland is on daylight saving time, Hawai'i is not, so add an extra hour of time difference between the Islands and U.S. mainland destinations. You may also find that things generally move more slowly here. That has nothing to do with your watch—it's just the laid-back way called Hawaiian time.

TIPPING

As this is a major vacation destination and many of the people who work at the hotels and resorts rely on tips to supplement their wages, tipping is common.

TIPPING GUIDELINES FOR THE BIG ISLAND	
Bartender	$1–$5 per round of drinks, depending on the number of drinks
Bellhop	$1 per bag, more if you have bulky items such as bicycles and surfboards
Hotel Concierge	$5 or more, depending on the service
Hotel Doorman	$1–$5 if he helps you get a cab or helps with bags, golf clubs, etc.
Hotel Maid	$1 per night, paid daily
Hotel Room-Service	$1–$2 per delivery, even if a service charge has been added
Porter at Airport	$1 per bag
Skycap at Airport	$1 to $3 per bag checked
Taxi Driver	15%, but round up the fare to the next dollar amount
Tour Guide	10% of the cost of the tour
Valet Parking Attendant	$2–$5, each time your car is brought to you
Waiter	15%–20%, with 20% being the norm at high-end restaurants
Spa Personnel	15%–20% of the cost of your service

INDEX

D

E

F

G

H

PHOTO CREDITS

Cover Photo *(Lava flowing from Kilauea volcano): G. Brad Lewis/age fotostock.* **Chapter 1: Experience the Big Island:** 7, *Douglas Peebles/age fotostock.* 8 (top and bottom left), *Big Island Visitors Bureau.* 8 (bottom right), *Photodisc.* 9 (all), *Big Island Visitors Bureau.* 11, *Big Island Visitors Bureau.* 12 (top left), *Photo Resource Hawaii/Alamy.* 12 (bottom left), *Cornforth Images/Alamy.* 12 (top center), *WaterFrame/Alamy.* 12 (bottom center), *Photo Resource Hawaii/Alamy.* 12 (right), *Douglas Peebles Photography/Alamy.* 13 (left), *Russ Bishop/Alamy.* 13 (top center), *Andre Seale/Alamy.* 13 (bottom center), *Hemis/Alamy.* 13 (top right), *Andre Seale/age fotostock.* 13 (bottom right), *Stephen Frink Collection/Alamy.* 14, *Photo Resource Hawaii/Alamy.* 15 (left), *SuperStock/age fotostock.* 15 (right), *WaterFrame/Alamy.* 16–18, *Hilton Hawaii.* 19 (left), *Photo Resource Hawaii/Alamy.* 19 (right), *Michael S. Nolan/age fotostock.* 20, *Bryan Lowry/Alamy.* **Chapter 2: Exploring the Big Island.** 23, *Joe Viesti/viestiphoto.com.* 46, *Big Island Visitors Bureau.* 47, *Russ Bishop/age fotostock.* 49, *Photo Resource Hawaii/Alamy.* 50, *Cornforth Images/Alamy.* 51 (top), *Big Island Visitors Bureau.* 51 (bottom), *Linda Robshaw/Alamy.* 56, *Greg Vaughn/Alamy.* **Chapter 3: Beaches:** 75, *Preferred Hotels & Resorts Worldwide.* **Chapter 4: Water Activities & Tours:** 91, *WaterFrame/Alamy.* 106, *Ron Dahlquist/HVCB.* **Chapter 5: Golf, Hiking & Outdoor Activities:** 111, *HTJ/HVCB.* 124, *Luca Tettoni/viestiphoto.com.* 125, *Jack Jeffrey.* **Chapter 6: Shops & Spas:** 129, *Hilton Hawaii.* 132 (top), *Linda Ching/HVCB.* 132 (bottom), *Sri Maiava Rusden/HVCB.* 133 (top), *leisofhawaii.com.* 133 (2nd from top), *kellyalexanderphotography.com.* 133 (3rd, 4th, and 5th from top), *leisofhawaii.com.* 133 (bottom), *kellyalexanderphotography.com.* **Chapter 7: Entertainment & Nightlife:** 147, *Hilton Hawaii.* 150, *HVCB.* 151, *Thinkstock LLC.* **Chapter 8: Where to Eat:** 157, *John Almarez/Four Seasons Hotels & Resorts.* 165, *Polynesian Cultural Center.* 166 (top), *Douglas Peebles Photography.* 166 (top center), *Douglas Peebles Photography/Alamy.* 166 (center), *Dana Edmunds/Polynesian Cultural Center.* 166 (bottom center), *Douglas Peebles Photography/Alamy.* 166 (bottom), *Purcell Team/Alamy.* 167 (top, top center, and bottom center), *HTJ/HVCB.* 167 (bottom), *Oahu Visitors Bureau.* **Chapter 9: Where to Stay:** 187, *Castle Resorts & Hotels.* **Color Section:** Akaka Falls, Akaka Falls State Park, Hamakua Coast: *Russ Bishop/Alamy.* Kona coffee beans: *Photo Resource Hawaii/Alamy.* The "Lobster Claw" *Heliconia* plant: *BIVB.* The Gemini and Canada-France-Hawaii telescopes at the summit of Mauna Kea: *SuperStock/age fotostock.* Lava flows at Hawaii Volcanoes National Park: *INTERFOTO Pressebildagentur/Alamy.* A pristine beach at Kua Bay: *Cornforth Images/Alamy.* A hot stone massage on the beach: *Sri Maiava Rusden.* Diver and green sea turtle: *Andre*

Seale/Alamy. Horseback riding in Waipio Valley: *Photo Resource Hawaii/Alamy.* Hula dancers: *Danita Delimont/Alamy.* Humpback whales: *Stephen Frink Collection/Alamy.* Driving through Waimea: *Photo Resource Hawaii/Alamy.* Rowing at sunrise, Kailua Bay: *Luis Casteñeda/age fotostock.* Lava rocks in the Waipio Valley, Hamakua Coast: *Cornforth Images/Alamy.*

ABOUT OUR WRITERS

Wanda A. Adams was born and raised on Maui and now makes her home on O'ahu. She has been a newspaper reporter for more than 25 years, specializing in food, dining, and travel. Wanda wrote the Lū'au and Hula features for this edition.

Don Chapman is the editor of the award-winning *MidWeek,* Hawai'i's largest-circulated newspaper. The golf writer for this guide, Don has played 88 golf courses in Hawai'i and writes about golf for a variety of national publications. He is also the author of four books.

John Penisten has written four Hawai'i travel guides, and his articles and photographs have appeared in *Hawaii* magazine, *International Travel News,* and various other outlets. For this book, John updated the Beaches, Water Activities & Tours, and Golf, Hiking & Outdoor Activities chapters. He and his wife have lived on the Big Island for over 30 years—and, despite Hilo's annual 126 inches of rainfall, they wouldn't live anywhere else.

Cathy Sharpe, who handled Big Island Essentials, was born and reared on O'ahu. For 13 years, she worked at a Honolulu public relations agency representing major travel industry clients. Now living in Maryland, she is a marketing consultant. Cathy returns home once a year to visit family and friends, relax at her favorite beaches, and enjoy island cuisine.

Cheryl Chee Tsutsumi has covered Hawai'i for numerous publications, including the *Honolulu Star-Bulletin, Hawaii* magazine, the *Chicago Sun-Times, TravelAge West* and *Hawaii Westways.* She is the author of nine books and the recipient of multiple awards from the Society of Professional Journalists and the Society of American Travel Writers. Cheryl wrote the Hawai'i Volcanoes National Park feature.

Amy Westervelt was lucky enough to spend summers growing up on the Big Island, and she now divides her time between Kona and San Francisco. She writes about travel and all things wedding-related for publications including *Travel + Leisure, Modern Bride,* and the *San Francisco Chronicle.* Amy wrote and revised the Experience the Big Island, Exploring the Big Island, Shops & Spas, Entertainment & Nightlife, Where to Eat, and Where to Stay chapters of this book.